Design Research

Design Research

METHODS AND PERSPECTIVES

Brenda Laurel, editor

The MIT Press
Cambridge, Massachusetts
London, England

Cover and book design: The Offices of Anne Burdick, Los Angeles
Designers: Anne Burdick, Stuart Smith, and Megan McGinley
Cover photo: © 2003 Susan L. Burdick

Library of Congress Cataloging-in-Publication Data
Design research : methods and perspectives / [edited by] Brenda Laurel.
p. cm.
Includes bibliographical references and index.
ISBN 0-262-12263-4 (hc : alk. paper)
1. Engineering design. I. Laurel, Brenda.
TA174.D483 2003
745.2–dc22   200359969
10 9 8 7 6 5 4 3 2 1

for the Lady in Des Moines

CONTENTS

CONTENTS

CONTENT CATEGORIES

	PEOPLE								FORM						
	CHRISTOPHER IRELAND	TIM PLOWMAN	BONNIE JOHNSON	ERIC DISHMAN	BRENDA LAUREL	CARLOS SANTOS	STACEY PURPURA	ABBE DON, JEFF PETRICK	LISA GROCOTT	DENISE GONZALES CRISP	ANNE BURDICK	RACHEL STRICKLAND	MICHAEL NAIMARK	EMMA WESTECOTT	ROB TOW
	23	30	39	41	49	55	63	70	83	94	101	118	109	129	135
RESEARCH METHODOLOGIES															
EXPERIMENTAL							○			○	○	○	○		○
QUALITATIVE	○	○	○	○	○	○		○				○			
QUANTITATIVE						○	○	○							
SPECULATIVE			○	○	○				○	○	○	○	○	○	○
EXPERIENTIAL		○			○							○	○	○	
PERFORMATIVE			○	○	○										
DISCOVERY-LED/POETIC									○	○	○		○	○	
FORMAL/STRUCTURAL										○	○	○	○	○	○
PROCEDURAL	○	○			○			○	○		○		○		
CONTEXTS															
COMMERCIAL	○	○		○		○	○	○	○						○
ACADEMIC		○			○				○	○	○			○	
EXPLORATORY	○	○	○	○	○			○		○	○	○	○		○
SUBJECTS															
DESIGNER			○	○	○			○	○	○	○		○	○	○
DESIGNED OBJECT	○		○	○	○				○	○	○			○	○
USER/CUSTOMER	○	○	○	○	○	○	○					○			
ORGANIZATION						○		○	○						○
DOMAINS															
PRODUCTS/SERVICES	○		○	○	○	○	○	○	○						○
THEORY		○	○	○	○				○	○	○	○	○	○	○
PRACTICE	○	○	○	○	○	○	○	○	○	○	○	○	○		○
GAMES/ENTERTAINMENT														○	
BRAND									○						

CONTENT CATEGORIES

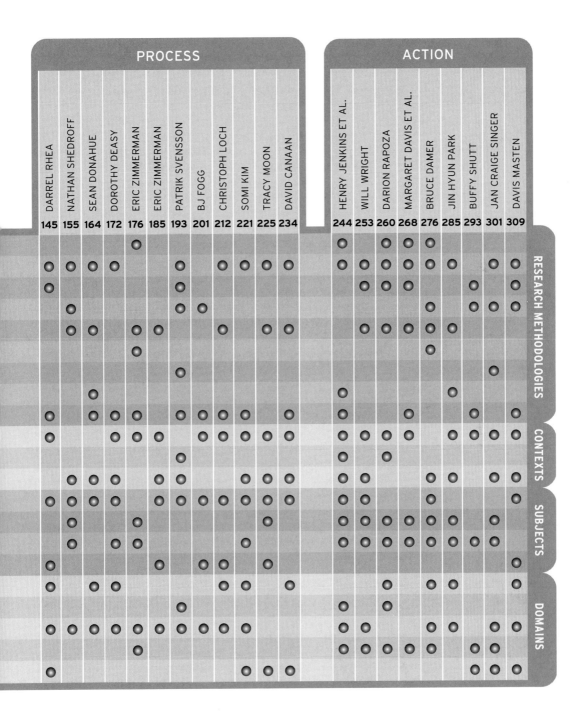

The Design Cluster

PETER LUNENFELD

Today, design is a category beyond categories. Search the World Wide Web for the word "design" and you get close to hundred million sites (twice as many hits as "god," half as many as "sex"). Marshall McLuhan coined the phrase "Gutenberg Galaxy" to describe the effects of the printed book on human culture [McLuhan 1962]. Astronomers group galaxies by clusters, and I would claim that now, we all live in the Design Cluster. While this means there is space in the Design Cluster to do extraordinary work, it also means that the territory is vast. And it is the very vastness of the territory that makes *Design Research* such an essential collection. The essays, case studies and provocations that editor Brenda Laurel has assembled here chart the nature and value of research done in the Design Cluster. There is a welcome openness to this book, for it begins with the understanding that no single research methodology could possibly account for the diversity of inputs and outputs to contemporary design practice and process. There are simply too many markets and media, clients and users, ways and means.

There are also too many definitions of design itself to pin down a definitive one. The great American modernist Charles Eames offered the following: "A plan for arranging elements in such a way as to best accomplish a particular purpose" [Eames 1972]. This definition situates design as a problem-solving discipline, with problems here defined mostly within market contexts. The 1980s and the 1990s saw an explosion of "personal" design to challenge this problem-solving methodology, which brought about debates on everything from legibility to the difference between "design with a small 'd'" and "Design with a capital 'D'" to the dissolving of the boundaries between art and design, and architecture and sculpture. More recently, Serges Gagnon has referred to design as "the cultural appropriation of technology," an intriguing place to start any investigation of design research [cited in De Winter 2002].

In the Design Cluster, pluralism and serendipity define ways of thinking by, with and through the idea of design research. Design research can fashion singularities that allow theory to morph into practice and come back again through the wormhole as something entirely new. Design research creates a place to braid theory and practice to make the work stronger. It establishes a demilitarized zone between makers suspicious of discourse and critical intelligence disdainful of the negotiations between designer and client. Design research is a method of invention that sides with finding out rather than finding the already found. Design research is not inherently good, nor is it inherently bad, but that doesn't mean it's neutral either. Obviously, design research will draw polling methodologies of the social sciences and the niche analysis of marketing surveys when it is appropriate, but as design research develops its own methodologies, its practitioners push farther afield. As this books demonstrates, the space of design research is as much like the novelist's library or the cook's kitchen as it is the scientist's laboratory or the marketer's phone bank.

Design Research regularly participates in the redefinition of the design process away from the stand-alone object and into the integrated system. Designers of all stripes regularly lament that they are seen by the rest of the world as stylists—pseudo-professionals brought in to smooth the edges, improve the palette and make the medicine go down more easily. By moving away from "mere styling" of the product itself and into the interlocking systems that manifest, support, constrain and envelop products, designers can rightfully claim lay claim to a much farther-reaching contribution. A commitment to design research as practice is a prerequisite for any kind of design entrepreneurship. Design Research helps to establish the right to a share in the equity when the profits are divided ➲212 LOCH, ➲145 RHEA.

There have been numerous attempts at defining what design research is and how to identify its methodologies, from László Moholy-Nagy at the Bauhaus in the 1920s, to Henry Dreyfuss's seminal study *Designing for People* in the 1950s, to the Royal College of Arts' Sir Christopher Frayling in the 1990s [Moholy-Nagy 1969, Dreyfuss 1955, Frayling 1993]. To draw from the most recent, Frayling identifies three key modes of design research: research *into* design, research *through* design, and research *for* design. Research into design includes the traditional historical and aesthetic studies of art and design. Research through design is project-based, and includes materials research and development. And finally, research for design is the hardest to characterize, as its purpose is to create objects and systems that display the results of the research and prove its worth.

This book organizes its methods and perspectives into four major sections: "People," "Form," "Process," and "Action." The importance of research into the design process, which includes the traditional historical and aesthetic studies of art and design, cannot be overstated. In *Design Research*, the essays that explore this terrain are in the section entitled "Process," and there are examinations of methodologies in the sections on "People" and "Form" as well. "Form" and "Process" incorporate project-based investigations into materials research and development. "Action" is a synoptic category that incorporates the understanding of people, form and process and that activates that knowledge as design.

We need new categories of design research because of the impact of digital technologies on the design disciplines over the past twenty years. The computer democratized access to the tools of the professional designer, brought about an amazing efflorescence of new styles, and made the Design Cluster much denser with people who define themselves as designers. Unfortunately, the democratization of digitization didn't go hand in hand with any kind of informed discussion of the history and discourses of design as a field. Knowing something about the ways in which designers from earlier eras were able to shift the dialogue from service to collaboration, staking out either new territory or reformulating the way the game is played—think Charles and Ray Eames—is essential to anyone who wants to make design research a major component of their practice ○83 GROCOTT.

With all the hype about new design tools (from Hypercard to Director to Flash to whatever's in beta today, to be released tomorrow, and a technological cliché the day after that) and the concomitant backlash against them, this is precisely the time to revisit the debates about deep design versus styling. But the very people who should be talking about this lack the historical and aesthetic background to see their work in larger contexts. For example, they probably do not have the vaguest notion of who industrial design great Raymond Loewy was, much less the fact that as early as the 1930s, he was talking about the designer's role in "reconciling" people to new technologies through the exterior styling of everything from streamlined locomotives to streamlined toasters. The idea of speed was as much the point as any real velocity [Loewy 1951]. This is not to endorse Loewy's position by any means, but it would make the discussions between partisans of the "new" and their detractors a whole lot more interesting. How about countering the banality of Web usability consultants by recasting Frankfurt School theorist Theodor Adorno's condemnation of functionalism? In the 1960s, Adorno was dealing with the unintended consequences of modernism's reductivism: the creation of boring and inhuman living spaces [Adorno 1997]. Connecting the dots from these historical arguments to a staff meeting is tricky, but it can be done. Essentially, it's about making history, theory and criticism viable in non-academic environments.

Another way of positioning design research in "Action" is to think about design as research. Design as research uses its own media to perform the investigations, expanding past the idea of market surveys, and god forbid, color preference charts. A flexible and ever expanding methodology of design as research is necessary to deal with a moment defined by pluralism and enlivened by serendipity. Design as research is a rational practice, but it is one in which emotion is allowed its own power and intelligence. This openness to braided modalities of thinking and feeling can offer the mid-career designer a way to escape from the prison of safe solutions that "always work." At the very least, design research saves us from reinventing the wheel. At its best, a lively research methodology can reinvigorate the passion that so often fades after designers "join the profession." Designers are so often the chameleons of system analysts, able to slip in and out of other people's lives, workplaces, and needs. If they are hard-working, inquisitive and lucky (yes, it takes at least this much), designers can find themselves working with a constantly changing set of subjects, clients, projects, dreams and nightmares.

Design research can indeed result in the positivistic production of beautiful, useful and better products. But, given a different set of data or expectations, design research can build in an inherent criticality that produces provoking, tactical and oppositional results. Design research can be a way out of the banality of making beautiful/making functional. Design research can save the newest members of the profession from the solipsism of youth—the never-ending allure of exclusively designing for yourself and your friends. And design research can even—with an even greater level of serendipity than usual—convince clients to do something that they wouldn't have had the wit or courage to pay for otherwise ●82 BURDICK INTRO, ●94 GONZALES CRISP.

One of the most impressive design research-based practices in the world belongs to the architect Rem Koolhaas. Koolhaas has built his worldwide reputation in large measure by designing and publishing the results of his research in provoking ways. From *Delirious New York: A Retroactive Manifesto for Manhattan* [1978] through *S,M,L,XL* [1995], a collaboration with graphic designer Bruce Mau, to *The Harvard Design School Guide to Shopping* [2002], Koolhaas has consistently deployed design research in three distinct ways: first, to understand the context of any building project he might wish to undertake; second, to develop the building's program itself; and third, in a reflexive way, as a selling tool for the research and the building themselves. I once watched Koolhaas analyze the evolution of architecture in response to the globalization of capital. He showed a Mercator projection with the Western Hemisphere on he left, Eurasia in the middle, and Australia on the right, Koolhaas began to speak of the dominant world currencies, reading from left to right, the dollar ($), the Euro (€), and the Yen (¥). In a brilliant inversion of the West's cartographic norms, though, the next slide placed Asia on the left, Europe in the middle, and the United States on the right, creating a new supergraphic of the currencies: ¥ € $, or, as Koolhaas calls it, "the global YES."

If we define a graphic of the "the global YES" as design research, it should be obvious by now that design as research is not the same as science as research. Of course, the people in the boardroom would doubtless be more comfortable with design research if it behaved more like science. Of course, design research and scientific research converge at times—especially in the research on materials and statistical analyses—but they diverge just as often. The scientific method is built on a base of testability and reproducibility: an experiment done in one place when replicated with the same set of conditions in another place by other scientists will yield the same results. This is the operating methodology of "normal" science, that day-to-day routine of life in the laboratory [Kuhn 1967]. In fact, most scientists never have an epochal "eureka!" moment in their entire career. But the testability and reproducibility of design as research is less important. Very often it is the sensitivity to social context and cultural moment that makes the results of the design research resonate with a public or a market. The same "solution" in another context or market could fall flat, or simply be seen as entirely derivative ●22 IRELAND INTRO, ●293 SHUTT.

These comparisons also bring up the distinction between pure and applied research. We tend to associate pure research with scientific fields like physics and mathematics and applied research with the engineering disciplines. Design and engineering have long been intertwined, so it should come as no surprise that design research, for the most part, functions as a variety of applied rather than pure research (a claim sometimes made for fine art practice). In the 21st century, the linear narratives of research progress are dissolving into decentered threadings, less branches off a main root than tide pools by the shore, or the rhizomatic growth of peanuts in the soil [Lunenfeld 2000]. As information and data about everything explode in a frenzy of rhizomatic connectivity, the very search for what to research becomes its own research issue. The research model becomes a design problem that can also function as its own solution.

This sort of recursive involution in the Design Cluster resonates with the recent call for moving from a blinkered fascination with IT (information technologies) to a more expansive field of ITCP (information technologies and creative practices) [Mitchell et al. 2003]. Design research can lead the way to new modes of engagement with computer-inflected technologies. Design research is a key part of crafting ITCP that moves from human-computer interface technologies to humane computer interface technologies. Even more important than improving our interfaces with machines is design research's potential contribution to improving our relationships with each other, our communities, our cultures and our democracies. Design is not only about serving the needs of business, but also about determining and working towards the greater good for society, government, education and the environment.

How can we harness the Design Cluster's powers and attractions to make the world a better (and perhaps even smarter) place? This isn't a new question, of course, as anyone who has studied the history of design can tell you. In fact, one of the guiding principles of modernist design was that its practitioners might be able to serve as conduits and refiners of complex information about social, aesthetic and scientific systems for mass audiences, thereby adding to the realm of knowledge and democracy. Think of Viennese designer Otto Neurath's universalized isotypes from the 1920s or the desire of architects to create better "machines for living." The kinds of utopian aspirations that Bauhaus designers and other modernists had for the field have been obscured by a miasma of Coca Cola campaigns and automotive styling, but perhaps it can be reinvigorated in this era of electronic image-making and vectoral world building. This is my hope, my ideal for design research in action. As John Seely Brown, the Chief Scientist of PARC Xerox, once told me, "theory and practice aren't enough; it's got to be theory, practice and purpose."

Research helps us to appreciate design's own intelligence, rather than simply appropriating its glamour (and let us not forget that both glamour and grammar have magic at their roots). The proliferation of networks of production and distribution makes it vital to train citizens to upload as well as download ◗276 DAMER, ◗164 DONAHUE. Investigations into potentially profitless arenas will still need to be undertaken to push the envelope of the research. As the authors in this book demonstrate, the pioneers of design research do not take the easy route. Our ethical imperative is to make sure that the design research we do contributes as much to art, science, and democracy as it does to someone's bottom line.

Muscular Design

BRENDA LAUREL, EDITOR

Not too long after the end of the 20th century, I was sitting in a meeting at Art Center College of Design to discuss the College's curriculum. Around the table were administrators, chairs, faculty members and students. As we spoke about reaching across departmental boundaries to offer more trans-disciplinary and foundational courses, a student in the Environmental Design department made a suggestion. "We need a course for every student in the college in their first term," he said, "that helps us to understand why we want to be designers."

I think that every designer dreams of making work that makes a difference. Most designers are aware of the common misconceptions of the profession. Designers are variously seen as decorationists, elitists or servants of the consumerist machine. When their work is directed toward the marketplace, they rarely participate in the "research" that determines what product should be produced for whom—or why. When their work focuses on the investigation of design through form and process, they often stand accused of irrelevance or indifference. When they found great movements like the Bauhaus, they may be seen as self-proclaimed dictators of style. Each of those attributions ultimately marginalizes designers and design.

Underlying the discourse in this book about design research is a deeper conversation about the "why" of design. In this book you will encounter forty different voices. Each has something to say about how we make ourselves better at what we do through research. Each approach is situated in a particular context and reflects a distinct purpose. The authors argue passionately with one other about the object, process and goal of design research. But every one of them will tell you that research is a key—in whatever form and for whatever purpose—to making design a more muscular profession.

Our book begins with a look at human-centered research. Immediately, we are off on a controversial discussion. To many, human-centered research is equivalent to market research; it smacks of commercialism and is rejected by many on those grounds. The traditional goal of market research has been to find ways to sell stuff to people. In the colloquial view, the function of market research has been to validate existing and proposed products and to figure out how to persuade people that they need to buy them. Occasionally, we think of market research as finding out what potential customers want. Here again, the colloquial view is overly simplistic. Customers typically can't tell you what they want, and they can't design a product, service or experience for you to sell them. If you had asked any number of people in 1957 what they would like to play with, none would have suggested a plastic hoop that they could rotate around their hips.

In the old model, market research was a back-end process, devoted primarily to the final stages of development including styling, packaging, branding, marketing and advertising. In the emerging paradigm, the process is being inverted, with design research as a front-end method, informing the development of products and services from the concept stage forward. In this way, design research can enable the product to speak for itself, freeing branding and marketing to move toward honest communication and away from persuasion and the creation of desire. Human-centered design research encompasses a set of methods and practices aimed at getting insight into what would serve or delight people. It investigates behind the scenes, looking at individuals, situated contexts, cultures, forms, history, and even business models for clues that can inform design. Furthermore, good human-centered design research amplifies the designer's ability to shape popular culture and to smoothly transmit values through design.

Designers have their own "old models" to contend with. Brand/identity designer David Canaan wryly observes that most designers seem to see their mission as "educating the general public about good taste." But over the last decade, the balance of power between those who sell products or services and those who buy them has undergone radical change. Thanks in part to the rise of the Web, communication between companies and audiences has moved from one-way persuasion to two-way dialogues about needs, desires, problems and dreams. Customer support, enabled in no small part by advances in telecommunications, has evolved to have ears and eyes as well as a mouth. The most stunning evidence of the growing power of the people may be the organized boycotts of companies over issues of child labor, animal treatment or genetic engineering—and the fact that many have achieved substantial results with large corporations.

While marketing, advertising, distribution and customer service functions have been forced to adapt to this new state of affairs, the design disciplines have lagged behind. Design curricula in higher education rarely include design research as a set of skills with extremely high strategic value. Designers need to understand the tools of research, how they are deployed, how they map onto the various stages in the design process, and how research findings can contribute to both innovative and evolutionary design practice.

Many years ago, I worked with a Jewish colleague who owned the biggest Swiss Army knife I ever saw. It was at least 2 inches thick, containing virtually every tool made for it. I asked him, "What is that?" He replied, "It's a Jewish army knife." Deciding to go for it, I said, "OK, so why do you call it a Jewish army knife?" Shifting from his vowel-neutral, California manner of speech into a thick Yiddish accent he replied, "Because you never know."

Designers find themselves in a similar predicament today. Beyond the massive changes in dynamics among customers and companies, we work in a context shot through with rapid, often unexpected change along several vectors. Previously unimaginable technologies—from MP3 to nanotech—are blooming like time-lapse flowers. Shifting conditions in trade, politics and culture are forcing radical changes in the business models and operating methods of companies. Designers today work in a transmedia world: brands spread like viruses from print into video, web, email, sports-arena banners, LCD billboards, temporary tattoos and signage on spacecraft. Transmedia forces are at work in areas beyond branding, in the design of products, services and properties as well. Who knew, twenty years ago, that franchises as unlike as Citibank and the Harry Potter would live in every media type from atoms to bits? What next? One goal of this book is to put as many tools as possible on your belt, because "you never know."

Designers work in a world in which the velocity and abundance of information are exhibiting non-linear growth. At the same time, the consolidation of ownership in many industries, from telecommunications and media to retail and agriculture, creates the paradox of translating more choices into less choice. The well-entrained consumer responds to increasingly spectacular and superficial stimuli. The necessary push-back from designers who do not wish to vanish into the shadows of giant corporations requires not only that we design wonderful stuff, but also that we do it in such a way as to transform the consciousness of consumers from conditioned response to active participation. Not accidentally, the same transformation serves the political need to transform an apathetic public into a body of informed citizens. What we do is both framed by and transformative of the context in which we do it.

When one steps back from the marketplace, things can be seen in a different light. While time passes on the surface, we may dive to a calmer, more fundamental place. There, the urgency of commerce is swept away by the rapture of the deep. Designers working at that depth choose to delve into the essence of design itself. Form, structure, ideas and materials become the object of study. In the section entitled "Form," you will meet some of those pioneers who are making exquisite journeys into the inner space of design. In counterpoint to the view that "you never know," these explorers suggest that we know a lot, and that we can be continually informed by the cycle of form-making and reflection.

The third section, entitled "Process," presents insights on how research can be facilitated, represented, propagated, understood and utilized successfully within a variety of contexts. Here you will find a strong emphasis on how design works within the framework of various kinds of organizations, and how we navigate structural and cultural obstacles as we bring the messages of design research forward. The final section, "Action," provides case studies of projects that reveal design research at work—how methods are chosen and deployed in specific contexts and for specific purposes.

Simply put, designers who can harness the power of research will help design to become a more muscular discipline, acknowledging and utilizing its implicit power in explicit ways. The value placed on designers' work will likewise increase, as independent creators, members of organizations and shapers of culture. A designer who knows how to deploy formal research appropriately may introduce strong new currents into the ocean of possibility. In the world of commerce, design research betters the odds for a successful, even delightful, match between an audience's needs and desires with a product, service or experience. Research can enable designers to invent products that people didn't even know they wanted—like the hula hoop or the Walkman. Of course, design research can fuel branding, marketing and advertising as well. Design research can function as the *corpus callosum* between development and marketing functions in a company, making formerly isolated (and therefore often adversarial) parts of the corporate "brain" able to work in concert through their connection of shared information to serve common goals.

Design has power; this has always been true. Design has consequences. The question is not whether consequences exist, but rather whether they are intended, by whom, and to what purpose. The challenge for designers is to claim and direct the power of their profession. From flying cars to brave new books to computer games, from industry to academia to the independent studio, designers today are employing a panoply of research methods to strengthen their work. This 21st century hodge-podge is beginning to coalesce into a coherent discourse. Our hope is that this book takes us a step further in that direction.

ACKNOWLEDGMENTS

Every author in this book cracked his or her cranium to produce excellent work within (or nearly within) the constraints of insane deadlines. I've never worked with a more diligent and interesting group of people.

Art Center College of Design has been a pillar of support in this effort. Art Center funded our authors' conference and covered the cost of the time and efforts of college staff and faculty who worked on the project. My heartfelt thanks to President Richard Koshalek for his support. Thanks also to faculty members of the Art Center's graduate Media Design Program Anne Burdick (a featured author as well as the glorious designer of this book) and Peter Lunenfeld for their writing, advice and support; to Chanel Holmes for her logistical handiwork; and to MDP alumni Sean Donahue and Jin Hyun Park for making us proud.

While this book contains articles by authors from many different fields, you will find that several articles are written by people from a company called Cheskin—the other pillar of support for this book. Cheskin, a consulting and research firm with over 50 years of history, is grounded in the recognition that innovation and success rest on in-depth understanding of people, their cultures and the influences that motivate them. Through "cultural sense-making," Cheskin has led the way in the transition from old-style market research to human-centered design research as we have defined it in this book. Cheskin people often donate their time to lectures and workshops for the Media Design Program at Art Center. Sincere thanks to Cheskin for contributing both human and financial resources to this project.

Special thanks to Rob Tow, author and silicon ronin, for devoting a great deal of time and effort to the creation and maintenance of the authors' website and discussion groups and for his invaluable discourse with me as the book took shape. Finally, my gratitude to editor Doug Sery whose Mercurial efforts for timely publication hereby invalidate any and all jokes about the metabolic rate of the MIT Press.

The Changing Role of Research

CHRISTOPHER IRELAND

Few designers today have the luxury of creating their own vision with no input from others. If they desire to attract and delight customers or audiences for their work, they need to understand the people for whom they design. That used to be much easier. The U.S. was a "mass market" and people acted in concert. They bought similar things, they listened to similar music, they watched similar movies, and they even praised similar gods. If a designer understood a small group of people—perhaps neighbors, friends or family—then he or she could design for them and still be relevant to millions of others.

But that has changed. The U.S. is home to over 290 million highly diverse people, and the growth trend is toward more diversity. Furthermore, very few mass movements exist anymore. People have learned to choose how they spend their time and their money based on their individual beliefs, their personal desires and their specific needs. While some decry the helplessness of the consumer at the mercy of big business, in fact, the balance of power began to shift over a decade ago and shows no signs of stopping. It is big business—or any enterprise hoping to capture people's attention—that now is at the mercy of their customers or patrons. How these customers choose can make or break a company, an institution or an individual artisan.

For a designer, this is a formidable world. It requires a keen understanding of people, cultures and belief systems that may seem completely foreign and unintelligible. It requires patience and an open attitude. It also requires skills and perspectives that are not traditionally taught in design school. Identifying, observing and interpreting human behaviors and attitudes toward design is a discipline in and of itself—it's not easy to "wing it."

On the pages that follow, you'll meet people who have built successful careers understanding people in order to improve and enhance design. They explain the techniques and the approaches that have worked for them and offer guidance on where the future is going. In total, they offer a wide variety of methods that help designers reach beyond the constraints of their individual world-views and into a new world of choice and diversity.

Qualitative Methods: From Boring to Brilliant

CHRISTOPHER IRELAND

Qualitative design research enjoys a controversial existence. Even among its fans, there's vigorous debate over how, why and when it should be done. As a result, the field is chaotic, with practitioners and methods ranging from inspired to inept. To some, qualitative design research is what a company does when it can't afford quantitative. To others, it's a simple way to prove that a favored design will work in the marketplace. To still others, it's a "disaster check" that must be completed sometime before the product ships. I wouldn't have been attracted to the field if these were the true definitions of qualitative design research. What has captured my attention, my time and much of my thinking for the past 15 years is the role qualitative research can and should play in the creation process.

I have a fairly traditional marketing background, including an MBA followed by several years managing consumer products. In that role, I planned product launches, managed advertising budgets, worked with research labs, worried about cost of goods and monitored my products' market penetration and competitive threats. But after a few years of doing these jobs, I realized that the part of product management and marketing that I most loved involved learning about the people who would eventually use my product. In particular, I loved learning about them by listening to them, watching them or experiencing their lives first hand. This approach, in all its complexity and breadth, is summarized in the term "qualitative design research."

At the time I made this realization (the mid-1980s), qualitative design research was a poor stepchild in the marketing family. It was disdained by most marketing managers as being unscientific and naïve. Moderators, the people who actually interviewed consumers, tended to be older, heavy-set women or professorial-looking men who were hired for their ability to follow a written guide and get everyone in the focus group to talk. Once the groups were complete, the moderator's job was done. They were rarely if ever invited to be a continuing part of the product development team. This seemed like a huge waste to me. Why wouldn't everyone on a product design or marketing team want to engage with their future consumers? Why wouldn't they want that perspective to guide them throughout the process? To me, this was the most fascinating aspect of creating new products and I couldn't conceive of delegating it to a powerless drone.

With that perspective in mind, I innocently set out to do qualitative design research the way I felt it should be done. Unbeknownst to me at the time, many other design professionals, social scientists and marketers around the country had come to the same conclusion and had begun to proceed down the same path. We all faced the same obstacles: clients typically had very narrow views of qualitative research, budgets were slim, projects were isolated from the overall development process, and expectations occasionally bordered on the unethical.

The first qualitative project I did was for Disney. They were redesigning their line of audiotape stories, and I'd been hired to conduct focus groups with moms to identify their design preferences. Although my client did not know it, I had never conducted a focus group before in my life. But I had managed a large product line and well understood the problems faced in a major redesign. Because of that, I was able to lead the discussion into very fruitful areas, often ignoring the guide that the client had created. I did this by paying very careful attention to each woman in the group, by considering her lifestyle and personality and by asking realistic, ad hoc "what if" questions and probing until I truly "grokked" how each woman reacted to the new design. Much to my surprise, the client told my partner I was one of the best moderators she'd ever seen. Ironically, by breaking the cardinal rules of moderation, I had provided my client with exactly what she needed and wanted.

Other practitioners were making similar changes to the highly traditional, time-honored focus group approach. Some started inviting clients to leave the backroom (that dark, cramped space behind the one-way glass) and become part of the group themselves. Others started bringing new exercises into what had been a "talk only" environment. They experimented with having people respond to phrases or ideas on cards, sorting them into piles or identifying other relationships between them. They tried having people create mosaics to express concepts they couldn't articulate. Some tried using music; others showed video or photos. All of us learned from each other and continued to push the discipline forward, tentatively publishing guidelines or speaking at conferences about what was working.

Focus Groups

Probably because they were so pervasive, focus groups received the most attention first. As a result, they've evolved into an extensive family of related methods. Their evolution seems quite logical in retrospect, although at the time, we were all just reacting to opportunities and the resources we had. Others may organize this differently, but from my point of view, the core qualitative methods deriving from focus groups happened in roughly this order:

Traditional focus groups   A gathering of 10 to 12 consumers who are led in a tightly scripted discussion by a trained moderator, usually for about 2 hours. Originally used for any topic or purpose, they are now recommended primarily when you want to generate ideas and/or expand understanding without needing to reach consensus. Focus groups have never been a good choice if your subject is sensitive or where responses are related to personal or professional status.

Mini focus group   A slightly smaller gathering of 6 to 8 consumers (occasionally fewer) who are led in a tightly scripted discussion by a trained moderator, usually for 1 to 2 hours. The same considerations of topic noted for focus groups apply for mini groups; however, since mini groups involve fewer people, they provide the opportunity for deeper discussions and questioning that is more specifically tailored to each person in the group.

1-on-1 interviews   One person interviewed by a researcher who is following either a tightly scripted guide or a loose outline. The duration of these interviews can range from 20 minutes to 1 or more hours. Individual interviews are ideal for learning exactly how each person feels and thinks about a topic or design, without concern for the influence of others (except the moderator's influence, which really can't be avoided). It's my personal preference for most topics related to design evaluation.

Dyads   Two friends interviewed as a pair by a moderator following an outline or lightly scripted guide, usually for at least 1 hour. Dyads, or "friendship pairs" as they are sometimes called, are a powerful forum for exploring issues that are difficult for people to articulate or for interviewing people who may be uncomfortable participating in research. For that reason, dyad interviews are frequently used with children and teens. The discussions tend to be animated, insightful and very candid (people usually feel uncomfortable telling lies in the presence of a friend). However, these are difficult interviews to conduct. Less experienced researchers will lead them as though they were conducting two separate interviews at once. The more experience practitioners know that the best dyads reflect the true interactions between friends, coached along by the researcher.

Super groups   50 to 100 or more people are gathered in a large auditorium to view ideas, products, designs or other exhibits presented on a large screen. One or two moderators lead the group from a stage. Usually, respondents are given devices which allow them to respond to and/or rate what they are shown. These groups tend to be short and highly focused since it's difficult to keep such a large group controlled for very long. While this approach provides rapid feedback from a large number of people, the questions must be very structured and there's no room to vary. Occasionally, smaller groups of people are selected to attend breakout sessions after the super groups.

Triads   Three people who are either similar to each other or are different in a specific way, interviewed by a moderator following an outline or lightly scripted guide, usually for about 1 hour. Triads provide the depth of 1-on-1s with a bit more breadth. If all the people in the group are the same, the dialogue can be generative (like focus groups). If they differ in some way—for example, if they are all IT professionals but from different sized companies—then their responses can be seen in comparison. Triads are more like 1-on-1s than focus groups, but they run the risk of group influence. They tend to be more appropriate and cost-effective for business-related topics than for consumer subjects. They're pointless if all three participants are distinctly different because the interview will then take as much time as three 1-on-1 interviews with less benefit.

Party groups   A group of people who all know each other gather together in one person's home and spend 2 to 3 hours conversing with each other and the moderator on a chosen topic. For sheer fun, party groups are my favorites, but they tend to work best for consumers (not business people) and for singular topics that benefit from deep, thoughtful and candid discussions. The researcher gets to see where and how people live, which can often add important dimensions to the topic. There's no backroom for clients, so either the client participates in the group or they watch video later. While party groups can generate exceptionally good insights, they are very hard to arrange and to manage. They can go badly astray if babies, household emergencies or excessive alcohol is present.

Online discussion groups   Still in its infancy and plagued with problems, this approach takes any of the methods described above and attempts to conduct it virtually. Currently, it primarily supports a text interface, which omits crucial body language that any good researcher needs in order to properly interpret what he or she hears. This context also favors fast typists—definitely not a representative group. As video conferencing matures and is integrated into online groups, they will become more practical and useful.

Ethnography

While focus groups were spawning this range of offspring, other qualitative methods began showing up and gaining credence. Thanks to influence from social scientists and academic professionals, the term "ethnography" starting popping up in design discussions in the late 1980s. At the time, one of the most common questions I got from clients was, "Just exactly what is ethnography?" I'm sure many others heard the same inquiry and we all tried our hand at crafting a reasonable response. In the context of design research, I found it most useful to define it as a research approach that produces a detailed, in-depth observation of people's behavior, beliefs and preferences by observing and interacting with them in a natural environment. In retrospect, I imagine that made it sound like I'd be wearing a safari jacket, stalking adult homeowners or teenaged fashion mavens with my field binoculars. In fact, it was just a first stab at a process that was in transition from its anthropological roots and hadn't yet been refined for a commercial market.

The growth and refinement of ethnography as an effective design research method owes a great deal to the few clients who risked their careers supporting this new approach. At the time, most marketers, product developers and designers were not trained to understand or ask for this type of information about people. When they got it, they rarely knew how to use it. To complicate matters further, there were no real standards or benchmarks to measure the quality of the work or to determine how much study was enough. Very few established research firms could afford to develop this new discipline, so its progression rested heavily on the efforts and investments of small entrepreneurial companies who believed in it. Along with my company, Cheskin, other important initiators of ethnography as a design research option were The Doblin Group, E-Lab, Fitch and IDEO. For a more in-depth discussion of the roots of ethnography and its current implications of design, see Tim Plowman's chapter later in this section ◗30 PLOWMAN.

Ethnography is still evolving in the commercial realm, but it's come a long way. Like focus groups, ethnography has generated progeny of various shapes and sizes that help round out its offering.

Field ethnography A person or group of people are observed by a researcher while they go about their normal lives. The duration of these observations can range from 1 hour to several days or weeks. Field ethnographies are ideal in early exploratory stages when a firm needs to learn more about the people for whom they are designing. However, traditional ethnographies take time; they rarely work well in a rapid paced development program.

Digital ethnography This is a more recent variation on traditional ethnography, using digital tools to speed the process without compromising the quality of the work. It typically follows a similar approach, observing people as they go about their lives, but uses digital cameras, PDAs, laptops, virtual collaboration sites or other technology to record, transmit, edit and present the information.

Photo ethnography A person is given a camera (still or video, film or digital) and asked to capture images of his or her life and describe them with accompanying notes. The images are returned to the researcher who then reviews them and learns from both the visuals and the related notes. This approach is highly useful when the presence of an ethnographer would drastically alter people's behavior (such as at a teen's party), or when it's not appropriate or cost-effective for others to be present (such as when someone is bathing, dressing or traveling). While this approach is engaging for both the researcher and the participant, its difficulty is often underestimated. Organizing and managing thousands of photos is a science requiring careful planning and strict guidelines. Interpreting thousands of photos is an art requiring years of practice, a keen sense of observation and a high level of consumer understanding to begin with. In other words, this approach is for pros.

Ethnofuturism This is a very young but rapidly growing variation that marries digital ethnography focused on daily activities and small details of cultural significance with a futures perspective that looks at major trends influencing and changing culture as a whole. It's most applicable for technology products that call for understanding of both the individual user's perspective and the "big picture," but also may be effective for other products whose success depends at least partially on trend movements.

"Real world" ethnographic enactments First popularized by MTV in their Real World series, this approach builds an environment for a person or people and then monitors them within it. It's been used by several technology companies hoping to understand how people's lives will change when their homes become filled with new digital appliances and distributed computing ◗41 DISHMAN. For those who have the budget and the time, this is both a fascinating and highly accurate method of research.

Personas These are scenarios or profiles created to inspire and guide design. They are typically visual and textual descriptions, but ideally, they are the results of studying real people. This approach was heavily used by advertisers in the 1980s and 1990s, but was popularized for technology design by Alan Cooper in his book *The Inmates are Running the Asylum* [1999]. Personas are less effective if the audience is diverse—by definition personas are narrow descriptions. They're best suited to homogenous audiences or niche markets. ◗70 DON, PETRICK

Participatory Methods

As designers and product developers learned to benefit from direct consumer feedback, they started crafting their own qualitative approaches. I'm personally indebted to the work of Liz Sanders, who pioneered "participatory" design methods while at Fitch and then later at her own company, Sonic Rim [www.sonic-rim.com]. Participatory methods involve consumers in the development of the products, services or brands they hopefully will eventually buy. They are inherently flexible, taking whatever shape they need to suit the designer's needs. The most common methods are not necessarily the best, but they are probably the easiest to conduct with consistent quality. With all forms of participatory design research, the challenge is to keep people's input fresh and representative. The temptation to turn consumers into designers is hard to resist, but that's a quick way to doom this type of qualitative research.

Development panel Groups of people are contracted for a period of time to evaluate and give feedback on various aspects of a product or service as it's developed. Their input can be offered in person, over the phone or online, but it's important that they have a good sense of what they're evaluating. I prefer to know as much as possible about the members of a development panel, so I typically start one with a thorough interview and photo ethnography. The panel members' feedback can often be improved by providing them with simple means of indicating their design preferences. Liz Sanders often used a felt board with cut-outs that could be rearranged. Others have let members draw, send photos or visuals, create collages or even make brief movies.

In-home placement People are given a product or provided with a service at an early stage of its final development and asked to use it as a part of their daily lives and then provide specific feedback on how it performs. This is a method that was perfected by mass marketers of consumer food and beverage products, but it's proving very useful for a wide range of designers. It's somewhat similar to software beta tests, but in this case, the people participating often have no previous experience with the product or service they're using. As such, they can be a good test market for how normal people will react to the product or service when it's fully launched. This is a sophisticated method that takes great discipline to use. In most cases, for it to really be beneficial, the company must be willing to revamp its product or service if needed, even though they've already invested significantly in its development.

As I hope this brief historical recap shows, the field of qualitative design research has become much richer, more refined and more effective over the past decades, largely due to the efforts of innovators and the clients that were willing to experiment. You'll hear from many of them in the following chapters as they illustrate the many diverse dimensions of this practice, including a few very new ones like "Informance" ❍39 JOHNSON, ❍41 DISHMAN, ❍49 LAUREL. I hope you find, as I have, that this is discipline is a complex, enticing and inherently exciting field. Quantitative research never deserved to be thought of as boring, and it becomes more brilliant every day as new strategies and techniques emerge from the innovative efforts of the design research community.

Ethnography and Critical Design Practice

TIM PLOWMAN

The philosophers have only interpreted the world, the point, however, is to change it. —Karl Marx

This chapter describes how ethnography, a research technique that originated in anthropology, has become an increasingly central practice for a variety of businesses and professions, including design. I was trained as an anthropologist at the University of California at Berkeley and conducted long-term fieldwork for my research in Brazil. I now work outside of academia primarily in technology, design and other areas of business. In this chapter I will briefly describe ethnography, a core anthropological research tool, and its role in research both in and out of academia. I will also explain how ethnographic techniques and social science theory are suited to enhancing design practice. I'll offer my own view of what the future relationship between designers and ethnographers might look like and what the two professions have to offer each other. Finally, I will briefly explore the potential for and promise of a critical design research practice.

Designed Artifacts, Culture, and the Study of Imponderabilia

At its core, anthropology is the study of human behavior—how people experience and make sense of what they themselves and others do. This is a very broad statement and, as such, a vaguely absurd claim. The terms "experience" and "making sense" comprise a large part of what social scientists like anthropologists generally call culture—the practices, artifacts, sensibilities and ideas that constitute and inform our everyday lives. The culture concept has been periodically championed, reviled, deconstructed, abandoned and reclaimed many times since it first came into use in the 19th century. I will simply use it as a heuristic for the sake of discussion.

As a working concept, culture includes phenomena ranging from how we tie our shoes to religious beliefs, flirting, the categories we use to parse the world, body piercing, and how we navigate an interface. Typically, we don't realize how and to what extent we are participating in and therefore shaping culture. It is so natural to us—our behaviors, feelings, thoughts, ways of doing, communicating, and understanding all things—that it is extremely difficult for us to step back from our everyday experiences and analyze these practices objectively.

The products of design, whether material like a bicycle or immaterial like a networked computing environment, engage humans through their utility as well as their cultural location—the "situatedness" through which designed artifacts recursively derive their meaning and are simultaneously the object of interpretation. In other words, "situatedness" means the multiple ways people consume and integrate designed artifacts into their lives through interaction (use and embodiment) and through their experience creates understanding.

One aspect of engagement with a designed artifact is through use. Don Norman has written extensively on the issue of product use and usability [1989]. Another dimension closely related to use is how products are experienced or interpreted. These are both deeply cultural activities. It is only recently that the design community has paid attention to the experience of designed artifacts and the impact of experience on consumption ●153 SHEDROFF. In late industrial capitalism, designed artifacts and the experience of them are sites through which people, to differing degrees, live facets of their lives. People live and dream through design. Designed artifacts are, in this sense, "materialized ideologies." Designed artifacts help to create our subjective experience by acts of what Louis Althusser [1972] called "hailing." These are acts of attracting attention (hailing), compelling individuals to generate meaning (interpretation) and behave in specific relation to designed artifacts. To a certain extent, our sense of self and identity flow from the raw material of design that permeates our high modernist world. This is something designers and social scientists need to consider.

In order to think about how design influences us and the relationship between design research and social science, we need to look briefly at the development of anthropology and, in particular, the research method called ethnography—a practice increasingly central to design research. In attempting to describe what he did during extended fieldwork in the Trobriand Islands, one of anthropology's founding figures, Bronislaw Malinowski, used the phrase, "the imponderabilia of actual life" to refer to a perspective that can only be obtained by living among indigenous peoples for long periods of time. By imponderabilia, Malinowski meant the daily life of the people, their ordinary behavior, which the "natives" themselves find difficult to explain or articulate: "[t]he final goal…is to grasp the native's point of view, his relation to life, to realise his vision of his world" [Malinowski 1922, 25].

Prior to Malinowski's pioneering work, early in the 20th century, most early "armchair" anthropologists received their information secondhand from missionaries, soldiers and traders and they did not hesitate to occasionally engage in questionable induction and wild speculation. Malinowski's corrective was simply to take the (then) radical step of living with the people he wanted to learn about and systematically document what he learned in great detail. It seems obvious now, but at the time, a host of prejudices and racist ideologies against living with the so-called "primitives" discouraged that option. But instead of somewhat blindly asserting what people beyond the Western world were doing, anthropologists began to gather firsthand information in order to develop more informed and nuanced theories about human behavior. And the way they gathered that information was modeled after Malinowki's ethnographic, on-the-ground approach in the Trobriands.

Like armchair anthropologists, designers, engineers and other professionals often face barriers (of a different nature) that prevent them from learning about the context and audience for their products, processes and systems. While the trend in design seems to be moving away from the armchair approach, the majority of designed artifacts are planned, prototyped and produced without the benefit of primary, ethnographic research on intended audiences and the context of use.

What Is Ethnography and How Do Academic Social Scientists Do It?

From Malinowksi's early excursions to the field, to the University of Chicago's "urban ethnography" of the 1930s and 1960s, to the present field of cultural studies, social scientists have typically used the ethnographic method for studying and learning about a person or relatively small group of people in order to theorize about culture at a more general level. Almost without exception, ethnography still involves the study of a small group of people in their own environment in order to test the ethnographer's hypotheses. Instead of looking at a small set of variables among a large number of people (the typical approach in survey research), ethnographers attempt to get a deep, detailed understanding of the life and circumstances of fewer people. Ethnographic accounts are both scientifically descriptive and interpretive. They are descriptive because they are designed to capture as much detail as possible, crucial to testing and developing theories. They are interpretive because the ethnographer must determine the significance of the detail in the relatively narrow scope she observes without necessarily gathering broad or statistical information. Ethnography requires analytic rigor and process as well as inductive analysis (reasoning from the particular cases to the general theories).

The practice of ethnography typically involves a range of specific techniques. These are applied as necessitated by the research objectives. The following illustration lists many of the specific research tools used when conducting academic ethnography. Academic ethnographers might use all or a few of these techniques when conducting long-term research. In contrast, the gray area indicates methods that are primarily used in commercial ethnography.

In and outside of academia, participant observation (in the upper right quadrant of the illustration) is regarded as both a core ethnographic practice as well as one of the most demanding techniques in qualitative research. In academic ethnography, participant observation often requires months or years of intensive fieldwork—partly because the problems are so complex, but also because it is thought that the researcher needs to become accepted as a "natural" part of the culture or context under study. The assumption is that this minimizes the impact of the researcher's presence and increases the likelihood that the observations

Research tools for conducting academic ethnography.
The gray area represents those used primarily in commmercial ethnography.

are of more or less naturally occurring phenomenon. The extent to which a researcher can actually become a natural part of the context in which the ethnographer is working has been debated on and off for the past 50 years within social science, yet ethnography continues to increase in popularity as a method.

Participant Observation as Ethnography in Business and Academia

A relatively recent incarnation of participant observation mandates that you immerse yourself into the flow of daily life, copiously documenting what you learn and what you think it means in order to tease out the strands of thought and action enmeshed in a given context. This differs from Malinowski's approach in that he saw his role as that of detached scientific observer, whereas this recent variant emphasizes a more interpretive approach. Advocating for this interpretive approach, Clifford Geertz used the term "thick description" and extended the idea of participant observation as a means of representing another's reality [Geertz 1973]. This technique has a strong grounding in both verbal and visual domains of experience. It also privileges another dimension not captured by the illustration above: empathy, the altered subjectivity that can come from immersion into a particular context.

According to this model, to the extent possible, when the people you are studying gamble on cockfights, as was Geertz's case in Indonesia, you gamble with them and run from the police with them when the game is raided. According to Geetrz, this single event allowed him to gain the trust and respect necessary to effectively conduct his research at the time. In his study of genetic scientists in France, Paul Rabinow [1999] went to work in their research lab and participated in their research routines as much as possible, including running a number of experiments. The notion of empathy and understanding through immersion in participant observation has a physical as well as cognitive component. Using embodiment and bodily practices as a means to gain insight requires the researcher to explore the physicality of experience. This variant has been used successfully in both academic and business contexts ⊙49 LAUREL, ⊙39 JOHNSON. The theory is that by engaging in their activities and observing where engagement is not possible, the ethnographer obtains deeper insight into the desires, beliefs, habits, motivations and understandings of behavior in a given context. The goal of immersion and thick description is to ensure that the resulting ethnographic representations are strongly interpretive and deeply germane, providing more comprehensive intellectual leverage for analysis and theory generation.

In contrast to academic ethnography where social scientists conduct years of participant observation, in a business context, ethnographies (read: participant observation) can last a half a day or even less. How is this possible? Ethnographers working in business are generally PhDs and typically manage this seemingly impossible feat by applying their methodological skill and accrued knowledge of theories of human behavior and social interaction. Through years of experience, trained ethnographers working in a business context also build up a great deal of knowledge garnered through numerous research projects about those segments of the population who are reliably of interest to business. A mastery of ethnographic techniques allows them to quickly gather relevant information, minimize the impact of their presence, quickly synthesize data and draw conclusions.

Academic and business ethnography also require a well-defined set of hypotheses and research objectives designed to test those hypotheses. In academia these research objectives tend to be complex and grounded in a body of previous research. You are expected to spend years or a career figuring out how to address them. Of course, this is a luxury of time that designers and developers do not have. Research objectives that designers have to deal with typically need to be defined in a matter of weeks or days. Accordingly, the goals of commercial ethnography are modest by comparison and therefore achievable.

When companies like IBM, IDEO, Apple, Design Continuum, Cheskin, Intel, Xerox, Herman Miller and Microsoft say they conduct ethnographic research, they are not conducting ethnographic research the same way as academic ethnographers are. These companies are using a few specific ethnographic techniques that make sense in a business context, as indicated by the illustration. It is simply not practical for business entities to engage in the same form or extent of ethnography as is practiced by academics. Despite the constraints imposed by companies seeking to earn a profit from their ethnographic activities, it is possible to successfully use abbreviated ethnographic methods as demonstrated by these companies and others, provided they are carried out by a trained ethnographer.

The use of ethnographic methods in conjunction with design problems— whether graphic, industrial, architectural or otherwise—can have a democratizing and potentially radicalizing effect on aspects of the design profession itself. With regard to designers, an infusion of insights flowing from social science provides opportunities for the profession to think critically about design processes, outcomes, and human interaction. Design process and practice have not historically coalesced, nor has the profession systematically codified its practices, in ways that accommodate critical reflection emerging from the application of ethnographically based analysis. It is simply not built into most design practices.

Ethnographers and other social scientists, on the other hand, also face their own set of challenges in being meaningful contributors to the design process. Most, but not all, anthropologists and ethnographers are trained to observe, analyze, theorize, and publish within the confines of academia or NGOs. This bias stems in part from the way ethnography and social theory is taught and practiced in North America and Western Europe. In other anthropological traditions, however, there is more emphasis on applying ethnographic insights to social contexts with real problems [DaMatta 1993]. This unwillingness or inability to move en masse into other spheres of social activity is changing slowly, but much of academic anthropology and holds an aberrant disdain for the business world. With its emphasis on popular culture, one might expect cultural studies to prove an exception to this trend. While a case might be made for engagement for the British variant of cultural studies, the American strain prefers to write in a specialized and coded vocabulary. I hope acceptance will grow as anthropologists and sociologists begin to recognize that the growing alliance among social scientists and all variants of designers holds immense promise for reshaping consumer culture in unexpected and positive ways.

Some social scientists have been deeply but narrowly concerned with products and design, but this has been largely in the form of critiques. The Frankfurt School was built around critical (and occasionally elitist) sociological analyses of modernist forms of mass production and consumption. More recently, Daniel Miller [1987] and other anthropologists have engaged in their own critiques of products that focus more on the consumption side of the equation as opposed to the production side. While these analyses are useful, they fail to robustly engage the design community and thereby limit their potential contribution.

Ethnography and Design: A Partial History and a Powerful Future

Many people identify the work done at Xerox PARC and other research labs in the early 1980s as the first use of ethnography in design processes, specifically system design [see Blomberg, et al. 2003]. While it is true that a number of anthropologists were hired by Xerox and carried out pioneering ethnographic research, it is important to identify important a few precursors to Xerox PARC's integration of social science and design. Broadly speaking, the antecedents to socially oriented design can be traced back to early Futurism, Constructivism and The Bauhaus School. Later, Germany's Hochschule für Gestaltung (HfG) Ulm, and the Swiss Kunstgewerbeschule, Basel also produced influential, socially/scientifically based design ❍94 GONZALES CRISP.

In 1955, on the other side of the Atlantic, Henry Dreyfuss published *Designing for People*. In it he argued that conducting field research was critical to successful industrial design. This position was based on the insight that industrial design should both help and delight people. To that end Dreyfuss engaged in any number of activities and contexts he thought relevant to the design problems he sought to solve. This ranged from driving a diesel train, to spreading manure, to washing clothes in order to design better products [Dreyfuss 1974]. Robert Probst, who eventually headed the Herman Miller Research Corporation, strongly advocated for field research that closely resembled participant observation. He emphasized capturing visual data and using cognitive models derived from interviews with the audience for whom he sought to design furniture [Rothstein 1999].

In a slightly different vein, the British sculptor Richard Wentworth has been taking a series of photographs called *Making Do and Getting By* since 1974. One could describe the photos as a visual notebook, or perhaps as a small anthropological investigation. The objects in his images fall loosely into categories of acts: piling, propping, wedging and leaning. A door is wedged open with a gumboot, the clapper of an alarm bell is silenced with a Fudge bar still in its wrapper, and a catering-size tin of peas is used as a cafe doorstop. Wentworth's visual anthropology carefully documents these *ad hoc* acts of design, demonstrating how people bend the world to their will by using their imagination [Wentworth 1985]. Similarly, Rachel Strickland's striking work on the Portable Effects project explores the relationship among cognition, material culture and problem solving using video as a research tool in the tradition of *cinéma vérité* ●118 STRICKLAND.

The introduction of social science theory and ethnographic methods into the fields of human computer interaction (HCI) and computer supported co-operative work (CSCW) represents a modest high point in transdisciplinary work (and much of this work was carried out initially at Xerox PARC). However, in general, the use of the sociological and anthropological literature has unfolded in extremely selective ways. Initially, engineers and computer scientists, as opposed to social scientists working in a research and development setting, borrowed from sociology and anthropology in the course of developing CSCW, GUIs and tangible computing. Social scientists, however, were soon drawn into service. The use of social science method and theory in this computer- and networking-based context was often aimed at pragmatically trying to improve these now commodified tools [Dourish 2001]. Ironically, the anthropological and sociological methods and theory that have been utilized were themselves socially decontextualized. The methods and theory used have largely been deracinated of considerations of phenomena like social inequality, gender, class, and, more generally, power relations. Historically, product and graphic design have followed a similarly narrow path and used a few research tools (and little theory) imported from or applied by social science practitioners.

HCI, CSCW, as well as industrial and graphic design have avoided or found little utility for theorists like Franz Fanon, Pierre Bourdieu, C. Wright Mills and Michel de Certeau, whose analyses possess a more deeply contextualized, critical perspective. Perhaps this is due in part to the density of their ivory-tower prose, but I suspect it is primarily because it is not immediately clear how to apply the work of these theorists to issues so intimately bound up in the generation of capital and social reproduction. Not only would design benefit from the introduction of powerful social theory into its practice, but social scientists, tending to write in technical and coded language (making their theories impenetrable to the general population) would reap rewards. The application and "materialization" of theory in design stands to clarify and operationalize theories, as well as to contribute to the development of alternative or supplementary criteria in the planning, crafting, manufacture and assessment of graphic and industrial design. Victor Margolin makes a similar argument in calling for a deeper assessment of "…the relation between products and how people construct ideals of human happiness…" and "…studies of technology innovation on which to base proposals for social policies or legislation that would link human well being to the presence or absence of particular products" [2002, 53].

Conclusion

In thinking about the relation between products and human happiness there is much at stake outside the traditional scope of design—macroeconomic and ecological factors some to mind. From an ethnographically based point of view, there are other considerations that come into play. I conclude by exploring the possible relevance of the ethnographic insights of French social historian Michel de Certeau for design [1998].

On cultural issues, de Certeau's originality lay in his refusal to endorse the old opposition of high culture versus popular culture and by extension the dichotomy of creative art versus mass production. Over the course of his research, he analyzed what he called the "operations" that people perform with designed artifacts and other cultural objects. What was at stake for him was the way people use some readymade objects, the way they organize their private space, their office or workplace, the way they "practice" their environment and all public space available to them including shopping malls, town streets, airports, railway stations, and movie theatres. This approach allowed de Certeau to focus his theorizing on the ordinary practices of people's everyday life. He replaced presupposition of passive mass consumption of objects and products with the assumption of large-scale, anonymous creativity by ordinary people. For de Certeau, every man or woman could be regarded as the "producer" of his/her own lifestyle through the art of recycling objects, adapting and transforming readymade products.

While it is true that ethnographic research results in better products and systems, it is not enough to produce better products and systems in the conventional sense. For designers and social scientists the question should become: how can we design artifacts so they radiate the degrees of freedom necessary to enhance the self-invention that de Certeau observed? Can the cross-pollination between these professions move toward the introduction of emancipatory content into designed artifacts? Can this direction comport with the business imperatives inherent in the production of goods and development of services? I think the answer is yes, but the questions are dauntingly complex and solutions will only come through sustained and hard work. The logical point of departure for engagement is increased social science and design collaboration, working towards the development of a robust, theoretically-informed, critical design research practice.

The Paradox
of Design Research
The Role of Informance
BONNIE MCDANIEL JOHNSON

Design research is inherently paradoxical: it is both imaginative and empirical. It cannot be simply empirical because the "typical" consumers that researchers need to understand are rarely able to articulate their needs ○47 DISHMAN.

Design researchers must go beyond what they can find: to see more than is visible, and to learn more than can be heard. Accordingly, design research is an act of imagination, just as much as design itself ○23 IRELAND. Yet it must also be grounded in empirical evidence, for no business manager wants to think that the research on which her profits depend is made up in the research department.

The metaphor of consumers as tribes of culturally unknown people has influenced much of design research today. Hence, ethnographic field methods and other techniques used by anthropologists provide disciplined approaches for research. The goal of ethnography is to understand what is foreign to one's own world view ○30 PLOWMAN. Some have used the expression "empathetic design" to express a more ambitious goal of seeing a situation internally; that is, as potential consumers will see it [Leonard and Rayport 1997].

The goal of "informance" (and its cousins, performance ethnography and design improvisation) goes beyond understanding consumers' culture or even having an "inside" understanding of consumers. Its goal is to create, through performance, characters that can speak about their world, express informed opinions about product features, answer questions about design possibilities, and even design products. Informance is a set of techniques in which actors and/or researchers study what is known about consumers and role-play potential consumers ○41 DISHMAN, ○49 LAUREL. Informance subsumes both ethnography and empathy. It begins with ethnographic study—questioning and observing people in particular consumer segments. Researchers move on to interpreting their data through empathy: seeing situations, uses, and elements as the studied consumers would see them. The next step is informance itself: acts of pretending which transform empathy into action.

Pretending has value in many ways for design researchers. It is a way of learning. Just as children pretend to be moms, dads and firemen as a way of learning how to be adults, researchers can learn how the world works for the people they pretend to be. It is a way of changing oneself. As people can change their negative moods by pretending that they are happy, researchers can change their attitudes and see values where they would not have otherwise imagined them. Perhaps most important, pretending allows researchers to give a voice to their understanding of consumers. These consumers become "we" rather than "they," and as such, join the design team.

Two situations especially call for informance. Design for entirely new categories of products calls for Informance because new kinds of products are particularly difficult for most people to imagine. Informance is also particularly useful with products for populations who have little in common with the designers. A product may be for a segment that is demographically remote from the designer; for example, 30-year-old designers creating products for people who are 70; or a product may be intended as "worldwide" and thus culturally remote from any individual designer.

Informance can take many forms; different forms are practical in different business situations. In his essay, Dishman describes the most elaborate form: "performance for an audience." To use these techniques, you may need to have assistance from someone who, like Dishman and Laurel, has professional training in performance. But as their examples illustrate, you can create informances using teams of researchers and designers, most of whom have no formal training. The great advantage of "performance for an audience" is that many people can be brought into the research and design process; for example, engineers who may be remote from the research process can be included in the audience and bring new insights and engineering components that improve the design.

A second kind of Informance, described by Laurel, is "design improvisation." Here there is no audience apart from the team members who are performing for each other. The advantage is that it requires less polish and probably fewer props. Sessions can also flow back and forth between improvisations and discussions of design implications and possibilities.

Informance can be part of the everyday life of design teams, and at its most casual level, it already is. Team discussions with improvised examples are an elementary form of informance. As researchers and designers discuss their potential consumers, some people will no doubt exemplify their ideas with comments about what Consumer Jane might think, and even mimic what Jane might say about a design feature. This pretense should be encouraged in team discussions. As team members bring rigor to their characterizations of consumers they have studied, they can bring consumers' voices into the meetings is a quite useful way.

In concentrating on the imaginative aspects of informance, I have not meant to neglect the importance of grounding the imaginative techniques of Informance in high-quality quantitative research. The people who are improvised must be drawn from scientifically selected samples to represent targeted consumer segments ○63 PURPURA. The idea is to allow typical consumers to say what they cannot themselves say by transforming them into characters in a performance. The power of informance lies in embracing the paradox: using a sound empirical basis as springboard for the skill of the researchers and designers to create characters.

Designing for the New Old
Asking, Observing and Performing Future Elders
ERIC DISHMAN

Designing for a Disruptive Demography

The beginning of the 21st century marks the end of the period of human
history with more young people than old, and for the rest of human
history, there are going to be more old people than young, unless there
are some very major surprises. —Joel Cohen, *Guardian*, August 2001
[Meek 2001]

While our Y2K worries about old computers "retiring" at midnight filled the cable TV channels, a more significant "old age" phenomenon snuck onto the scene with hardly a headline: the dawn of the age of the aged. Already over-burdened healthcare systems will face a worldwide wave of retirees who will live longer, cost more to treat, and demand new goods and services to help them stay active and independent. What will this age of the "new old" look like? How can design research inform the next generation of technologies to support this next generation of elders?

I started asking some of these questions at Interval Research in a 1993 project called ElderSpace. Here in 2003, I am again trying to design technologies for future elders in an Intel Research project called Proactive Health [www.intel.com/research/prohealth]. I will use these two projects to describe diverse techniques for conducting design research into peoples' everyday lives. In particular, I will explore how theatre, or what I have called "informance design," provides a powerful tool for understanding the interaction infrastructures upon which new inventions are built. Along the way, I will also promote aging-in-place as a design space worthy of more attention.

Case Study: The ElderSpace Project at Interval

Why are we working so hard to build a better nursing home? Why aren't
we doing everything in our power to design technologies that help
people grow old at home, instead of imprisoning them in institutions?
—"Bill," Senior Engineer at Interval Research, September 1993

Bill's provocative questions came as we were tearing down foam-core walls that we had constructed in three Interval conference rooms to simulate a more empowering, efficient nursing home of the future. Standing literally upon the rubble of the ideas that we had prototyped, I stared at Bill with dread and dismay. He was right: we had started with the wrong research question.

ElderSpace emerged from early Interval study of the residents and staff of a nursing home called "Live Oak". After weeks of analyzing video and photos from the facility, five of us—three social scientists, one artist, and an industrial designer—set out to produce what I called an "informance" or "informative performance" [Burns et al., 1994; Dishman, 2002]. Heeding Brenda Laurel's call to action in *Computers as Theatre*, we were ready to "improve the quality of human-computer experiences through new approaches to their design ... to create new visions of what people can do with computers" [Laurel 1991]. We were determined to move well beyond the personal computer, which was hardly "personal" or commonplace for anyone other than office workers in 1993. For that matter, it was also uncommon to imagine nurses (who today are still mostly women) and elderly residents (also mostly women) as the intended users.

Humans are inadequate proxies even for people who are exactly like us. We are impoverished proxies for people who differ from us in so many ways. In ElderSpace, we were mostly in our 20s and 30s and, except for knowing our grandparents, were effectively clueless about the often invisible lives of elders and the staff who care for them. To explore these unknowns, each of us adopted a character—what have been called "personas"—based upon representative combinations of actual people we had studied. For two weeks, we tried to recreate for our own young, able bodies what some of the age-related effects of physical and cognitive impairment, loss of hearing and vision, and social isolation might be like. We brainstormed and built concept prototypes for our personas, using improvisation techniques and acted-out storyboards both to inspire and to constrain our ideas. Each designer-actor advocated for his or her persona and how each invention would fit or fail within the larger social system of a place like Live Oak.

"Susannah" (played by Karen Wieckert) and "Joe" (played by Colin Burns) use a video link between their resident rooms in Interval's ElderSpace informance in 1993. We combined cardboard props with working prototypes in a conference room to simulate this nursing home of the future. They used the video link to check in on each other several times a day.

The first phase of this informance was all about using theatrical techniques—using live bodies interacting in real space and real contexts with props to produce a plausible story—as part of the design process itself. We could have stopped with the rich portfolio of concepts we had produced—wireless ear buds, wearable microphones and medical sensors, object- and people- tracking systems, smart paper, and immersive video conferencing. But we decided that the best way to share our design ideas with our colleagues was to create a "Live Oak 2003" drama.

Why bother going through the trouble of scripting, memorizing, embodying and acting out the lives of these personas in a fully staged set? For us, the second phase of the informance was about iteration, instantiation, and integration.

Becky Fuson played the part of a nursing home administrator in Interval's 1993 ElderSpace project. We prototyped a wall-sized nurses station (designed by Colin Burns), which represented the location and health status of the residents and staff on a large graphical map of the imagined facility. The system was mostly imaginary, but showed enough of the concept to spark Interval engineers to start designing biosensors and location tracking technologies that might ease the administrative burdens of the many actual nursing home staff members we had studied.

What came to be known as "the show" gave us another chance to revise our concepts, forced us to move the ideas from paper to tangible prototypes, and challenged us to consider just how all of those technical and social systems might (or might not) work with one another.

With a mix of foam-core walls and computerized prototypes, we constructed three different environments for our five personas. "Joe" lived in a single-resident room with a video link to other residents. He was fairly mobile but had difficulty hearing. "Susannah," quite articulate and physically active, was virtually blind even with her glasses, while her more silent roommate, "Molly," was confined to her wheelchair with what may have been early-stage Alzheimer's. Each of them had a wall-sized screen interface of her own. The third room was the caregivers' station where a central communication system and wall-sized patient monitoring projection kept the staff—"Donny, Judy, and Becky"—quite busy with a range of triaged prompts to help them get through their day.

The show went something like this. With her wall-sized mural interface, Susannah "watched" soap operas recorded on her hard drive, made a Star Trek-style call to check on Joe, put in her eye-drops thanks to a whispered alert from an automated medicine tracker, and exercised with her friends online through an international "Seniornet." Molly was able to read an interactive *People Magazine* with video segments, to call for help at any moment, to have a hands-free conversation with the facility's chef, and to go on a virtual window-shopping trip at the mall with her grand-daughter. Joe played along with *Jeopardy* at his own pace, joined the video call with Susannah, and then showed off tagged paper photos of his old home which magically brought up digital versions on his wide screen. Donny, Becky, and Judy each attended to the residents' needs, constantly informed of emergency conditions by their wireless microphone/earbud system linked into the main computer and to each other.

We cast the fifty or so Interval audience members as themselves—as technology researchers studying a nursing home—so that they could ask questions about the technologies without breaking the continuity of the scenes. The informance lasted twenty minutes, but we ran it three times back-to-back so each audience member could see what was happening in the different rooms "simultaneously." Everyone attended all three versions, except for three people who later said the foam-core environment was "too real" and "too much like a nursing home" for them to deal with. Following the show, we tore down the set to launch a brainstorming session with all of the attendees about how to make some of those prototyped concepts into real technologies.

So did the ElderSpace informance work? We did not go into the elder facility business, but that was never our design goal. Several of the technology concepts—especially around contextually-aware computing and tangible user interfaces—were taken on by other projects in the lab. The five designer-actors reported that they learned more by "doing" and "being" those characters than they could have by any other means. Most of the audience felt deeply engaged with the issues of social isolation, independence and health monitoring that we brought up. As a design process, most saw informance as having enormous power in two areas: 1. helping the designer to consider how each individual user is embedded in larger social systems; and 2. forcing us as technologists to evaluate the whole electronic ecosystem and interaction infrastructure when trying to bring in new technologies. And as I stood listening to Bill's questions amidst shredded pieces of foam core, disconnected computers and whiteboards filled with ideas from the Interval audience, I walked away with a new research question that did not stop haunting me.

Case Study: The Proactive Health Project at Intel

I pleaded with my children for years not to put me in an institution. Now that I am here, I wish I had come a decade ago. The hassle of taking care of my house is gone. The yard mowing is gone. The loneliness is gone. You ought to be convincing all those other 70-year olds to stop putting every penny into caring for their homes and to come to a place like this where the home cares for you!—"Mark," Senior Citizen in Intel Research Study, March 2003

Questioning our questions is the most important thing we can do in any design research project. ElderSpace left me convinced that systems to support future elders should empower them to stay in their own homes. But Mark, a retired 79-year-old jewelry maker who lives in a high-rise retirement center, made me rethink that assumption during our recent Proactive Health studies at Intel. We do design research with real people for exactly this reason—to have our questions, ideas, prototypes and interfaces held up to the scrutiny of a diverse set of potential future customers so we can make better choices.

Thanks to Mark and many like him, we have come to understand that aging-in-place is really about giving people choice and that "home" must include all types of elder care facilities. Our recent focus groups with people in their 50s (future elders) and 70s (today's elders) revealed that we must also expand our definition of "healthcare." While these groups did ask for medical diagnostic devices and pill reminders, they also demanded tools for psychological support, promoting good fitness and nutrition, fending off social isolation, coping with loss of memory-hearing-sight and staying engaged in the world with a sense of purpose. These design themes echoed ElderSpace from ten years earlier. Bonnie Johnson, my mentor at Interval, always used to say: "Focus on peoples' enduring concerns."

BACKGROUND	EXPERT INTERVIEWS	2 dozen audio/video taped 1-2 hour interviews with Alzheimer's experts, cognition experts, geriatricians, home care nurses, etc.
	LITERATURE REVIEW	Hire consultants to review medical, popular and financial literature on cognitive decline; team to read top 3 works in each category
	WAKE-UP INTERVIEWS	Initial "pilot" phone and in-home interviews with elders and adult children dealing with cognitive decline; recruited by friend-of-friend
EXPLORATORY	CAMERA SURVEYS	Recruit 4 "segments" based on cognitive decline: send 24-roll disposable camera with 24 survey questions to about 100 households
	FOCUS GROUPS	Select "extremes" and "norms" to attend 12-person focus groups based on healthy aging, early stage decline, mid-stage and advanced
	CONTEXTUAL INTERVIEWS	Follow up in-home Interviews with 12 households for each segment: in-context discussions, show home and artifacts, videotaped
	SHADOW STUDIES	Choose 1-2 households from each segment for in-depth; we live with family for 1-3 days; observe with field notes and still photos
	LONGITUDINAL INTEVIEWS	Continue occasional follow-up contextual interviews with 2-3 households from each segment; note changes over time
	SURVEYS	Take key findings—such as day to day variability of cognitive disease—and survey larger numbers to see if it is broader discovery
CONCEPT	STORYBOARD SKETCHES	Cartoon-like drawings of future technologies used to help manage cognitive decline: shown to elders in interviews and focus groups
	INFORMANCE/FOCUS TROUPES	Invite key 2-3 households from each segment to theatrical show of key concepts/themes/prototypes for critique and brainstorming
	PROTOTYPE TRIALS	Deploy anything from "Wizard of Oz" to working prototypes of, for example, safety monitoring systems in 12-24 actual households

This represents the ideal model of methods and techniques used in Intel's year long Cognitive Decline study.

So how do we go about understanding these enduring concerns? Doing design research in a results-oriented, quarterly-driven company like Intel means we rarely have the resources to do full ethnographic, participant-observer field studies that sometimes last weeks, months, or years ❯30 PLOWMAN. I suspect the vast majority of so-called "corporate ethnographies" are similar to the structure we are using for our "Cognitive Decline" (CD) study. The table above shows an idealized, simplified model of our year-long CD study. Our funding and our findings will dictate how close we hold to this plan.

We are currently in the middle of the CD study. After background research that included expert interviews, literature review, and numerous in-home visits with friends who are experiencing cognitive decline as "patients" or "caregivers," we moved into the more formal, but still exploratory study of about 50 households. The crux of this phase has been exploratory focus groups followed by 3- to 5-hour contextual interviews (described below) that are videotaped and photographed with people interacting with their "stuff" in their homes, offices, cars or wherever appropriate. We have followed up with several households using two-day long "shadow studies" with more observation, less interview. These provide a deeper sense of daily routines but also day-to-day, weekend versus weekday, and seasonal differences that may be important.

In Intel's Cognitive Decline study, we conduct contextual interviews in the homes of Alzheimer's and other patients who are dealing with cognitive decline. We take hundreds of photos of these homes to help remind us of the challenges that our end users face. In this case, Bob's daughters have placed notes all around his house to try to help their Dad stay safe and independent. It is hard for him to remember who is a "stranger" and who is a friend or family member.

"Carl", one of the participants in Intel's Cognitive Decline study, shows me his wood shop and electric saws with great pride. These days he has very few projects to keep him busy and to give him a sense of purpose. His family and friends are frightened he may hurt himself on the tools in the basement; his wife often sits for hours just on the other side of the basement door so she can hear if things are okay.

Contextual interviews—our primary tool of the trade—are essentially structured conversations whereby we use a list of about twenty themes (e.g., daily routine, privacy, technology usage, etc.) as suggested topics, but often the tour of a person's home will lead us into a "deep dive" on their key issues. In a recent visit to "Carl," an early-stage Alzheimer's patient in Rochester, New York, I spent an hour in his basement talking about his woodworking hobby. He used to have a "purpose jar" in which his friends and family placed requests for him to build toys, cabinets or fence posts. These days he has no sense of identity or usefulness because no one asks him to build anything for fear of him hurting himself on his electric saws. In every household, we now look for the metaphorical equivalent of a "purpose jar" and try to imagine how technologies might support such higher-level needs.

It is critical to understand both what people say ("I exercise for an hour every morning") and to observe what they do (he walks slowly around the basement for an hour while listening to music). For almost every story someone tells us or for every claim they make ("I can use the remote control just fine"), we, as researchers, are constantly asking, "Can you show me how you do that?" Sometimes it is a matter of understanding the specifics of what they are referring to. Other times it is a matter of their over-representing their abilities or being in denial about some issue, which becomes plain to see as they struggle with the remote control. Our goal is not to embarrass them or "call their bluff" but to listen intently between the lines of their words and actions for what they value, what they fear, what they hope for.

When doing contextual interviews, we try to capture multiple and competing points of view. In the CD study, we tack back and forth between studies of boomers (the cohort) and today's elders (the lifestage) to get a sense of how boomers' expectations for aging mesh with the practical realities of people already experiencing aging challenges themselves. Furthermore, we interview and observe anyone who is relevant in the chain of care: the boomer or elder with decline, neighbors, friends, family members near and far, doctors and nurses, even their online support group. Every design research project must consider how the research participants are embedded in a larger social system and how to study the network of key players who inform the user's values, beliefs, actions, lack of action and stories.

We often hear very different versions of a story depending on who is present in the interview. With his wife sitting on the sofa next to him, a man with early-stage Alzheimer's recently proclaimed to me: "I'm doing fine—my memory is still good most of the time." Hours later, with just the two of us, he admitted "I'm having lots of trouble with my memory, but I can't let my wife know because it will just destroy her." Towards the end of the interview, his wife whispered to me: "He is too embarrassed to tell you the real problems he is having—he even hides it from me because he is worried I will have his driver's license taken away or put him in a home." This kind of face-saving is not unique to the extreme circumstance of cognitive decline; I have heard similarly discrepant stories from different family members about everything from how they mange their calendar to deciding upon what car to buy to whether or not they watch television.

We are currently moving from exploratory research to concept feedback research to elicit input from boomers and elders on our early sketches, storyboards and prototypes. The biggest challenge here is helping them to imagine beyond their current concepts of aging, healthcare and technology. "Mary," a 78-year-old caregiver for her husband who has dementia, told us a year ago in response to our wireless safety monitoring concept: "There is no way I would let a system track our whereabouts and what we're doing. I don't want some strangers knowing everything about me and my family." Unfortunately, her husband has declined to the point where Mary has to sit with him twenty-four hours a day. When we arrived for our latest visit, she met us at the door: "Give me that wireless safety thing you showed me last time—I never imagined it would get this bad!"

We often find people unable to step out of their current experiences to be able to give a fully considered critique of an idea. They cannot conceive of new technologies much beyond their personal computers. They cannot understand privacy concerns beyond those they face already. If healthy, they cannot imagine the need for systems to help them get dressed in the morning or to make tea. This brings us full circle to the role of informance discussed in ElderSpace. We are in the midst of scripting "the next show," this time with caregivers and patients who are grappling with the nightmare of Alzheimer's. We will ask them to react to a future made real for them by actors with cardboard props and "Wizard of Oz" prototypes. And in the ways they so wonderfully always do, these future elders will force us to face the strengths and weaknesses of what we have imagined—and to rethink our research questions and assumptions again.

A Framework for Asking, Observing and Performing

We actually used some kind of video screen to watch each other open presents together at Christmas. I was in North Carolina, and Eric was all the way in Portland. Who would have ever imagined we could do such amazing things! I never thought it possible!
—"Jack," my grandfather, December 2001

Until time travel is perfected, we have no choice but to use every research method at our disposal to help us make an informed and empathetic guess, as best we can, about what needs, aspirations and values our future end users will have in the time when we believe our product will exist. Understanding future elders provides an extreme case of what designers must do all of the time: anticipate how some future group of people might discover, learn, buy, use and dispose of

The Ask, Observe, Perform framework is appropriate to use at all phases of design research, whether when just starting "exploratory" research to understand people, or getting user input on concept prototypes, or even testing/trialing nearly-finished products and marketing messages.

some product/creation we believe we invented for them. These two Interval and Intel case studies have touched upon a potentially confusing mish-mash of methods—expert interviews, focus groups, ethnographic field research, informance design, personas, storyboards and tons of iterative prototyping. A simple framework I use for almost any design project may help: "Asking, Observing, Performing."

Asking is about understanding the opinions, life stories, enduring concerns, everyday activities and core values of people, whether at the beginning of a project when defining the research questions or at the end when soliciting their feedback about a concept, interface or product. Observing real people in real contexts is a critical complement to asking, to help identify patterns and extremes of behavior, unarticulated needs, and places where peoples' actions and stories about what they do differ in important ways. Performing is about designers acting/testing out the future lives of their imagined end users, as well as getting those users themselves to embody and critique plausible future scenarios using concept, prototype and product level "props" to simulate future technologies.

As simple as the framework seems, Asking, Observing, Performing is never so neat and sequential in practice. Nor does it provide a cookie-cutter approach that works for everyone and everything. Literary scholar Terry Eagleton reminds us that "it is not a matter of starting from certain theoretical or methodological problems: it is a matter of starting from what we want to do, and then seeing which methods and theories will help us to achieve these ends" [210]. Design research methods are themselves "products" that need to be designed for different audiences, purposes and contexts—it really does all depend on what you want to do.

Through design research, I believe we have the capacity to imagine, invent and iterate our way out of a demographic/economic crisis that hopefully all of us will be able to look back on with a smile when we are in our 90s. On the way, we will have to ask different questions about what we mean by "home," "healthcare," "old" and "computer." And if we ask about, observe and perform the contexts of future elders, we may share in my grandfather's awe at the amazing things we have invented—at the products and services that we never thought possible.

DESIGN IMPROVISATION
Ethnography Meets Theatre

BRENDA LAUREL

Theatre has been an explicit part of my life since I stuck my nose up to a glitter-and-glue star on a backstage flat in my junior high school. I did both undergraduate and graduate work in theatre, and working in the field of computer interaction design has been a long, strange and not altogether unrelated trip. One comes to understand, through intuition, observation or even critical theory, that we perform ourselves, and that within the construction I call "me" are several different characters—mom, teacher, partner, friend, daughter, shopper, fan, person waiting in line, rider on the subway or user of a computer. While core characteristics run through all these performative selves, we may see by simple reflection how who we are—and who we are performing—is highly situated. When we observe those around us, we see that context creates some common performative (and experiential) threads among people in any given situation. This observation leads to two sorts of challenges for designers: to notice how a person interacts with a situated context, and to design objects and experiences that enable people to perform themselves somewhat differently in those same situations—with greater pleasure, ease or agency.

Eric Dishman turned me on to the idea of performance ethnography when I met him at the University of Texas at Austin in the late 1980s. As a practice that evolved in the discipline of anthropology, performance ethnography attempts to understand observed experience by memorizing and performing it. An interesting connection with the theatrical practice known as "Technique Acting" is implicit in this process. The well-known James-Lange Theory of Emotion would predict that if we can mimic a person's physical postures, facial expressions and expressive gestures, we can invoke physiological reactions in our own bodies that map to the subject's emotional states. Technique actors use gestures, facial expressions, posture, gait and other physical transformations, both to represent characters and, secondarily, to physiologically induce emotional states. With the addition of spoken words and semiotic gestures, performance ethnography—like technique acting—becomes a cognitive as well as an emotional tool for understanding people (or characters) in situated contexts. The technique has been appropriated by students of human behavior and popular culture. The idea of "informance," as described by Eric Dishman and Bonnie Johnson in this book, is an understanding of performance ethnography as a tool for design research.

At Interval Research, where I worked with Bonnie and Eric, we latched onto "informance" as a significant research technique. I taught a basic workshop in theatrical improvisation to all interested scientists in the lab. The class involved basic theatre games, performing observed characters and working with masks. Several of our improv-trained researchers became participants in the informance activities staged by Bonnie and Eric. Eric was also an informance subject in the early investigations that led to Purple Moon (a transmedia company that created games, web activities and tangibles for girls), performing a preteen girl in several situations. He would blush, I'm sure, to know how good he was at it. We went on to use informance techniques with designers and developers after Purple Moon had "spun off" from Interval Research.

After Purple Moon was acquired by Mattel, I became involved as a part-time instructor at Art Center College of Design in what was then called the Communication and New Media Design graduate program. During that time, I consulted on the design of the curriculum that now guides the department I chair, the graduate Media Design Program. One of the courses I developed in the process was a workshop in Design Improvisation. The workshop focused first on basic improvisational techniques and theatre games, then on performance ethnography. I asked students to document people "having trouble" with technology in public places. The documentation medium of choice was digital video. Then we proceeded to figure out how we could use the mindset of the improvisational actor—optimized for invention and creativity—to go a step beyond performance ethnography to improvisational design.

Let's say that you have captured an interesting scene on video and that you have memorized it and can perform it from the perspective of its main character. That's performance ethnography. Then let's say you take it a step further and speak the character's thoughts aloud as you perform the scene. That's what Method actors would call "speaking the subtext"—a technique where actors verbalize the characters' thoughts, interspersed with the actual lines of dialogue. Ironically, this aspect of Design Improvisation appropriates practices from Method Acting as promulgated by Constantin Stanislavski as a reaction against the Technique Acting that was standard practice in the early 20th Century. In performance ethnography, the "lines" are not derived from a script, but rather from what the subject actually said during the event being studied. Improvisation with vocalized subtext can help design students to pinpoint their understandings of the cognitive as well as the emotional aspects of the subject's experience. The student is then asked to perform the scene again, improvising solutions to the problems encountered by the original subject "on the fly." Such preliminary design improvisations are rough and often illogical, but they stimulate creativity and often lead designers into new solution spaces. At this point the designer may step back and deploy more traditional design skills to visualize a new technology or interface that may banish the original subject's difficulties.

CONT'D ON P. 54

Eun-Kyung Chung, a Design Improv student who earned her MFA in Art Center's Media Design program in 2000, chose to explore the plight of soft-serve ice cream servers. Eun-Kyung walked through each step of the process I have just described. Below are images taken from her work and a transcript of her comments.

Above: The employee takes an order from the customer. He then turns his back to the customer and walks to the soft-serve machine. After making sure he has the right flavor, he then has to hunch over for several moments in order to dispense the ice cream completely.

The employee has to hunch over for several moments in order to dispense the ice cream completely.

Doing this many times throughout the day is likely to lead to chronic back pain, and the customer can't see the performance.

My design solution enables the employee to face the customer the entire time.

Left: In my design, the soft-serve machine is located overhead, and extends down to the eye level of the customer. This is also where the product dispensers are. After choosing a cone the customer picks a flavor seen through clear windows located above the dispenser by pointing to it.

My design makes it easier for the employee and gives him a chance
to perform for the customer.

Perhaps the most evocative insight from this design improvisation process was not simply that the workers had less than optimal ergonomic conditions. Rather, it was the performative nature of their work—glimpsed even when they were in torturous postures—that took center stage. Soft-serve ice cream as virtuoso performance!

A final design improvisation integrates the designer's solution into a performance of the original subject in the same situated context but with new interfaces or affordances. The final improv allows the designer to explore the design solution in all sensory and cognitive modalities. Iteration may be required to arrive at a solution that solves all the problems, but the bulk of the redesign job has been done—with the designer's intuitive, haptic and emotional capabilities fully engaged in a way that cannot be achieved through mere graphic design or well-plotted "user scenarios." While the actor uses empathy to perform dramatic characters in scripted situations, the designer uses empathy to perform design solutions that are drawn from deep identification with real, individual people in specific situated contexts in the real world.

Leading people away from performing "consumer," "worker," or any other role in a way that is unnecessarily constrained is an enduring goal in my work as a designer and a teacher. "De-humanization" isn't quite the problem: I don't mind being de-humanized (or "fishified," if you prefer) in order to breathe underwater when I'm snorkeling, for instance. More to the point is the sort of flattening that comes from being reduced to a role that does not admit of such natural characteristics as curiosity, the desire for freedom or the ability to exercise creativity and self-expression. Getting inside the body and emotions of a person performing as a postman, a computer-user or an ice cream server can help us as designers notice what we might design to make the role one that would be more enjoyable and rewarding to play.

Hispanic Culture in Design Research

More than Language

CARLOS SANTOS

As a bilingual researcher, I am frequently asked to conduct research focused on the Hispanic Market in the United States. This is not surprising; according to recent census figures, Hispanics now make up the largest minority in the United States. More than 37 million Hispanics reside in the U.S., a 58% increase between 1990 and 2000. The combined buying power of U.S. Hispanics is estimated at more than $450 billion. Corporations are naturally interested in the potential opportunities this market offers, and they conduct research for product design, branding and marketing with Hispanics in order to better target their products or services.

However, as gratifying as it is to conduct research with Hispanic participants, it can also be a frustrating experience if one is trying to apply General Market approaches to the Hispanic consumer. In Hispanic research, as with any other research, the GIGO principle (Garbage In, Garbage Out) applies.

Here then are the top five things to be aware of with Hispanic research in order to minimize GIGO. Under each of the five main points, I have described some common mistakes.

Language

Think like a wise man but communicate in the language of the people.
—William Butler Yeats

Marketers and designers are aware that in-language communications play a vital role in the design of a product or service for the Hispanic Market. Therefore, it is not surprising that the most common objective driving research with Hispanics has to do with issues around "Spanish language." It is also an area where most research and design "issues" occur. Some of the most common mistakes include:

MISCONCEPTION FOCUSING ON WHICH LANGUAGE (ENGLISH OR SPANISH) RATHER THAN WHEN AND WHY IT IS USED

It is well documented that most Hispanics in the US, even those that have spent a significant amount of time in this country, still prefer to speak in Spanish. They view Spanish-language television, speak in Spanish with co-workers and listen to Spanish-language radio. In other words, it is possible to survive in this country, even if you don't speak English.

However, language is not a binary, either/or variable. Even with consumers that are considered "Spanish Dominant"—a term referring to individuals that have a strong preference for Spanish for most communications—English may be used in certain situations. For instance, a basic transaction such as a purchase may be possible in English. Asking for more information about a new product is more likely to occur in Spanish.

MISCONCEPTION EQUATING ENGLISH COMPETENCE WITH ENGLISH PREFERENCE

This is a common assumption among designers and marketers. The fact that a consumer is capable of speaking English does not necessarily indicate the desire or the preference to do so. Hearing a familiar language is comforting and reassuring to most people. This is particularly important for Hispanics that may be new to the area, or who are self-conscious about their language skills.

The comfort of language comes from its associations. Hispanic research participants speak of language as being more than a means of communication. It is a connection to their culture, their parents, their ancestors and their history. It is a part of who they are, who they were and who they will be.

Comfort is also a matter of having confidence in what is being communicated. Hearing something in Spanish provides a level of comfort regarding comprehension for many Hispanic consumers. If it's in English, they might think they understood, but if it's in Spanish, they'll know if they understood. This is a very reassuring aspect of using Spanish with Hispanic audiences, when appropriate.

MISCONCEPTION ASSUMING THAT LANGUAGE PREFERENCE APPLIES EQUALLY TO ALL MANNER OF COMMUNICATIONS (SPEAKING, LISTENING, WATCHING, READING)

If most Hispanics prefer to speak Spanish given the choice, then a logical assumption might be that they also prefer to read in Spanish. This is not necessarily the case, as many immigrants arrive with a limited education. Research needs to understand whether print is an appropriate medium when addressing the language issue. The same applies to other media, such as the Internet, newspapers and radio.

MISCONCEPTION ASSUMING THAT ALL HISPANICS SPEAK THE "SAME" SPANISH

This seems like a reasonable assumption, until one starts to actually think about the composition of Hispanics in the United States. Mexico is the country of origin of most Hispanics in the U.S. There are also Hispanics from Central America, South America and the Caribbean. The languages spoken in some of these countries have been influenced by Spain, Portugal, and France, as well as African dialects, Dutch and English.

In other words, there is a lot of variability from country to country, and indeed, region to region. A very common term used in Mexico could be meaningless or even insulting if you are from Argentina or Ecuador. Research can assist the designer in understanding if the intended message or information is comprehensible to a wide range of countries of origin.

Applying Knowledge About the General Market to the Hispanic Market

Simply applying General Market strategies or designs to the Hispanic Market is problematic. The most common reason for making this generalization is to save time and resources. However, this short-cut can significantly affect every aspect of a product or service, from basic design to marketing principles such as awareness and product adoption.

The simple application of General Market strategies to the Hispanic Market is often based on the assumption that cultural groups "assimilate" into the U.S. culture, and that this assimilation occurs over time. However, significant research shows that time in the U.S. does not necessarily lead to assimilation [Yankelovich-Cheskin]. While 2nd- and 3rd-generation Hispanics are likely to assimilate due to the influence of school, media and friends, most Hispanics that arrive in the US after ages 12 to 18 are more likely to retain their original cultural perspective [Yankelovich-Cheskin]. Other factors such as which region of the country they reside in and the availability of a cultural enclave also play a role, but research has shown that the majority of Hispanics in the U.S. identify primarily with their home culture.

This cultural association drives the need to understand the influence of culture on design and marketing criteria. However, there are very common mistakes made in this regard.

MISCONCEPTION EXPECTING THAT GENERAL MARKET MESSAGES WILL RESONATE WITH HISPANICS

Companies may think that translating the message of a successful campaign or other communication into Spanish is sufficient to "tailor" it to the Hispanic Market. Language issues aside (see Language section above), this approach overlooks many other elements likely to be contained in a message.

For example, a commercial with a blond, blue-eyed woman in a business suit and carrying a briefcase touting the gentleness of her dish soap may have gained 10 points of market share. However, a Spanish voice-over is not sufficient to make this message "culturally relevant." Yes, the fact that it's in Spanish is helpful, but there is likely to be a "cultural disconnect" if your target is defined as "Hispanic stay-at-home housewives with 3 children under the age of 10." The message will be lost even when the audience for whom it's intended can understand the words if they can't relate the words to their own situated context.

Aside from relating to the situation, the message also needs to play on cultural values. A message that shows a couple on the verge of having their last child "leave the nest" and move on to enjoy "life without the kids" would fail miserably with Hispanic audiences. That is because it completely ignores the significance of family among Hispanics.

MISCONCEPTION APPLYING GENERAL MARKET SEGMENTATIONS (E.G., BABY
BOOMERS, EMPTY NESTERS, ETC.)

Segments from the General Market may not map directly or appropriately to the
Hispanic Market. Segments should be based on meaningful and discriminating criteria that explain the segments. General Market segments such as "Baby Boomer"
completely overlook relevant cultural issues such as language, country of origin, etc.

MISCONCEPTION ASSUMING THAT THE HISPANIC MARKET IS AS "KNOWLEDGEABLE"
OR "AWARE" OF AVAILABLE PRODUCTS/SERVICES AS THE GENERAL MARKET

Another common mistake is to assume that the Hispanic Market is "up to speed"
with regards to product adoption and product awareness. Some individuals within the research community have gone so far as to describe the Hispanic Market as
being anywhere from 10 to 20 years behind the General Market in terms of technology or product adoption.

This is not a truism, however, and research helps to determine whether
this is indeed an issue that needs to be factored into an organization's planning.
For example, PC penetration in the Hispanic Market is lagging behind the General
Market, but DVD player adoption is very close, if not further along, with Hispanics.
Why such a disparity? Some of the factors are the availability of discs with
Spanish language options, as well as the economic savings of watching a movie at
home as a family rather than going to the theater.

Participant Recruiting Criteria

The mistakes don't end when firms acknowledge that Hispanic research is valuable to aid in product design or messaging. An understanding of the Hispanic
Market is required in order to make appropriate decisions regarding the criteria
that will be used to define the target audience. However, just as applying General
Market knowledge can be a pitfall, applying General Market definitions has the
same problems.

MISCONCEPTION REPLICATING GENERAL MARKET DEMOGRAPHICS FOR HISPANIC
RESEARCH

If one were to look at the distribution of household income in the U.S., certain
amounts represent Median or Mean income levels. If those same levels are used to
recruit for the Hispanic Market, it is possible that one would have very different
respondents. For example, the median income for the General Market is more
than double that of the Hispanic Market.

Other key differences exist in terms of age, education, household composition, occupation and marital status. Even though one key objective of any
research is to obtain data that is applicable to a specific audience, issues surrounding target audience definition are often overlooked.

MISCONCEPTION EXPECTING TO UNDERSTAND THE HISPANIC MARKET WITHOUT TRYING
TO UNDERSTAND THE DIFFERENCES AND SIMILARITIES THAT EXIST ACROSS MARKETS

Some examples of this are assumptions that Hispanics of Mexican descent in Los

Angeles share similar views with Mexicans in Chicago or Dominicans in Miami. Just as region of the country plays a role in the General Market (why do research in Atlanta and New York?), it also plays a role in the Hispanic Market. Los Angeles has a large and well-established Mexican community. In Chicago, the community exists, but it is spread out and not as overtly defined as that in Los Angeles.

Not only might there be some regional differences, but, as in the discussion of culture and language, there are also differences based on country or origin. Research needs to be designed to address these differences where appropriate, by ensuring representation of relevant countries of origin in the target definition.

MISCONCEPTION ASSUMING THAT ACCULTURATION IS A LINEAR PROGRESSION: SPANISH DOMINANT→SPANISH PREFERRED→BILINGUAL→ASSIMILATED

This is an issue that crops up repeatedly when recruiting participants for design or other product research. The assumption is that Hispanics that have been in the U.S. longer are more likely to speak English (true), and that they are more likely to "think" or "behave" like the General Market (false). Therefore, one must recruit individuals that have just arrived in the U.S. in order to obtain feedback from "Spanish Dominant" consumers (false).

Recruiting participants that have recently arrived in this country would actually be inappropriate, unless the objective is to understand how they adapt to their environment. Otherwise, recent arrivals have little experience with the wide variety of products, brands, distribution channels and media that are available in the U.S. Therefore, they would have little to offer regarding products or services.

Typically, questions regarding language usage and preference, in-language media consumption and time in-country are all used in combination in order to properly select the appropriate type of research participant.

Research Methodology

In addition to carrying over misconceptions regarding language, culture and demographics, there are also misconceptions concerning the appropriate methodology to use when researching Hispanics (and other cultures as well). While typical methodologies such as focus groups and surveys can be used with Hispanics, one must tailor them for the audience in order to obtain meaningful results. This begins by selecting the appropriate research methodology for the objectives as well as for the target.

MISCONCEPTION ASSUMING THAT THE SAME INTERVIEWING TECHNIQUES USED IN GENERAL MARKET WOULD CREATE SAME RESULTS

By now a theme should be evident that whatever works for General Market does not necessarily work for the Hispanic Market. For example, conducting mixed-gender or mixed-acculturation groups is more problematic in the Hispanic culture. Typically, females are more restrained in a mixed-gender group and will likely defer to the males. This aspect becomes more pronounced as one moves down the socio-economic scale.

Likewise, acculturation level is very likely to affect knowledge and experience concerning brands and products. Also, less acculturated individuals will likely defer to more sophisticated participants, particularly when questions of language are posed before the group. Typically, questions regarding language usage and preference, in-language media consumption and time in-country are all used in combination in order to properly select the appropriate type of participant.

Finally, presenting the same stimuli used in the General Market phase of study for the Hispanic phase can also be problematic. Given the relatively low education levels in the Hispanic Market when compared to the General Market, questions, stimuli and concepts have to be presented in a simple yet meaningful manner. Complex rating schemes and unanchored scales can present significant challenges to participants.

For example, social politeness in Mexico can affect the responses to attitudinal measures. This is often referred to as a "positive response bias." This is the reason why 10-point scales are used more commonly with Hispanics than 5- or 7-point scales. The 10-point scale permits greater differentiation at the upper end of the scale. However, some firms insist upon using a 5-point scale, because that is the scale that is used for their General Market studies.

MISCONCEPTION ASSUMING THAT ANYONE THAT SPEAKS SPANISH CAN CONDUCT THE RESEARCH

As discussed previously in the section, the issue is more than simply being able to speak the language. Nuances concerning culture, social interactions and group dynamics in the context of Hispanic participants are critical to the quality of the information. This includes surveys as well as focus groups.

Simply translating a survey is insufficient. The questions also have to be worded in a culturally sensitive manner so as to be understood by Hispanics of different origins. A term as simple as "grocery store" may have very different meanings for participants from Mexico and those from Costa Rica.

Some words in the English language don't have a direct translation into Spanish. Descriptive terms must be used to ensure that the participant is being exposed to the intended message or question. This process tends to add time to both qualitative and quantitative research. Roughly speaking, the amount of material one can cover in a 15-minute English-language survey will require anywhere from 20 to 25 minutes to conduct in Spanish.

Impact on Marketing and Consumer Behavior

Not only does culture impact designing and conducting research with Hispanics, it also affects the outcome in terms of marketing or product development strategy or tactics. Raising awareness, motivating trial or repositioning a brand still apply, but the means to do so needs to take cultural nuances into account.

For example, the role of brand is much stronger among Hispanics, and there are numerous examples of brand loyalty that extend from generation to generation. References to "what my mother uses" or "what I remember as a child" are very strong influencers of brand perception.

Also, what the user perceives as a desirable product attribute may run counter to what the manufacturer is intending for the product. A classic example is "environmentally friendly soap" that produces fewer suds. This product can fail miserably in the Hispanic Market because girls in Mexico are taught that "suds equal clean." Therefore, the lack of suds means the product "doesn't work" in the mind of the consumer, even though the clothes are technically "clean." Or the customer is unhappy because they have to use four times the normal amount in order to achieve the desired level of suds, which ends up making the product more expensive to use. Putting an "educational" label on the product isn't going to be very helpful if it's in English.

Motivating brand-switching behavior often requires extensive discounting or education in order to convey the benefits. For example, Hispanics of Mexican descent don't tend to use coupons as often as one would expect given the economic levels. Therefore, a blanket "coupon" strategy needs to be evaluated before implementing among Hispanics.

Following are some other elements that one should take into account when designing products or services for Hispanics.

BRAND OVERLOAD

In most Latin countries, the number of available brands is significantly lower than in the U.S. This is especially true in smaller towns and villages. When a Hispanic housewife goes to the supermarket for the first time in this country, she is likely to be overwhelmed by the number of choices available in almost every product category. Brands that are also available in her country of origin are therefore likely to be selected by default, simply due to lack of awareness regarding brands and associated brand imagery. Not only are the brands unfamiliar, but brand promise and legacy are also meaningless to this consumer.

PURCHASE INFLUENCERS

Given the strong sense of community, Hispanics are likely to rely on their own for product and brand information. "Community Marketing" is a term used to represent the idea of working within the existing Hispanic community framework to disseminate marketing communications. This is a useful approach for new products or services, as word of mouth from a trusted family member or friend is likely to carry significantly more weight than information from a salesperson or manufacturer.

The presence of children is also a significant influencer. The Hispanic culture tends to be very aspirational in terms of providing a "better life" for their children. For this reason, personal computers are present in many Hispanic households, but they were obtained primarily to benefit the children. Relatively few housewives access the Internet or use email; therefore, a program that relies on email or the Internet is likely to limit the target significantly. Designers and manufacturers need to be aware of the purchase influencers for their product or service, as these can vary significantly from one product category to the next.

All in all, designing products and services for Hispanics is like doing so for any other target market. The key is to avoid mistakes based on cultural ignorance in order to maximize the return from your research budget. Simply translating a commercial, ignoring cultural relevance in a marketing message, or foregoing research with Hispanics may save time and money in the short term, but long-term competitive advantage comes from research that illuminates key cultural differences.

When I was 5 my father taught me a saying that I still use when explaining to clients the long-term value of up-front work.

"Trabajo bien hecho es buen trabajo."

"Work done well is good work."

Think about it.

Overview of Quantitative Methods in Design Research

STACEY PURPURA

Using statistics to improve design seems to contradict the field's inherent freedom and creativity. Yet the field of design often uses quantitative research to inform anything from practical considerations (i.e., time-to-task completion) to refining theories about interactions with designed objects through the validation of exploratory research findings. Through quantitative studies researchers and designers can link attitudes to behaviors and set benchmarks to gauge improvements. This chapter provides an overview of how quantitative design research helps us understand how to make things simpler and easier to use, how quantitative research can be used to find the "best" product by a nose through the use of experimental design, and how it can marry attitudes and behaviors in a way that can inform design decisions. While qualitative research that casts a wide net and gradually refines its research objectives, quantitative research is used once research objectives are defined.

Most of my personal experience with quantitative design stems from the development and enrichment of technology-based products and experiences. During the past few years I have lived in the rarified air of Silicon Valley, and although those years saw the deflation of eCommerce and web design, they are also the years during which principles of design and design research came to the fore. As a rising tide raises all boats, during the unharnessed development of the web successful developments came about through an unflinching emphasis on iterative design and user or consumer experience. In this case, "experience" is understood by marketers and designers alike as extending beyond a person's immediate interactions with a product to all experiences with that product in all of its incarnations. In the past years, we learned through clicks and mortar that experience can be virtual as well as physical. For example, a poor experience with a website for a certain brand could lead to a perceived poor experience with the product itself. Design isn't merely about the object but the extensions of the object through its communications with the end user. In this spirit we will explore quantitative design research in different permutations for finding the right audience, identifying their needs, testing usability, and conducting validation and brand research.

Whereas qualitative research is typically used for casting a wide net on a topic, the exacting nature of quantitative research is used to pin down the details

BEGINNING
Assessing the Potential Market and
New Product Opportunities; Needs of the
Consumer (subconscious and unmet)

MIDDLE
Feature Testing, Usability Testing

END
Refining Messaging and Branding

Quantitative Research in the
Design Process

of the research. Iterative design moves projects forward without leaving the end user behind. Research is often left until after the product is well past the design stage and ready to bring to market. But there are certain phases at the beginning, middle and end of the design process when quantitative design research can successfully inform the design of products and processes. This isn't to say that quantitative research should take the place of qualitative research, but that it has a distinct place and value of its own, especially in an iterative design process when you are looking for incremental gains and benchmarks.

Research at the Beginning: Working with Thought Leaders

It's great to use research to understand your potential market, but what if you don't really know what your market is, or worse, what your product is? Can you still benefit from doing research? The answer is an unequivocal "yes"—if you do it properly. The "beginning" refers to the concept stage when ideas are most mutable and fragile. At this stage, researchers and designers must tread lightly to ensure they don't kill good ideas. Going out with a color-preference survey to an undifferentiated mass audience would be inappropriate or even damaging at this stage. At the very earliest stages of the design process, certain market segments should be tapped: early adopters and the fringe. For the remainder of this chapter we will follow a hypothetical "bleeding edge" technology/clothing/housewares company trying to get a product to market. In reality this process would inevitably be iterative and cyclical, but in the interest of time I'm going to run straight through without the Chutes-and-Ladders game that usually takes place in iterative design.

> Company Y decides that they want to develop products based on smart fabric with embedded computer chips. The problem: Company Y has not yet decided what kinds of uses this new type of fabric has or what kind of functionality the chips that are embedded in it will have. At this stage they have only conceived the idea and think it is time to send up a trial balloon. Company Y's first challenge is to make sure that the right people see the trial balloon.

TALKING TO THE RIGHT PEOPLE

The general population has a tendency not to use or adopt products until they are proven. Logically they are not the target for early research, since they are not really the target audience for an innovative product when it first comes out. However, early adopters and people on the fringe tend to find new uses for old products and adopt emerging products at the earliest stage or generate new ideas. Thought leadership isn't a democracy.

Leaders can be identified through key characteristics such as a propensity to learn and an avid love for all things new. If you are planning on doing research with this population I recommend taking the time to get to know this very special audience through a qualitative study. Their experiences differ from ours—well some of ours, anyway—and therefore they may have different criticisms, ideas or uses for products, and they have an inclination to like change. Once you know where they are coming from you will know what you can ask them. In the world of research these people can be identified and used as a barometer for all kinds of emerging ideas, typically through concept testing.

CONCEPT TESTING

Concept testing allows you to take a few ideas out to your audience of early adopters and put them to task. One of the benefits of doing a concept test quantitatively is that a clear winner usually emerges from a few concepts. In concept testing, you are going to have to help respondents along with some kind of stimuli—words, pictures, or a rough prototype. Don't waste their valuable input on something they can't envision. Stimuli can be based on brand-new ideas or old ideas repackaged in a new way—just make sure that the stimuli capture the essence of your idea. The most useful questions at this point are how unique and relevant the concepts will be to the audience. Concept testing can provide direction when two or more contenders are in the ring and there is no clear winner.

Company Y knows their capabilities for creating computerized fabric but cannot decide between computerized clothing or computerized towels and bedding. There is little contention that the material in the product will have some computerized functionality but a map of the market is unclear. Company Y performs a concept test to see which of these uses excites their core early adopters most. As a result of concept testing they have a clear idea that, while it is nice to have a towel that will fluff itself according to how wet or dry you are, the concept of having clothing you can communicate through is rated as significantly more unique and relevant to most early adopters. Their next step is to understand what features could be included (and which should not be) to flesh out the concept of communications togs.

FEATURE TESTING–BEGINNING TO MIDDLE

Features can make a product; they can also overload and destroy it. Occasionally designers have absolute creative freedom to include or exclude features based on their own sense of what makes a design sing, but these opportunities are rare.

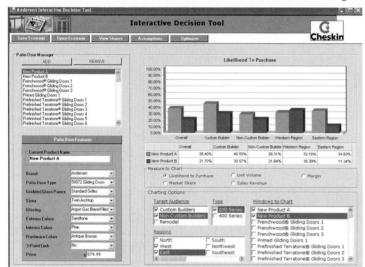

Another way to understand which features hold water is through a discrete choice analysis. This type of study controls respondents' exposure to specific features or concepts of a product that are then tested against one another. Feature testing should be used, like concept tests, when there is no clear winner from qualitative research, and especially if pricing is an issue in the development of features. The name "feature testing" may be misleading, because the goal is actually to understand how people will react to the entire package, with all of the features included, sometimes

An interactive tool to represent potential customers' responses to product features.

accompanied by a price tag. Respondents will be exposed to a single example of each of the hypothetical designs one at a time. This is best done through computer simulations; otherwise, such tests can make the development process very expensive. Based upon the results of feature testing, the designer or researcher will be able to understand which features are deal-makers and which features are potential deal-breakers and at what price.

Company Y is now thinking about the actual design of the product. Where should they put the computer chips and where will they allow the communications functionality to reside? Will consumers tolerate having wide lapels on their talking clothing for better reception? Will they want clothing that will allow them to have a private conversation? Can clothing that meets consumers' desires for certain kinds of functionality be fashionable? What design features will satisfy that goal?
Company Y takes their hypotheses and generates models with them, creating models with different combinations of features. Then they launch a computer survey that allows consumers to view the models and to evaluate not only the features, but the entire package. Company Y then has a clearer idea of what their customers would tolerate, what they would actually enjoy and how much the product will be worth to them once it is actually on the market.

Research at the Middle: Usability

Usability studies tend to be quantitative in a different way than many market researchers think because they need not employ 30 or more subjects. The sample size for these studies may be small, but they can generate a large amount of data. Their insights come from metrics such as time-to-task. The value of such studies is the ability to determine whether a product is usable in a timely enough manner to satisfy the audience to which it is geared.

Time-to-task methods will always require a prototype near completion so the user can be seen in action. Designers may use information from such studies after the basic work of design is completed. If a designer feels that the design is only about 80% effective, data from such studies may enable them to inch effectiveness up incrementally by 10% or more. This is the best use of usability studies that employ metrics such as time-to-task.

It's important to remember that usability testing is not "likability" testing. Someone may like the cornflower blue icon today and hot pink tomorrow, but Usability research is focused on helping the designer make the product more compelling and usable through little tweaks to its functionality.

While natural work environments should be used during the contextual design phase of the research, usability studies are best performed in a controlled environment such as a laboratory. Because the goal of time-to-task research is to assess how long it takes a subject to complete a particular task (which may be one in a series of tasks to complete an entire experience), it is ideal to not have the participant interrupted. The focus of usability research is on the in-depth detail of the user's interaction with the product. Small, incremental gains may seem ridiculous when we are talking about products designed for leisurely use, but imagine a situation where time is of the essence—the emergency room for example, or a diabetic's need to inject insulin. Incremental gains in a time-critical task may turn out to provide tremendous gains for individuals.

Company Y has developed a prototype, a model of the communicative clothing, with the optimal features they have identified included in the physical model. Company Y can now test this with individuals and assess whether or not the clothing is operational. How long does it take, for example, for one of their customers to figure out how to send a message? If it is an option, how long does it take for customers to enter text? The point of these timed exercises is that all of the features may be in place but none of them may be working appropriately for the user in a timely manner. Obviously, the design will fail if it is simply too difficult to figure out or use. After testing, Company Y discover it happens to have had a resounding success with the wide lapels and collar model, because customers can turn their collars up to listen to incoming messages as quickly as the message comes in.

Research at the End: Validation and Standardization

At the end of the product development or research cycle you may want to validate your findings with the relevant audience. Quantitative validation means that you are confirming what you heard from a smaller group of people with a larger and hopefully representative group of people, if you have designed the study correctly. In order to validate findings from qualitative studies, a sample of at least 30 individuals should be used. These individuals must be exposed to the same types of stimuli you used in the qualitative phase.

DON'T EXPECT TOO MUCH

Depending upon the stage of the project, validation studies can be enlightening or disastrous. The reasoning behind validation is to confirm what you think you learned from the qualitative stage of your studies. But using quantitative measures to test your hypotheses is a little like feeling the trunk of the elephant or shining your flashlight on a certain place in the darkness—you aren't going to sense as much as you did with your qualitative study. This is intentional; the goal of quantitative study is to reduce rather than to add complexity. The interaction of qualitative and quantitative studies within an entire research process is a dance of expansion and contraction of possibilities, but always moving toward an optimized design.

Let's say we tested a prototype amongst a core group of users. The users of this prototype were in direct contact with a model. Hopefully, they were able to describe their responses in detail, and you were able to observe nuances of how they interacted with the model. Asking directed, standardized questions about their experience or observing subjects' experience with a limited set of features reduces the points of possible contact with the subjects. Result: one level of juicy complexity removed. Given the timeframe and the larger sample size, users will, in all likelihood, not be directly interacting with the prototype itself in the same way they had been during the qualitative phase. Result: another level of complexity and interesting findings is lost. This is a fair bargain at this late stage in the process because in exchange for the reduction of complexity you receive defined benchmarks from which to take steps for improvement.

A quantitative study necessarily limits what you are able to investigate, and it's important to recognize that you are working within a set of defined parameters. Constraints can be good and instrumental in focusing a product. The neatness and measurability of quantitative work necessarily means a trade-off between depth and breadth.

Research at the End (and at the Beginning): Segmentation and Brand Experience

Although it may not immediately come to mind, we can use numbers to uncover who our audience is and how they relate to a particular product and brand. Quantitative segmentation using advanced statistical techniques can refine and define an audience. Segmentation studies examine how certain groups of people hang together ⏵253 WRIGHT. For design purposes, we can uncover how these groups cluster together according to different attributes such as demographics, behaviors or attitudes. Using segmentation analysis it is possible to pinpoint key segments, such as the early adopters discussed above, and from there measure and improve their brand experience to develop stronger loyalty and wider adoption and usage. The advantage of quantitative segmentation in this regard cannot be understated. Understanding an audience in depth is key to making improvements, incremental and otherwise. The task is vastly easier when it can be clearly stated with whom a brand or product is excelling and with whom it is falling short. The objective of segmentation research is to get a picture of the general audience and the sub-audiences for a product or a brand.

To be most useful, segmentation studies should ideally take place after the product has gone to market. A segmentation study can tell you who your core audience is and who are the malingerers on the outskirts. It can also tell you who likes to use your product, how much of the market share they make up and how much they buy. Segmentation can also show you how to make your brand stand on its own. For example, brand maps are a terrific way to get a read on brand territory. At a glance, you can see which brands share, or have ownership over, traits typically associated with a group of brands. For example, a clothier may want to know which brands in the brand space are associated with being high-end, youthful, mature, trusted, sexy or classic. Some brands often share the same attributes with other brands, while other brands have sole ownership over a brand trait.

Company Y is now marketing their wide-lapelled smart clothing to hip young people, but they want to expand their audience. What is the next group they can take it to? Who is the best audience? They perform a segmentation study and discover that older people who are slightly techno-phobic also like the clothes. It's also uncovered through the segmentation that business people on the go can be another market for their products. At this point the company can go back to the drawing board to find ways to appeal to these new markets through specific changes in both product design and branding.

Quantitative methods have contributions to make at every stage of the life of a product or brand. They also provide information necessary for the renewal and change that characterizes the life cycle of a successful company.

User Requirements

By Any Means Necessary

ABBE DON & JEFF PETRICK

STRATEGY → REQUIREMENTS → DESIGN → BUILD → TEST → LAUNCH

Introduction

In an ideal software product development process, user requirements are generated in the requirements phase alongside marketing and technical requirements
and focus directly on the users of a product—their behaviors, goals and needs.
Gathering user requirements is a highly collaborative process among the designers and the rest of the product development team (marketing, engineering, con-
tent/editorial, executives) as well as between designers and customers. Based on
an amalgamation of market research (demographics, technographics, focus
groups, market segmentation) and design research (user interviews, contextual
inquiry, competitive product analysis), user requirements function to make sure

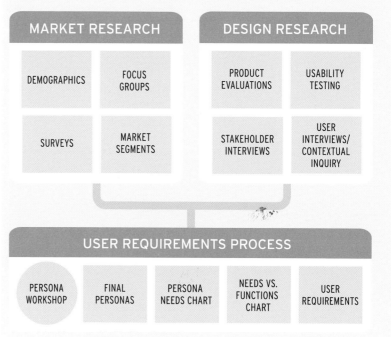

that business and marketing goals are aligned with end-user goals and needs.

Unfortunately, designers are often brought in too late in the process—after the strategy and requirements phases—and are then told that there is no time, no budget, no need or simply no interest in design research or user requirements. Regardless of when the designers are brought into the process, it is essential to develop even minimal user requirements quickly and by any means necessary in order to meet the goals and needs of the target audience.

Collect and Analyze Market Research

The user requirements process begins by gathering and absorbing existing market research and augmenting those findings with targeted design research. Market research focuses on general trends and patterns rather than the goals and needs of specific users. It does well at providing the marketing team with insights into expected usage patterns of a product and how to create targeted messages that will appeal to specific market segments.

However, market research does not do as well at providing designers with focused insights into the specific behaviors of users within these market segments. The subtle but important distinction between what marketing needs from user research and what designers need is a crucial point to clarify with key stakeholders as early as possible in any project.

Various types of market research may be provided to designers: Demographics describe the age, gender, income, ethnicity or other quantitative characteristics of the target market. Technographics describe the technological characteristics of the targeted audience such as computer and monitor types, processor speed and operating system, type of Internet connection, and other technologies used by the target market such as cell phones, PDAs or wireless devices. Focus Group findings capture feedback about market concepts gathered by marketing from interview groups. Surveys enable marketing to gather quantifiable feedback about market concepts from a broader audience than a focus group.

If you are not provided with marketing research documents, you'll need to ask for them. Cull through them with specific questions in mind:

- Who is your market?
- How is it segmented (if at all)?
- Which market segment(s) has the business identified as primary? Which are secondary?
- What are the demographic and technographic characteristics of users in these segments?
- What are the existing or expected usage patterns of these users?
- How are the needs of these segments currently being met?
- Which competitors are also vying for these segments and how are they currently attempting to meet their needs?

TIP For free demographic data for the United States, start with the US Census Bureau at www.census.gov. Additional information about specific industries can often be found at nonprofit organizations, such as The National Center for Educational Statistics www.nces.ed.gov or The National Center for Health Statistics www.cdc.gov/nchs. Using a web-based search, type in the industry you are interested in plus the term "statistics" to obtain a variety of free or inexpensive reports.

TIP If you are designing an Internet based product, The Pew Internet and American Life Project has free, up-to-date technographic reports available at www.pewinternet.org.

Identify Market Segments

Market segments can be your best friend or your worst enemy. They are often represented as a matrix based on the most significant market research variables. Prioritizing market segments helps to focus your design research and your persona development; however, there is rarely a one-to-one mapping between the number of market segments and the number of personas.

Even if the marketing team has not defined formal market segments, they may be able to explain their working assumptions. Key stakeholder interviews may also provide a sense of which customers the executives intend to focus on. Drafting a market segment matrix gleaned from market research and the key stakeholders can help you and your organization come to a common understanding of your target customers.

Keep in mind that when you present this initial draft you may encounter some resistance. You don't want Marketing to think you are stepping on their toes, so always keep them in the loop about what you're doing and why you're doing it. In the end, you both want the same thing: to understand your target audience so that you can design and market a useful and usable product.

Following are some examples of market segment matrices. Each axis represents the most relevant variables from the market research. In the case of the travel company, the horizontal axis represents the customer's interest in and familiarity with the product. The vertical axis represents the customer's lifestage. The x's represent the segments with behavioral characteristics distinct enough to warrant the creation of personas (more about developing personas follows). The gray represents those segments which, after prioritization based on market research and core business competencies, were seen as falling outside of the company's "sweet spot"; therefore, no personas were needed for these segments.

EDUCATIONAL SOFTWARE PUBLISHER

	REJECTER	INTENDER	REPEATER	-PHILE
PRE-FAMILY				X
FAMILY		X	X	
POST-FAMILY		X	X	

CABLE CHANNEL FOR KIDS

	DISINTERESTED	RESPONDERS	ACHIEVERS
K-5 CLASSROOM		X	
6-8 CLASSROOM		X	
LAB TEACHERS		X	X

TRAVEL COMPANY

	BOYS	GIRLS
6-9 YEARS OLD	X	X
10-11 YEARS OLD	X	X
12-14 YEARS OLD		

Conduct Design Research

Design research is informed by the available market research. Before embarking on independent design research, absorbed everything you can regarding the target market, the customers and the competition. The reason for this is two-fold: your research will be more focused and your credibility among other groups will increase, because you have shown that you value the work that has already been done. Sometimes your independent design research will challenge preconceived notions about the customers and the product, so it's best to be well prepared before presenting any findings.

In this section we've included types of design research that we've found particularly helpful. There might not be time for all of it, but doing some of it is better than doing none of it. If you only have time or budget for one form of design research, we recommend the user interviews. Reading reports on interviews that other people have conducted is valuable, but nothing compares to the insights gleaned from actually seeing and hearing real users talk about their goals, needs, frustrations and current cognitive models.

PRODUCT EVALUATIONS

Product Evaluations of your company's existing product and competitors' products are often useful to get an overview of the field. These evaluations can be loosely based on heuristic methods [Nielsen]. They are meant to provide direction for areas to explore in user interviews stakeholder interviews and usability testing.

TIP The use of heuristic methods is not intended to make the process academic. Rather, using such methods is meant to ground the evaluation through a set of pre-defined metrics. By establishing the metrics or "heuristics" up front, you prevent the evaluation from becoming an unstructured critique or an expression of personal preference.

TIP Create heuristics that are meaningful to your specific product and familiarize others with them before the evaluations begin so that other groups are more likely to embrace the final results.

USABILITY TESTING

Usability testing of your company's existing product can give you invaluable design insights. Through one-on-one testing that asks targeted users to perform specific, primary tasks and employing a "talk aloud" protocol, you will be able to see if the user's cognitive model matches the model of the product. Often, the team that worked on a product can no longer be objective about what's working. This type of test can provide a fresh set of non-biased eyes.

TIP You may include a limited number of qualitative questions that will help inform future design research, but don't let these questions sidetrack the users from their primary tasks.

TIP Employ "guerilla" testing techniques if money and time are limited. You don't always need formal recruiting or testing facilities. Use your personal network to find unbiased people to test. Use a conference room as a testing lab. Any testing you can do is better than no testing at all.

STAKEHOLDER INTERVIEWS

Stakeholder Interviews with key executives and subject matter experts are often a quick way to understand the product's strategic direction. These work especially well if you are new to a project, as you can quickly find out about "sacred cows" that others may already take for granted. Include interviews with the CEO/President as well as senior Marketing and Sales executives.

TIP After the interviews, be sure to write down everything you've heard in an informal report and then distribute it. Sometimes even key executives aren't aligned regarding a product's strategic direction.

TIP If there's an existing product, perform more tactical interviews with key product development team members to learn about the pitfalls to avoid for the next version.

USER INTERVIEWS

User Interviews provide directional design input. You are not trying to get the user to tell you how or what to design; rather, you are trying to elicit their goals and needs by focusing on how they perform their current tasks independent of the specific product being developed. Armed with this information, you'll be able to tease out their cognitive model, which is invaluable in setting design direction. Conducting the interviews in the context in which the product will be used can add a richness of detail which might otherwise be missed.

TIP Conduct interviews in pairs (dyads) because you can cover more people in less time ◗23 IRELAND. Additionally, they help generate more authentic discussion, as people are less likely to second-guess what the interviewer wants to hear when a peer is in the room.

TIP Any interaction with real users in any context is better than no interaction at all. If you cannot go to the user's environment or even meet them in person, try doing the interviews by phone. If neither of those are an option, get creative. For example, listen in at a "customer call center" as a way to get access to customers and hear the kinds of issues and challenges they face.

Synthesize the Research into User Requirements

Once the market research has been absorbed and design research conducted, it is necessary to synthesize the data into a form that can be used by the entire product development team. We do this through the use of personas. Our process for arriving at and defining personas is a modified version of the one first outlined by Alan Cooper in *The Inmates Are Running the Asylum* [Cooper 1999] and refined with Robert Reimann in *About Face 2.0* [Cooper 2003].

Personas are not an end but a means to tease out and identify user needs. These needs can then be used to develop, validate or prioritize new or proposed features and functions through the creation of a Needs Versus Functions Chart.

The combination of an executive summary of the market and design research, the Personas, and the Needs vs. Functions Chart and will make up the final User Requirements Report.

Create Personas

Personas are archetypal users with specific goals and needs based on real market and design research. They often include:

- A name
- A photograph
- Demographic characteristics

- Technographic characteristics
- Behavioral characteristics
- Barriers and/or challenges
- Specific goals and needs

The ultimate goal of personas is to identify specific user goals and needs, so that they can be aligned with business needs and technical goals to create an agreed upon, prioritized list of features and functions. To this end, the personas provide a common understanding of whom the product is being designed for. This understanding will prevent the project team from making decisions based on personal preferences and biases, thus helping to curtail "feature creep" and feature debates.

CHOOSE PRIMARY AND SECONDARY PERSONAS

Cooper recommends that designers limit their personas to one to three primary personas and perhaps two to three secondary personas. Narrow the number of personas by using the Market Segments Matrix (see above). While you will rarely need a persona from each segment, some targeted segments may require multiple personas.

Secondary personas, on the other hand, are often users who are in a particular role rather than a market segment. For example, in the case of education software, the primary users of the product are classroom teachers, but a superintendent or principal must have administrative functionality to activate, monitor and track learner progress. To address the needs of an administrator, a secondary, less robust persona can be created.

AVOID COMMON PITFALLS

The first place personas go astray is when business goals are confused with user goals. For example, a business-driven goal might be "user needs an easy way to get to personalized marketing messages." No user starts out thinking, "Hmm, I'd like to read messages prepared for me by marketing." This is a feature looking for a goal.

A valid user-driven goal, on the other hand, might be "user wants to be alerted when the best price becomes available." A feature that meets this goal would be personalized messaging.

The second place personas go astray is using a proposed or existing feature to define a user goal. A sure-fire way to defeat the success of personas is to define the goals and needs in terms of functionality that already exists.

PREPARE FOR OBJECTIONS

When introducing Personas to an organization, you may run into quite a bit of resistance. Common objections include:

"Marketing already did this." Market research is crucial input to this

process, but not sufficient as it is not focused enough on customer behaviors to provide necessary design insights.

"We have a lot of experts here so we know what our users want." These experts are included in the Stakeholder interviews.

"Everyone is our user." Market Segments help even large consumer companies organize and prioritize their customers.

"How do you know who the users are and what they want?" Designers don't know who the users are or what they want until they internalize the market research, perform the design research, and synthesize that data into personas.

"This feels silly. It's just a creative writing exercise based on made-up data." It is imperative that the personas be based on real data from both market and design research. Pruitt and Grudin of Microsoft have gone so far as to create a "persona foundation document" in which they take every single description in a persona and map it back to its original data source [Pruitt 2003].

"I did these before and they just weren't useful." It is likely that previous projects hit the three primary pitfalls outlined above: they weren't based on real data, business goals were confused with user goals or current features were used to define user goals and needs.

"There's just not time." We have consistently found that if you do not do this before the design phase, you will hit repeated roadblocks that require you to try to create this crucial understanding of the customer "on the fly." You will save time by taking time for this up front.

CONDUCT A PERSONA WORKSHOP

Ideally the personas are fleshed out as part of a collaborative workshop with at least one representative from each area, such as engineering, content, design, marketing and the executive team. The workshop is the process by which personas emerge: the means is as important as the end. Below are some tips for maximizing the success of such a workshop.

- Evangelize personas before, during and after the workshop.
- Do a presentation on the Persona Development Process before the Persona Workshop. Explain the process and the reason for using personas. Be sure to set expectations for the upcoming workshop and make the relevant research documents and background articles available.
- All team members who agree to participate must be familiar with previously conducted market and design research so they can make informed recommendations.
- Create posters with salient market research data for workshop participants to easily refer to.
- If you have quotes from user interviews, enlarge them and place them on the walls for inspiration.
- Seed the personas before the meeting so that the group can get traction immediately.

The workshop team will fill out the remaining demographic and technographic details for the persona. They will identify the barriers and frustrations of the persona and determine the persona's primary goals and needs.

COMPLETE THE PERSONAS

The final personas are vetted, compiled and completed by the design team. The final deliverable often includes a persona "menu" which is a one-page document containing a summary view of all the personas. The summary view for each persona often includes:

- A name
- A photograph
- Key demographics
- Key technographics
- Primary goals or needs

The persona menu should be included with subsequent design documentation and be present at design working sessions and design critiques, so that the needs of specific personas can help inform decision-making.

Prioritize Persona Needs

Once the personas have been created, use them to prioritize needs in relationship to features and functions. Although personas have unique and distinct goals and come from unique demographic or even technographic situations, they often share common needs.

STEP 1 Create the Persona Needs Chart and identify which personas share each need. (Note: Some needs may be shared by all personas while some may be unique to a single persona.)

PERSONA NEEDS					
	PERSONA 1	PERSONA 2	PERSONA 3	PERSONA 4	PERSONA 5
NEED 1	X	X	X	X	X
NEED 2	X		X		X
NEED 3		X	X	X	
NEED 4	X		X	X	
NEED 5	X				
NEED 6		X	X		
NEED 7				X	
NEED 8			X	X	X
NEED 9	X	X			
NEED 10	X	X	X	X	

STEP 2 Sort the list so that the needs shared by the most personas are shown at the top. (Note: Sorting the personas and their needs in other ways will help you see patterns and understand their similarities and differences.)

PERSONA NEEDS SORTED BY SHARED NEEDS					
	PERSONA 1	PERSONA 2	PERSONA 3	PERSONA 4	PERSONA 5
NEED 1	X	X	X	X	X
NEED 10	X	X	X	X	
NEED 2	X		X		X
NEED 4	X		X	X	
NEED 3		X	X	X	
NEED 8			X	X	X
NEED 9	X	X			
NEED 6		X	X		
NEED 5	X				
NEED 7				X	

Create a Needs vs. Functions Chart

It is extremely rare that a design team is put into place before the marketing team has created a marketing requirements document (MRD). The MRD almost always includes a prioritized outline of features and functions. However, the marketing priorities don't always map to the user needs and priorities. Also, there may be items in the MRD that don't map to a user need at all. Similarly, there may be user needs for which no features or functions have been conceived.

One way to analyze this is to take the Persona Needs Chart and add another column to it for features and functions. Place the outline number of each feature and function in the appropriate row to map it to the user need or needs that it meets. This helps the cross-functional team to understand the relationship between marketing goals, business needs and user needs.

The Needs vs. Function chart will also give the whole team a formal model by which to decide how to address those needs that aren't met by a feature/function or what to do with those features/functions that do not meet a user need. It may be that a user need was overlooked. It may be that the feature is truly innovative and should be kept in the product. Or it may be a pet feature of a stakeholder. Identifying these early will streamline the design process by reducing feature debates.

PERSONA NEEDS VS. FUNCTIONS

	FEATURES	PERSONA 1	PERSONA 2	PERSONA 3	PERSONA 4	PERSONA 5
NEED 1	1.0, 2.1.1	X	X	X	X	X
NEED 10	4, 5.1, 6.2	X	X	X	X	
NEED 2	3.1, 4.4	X		X		X
NEED 4	3.2, 7.1	X		X	X	
NEED 3	1.2, 1.3, 3.5		X	X	X	
NEED 8	4.1			X	X	X
NEED 9	6.3, 7.2, 8	X	X			
NEED 6	4.3, 6.3, 8		X	X		
NEED 5	2.3, 4.1, 5.2	X				
NEED 7	5.3, 6.0, 7.1				X	

With this final step, you have integrated data from all points in the organization and from all relevant user perspectives. The success of this collaborative process will go a long way towards ensuring the success of the final product design, and it will likely reduce organizational resistance and foster good collaboration the next time around.

Design (As) Research

ANNE BURDICK

Research is only as good as its interpretation. If the data that designers have to work with is as rich and relevant as that presented in this volume, it is absolutely essential that the working material of design used in response—whether a new software application, cinematic language, or typographic form—be the result of similarly rich critical investigation. Therefore design requires a space—the research lab—for design risk-taking, speculation and discovery, not only for specific applications but also to expand our knowledge of design itself.

The set of projects that make up this section are just a sampling of the broad array of concerns that can drive such investigations. All deal with complex issues of representation as defined through form. Can one create a visual-verbal form of writing? ❍101 BURDICK Where is the overlap between rationalism and decoration? ❍94 GONZALES CRISP How can we exploit the distance between representation and reality to reveal aspects of 3-D perception? ❍109 NAIMARK How can computer-based polylinear filmmaking reflect lived experience, outside of narrative? ❍118 STRICKLAND Such research questions are qualitatively different from those of user testing and human-centered research. The most significant difference is that the experiments developed in response to or in tandem with these questions use the act and material of design as the means of investigation. It is through making (rather than observing or interviewing) that these contributors generate new information.

All designers engage in creative exploration in the process of designing, but the difference between design that is simply design and design that serves as research has to do with the goals and outcomes of each. Designers who are conducting research through their creative practice create work that is intended to address both a particular design brief and a larger set of questions at the same time. In most cases, the inquiry is sustained over a period of time and the designers create a body of work in response—projects and practices that serve as experiments through which they interrogate their ideas, test their hypotheses and pose new questions. Critical reflection is a necessary component of a design research practice. Designers must be able to articulate their questions and conclusions, particularly in contexts such as this book.

The value of such formal investigations is not only to advance the array of choices designers have to call upon when in the act of designing, but also to advance the scholarship of the disciplines that make up design—to develop a critical understanding of the work we do and the objects we create. The projects within this section exist primarily in contexts outside of the mass market, in the more rarefied realms of academia, Literature, corporate research culture, documentary film, High Design and Art. Peers, scholars and critics define their value in addition to end users. This secondary community places a high premium on work that challenges and questions. It is necessary that such cultural arenas exist away from the concerns of popular culture and the marketplace—as incubators and hothouses for the difficult, the unresolved, the overly complex and the unconventional.

Speculation, Serendipity and Studio Anybody

LISA GROCOTT

To state that I once hated graphic design is neither provocative nor original. Many graphic designers before me have felt the physical and creative malaise I experienced after twelve-hour days of mouse-clicking week in, week out. This chapter describes the creative equivalent of a recovery program for disenchanted designers. This story narrates how my colleagues and I conceived of an ongoing research project that positioned our studio practice as the research subject, our professional dissatisfaction as the primary issue, and creative speculation within the workplace as our key argument.

After graduating I had a series of in-house jobs, so although I couldn't even complain about hours spent costing budgets or tolerating clients, I was still disillusioned by a profession that seemed to only fractionally be about designing. You see, as a student it was the verb that I had fallen for—not the typefaces, the software or the paper samplers—I fell in love with the process of creating designs, from the slow-burning hours of contemplation, the heady rush of possible ideas, to the focused micro-world of refinement. But driven by a weekly production schedule my designs had become more formulaic—consequently my job dissatisfaction intensified. It became obvious that I needed to reclaim a design process that valued speculation, an experimental yet investigative space, where design could once again reside in what Clive Dilnot refers to as the "realm of possibility" [Dilnot 1998, 24]. Unoriginally, my response was to enroll in grad school.

To escape operating systems and production deadlines, I chose a fine art program where I could explore communication and authorship, while dreaming big and remembering the potential of the creative process. As I was organized and good at thinking strategically, I was confident I would be the model student—until it became apparent that these qualities were more a liability than an asset in the context of a painting master's degree. One day when presenting my ideas and plans for the whole semester, the look on my supervisor's face confirmed the disturbing extent to which my professional life had trained me to efficiently predetermine every phase of a project. Unfortunately, it took the duration of my masters to unlearn the insidious habit of projecting outcomes before I had even started creating, but in the process I began to identify the distinctive quality of discovery in art and design. By experimenting and investigating ideas through my form making, it became possible to surpass superficially reworking the familiar, to explore and discover the unfamiliar. Terrence Rosenberg theorizes this experience by critiquing the way a straight line of intent defines a narrow focal channel for speculation, instead advocating a poetic research method where non-linear links seek alternative paths to those predicted from the outset [Rosenberg 2000, 5]. Simply translated into industry speak, this discovery-led process can herald the distinction between simple invention and true innovation.

Doing time within an institution that advocates an iterative, discovery-led process for designing unfortunately also sets up a stumbling re-entry into a commercial world that insists on abruptly reminding us that the client's deadline was always yesterday. It became immediately apparent that if my retreat to the academy were to be of sustaining value, I would have to reconfigure my professional practice to continually accommodate a space for speculative design inquiry. In setting out to foster a culture of research within a professional studio I hoped to weave together the time for experimentation and reflection afforded within the academy, the framed critical inquiry of the research lab, and the professional imperatives of the corporate R&D department.

In establishing Studio Anybody, a small independent graphic design consultancy with five equal partners, it became a commercial imperative that we not divorce the value of the speculative research from the specific realities of a corporate environment. We were convinced that if practitioner research intended to build strategic knowledge about design—the central contribution of most research—it made sense that the research be through the activity of designing. While not contesting the contribution of the theoretician's research about design or the marketing department's research for design, we were interested in the space between the academy and the user, where the professional designer deploys studio-based research to actively investigate the activity of designing. If the graphic design professional "community of practice" ultimately values creative, innovative design, it is important that the community's investment in research aligns with this professional endeavor and extends to research *through* design. The Studio Anybody case study presented in this chapter references a diversity of research findings that will hopefully illustrate how tacit understanding about creative speculation can inform and enhance tangible knowledge about design practice.

In what ways can a professional design studio foster a speculative culture?

At Studio Anybody we were young enough to be naïve about business models, yet experienced enough to be cynical about business practice. Our desire was to develop, implement and reflect upon a critically enhanced practice model that accommodated a discovery-led process. To do this we deployed cyclical, action research where the process of designing the artifact constituted the research methodology [Seagro and Dunne 1999]. The research study intended to explore a particular and subtle configuration of inter-related and inter-dependent design activities that sought to "naturalize" the professional relationship between speculative research and commercial activity.

Our first move was to develop a space for speculation by initiating a stream of design projects that were authored and funded by the studio. We believed that the pure, client-free space of the studio-initiated projects would help us to elucidate in what ways, and to what extent, the design process we adopt directly informs the artifacts we create. The original business model hoped that the rhizomatic, poetic nature of the speculative stream would generate a reservoir of ideas that could be drawn on by the commissioned client stream—ultimately valuing the accounted-for hours on our timesheets [Rosenberg 2000]. The studio's main presumption was that the prescribed nature of the design process down the path most traveled was an account management method that sought to provide the client with something known and familiar, but expediently constrained designers to design around what they already knew. If we could only decelerate the process enough to experiment and reflect outside of the time-starved treadmill of client projects, we thought, we could better understand how to polish and reclaim an iterative, creative process within a commercial context. The relative professional value of the study would depend upon whether the poetic process could afford the designers enough contemplative space to explore and refine culturally more effective communication. In turn, the study might confirm speculative research as an investment that offers direct return on enriching the professional culture and enhancing the commissioned projects.

What role can speculation play within workplace education?

By now I was both director of a graduate program and a partner at Studio Anybody, so I was not interested in accepting the didactic rationale that positioned academic speculation in opposition to professional application. I wanted to know if it were possible that the blue-sky experience of pure speculation could reveal to designers a reality about design that we often shortsightedly compromised in our never-ending quest to seduce new clients with bigger budgets.

Designers' initiating their own speculative projects is not in itself a new idea; from underground zines to internationally distributed publications, it is easy to find examples of designers creating a client-free space. More challenging, perhaps, is finding critical speculation that would fall within the research notion of scholarship, where outcomes are critiqued and disseminated within the relevant community. For this reason, we framed our research questions and methodology in association with my other workplace, RMIT University, because the educational context for research would situate our ongoing analysis and reflection within a community of scholarship. The formal research culture of the academy asserted that the professional research be more than just indulgent, introspective speculation, calling the designers to articulate the project's purchase, not just for enhancing our client work, but also for its contribution to the greater community of practice. The culture of learning and research that the university modeled became increasingly woven into the fabric of the studio. Our declared scholarly agenda internally

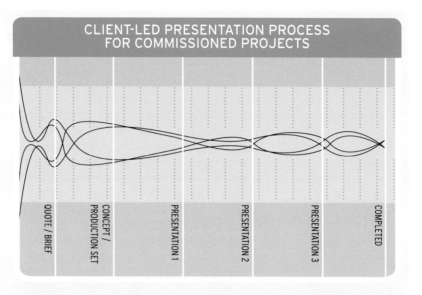

**CLIENT-LED PRESENTATION PROCESS
FOR COMMISSIONED PROJECTS**

QUOTE / BRIEF · CONCEPT / PRODUCTION SET · PRESENTATION 1 · PRESENTATION 2 · PRESENTATION 3 · COMPLETED

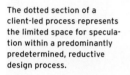

The dotted section of a client-led process represents the limited space for speculation within a predominantly predetermined, reductive design process.

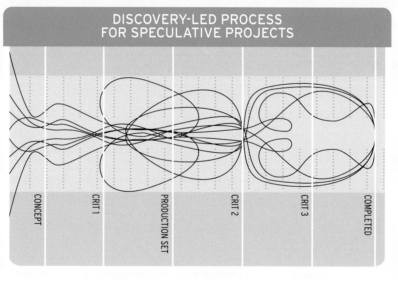

**DISCOVERY-LED PROCESS
FOR SPECULATIVE PROJECTS**

CONCEPT · CRIT 1 · PRODUCTION SET · CRIT 2 · CRIT 3 · COMPLETED

The dotted section of a design-led process represents the possibilities afforded within the space for speculation in this poetic, iterative design process.

directed the practitioner/researchers commitment to critical speculation, while externally building and sharing strategic knowledge about the business of communication design.

This chapter specifically refers to the studio's initial research study, which was framed by the big-picture question: what happens when discovery-led research becomes an integral component of professional graphic design practice? In the initial stages the research bluntly impressed broad structural and procedural changes onto the conventional business model, whereas within this cycle of action and reflection the latter stages of the study determined a shift toward a more complex and subtle reconfiguring of the professional design process.

Could critical speculation be the foundation for a business strategy?

For phase one of the study, we responded to our ambitions to develop an enhanced critical/creative/professional position by authoring, designing and disseminating studio-initiated, client-free projects. The speculative stream of experimental projects was conceived to power the creative process and formal language behind our commissioned client projects. For the first few years the Studio disseminated these projects through public and exhibition spaces, because we believed this client-free environment afforded the researching designers a contemplative space to develop our own body of work. The extended timeframe of the projects supported a discovery-led process, where the outcomes were not predetermined and the designers could embrace an iterative practice. This accommodated revisiting and further investigating conceptual and formal threads that began to run through all our projects. Within a short time, qualitative evidence implied that the adoption of a poetic process was directly improving our job satisfaction, critical reflection and professional development. The luxury of being able to resolve projects to our satisfaction motivated us to learn new software, negotiate healthy collaborations, refine experimental form and, most noticeably, to collectively develop a body of work that forms the basis of the conceptual threads we still return to today. We were seduced by authoring our own content, and with a newfound confidence we proceeded to design projects that accelerated our practice faster than if we had relied on clients to give the young studio a break. The following projects mark and highlight three particular phases the research study moved through, revealing how the commercial and cultural design strategies, conceived as practical experiments, continued to enhance our professional practice in a multiplicity of ways.

To what ends can play be good business practice?

Clearly and immediately the projects began to inform the commissioned work, most noticeably with the public projects inadvertently operating as a new business strategy. *La Lala La* was one such public project that attracted our first international campaign. Our relationship with Mooks Clothing Co., like other accounts

Research for new business
strategy.
Left: Detail from *La Lala La*
studio-initiated public project,
1999.
Right: Detail from Mooks
Clothing Co. fall/winter catalog,
2000.

introduced to us through the public projects, profited from being founded on the clients heightened expectations of the ideas we played with in our authored projects. The 1999 *La Lala La* project explored foiled romantic love through a world of pop culture. As the Studio splits into romantics and cynics, we conceived of this exhibition around the idea of how your reading of music and movies emotionally responds to the state of your love life. The installation presented mixed tapes behind glass cabinets that, at one end, had love songs like "Endless Love 2" on cassette labels, while break-up songs like "There Is No Me without You" were pasted over the tapes as you walked through the exhibition space. Printed dropcards reproduced the song titles and were distributed around cafés and bars, leading the audience to a web animation that explored similar territory by playing out the getting together and breaking up of a relationship—illustrated by the video rental transaction history of two people. When Mooks Clothing Co. came across *La Lala La* they responded to the playful intimacy of the open-ended pop cultural references, recognizing how successfully the humorous, familiar tone of the communication would engage their diverse audience. Our working relationship with the street-wear label was founded on their appreciation of our conceptual threads, so this new account became an invitation to revisit and refine them further—speaking to their audience through an excessive collection of pop illustrations that, like the exhibition, invited each individual to complete the narrative.

With the Studio receiving good publicity and drawing in like-minded clients, the designers felt inspired and challenged—it appeared as if the research study's practice model of speculative public projects alongside commissioned client ones was a success. Yet, although job satisfaction was everything when we started, we soon began to ask to what extent had the Studio's business practice really been enhanced? There was no real critical leverage from this improved client list if the studio model continued to artificially distinguish between the pure studio-initiated projects and the real-world jobs. The studio could continue to author public projects that influenced the conceptual, formal and material literacy of the design projects, but how did this educate us about the professional practice of design? What was the relevance of this structure if the designers were not convinced that the discovery-led process could ever translate to the structured schedule of a client relationship? If this practice model was to have fiscal purchase, it was imperative we distill what we knew about the speculative process to find a way to embed this sustaining, rich way of working into our client projects.

Is speculation time central to the contribution and merit of any designed artifact?

The consequences of promoting speculation outside of the client projects raised questions, during a critique within the academy, about the current Studio structure. Dutch graphic designer Linda van Deursen questioned the instrumental structure that divided the studio-initiated from the client-led projects, since, she argued, the potential of design lay in unfamiliar outcomes. Van Deursen lamented that the commissioned projects seemed well worn, like she had seen them before. Her argument was simply that innovative, engaging design required time for experimentation, so design would always be reduced to predictable solutions if designers attempted to shortcut this process. Although we concurred with van Deursen's critique, it was still daunting to contest the didactic studio model that, although it may have compromised the client projects, had significantly secured a safe haven for experimentation. Dutch designers are often empowered by the commissioning client to develop the design independently, whereas we were not so sure it was possible to protect a discovery-led process if we were to conform to the work-in-progress client presentation culture of Australian design. What would enhance the design process and outcomes further—greater authority for the designers or a tighter collaboration with the client? Although we hoped to contest the deferential service model, we had too much invested in a discursive creative process to feel comfortable acting out the role of the authoritative designer. If these options were not mutually exclusive, could we negotiate an inclusive relationship with clients that supported the democratic, propositional style of the designs we created?

Phase two of the research study addressed this issue by swinging away from structural models to reconsider how we facilitated the design process with our clients. We had to learn how to negotiate and assert a new kind of client collaboration that would legitimate speculation within the commercial projects. A long-time client, the design-literate director of the media arts foundation Experimenta, became our first guinea pig. An open discussion of our respective reservations was initiated, pointing out a desire to include the client in the process, but at the same time assert authority over how we directed that process. The Board of Directors was asked to give us the creative license they would unquestioningly extend to artists selected for exhibition, relinquishing their right to assert decisions throughout the development of the design. The proposition was that a poetic process that afforded the designers time to see where the process would take them would best support the production of critically intelligent and effective communication that would serve to do more than just announce their international exhibition.

Central to developing a new account management model was our decision to abandon the convention of showing the client a range of options, liberating the designers from the outset to pursue ideas in which they collectively saw merit. We also dismissed the client presentation model that reduced the design process to a series of formally approved decisions at each stage of the project, since it limited the design to something familiar that you could be assured would work. But we wished to meet regularly with the client, so we consciously referred to the meetings as critiques and adopted a discursive culture where ideas were openly rejected, recanted or revisited as the project evolved. Similar to the way we negotiated the studio-initiated project critiques, our commitment was to listening and considering the client's comments alongside the designer's, in a spirit of partnership where all voices were equal.

This model allowed us to develop a concept for the exhibition called *Waste*, where we recycled formal ideas tested in an earlier studio project and renegotiated the production budget around repeatedly reusing the print plates. By allowing the studio to work on the same critical terms as the artists, albeit relative to design criteria, the commission expanded and challenged the audience's perception of the role graphic design can play. With consensus from the client and the design community that the process had allowed the work to rise above the standard of previous work the client had commissioned, it began to seem possible that a commercial design process could sustain both a designer's creativity and engage the client's audience.

Research for Formal Reservoir.
Left: Detail from "He thought,
He felt—Something" studio-
initiated poster, 2001.
Right: Collection of promotional
material for Experimenta's
Waste exhibition, 2001.

To what extent can a discovery-led design process be deployed in commercial practice?

In this phase we had successfully renegotiated our client relationships, but now we had to address the other half of the speculation equation and accommodate the poetic nature of discovery in our client projects. Although being allowed to run with one idea had assigned us more authority, the process had still precluded speculation beyond the front end of the project. What became essential in phase three was our ability to intuitively and analytically articulate to our clients the nature of the pure design process the studio-initiated projects had privileged us to experience. We needed to consider whether a client could be persuaded to value unplanned, unsettling, unfamiliar discovery. Unable to contrive this next step, we just had to be open to serendipity at any stage within the process.

The opportunity came along with the arts program for the Melbourne Fashion Festival, when one day after the final design had been approved but before production, we joked amongst ourselves about an alternative idea we should have proposed. The festival director and program curator had both endorsed a beautiful, safe design that was intentionally restrained to take on the theme "Excess and Exuberance"; our new idea was to controversially illustrate the excessive consumer hype and marketing budgets that drive the fashion industry. Our quipped idea was a critique of the ever-increasing power afforded sponsors in the communication material we produced for the festival—and as soon as we thought of it we knew it could work. As we began to mock up the new idea, I had to

Research for Cultural Critique. Left: Detail from work-in-progress Melbourne Fashion Festival arts program, 2003. Right: Last-minute design for Melbourne Fashion Festival arts program, 2003.

defend our position to our nervous project manager, who was not convinced I could persuade a client that an innovative design process, by necessity, had to accommodate happenstance. Rewardingly, however, the client required no persuasion, immediately valuing the cultural commentary of the unfamiliar design and recognizing the enhanced communication of the last-minute idea.

Although this research study formally concluded some years back, strategic knowledge continues to be revealed, because the Studio agenda of research, learning and innovation cultivated the designers' sophisticated, experiential understanding of how to observe the nexus between commercial practice, creative process and the designed artifact. As the director of a graduate program I always questioned whether integrating research within a professional environment could soften the demarcation between the discrete, experimental experience of grad school and the applied, commercial context of the profession. The research study presented here convinced me and my colleagues of the personal and collective value of research through design. Our commitment to research is currently represented by a series of more specific, short-term projects in diverse areas such as exploring a discursive form of graphic activism and questioning how sub-cultures and mainstream culture talk to each other. Perhaps, after all, undertaking research training within the workplace can offer a positive model for fostering lifelong learning beyond the walls of the academy.

In writing up and disseminating this particular study to the professional community, we are conscious that project-based design research is often undermined by a misguided attempt to abstract findings to meaningless generalizations of practice. For these reasons the rich reflections presented here intentionally acknowledge the situation-specific, unique nature of every design situation. However, we consider many of the strategies and observations documented to be scalable to larger companies or transferable to other design disciplines—because designing is all about possibilities and should never be reduced to a twelve-step program.

Toward a Definition of the Decorational

(In Real Time)

DENISE GONZALES CRISP

Someday I hope to be able to quote myself. —Denise Gonzales Crisp

I am at the beginning. Yes, right this moment, starting on this page I set out to understand an impulse, to investigate something I suspect to be true about graphic design. I have an hypothesis of sorts. That's something. Maybe it's not much more than a hunch, a sense. Maybe it's just a hope. But it could evolve, as pronouncements will, into a theory, a model methodology, a revolution! I have named this hypothesis the "decorational." This is where I am.

I am also, just now, stepping into what I will claim as my design research. I am not a scientist or systems analyst or an historian. But I am a designer—predisposed to invent, to make something out of nothing, to connect things to other things to surprising, and if I may say not untrue, ends. My design, my experience, perspective and values all crowd this threshold, this now moment. The means, the hypothesis and the intent convene here to spark a departure toward the unknown.

My inquiry then is two-pronged: the content of the research and the process of making it research are emerging simultaneously, in real time. And so the goal is two-fold. To give substance to the hypothesis so a theory of the decorational might serve the discipline, at least moreso than if it were to remain in my head. And to demonstrate that design itself can be research, or that design research is this, here. Right now…

My position is predictably unformed and likely unsatisfactory. So be it. I am alone in my laboratory, examining what I know, holding it up to existing knowledge. I am working on my experiments, a bit mad in this way, insulated. Not unlike Le Corbusier who in 1925 asserted that "we have now identified decorative art as commensurate with the art of the engineer" [Corbusier 1925, 76].

Just before that he wrote (as if to ground his claim in logic): "Since we are sensitive to the harmony that brings repose, we recognize an object that is in harmony with our limbs. When a and b are equal to c, a and b are equal to each other. In this case, a = human-limb objects; b = our sense of harmony; c = our body. Thus human-limb objects are in accord with our sense of harmony in that they are in accord with our bodies" [76].

I trust you will believe me when I say I am no Corbusier. Unlike him, I value ornament for its own sake. But like him I believe designers invent out of one

Transformations, 2001/2002
lecture series poster. Organic
structure in space digitally constructed from cloth.
27" x 39", 5-color offset litho.
Client: Southern California
Institute of Architecture.
Design: D. Gonzales Crisp.

moment toward a truer one. His ideal cities *(contemporaine! radieuse!)* were necessary fantasies and finally radical alternatives for radical times. "If the hard life of this machine age makes us bitter that is because a page has been turned; we have a new existence, one which is not so very playful" [42].

The machine proposed solutions that could deliver us from tortured frivolity: "Purity, economy, the reach for wisdom. A new desire: an aesthetic of purity of precision, of expressive relationships setting in motion the mathematical mechanisms of our spirit: a spectacle and a cosmogony" [114]. Tools constructed from material and manufacturing truth would extend human reach: "The steel in our hands was the machine; with the machine came calculation; with calculation, the solution of a hypothesis; with the solution of a hypothesis, the resolution of a dream" [51].

In 1928, cowhide, steel and chrome tubing coalesced in what we might call a chaise lounge, what Corbusier named a "relaxing machine." Hyperbolic, critical, righteous, contagious: his ideas were extreme and—as with most research—manifest a finite perspective. The micro view necessarily shuts out other views for the duration of its discovery. Like Corbusier (but not) I have my suspicions, my experiments, my radiant microcosms representing what I see as possible and necessary in the now world.

My hypothesis of the decorational leads me here: "Modern decorative art is not decorated" [84]. Corbusier theoretically dismantled ornament in his series of 1925 essays collectively titled *The Decorative Arts of Today*. Before Corbusier was born his beloved machines were stamping out versions of Louis XVI chairs like so many pennies. Rabid automation (and exploited labor) of bad-quality goods is exactly the sort of thing that motivated the Arts and Crafts movement's various attempts to reinvest handicraft with honor and social value—anathema to machine manufacturing of the late nineteenth century. So ornamented chairs, rugs, spoons, even buildings—stuff made by craftsmen of conscience—carried anti-technological sentiments. All well and good, and thank you mister Morris & Co. for caring. But.

Decorative arts were anti-technology and therefore useless to Corbusier's future. The technology train had already left the Gare du Nord. No looking back. His was the age that witnessed and survived the First World War: "1914: the event that upset everything . . . . The old world was shattered, trampled on, rejected, buried . . . . While the event took its course, technology could dare everything" [141]. Any lingering decorative impulse would need to conform to a steely techno-logic that not only expressed modern life, but promised to redeem it.

I wonder what the young Corbusier would think of our computing machines, our sleek tablets that spin bits of light and time into entire worlds. Digital space, digital products, and physical products conceived in digital space are formed in ways unique to the dynamic capacities of the CPU. Would Gehry's frozen liquid Disney Hall exist in real Los Angeles space if not for the digital? A knotted web of steel lies beneath waves of titanium and belies the economy and vertical simplicity of Corbusier's blessed I-beam. Is this architecture decorative? Arguments I will entertain elsewhere allude to the possibility [Foster 2002]. At base, the decorative is now exuberantly technological.

Toward a Definition of the Decorational
I suspect it is time to move the computer past the "machine age," derail the persistent perception that it should only reproduce form languages originally invented for another techno-logic.

2001/2002 Art Center recruitment catalog, cover and spread. Patterns digitally constructed from details of student work. 10" x 9.25"; five 48-page booklets bound with industrial staples, 4-color offset litho. Client: Art Center. Design: D. Gonzales Crisp, E. Gladstone, Y. Khan.

Adolf Loos wrote "Weep not! See, therein lies the greatness of our age; that it is incapable of producing new ornament. We have outgrown ornament; we have fought our way through to freedom from ornament. See, the time is nigh, fulfillment awaits us." This spectacle of a statement was first published in 1908, but the time was not quite nigh. Seventeen years later Corbusier perceived "no mystery in the crisis of decorative art; the miracle can occur of an architecture that will be, the day when decorative art ceases to be" [Corbusier, 181]. Evidently the apotheosis had yet to be realized. These architects seem mighty anxious for the day when marble, glass, steel and stone could finally complete the job of glorifying modernity, the day when nothing insignificant could detract from their pure and clear purpose. Allow me to speculate: if they could possibly have kept women with unnecessarily large hips and fancy hats from walking within view of their buildings I think they might have.

Oh pardon me. Am I indiscreet? Outrageous? Leave me alone. I am in my laboratory.

> *Toward a Definition of the Decorational*
> *I suspect that functionalism—historically fixed in the physical*
> *world and powered by an economy of materials and means—*
> *is by now a quaint ism in need of a nice pair of earrings.*

"Form follows function" is the familiar slogan promulgated by modern architects and a century-plus of designers. It is the tagline that continues to criminalize the decorative. "Much of the time, form is nothing more than an educated guess about function…" argued architect Peter Blake in 1974. "…Much of the time, for better (but probably for worse) form follows the mortgage interest rate. Much of the time, form in modern architecture is anti-functional. Much of the time, this may be all to the good" [Blake 1974, 28]. "All to the good" means in spite of—or maybe because of—modern architecture's limits, options for lifestyles emerge organically and therefore creatively within concrete cracks. I am speculating again here: it is there in those cracks that the decorational survives.

In the 1960s and '70s, *Vogue* used monolithic modern buildings as fashion backdrops, often as counterpoint to flagrant chiffon or kooky prints. This contribution to superfluosity wasn't how these resolute symbols of urbanity and commerce were meant to "function." But business reconfigures everything and anything for profit. Mies van der Rohe's sheet glass façade serves as a Victoria's Secret storefront and as I dance past it my reflection interlaces with pretty product. Functionalism is decorated by capitalism, and desire.

> *Toward a Definition of the Decorational*
> *I suspect that to be taken seriously a graphic designer must favor a*
> *rationalist aesthetic.*

Modern graphic design adopted principles of modernist architecture. I will venture here that by the time commercial art began to identify itself as "graphic design" in the mid- to late-1920s, high design had already abandoned decoration (last seen on a platform of a neo-Corinthian train station fronted by statues representing nine great European cities, her pointlessly embroidered hanky waving moist farewells).

Decoration is not simply frivolous, however. It represents a crime of excess (a doomed love affair slathered over torment). So it would seem that the course of modern design ideology in general, led by architecture, sidestepped the need for a theory of ornament in graphic design. I am still looking for essays arguing against or for ornament in graphic design as vehemently as those arguing about it in architecture at the beginning of the century. Could a relative lack of discourse mean that decoration in graphic design is just fine? Trust me, it is not just fine. Graphic design of consequence—and simply moving product doesn't count—is not overtly adorned. The course of clear communication cannot be cluttered with curlicues.

How can this be, a theory of graphic design, of commercial art, *sans* embellishment? Germany's Hochschule für Gestaltung (HfG) Ulm, and the Swiss Kunstgewerbeschule Basel. That's how. In the 1950s and '60s Max Bill, Otl Aicher, Armin Hofmann, Emil Ruder et al. stood alongside Corbusier and Mies as researchers theorizing design's role in post World War II society. In particular, HfG Ulm developed approaches that would strengthen design's significance to culture, and to ever-expanding industry. 1958 curriculum copy read: "The task of this department is to design images in accordance with their function ... typography, graphic design, photography, and exhibition design are treated as a single area, which will shortly be augmented by ... motion pictures and television. The term 'visual communication' has emerged to denote this area, in accordance with international usage .... To this end methods must be evolved that take account of the advances made in recent decades in the theory of perception and meaning" [Ulm Design, 140].

But design's partnership with the social, linguistic and physical sciences was not a natural one, even as late as 1965. Core faculty Guy Bonsiepe wrote in the institution's journal *Ulm* "... tension and hostility spring from the fact that the HfG pays more attention to the question of how design relates to the sciences than to the question of how design relates to the arts" [151]. While Basel teachings reinforced the more familiar values of the Bauhaus—the project that brought art to industry—faculty at Basel did experiment with ideas such as mathematical systems (rumor has it typographer Emil Ruder walked around campus in a white lab coat). The influence of these and other institutions further ossified the "form follows function" logic by giving it a scientific face. Enter "design science," that is, systematic and comparative methods applied to determine and construct systems that would solve so-called problems.

Magazine covers: 2 of 4 embellished quarterly mastheads and other fancy typography. 9.5" x 10.625", 4-color offset litho. Client: *Artext Magazine.* Design: D. Gonzales Crisp.

Toward a Definition of the Decorational
I suspect that the rationalist aesthetic as theorized and practiced by mid-century modernists is not only of a different time, but of a different place, a different gender, a different ethos.

Different than Corbusier's singular vision but similar in impulse, HfG Ulm and the Basel School were design laboratories setting forth and testing what might be true. They generated imaginative (for the time) ideas, made relatable objects, built a case for their research, and sold it to the client, the sponsor, the press and the public. Now their processes and products are what continue to inform most design study, and what establish the limits of practice.

The forms and functions of design are instigated by design research, by designers' drive to communicate their place and moment truthfully through the material world. Corbusier's theories responded to his modernity. The form languages founded in Basel and Ulm gave shape to the concepts of corporate identity and public information, ideas that coincided with the birth of global trade. Each literally designed the future for which their moment would eventually be history.

Today! I seek what was left on the platform to wither. Since 1925, ornament has served many with dignity: W.A. Dwiggins, Fredrick Goudy, The Eameses, Wes Wilson, Herb Lubalin, April Greiman.

And today! The decorational identifies and responds! (You see how, as I near the end of my investigation, I am given to assertion, to hyperbole? I am in my laboratory.) The decorational dares the attempt to be true to now. It honors

Detail of a poster, *What I Was Doing When I Should Have Been Listening*, announcing a presentation of work by D. Gonzales Crisp to the Art Directors Club of Tulsa, 2003. Digitally constructed from doodles. 28" x 19", 4-color offset litho. Design: D. Gonzales Crisp.

many meanings in many forms; honors histories and contemporary currents, communal and technological invention. The decorational intends to engage the discourse of ornament with that of rational design. The decorational finds pride in craft, joy in materials (Our material is digital! Our digital is material!). The aim is not nostalgia, nor pastiche nor irony, but to reflect and be the complexity of our time (which could be nostalgic! ironic!).

There it is. This now. I have initiated the argument and presented my experiments and find myself here, some weeks and pages later. And so I begin.

ESSAY STUDY: What is decoration in graphic design? What is ornament? By accepting one or both as integral to communication, will they cease to be decorative, ornamental, superfluous?

ESSAY STUDY: The decorational is alive and well on the wwweb. Groups are developing form vocabularies that intricately weave information, simulate physical surfaces, create complex pattern, animate the figurative and the abstract. Proponents are growing in number. Identify the decorationalists!

ESSAY/DESIGN STUDY: Document decoration's communicative value that speaks to complexity and diversity.

ESSAY/DESIGN STUDY: Meet need with delight!

DESIGNWRITING

ANNE BURDICK

How might writing change when design is an integral part of its conception? This is the primary research question that I've explored through design (as methodology and outcome) in a range of projects over the past ten years. The exploration hit its stride through design-writing-programming collaborations that took place in the electronic realm; inevitably, that experience fed back into the print environment. The issues turned out to be surprisingly similar, but shifting between media brought key questions to the fore; specifically, those related to the materiality of writing, the possibilities and limitations of various media types, and the ergonomics and cultural conventions of reading.

In the mid-1990s, I came across Jay David Bolter's conception of a "writing space"—"the physical and visual field defined by a particular technology of writing" [Bolter 1991, 11]—which altered my thinking about writing and design significantly. "Different conceptual spaces foster different styles and genres of writing and different theories of literature" [Bolter, 11] Aha! Instead of designing "pages," "screens," or "chapters," I was *designing spaces for writing*. Thinking about these conventional forms—from pages to essays to poems to lists—as containers that have a predetermining effect on the kind of writing that can take place within them allowed me to pose the questions: If we change the attributes of the space do we necessarily change the writing? What if one were to design a space first, and fill it with writing second? What happens when the two are developed in tandem? What are the possibilities for imagining new ways of seeing/reading/writing?

My experience in collaborations with expansive thinkers from literary criticism and linguistics led to additional questions: What role does representation play in the semantics of writing? How can designers and writers take advantage of the interplay between writing structures and visible form? What are the unique capabilities of different media types and how can design and writing work to exploit them in innovative ways?

CONT'D ON P. 108

In the following examples,
spatial relationships, visual style

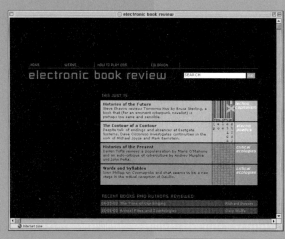

Left: The splash page, showing the most recent postings.
Below: The "weavemap" is an interface to the entire contents of *ebr*, one which is generated dynamically according to the reader's selections. The weavemap's topography indicates each essay's multi-levelled affiliation with the site's various "threads" or themes. Each essay is also represented by a word-string, a 16-letter placeholder written by the editor. The wordstrings combine with the colored weave to create a visual-verbal tapestry, an always changing representation of the site's contents. Below, top: in default mode, the contents are sorted by date. Below, bottom: the reader sorts the contents by the thread "music sound noise."

electronic book review,
(ebr), is an online literary journal dedicated to promoting print/screen transformations and weaving new modes of critical writing into the web. Since 1995, it is one of the primary sites for creative, media-specific literary criticism and electronic literature.
www.electronicbookreview.com

and organizational logic are
equal in semantic significance
to word choice and sentence structure.

post-singular

nodal

technocapital

AVAnt

betweenness

reverbal

touristy

immeasure

animot

Above: A detail from the weavemap showing its "random poetry."
Right: A detail from the weavemap showing the wordstring list that represents "music sound noise" in the abstract.

music
sound
noise

web

crunky

poem

msn

legalistic

medieval

discovery

(Zoo)!

undigitized

grammatical

operatic

domestic

recombinant

subjective

acoustic

electronic book review

Tattoo it in Skin: A Literary Prediction   Rob Wittig

atom one, the troubadours

The troubadours invented love.

Or, at least, that's the CLAIM that every scholar who writes about the 12th century explosion of song writing in southern France at first repeats...... then backs off of.

"It's probably not EXACTLY true," they'll waffle... "but it's close enough for Jazz."

What IS unquestionable is that every theme of every love song being played on the radio at the moment you read this - country, rock, standards, hip hop, dance, in every Western language - can first be found in troubadour lyrics . . .

- My beloved doesn't love me and I'm going crazy with grief

- I know that loving you is against all the rules, but our feelings are more important than anything else

electronic book review

Tattoo it in Skin: A Literary Prediction   Rob Wittig

atom one, the troubadours

The troubadours invented love.

Or, at least, that's the CLAIM that century explosion of song writing then backs off of.

"It's probably not EXACTLY tru Jazz."

What IS unquestionable is that played on the radio at the mom standards, hip hop, dance, in e in troubadour lyrics . . .

- I know that loving you is agai important than anything else

- You are so lovely that lookin

- My love is so strong it has tak of us

- One glance from you would m

- Spring time is the season of l

(e l e c
p o e t t
i r
c o
s)

electro
poetics

medieval

parodic

betweenness

written

tropical

technographic

literal

not an end

sited

cyberdebates

bulldozed

AVAnt

hybrid

open-ended

encyclopedic

blogstyle

Above, top: The essay view includes icons on the right that represent an essay's thread affiliations.
Above, bottom: Clicking on the thread icons reveals a pull-down menu showing the wordstring list for that thread. The list is a series of links to the individual essays, allowing users to move laterally through the site's contents.
Right: A detail showing the wordstring list for "electro-poetics." Navigational elements double as literary devices.

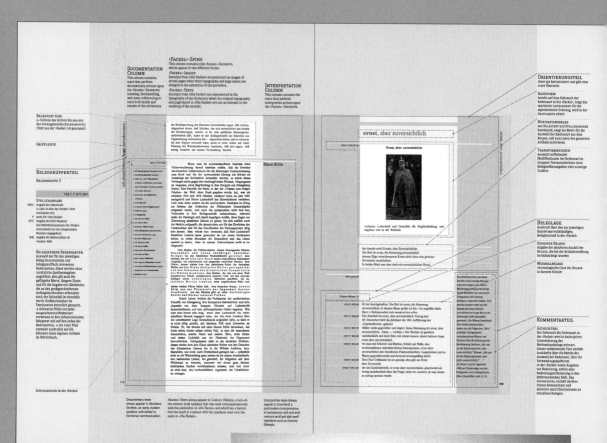

DOCUMENTATION COLUMN
This column contains texts that perform documentary actions upon the ›Fackel‹-Excerpts: indexing, documenting, and cross-referencing to texts both inside and outside of the dictionary.

›Fackel‹-Spine
This column contains only ›Fackel‹-Excerpts, which appear in two different forms:
›Fackel‹-Images
Excerpts from ›Die Fackel‹ are presented as images of actual pages when their typography and page layout are integral to the semantics of the quotation.
›Fackel‹-Texts
Excerpts from ›Die Fackel‹ are represented in the typography of the dictionary when the original typography and page layout in ›Die Fackel‹ are not as relevant to the meaning of the excerpt.

INTERPRETATION COLUMN
This column contains the texts that perform interpretive actions upon the ›Fackel‹-Excerpts.

ORIENTIERUNGSTEIL
dient als Artikelkopf und gibt eine erste Übersicht

BASISFORM
beruht auf dem Gebrauch der Redensart in der ›Fackel‹, trägt das markierte Leitelement für die alphabetische Ordnung, wird in der Griffleiste zitiert

MOTIVATIONSBELEG
aus Belegtext und Stellenangabe bestehend, zeigt ein Motiv für die Auswahl der Redensart aus dem Korpus, soll zum Lesen des gesamten Artikels motivieren

TRANSFORMATIONEN
Auswahl auffallender Modifikationen der Redensart im knappen Textausschnitten ohne Belegstellenangaben oder sonstige Zusätze

BELEGLAGE
Angabe der absoluten Anzahl der Belexe, die bei der Artikelerstellung berücksichtigt wurden

ENFASSTE BELEGE
Angabe der absoluten Anzahl der Belexe, die bei der Artikelerstellung berücksichtigt wurden

MINIMALBELEGE
chronologische Liste der Belexe in kurzem Schnitt

KOMMENTARTEIL
Geckichteil
Der Gebrauch der Redensart in der ›Fackel‹ wird in deskriptiver Unterstützung des Motivetionsbelegs erörtert.

BELEGTEXT-Ende
(= Schluss des letzten Belexes aus der vorangehenden Beleggruppe); (Text aus der ›Fackel‹ ist gescannt)

GRIFFLEISTE

BELEGGRUPPENTEIL

BELEGGRUPPE 9

1921; F 577,946.

STELLENANGABE

BELEGKONTERNE REDENSARTEN

Seitenumbruch in der ›Fackel‹

ernst, aber zuversichtlich

Ernst, aber zuversichtlich

Blaue Brille

Documentary texts always appear in Akzidenz Grotesk, an early modern typeface well-suited to functional communication.

›Fackel‹-Texts always appear in Century Oldstyle, a turn-of-the-century book typeface that was used contemporaneously with the publication of ›Die Fackel‹ and which has a history that has much in common with the typefaces used over the years in ›Die Fackel‹.

Interpretive texts always appear in Crée Serif, a postmodern interpretation of anonymous 19th and 20th century serif and slab-serif typefaces such as Century Oldstyle.

The *Fackel Wörterbuch: Redensarten* has been called "the apotheosis of the book." This unconventional 1,200-page dictionary is based upon the use of idioms in Karl Kraus's *Die Fackel*, an early 20th century journal of media criticism. The dictionary's unique diagrammatic structure and visual strategies were a direct response to the book's complex and varied contents.

PHOTO: SUSAN L. BURDICK

Top: One of the "Exploded Entry" spreads from the dictionary that provides an example of the book's complexity. The dictionary contents are divided into three columns that facilitate multi-directional reading. Typographic coding further indicates the function of each textual unit.

In order to maintain the materiality of the original source material, images of the quoted texts

are integrated into the layouts of the following projects.

Right: The center column of the dictionary pages carry excerpts from the dictionary's corpus, *Die Fackel*. The two pages shown here include both "Fackel-texts," excerpts which conform to the typography of the dictionary, and "Fackel-images," reproductions of the actual pages of *Die Fackel*.

Below: Two "Fackel-images": The graphical layout of each is integral to the semantics of its text. At left, Karl Kraus used a diagrammatic display to juxtapose appropriated newspaper ads. At right, Kraus included the silence of the blank page to indicate the absence of material censored by the government.

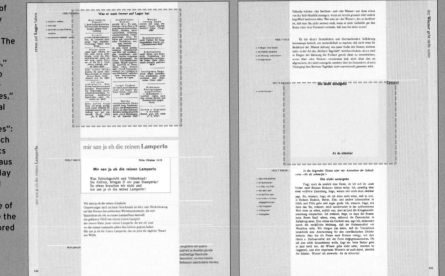

Writing Machines, a Mediawork Pamphlet by literary critic N. Katherine Hayles, combines both a book and a web-based supplement. The text addresses materiality in the critique of literature, from artists' books to e-lit. The design of both the print and web components emphasize the status of each as a navigational interface and a tool for reading, embodying the theory on both the macro and micro levels.
www.mitpress.mit.edu/mediawork

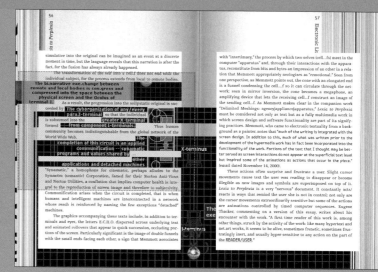

Above: A spread showing how visual slices of quoted material are woven into the body text in place of conventional text-only quotations. In this example, the original was a web project called *Lexia to Perplexia*.
Below: Detail shown at actual size.

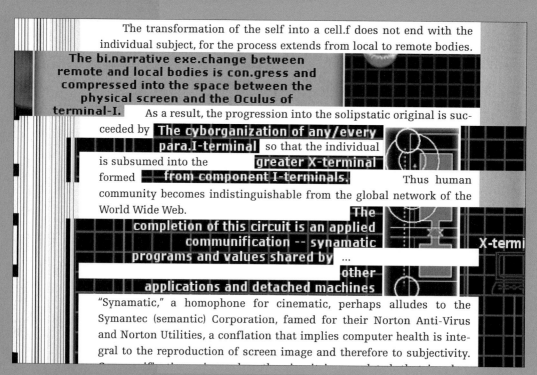

The transformation of the self into a cell.f does not end with the individual subject, for the process extends from local to remote bodies.

The bi.narrative exe.change between remote and local bodies is con.gress and compressed into the space between the physical screen and the Oculus of terminal-I. As a result, the progression into the solipstatic original is succeeded by **The cyborganization of any/every para.I-terminal** so that the individual is subsumed into the **greater X-terminal** formed **from component I-terminals.** Thus human community becomes indistinguishable from the global network of the World Wide Web. **The completion of this circuit is an applied communification -- synamatic programs and values shared by** ... **other applications and detached machines**

"Synamatic," a homophone for cinematic, perhaps alludes to the Symantec (semantic) Corporation, famed for their Norton Anti-Virus and Norton Utilities, a conflation that implies computer health is integral to the reproduction of screen image and therefore to subjectivity.

VISUAL-VERBAL QUOTATIONS

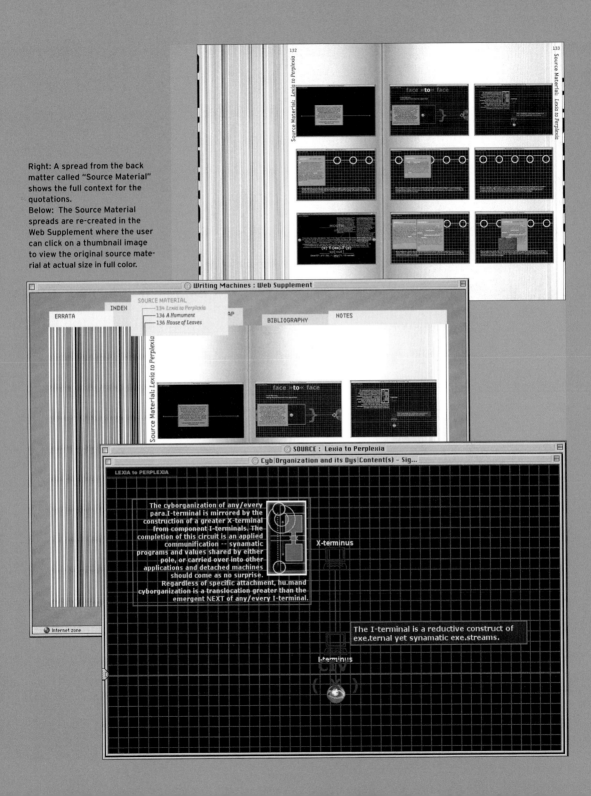

Right: A spread from the back matter called "Source Material" shows the full context for the quotations.

Below: The Source Material spreads are re-created in the Web Supplement where the user can click on a thumbnail image to view the original source material at actual size in full color.

The work shown here explores these questions and ignites others. Of course this is just a glimpse into the complexity of the individual projects, the highly involved process, and the theoretical issues that are raised with each. Nonetheless, these examples introduce a number of material-linguistic innovations that demonstrate the way in which design can be used as an investigative tool when the goals are larger than the practical implications of the individual project itself. I've called the process and product DesignWriting.

DesignWriting is defined as written communication that depends as much on verbal content as it does on visible form to convey the full breadth of its meaning. Examples of DesignWriting are most frequently found in popular culture where words and images mix freely, such as comics or advertising. Poetry, hypertext, charts and diagrams are examples from the more conservative realm of scholarly discourse. It is in this land of "serious writing" that my design research activities take place.

DesignWriting in action requires that both words and visual form be developed in tandem, either by a single author or through tight collaboration. My DesignWriting process begins with a close reading of the content—which doesn't mean subject matter as much as writing strategy: the internal rhythms, sequence of ideas, range of voices and organizational logics—in order to develop visible form that is specific to each project. My goal is to interpret, through structure and form, the nuances, opportunities and semantic requirements of each unique piece of writing. Ironically—or obviously—it is through focusing on the micro that I have been able to create innovations that answer to the macro: imagining new forms of writing through design.

Sensory Anomalies

MICHAEL NAIMARK

Mediated Sensory Experience

The work discussed in this chapter can be seen as experimental design research, exploring formal aspects of time, space, place, movement and perception. The nature of mediated sensory experience is central to such explorations.

Mediated sensory experiences are never perfect, in terms of being indistinguishable from unmediated first-hand experiences. These imperfections, the sensory anomalies, range from distractions and violations to poetry and metaphor, depending on the complex relationships between media, content and audience. For new media, these relationships are largely unexplored: we learn as we go.

The single biggest difference between first-hand and mediated experiences is whether sensory anomalies exist. There are none in first-hand experience. Such anomalies always have explanations: the window allowed me to see but not hear, the ventriloquist is talking not the dummy, and the elevator changed floors when the door was closed. The physical world obeys the laws of science. When we experience anomalies in the physical world, it's due to human hardware or software issues, such as blindness or psychosis, not because of the environment.

Now consider montage. In the blink of an eye, the movie audience is transported across space or time, an entirely impossible event in the physical world. The same holds for optically changing scale, for compositing together different audiovisual elements, and for generating photo-realistic fantasy characters and places. We would question our senses, or our minds, if we saw a giant human head staring through our living room window, or if we came upon the Eiffel Tower in a cornfield, or if Bugs Bunny hopped by. But we totally accept, indeed enjoy, such anomalies in the movies and in other media. These anomalies are intentional, meant to create metaphor and poetry.

"Virtual Reality," in its theoretical construct, is the merging of the feeling of first-hand experience with the freedom from physical-world constraints. The ultimate VR experience may have dungeons and dragons, it may have "cartoon physics," or it may simply transport us to another place or another time. In all cases, the goal is indistinguishability from first-hand experience in the physical world: "just like being there." Such VR doesn't exist and may never (at least not without electrodes). So for now, we live with even the best sensory media having some degree of anomalies. These anomalies are not intentional, and entire industries exist to make higher resolution cameras, better synthesized lighting models and auto-stereoscopic displays. The goal is not about creating metaphor and poetry but about re-creating a multi-sensory experience that is as consistent as possible.

So some anomalies in sensory media are intentional while others are not. What gives?

Rather than propose Big Answers, I present here a series of small observations. Over the past two decades I've explored how new media technologies can expand "sense of place."

These projects, being experimental in nature, have been opportunities to both transcend and exploit sensory anomalies and to watch what happens. Here are some notes and observations about these projects from which readers may draw their own conclusions.

Anomalous Space

DOME PROJECTIONS

Like montage, mediated experiences may offer ways to experience space one might consider superior to unmediated experiences, anomalies be damned. Some work, some don't, and there's no way to know except by experiencing them.

Dome Projection

In 1978, as a graduate student at MIT, a visual riddle became a haunting obsession. Suppose one placed a 180-degree lens on a camera, pointed it straight up and shot a picture, then projected it onto a dome with the same fisheye lens. For viewers inside the dome looking outward, the image would more-or-less "read" correctly. But what if the image was projected on the outside of a little dome, and viewers were outside the dome looking inward? My obsession, particularly at a place like MIT, became contagious and the subject of cocktail chatter. Some of my colleagues thought the image would look as natural as sitting in a planetarium but from a "God's eye" view. Others were convinced the image would be gobbledygook.

So for the next month, I built a simple camera and display system. I rented a large, expensive fisheye lens, mounted it on a Nikon 35mm still camera, and shot lots of images in a variety of settings and situations (more on this in a moment). The metal back of the camera was replaced with a custom-made optical glass mount and the camera was mounted vertically with a strong light source underneath aimed through the glass. A 36-inch acrylic dome was sandblasted to act as a rear screen, mounted on top of the lamp/camera/fisheye lens system, and the processed film was reloaded into the camera. *Voilá*, an inside-out dome projection!

The documentation image shown here may look impressive, but the reality is that poor Ann Marion, another MIT graduate student, sees nothing: her eyes are straining to focus close-up on imagery that is far-field, and the image itself is curving in all the wrong directions. Some observers claimed partial success for interior imagery, where the wall and ceiling lines along the dome's surface could be mentally "flipped" like the Necker Cube illusion. But for the most part, there was no miracle "inside-out" illusion many of us hoped for.

The *Dome Projection* did have one noteworthy feature, though. At the time, I was involved romantically in an intense but confusing relationship. During the week of shooting, there we were, standing in an embrace, when I reached for the camera, placed it between our faces, and snapped. The image projected on the dome shows her face on one side and mine on the other. If this were projected inside a planetarium, we would indeed be facing each other, but on my little dome projection, we appear to each be facing away, backs to each other. "I guess this sums up our relationship," she said upon seeing it.

DISPLACEMENTS

During the same period, I was exploring how to add spatiality back into cinema by moving the projector the same way as the camera moved during filming. That movie cameras can move but movie projectors don't is itself an anomaly, and when a movie projection moves the same way as the original camera movement, a very natural-looking "flashlight effect" occurs. A simple demonstration can be made by filming with a movie camera on a slowly rotating tripod, then projecting the movie on a slowly rotating turntable. This became the basis for an art installation.

The idea was to design an Americana-style living room, mostly from Salvation Army furniture, inside the exhibition space, then film it with a rotating movie camera from the room's center. After filming, only two changes were necessary: the camera would be replaced with a loop projector on the same turntable and the entire contents of the room would be spray-painted white. The projector would project everything back onto itself, now acting as a giant, custom-shaped projection screen.

Displacements

Projecting an image onto a screen the same shape as the image enlivens it to perfect three-dimensionality. Such a technique is used by Disney in the Haunted Mansion to project a woman's face onto a face-shaped mask. This effect is so strong that small anomalies, such as her moving lips, go unnoticed. Most people erroneously believe they're viewing a hologram (which, to anyone in the field, is nonsense).

I produced this living room installation three times over a four year period, each time walking the plank a little further away from verisimilitude in favor of sensory anomalies.

The first installation, obediently entitled *Moving Movie*, was almost entirely motionless, insofar as the rotating movie projector simply projected rotating imagery of the stationary furniture that occupied three of the four walls. In what felt like a total violation of the concept, I filmed a performer walking along the fourth blank wall. Though she added some motion, and maybe even some emotion, she appeared simply as a flat projection in an otherwise 3D projection environment.

The following year I produced the installation again, this time deciding to integrate live performance even though I was apprehensive of the anomalous look of people in the movie (especially knowing that I could not paint them white as well). This second installation, with another general title, *Movie Room*, also had one blank wall, where three performers did such actions as spray-painting graffiti as the camera panned by. One insisted on actually sitting on the sofa during filming, to which I finally succumbed. Another snapped a Polaroid picture and stuck it on one side of the blank wall during filming. I decided, after a great deal of "art anxiety," to keep the Polaroid unpainted. In the end, I was indebted to the performers. The graffiti action was striking but safe. The performer on the sofa appeared nicely ghost-like (an anomaly!) on top of the very real-looking sofa. And the image of the performer holding the image of the Polaroid, walking toward the actual Polaroid, and placing it there—witnessing the moment where the image and object became one—was spine-tingling.

This displacements/convergence anomaly became the basis for the third installation. This time, no holds were barred on violating the formalism of 3D representation. Another living room was installed, this time along all four walls. Lots of movable props: sweaters to take off, a purse, a globe to spin, junk food on the coffee table. Two performers were carefully scripted to move things during filming. Ten rotations were filmed. This installation was still about adding spatiality to cinema with the rotating and 3D projection, but it was also about the displacements. The piece, entitled *Displacements*, was final.

Anomalous Time
MOVIEMAPS

A motion picture film can be viewed forward or backward at any speed, even though there's only one "correct" (non-anomalous) speed, at least if "real-time" playback is the goal. But motion picture film can be triggered by space instead of time, measuring "frames-per-feet" instead of "frames-per-second." Such is a "moviemap."

A moviemap is a kind of interactive travel experience made by carefully pre-recording paths and turns, then accessing the material in such a way to give the participant control of speed and direction. The first moviemap was made of

Aspen, Colorado, by filming up and down every street and filming every possible turn through every intersection, using a special camera on top of a moving vehicle, triggering one frame every ten feet by a fifth wheel. The camera vehicle drove down the center of the street, and filming took place between 10am and 2pm to minimize shadow difference. The *Aspen Moviemap* was an MIT-based project two decades ago. I was on the original team and continued making moviemaps professionally.

In a word, the trick to making effective moviemaps is seamlessness. Great care must be taken to insure that the film footage of moving along paths, and particularly, cutting from a path sequence to a turn sequence and back, is as visually matched as possible. Driving down the exact center of the streets and using gyro stabilized camera platforms help, but perfect "match-cuts" are never perfect.

Consider the anomaly that results from passing someone walking down the street during filming a moviemap. Since the control of speed and direction is made by changing the playback speed of the storage medium (e.g., laserdiscs), the real time nature of the walking person is lost. If the participant decides to "travel" more slowly, the person will appear to walk more slowly. If the participant decides to travel backward, the person will appear to walk backward. One solution is to make sure nothing moves during filming. The ideal solution is to digitally isolate transient objects from the imagery, a non-trivial and state-of-the-art problem.

Another time anomaly is sun and shadow. If a particular path sequence was filmed at 11 am one day and a corresponding turn sequence was filmed at noon, the shift of the sun and shadows will be apparent. Even a few minutes makes a difference. Cloudy days help, but less than one might believe.

It's important to provide enough visual seamlessness to maintain overall spatial continuity, but from there, things can be stretched. For example, the *Golden Gate Flyover* is an aerial moviemap I directed in 1987, on exhibit at the

Golden Gate Flyover

Exploratorium. We used a gyro-stabilized helicopter camera and carefully filmed along a ten by ten-mile grid, at one-mile intervals, from 1,000 feet above sea level, always centered on the Golden Gate Bridge. Since we could fly at a precise ground speed, the camera filmed at a slow but constant frame rate equivalent to one frame every 30 feet. The interface was simply a trackball, and moving it allowed participants to "travel" over the Bay Area at speeds topping one mile per second. The result was a "hyper-real" experience, impossible in the world of first-hand experiences, unless you're a superhero.

Be Now Here:
Dubrovnik

BE NOW HERE

Another upside of anomalous time, in theory, is that it allows us to experience more than one slice of time simultaneously. Consider, for example, a Breugel painting with dozens of people all in the same scene. Chances are slim that Breugel looked out his window one day and actually witnessed a hundred children playing in the street. More likely, his subjects appeared over time (or in his imagination) and Breugel used a single canvas to place them all together. A similar phenomenon was incorporated in my 1995 immersive installation called *Be Now Here.*

Be Now Here:
Timbuktu

Be Now Here is a stereo-panoramic installation of public plazas in beautiful but dicey areas, specifically, UNESCO-designated World Heritage Sites In Danger. Like *Displacements*, a slowly rotating camera was used for filming, but with two cameras side-by-side for stereoscopic 3D. Unlike *Displacements*, rather than rotating the projector, *Be Now Here* rotates the audience, who stand on a 16-foot-diameter floor rotating in sync with the panning scene. The effect is similar to the "moving train illusion" we've all experienced when the train next to ours pulls out of the station and we think our train is moving.

For each of the four endangered locations, five scenes were filmed from exactly the same spot, where the tripod and camera system didn't move a millimeter. The result was perfect match-cuts from one time of day to another, with only transient objects and light changing. A simple input pedestal located in the center of the floor allowed participants to change location and time of day. Participant wore inexpensive polarized 3D glasses. Four-channel location sound added to the ambient feeling of "being" in these four endangered places.

Changing times of day in *Be Now Here* was magic. Like conventional montage, the world changes in the blink of an eye. But here, only time changes, while space stays exactly as it was. If the cameras had moved even a few inches during production, the magic would have been lost: the perfect registration of the buildings, trees, and mountains became the visual foundation on which the time anomalies comfortably rest.

Several years later, the *Be Now Here* footage was used for a space-time experiment, whereby three projectors were placed side by side to make a 180-degree composite image. Since the cameras rotated once per minute, offsetting the same sequence by 10 seconds resulted in a 60-degree shift, and thus a 180-degree image can be made with the same footage offset by 10 and by 20 seconds. If the footage contained little motion, the triptych projection appeared credible. With prominent motion (such as a camel caravan in Timbuktu), the projection appeared broken due to the repeated action every 10 seconds on all three screens. But with lots of non-prominent motion (such as a crowd scene in Jerusalem), the repetition appeared unnoticeable.

Slightly more daring, it was possible to make a triptych of the same place but of three different times of day, as shown here in Timbuktu and Dubrovnik. The sun, sky and people dramatically change. But even with such anomalies, the "placeness" apparently remains.

Anomalous Interaction

KARLSRUHE MOVIEMAP

The hardest part for many artists making interactive work for the first time is the realization that the audience matters and that their behavior must be taken into account. The extreme traditional view is that artists (unlike designers) work from an internal drive, independent of any audience. Think Michelangelo or Van Gogh. But the rules change when an interactive artwork "asks" its audience to participate.

In 1989 I had the opportunity to make an immersive moviemap installation. Unlike past moviemaps, which were viewed on a small screen, the *Karlsruhe Moviemap* was filmed with a wide-angle lens and projected onto a large screen. The moviemap, based on Karlsruhe's famous tram system, allowed participants to control speed and to chose which way to go at each track intersection. A tramcar was used for filming—the camera was triggered by the tram's

Karlsruhe Moviemap

odometer—and the tracks assured unrivalled registration and stability of the footage.

A kinesthetic input system was built for the installation. Since the immersive image would create a visceral experience, why not get the whole body into the act? The input system was designed around a raised floor, with three illuminated foot switches in front to choose left, center, or right directions, and a broomstick-length speed lever that pivoted forward and backward. Participants held the lever to control speed and used their feet to control direction.

Bad idea. I watched in amazement and embarrassment during two public exhibitions, as participants mastered the speed control but stumbled around the floor looking for the foot switches. It turned out that, precisely because of the hypnotic, immersive quality of the screen, the last thing people wanted to do was to look down. By the third show, the raised floor was replaced with a modest but easy-to-use pedestal with hand controls.

SEE BANFF KINETOSCOPE

Our senses work together to form a single integrated experience. Even with some anomalies, little bit of parallel support goes a long way. Using a variety of sensory modalities was explored in a project called *See Banff.*

See Banff was a stereoscopic moviemap made in 1993. It was a simple moviemap—single paths only, no turns—of scenes from the Banff region of the Canadian Rocky Mountains. A portable camera cart was built from a 3-wheeled "baby jogger" on which a stereoscopic pair of stop-frame cameras were mounted, triggered by one of the cart's wheels. Based both on the concept of parodying tourism and on the technical requirements, the system was packaged in a hundred-year old style kinetoscope cabinet. It included a lever for selecting scenes, special 3D optics hidden in the eye hood, and a crank with which the participant could "travel" back and forth along the pre-recorded paths. It's the crank that became the center of anomalous attention.

Since the moviemap sequences were all of finite length, the question arose of what to do with the crank when the scenes came to an end. One solution was for the image to simply go black, but this was unsatisfying. A better solution, it seemed, was for the crank to automatically freeze. A force-feedback brake was attached to the crank. When the first or last image of a sequence was viewed, the brake would switch on and the crank would lock up.

The effect was so effective that when the force-feedback was disengaged, something felt wrong. Obviously, a mental model of film mechanically transported through the device, with a beginning and end, was strong, and it was amplified

See Banff
Kinetoscope

when the eye and hand received consistent signals.

But there was a small problem. The force-feedback brake was only so strong and could be over-ridden. An engineer colleague, Bob Alkire, had a curious suggestion: he said add an audio "pop" in sync with the brake engaging. Easy enough, so we did. The wooden cabinet was resonant, so the pop could be felt as well as heard. Magic! The result, based purely on adding an additional parallel sense, was that people actually thought we installed a more powerful brake.

But the problem didn't entirely disappear. Anyone (big males in particular) could still force the crank to move when the brake was engaged. An even more curious solution was proposed by Joe Ansel, former exhibit director for San Francisco's Exploratorium. He noticed that a mechanical bearing coupled the wooden handle to the crankshaft, allowing participants to grip the handle while turning it. He said "take it out." Everyone was puzzled. Joe explained that without the freely rotating bearing, participants would have to hold the handle lightly, to let it rotate under their grip. Joe's solution worked like a charm. The "light-handedness" made the brake feel even stronger. And the cost was, well, a negative number.

So in the end, the least anomalous interface required a force-feedback brake added, and an audio "pop" added, and a mechanical bearing subtracted. Who knew?

Violation or Metaphor?

Sensory anomalies are funny things. I once slowed down the real-time motion of a film in an art installation to half speed, resulting in everyone appearing to move in slow motion. I had my reasons, but a colleague, a well-respected engineer, was shocked, as if I had violating something.

I had.

Metaphor to some is violation to others. "Faithful representation" is a noble engineering goal, but things aren't quite as clear in art and design. To confuse—or clarify—things further, good metaphor can often be a form of shorthand. If we share similar cultures, backgrounds or personal experiences, metaphor is a form of abstraction of compression. So in the end, the degree of faithfulness and the degree of violation depend on what we want to say. Sensory anomalies sit on both sides of this fence.

Spontaneous Cinema as Design Practice

How to Walk Without Watching Your Step

RACHEL STRICKLAND

A movie may be regarded as an intention to register something that is fleeting—elements of a process, for example, a response to prevailing conditions; or to reveal something that is otherwise invisible—drifts of a wind, the relationships that impart structure to an environment. Employing a perspective that corresponds to our bodily experience of the physical world, the movie also manifests an ordinary development of awareness—such as the flights and fixations of its cinematographer's attention, or someone's mental construction of a sense of place.

When referring to moviemaking as a method of design research, I am not considering instances when the camera is treated essentially as a mechanical apparatus for data-gathering or record-keeping. Like footage from surveillance cameras, such evidence may be intended for nobody's review except in the unlikely event of a bank robbery. Sometimes hapless summer interns are put to work transcribing the dialogue.

One evidentiary application of motion photography in service of design that nonetheless begs mention is the time-lapse studies of New York sidewalks and plazas that were produced by sociologist William Whyte's *Street Life Project*. For some 16 years beginning in 1969, Whyte and his research assistants employed interval recording techniques with super 8 film to track the meanders of New York pedestrians. By accelerating gradual and intermittent developments to a threshold of perceptibility, these time-lapse film sequences yielded provocative data about a category of human nature that had never been systematically examined. In keeping with Whyte's hypothesis that the main thing which attracts people is other people, his work demonstrated a method of predicting and measuring physical characteristics of places that attract many people to one place or another [Whyte 1988].

Neither do I regard as design research those declarative movies that are produced for the sake of illustrating a concept, or for presenting what the moviemaker, or the moviemaker's employer, already knows. Rather the purpose of my meditation in this writing is to reflect on the sense in which cinema may be pursued as exploration—articulating a language of direct physical experience with space and things and people, bringing all one's faculties to bear in an effort to become incorporated in a situation that is unfolding. It is a matter of using your eyes and ears to respond to emerging patterns and developments in the situation, and of moving the point of view to account for some several forces beginning to be examined from one instant to the next. Such an exploration extends not only to the subject of observation and the process of observing, but to cinematic aesthetics as well. It exercises sensory-motor and narrative systems of intelligence simultaneously.

Observational cinema has a particular affinity with design thinking in the ways that it complies with humans' innate aptitude for inferring continuity, for discerning relationships among phenomena and imparting structures to experience, for dwelling in the alternating currents of ambiguity, for making sense through association, combinatorial play and projective construction.

Disclosure

Although a drawing or photograph may contain a great deal of information about a place, it does not begin to describe how the place works—the comings and goings and dwellings of people there, or how events take place, or how an environment responds to weather and seasons and times of day. Because motion picture media offered a way to explore and represent the dynamic and ephemeral dimensions of architectural space, I began making films while I was a student in architectural design. My thesis project employed Super 8 film to observe an outdoor market in Rome's Campo dei Fiori. The life of the market unfolded in a setting whose territorial demarcations and circulation zones were re-created and dismantled on a daily basis. The film experimented with mapping architectural definitions of space to cinematic structure.

I might also mention that I have never written a film script. My filmmaking was rooted from the beginning in *cinéma vérité*—a method of documentary filmmaking that emerged in the 1960s, which favored spontaneous observation of everyday life over the reenactment of events. From the perspective of the audience, *cinéma vérité* was striving to be a kind of motion picture that would be self-revealing and permit discovery on the part of viewers. And because I was interested in using cinematic media to communicate about places, I have spent many years pursuing a way of making movies whose construction would be more like architecture than narrative.

"But isn't a place just a container for stories?" is the question a television writer asks me. If you know any place in particular, if you ever got lost somewhere, perhaps you would be willing to consider with me that it has several other dimensions. When you look at a building, what anyone can see is the walls and the roof and the windows and doors. It is difficult for some people (including architects) to see that the subject of architectural design is not these walls and windows and doors, but rather space—which is the thing that you neither see nor bump into.

"It is not easy to orient yourself in a whole which is made up of parts belonging to different dimensions, and nature is such a whole, just like art, its transformed reflection," observed Paul Klee. "It is hard to gain an overall view of such totality, whether it be nature or art, and it is still harder to communicate the view to others" [Klee 1924]. The trouble with our thinking is that we are tempted to orient ourselves within a closed system that would have a finite number of known dimensions. Yet experience does eventually project anyone, kicking and screaming, into those others. Wanting to capture and articulate a kind of experience that belongs to many different dimensions was the motive that attracted me from the outset of my career toward polylinear potentials inherent in computer-based interactive cinema.

My credentials as a research videographer and my sense of the job description have acquired definition during 15 some years in the service of Silicon Valley research labs, including Atari, Apple, Paramount Communications and Interval Research Corporation. I need not enumerate the various duties of a research videographer's job, but merely mention two kinds of research activity that have often been intertwined in my experience: The first one you might call fieldwork—using video to observe and capture aspects of the everyday life of people outside the research lab as a way of informing design projects undertaken by the lab. The second takes the form of new media prototyping, which is to say exploring and modeling future ways that people might interact with cinematic media.

Portable Effects is one example of a project that has pursued both these lines of research simultaneously.

Who is Designing What for Whom?
Observing Design Practice in Everyday Life

Portable Effects is an interactive video exploration that examines people's portable architecture—the collections of things that individuals carry everyday, and how they carry these things. "Portable architecture" is a phrase for expressing the miniature, mobile piece of our environment that we take with us from place to place. This phenomenon was rendered salient to me during a sojourn in

Portable Effects: A Survey of Nomadic Design Practice. Video frames.

Portable Effects: A Survey of Nomadic Design Practice. Video frames.

Kyoto in 1984, through encounters with a culture that is enormously sophisticated in the ways of folding, stacking, rolling, nesting, carrying, miniaturizing and transforming things. Several years later when Apple was developing the Newton, and other manufacturers were tinkering with similar visions of handheld computing devices, I began to videotape scenes of people and the things they carry, as a way of learning about design strategies of ordinary people in everyday life

Between setting forth in the morning and returning home at night, each person lives nomadically for several hours a day. You can't take everything with you—neither in your backpack nor in your head. Identifying essentials, and figuring out how to contain, arrange and keep track of them as you go, are instances of design thinking.

A collection of more than 100 of these nomadic portraits that I videotaped over the course of several years formed the basis for the experimental cinema project I subsequently directed at Interval Research Corporation. A portrait (like a place) is another kind of structure that is not a story. Look at images in the studio photographer's window to see what I mean, or consider any other rendition of a character whose development does not revolve around a plot. As we accumulated these video portraits, it became increasingly obvious that they were not going to add up to a feature-length documentary with a beginning and a middle and an end. The richness of the video material has a great deal to do with the range and diversity of the people who are its subjects. But how could we give viewers access to this richness without making them watch portrait after portrait for hours on end? How could we enable product inventors, for example, to pursue the threads of their own interest and to discover patterns among the various collections and design strategies?

Because computers do not know how to make sense of video content, an annotation language is required for imparting an underlying structure to the data. This structure might never be visible to a viewer, but it enables noteworthy connections in the material to surface when the viewer happens to be noticing. The

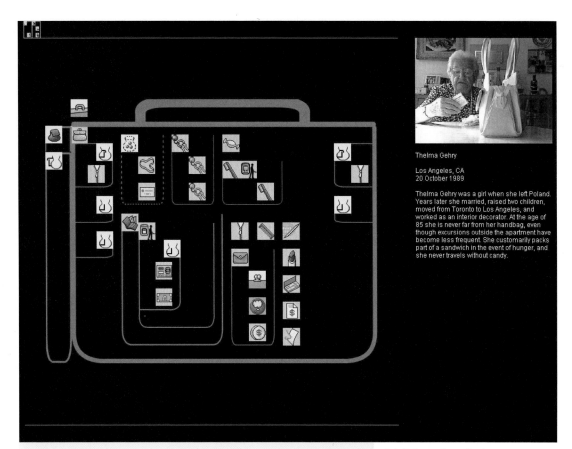

Thelma Gehry

Los Angeles, CA
20 October 1989

Thelma Gehry was a girl when she left Poland.
Years later she married, raised two children,
moved from Toronto to Los Angeles, and
worked as an interior decorator. At the age of
85 she is never far from her handbag, even
though excursions outside the apartment have
become less frequent. She customarily packs
part of a sandwich in the event of hunger, and
she never travels without candy.

One visual strategy for retriev-
ing video clips on the fly is
exemplified by the BAGviewer,
which uses annotations in the
database to dynamically com-
pute a graphical diagram of the
subject's portable architecture.
This diagram lets you see the
bag structure inside out, revealing nested relationships among
containers, compartments and
objects.

Portable Effects annotation language is a special dialect of *Media Streams*—a system that was developed by Marc Davis for his Ph.D. at the MIT Media Lab, in collaboration with Brian Williams and Golan Levin [Davis 1995]. Our ontology of
portable design has evolved on the basis of evidence we observe in the videos.
Grammatically speaking, the annotations are constructed very much like sentences, with subjects and verbs and objects. Using annotations in the database to
automate retrieval, our explorations in video form developed a series of polylinear
cinema prototypes for interactive viewing, experimenting with cinematic linkages
among scenes through invisible annotation hierarchies and "Seamless
Expansions." A Seamless Expansion employs the syntax of cinematic construction, or montage, to sustain perceptual continuity while a viewer modifies the
flow of an audiovisual stream [Gould and Strickland 2002].

　　　As designers operating in corporate culture, we are bound in our education
and practice to accede to the tenets of capitalism. We serve an economic regime
that relies on exploitation of people and resources. No matter how benign or

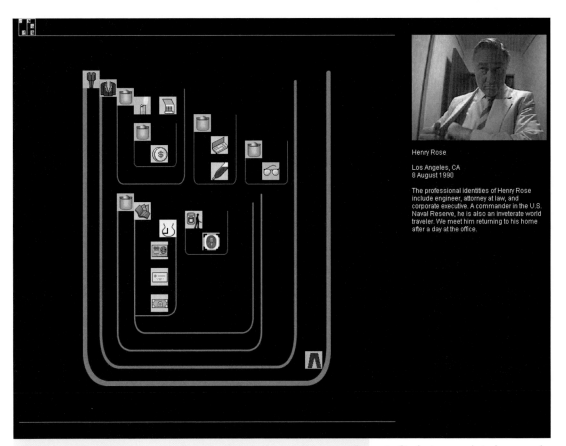

Henry Rose

Los Angeles, CA
8 August 1990

The professional identities of Henry Rose
include engineer, attorney at law, and
corporate executive. A commander in the U.S.
Naval Reserve, he is also an inveterate world
traveler. We meet him returning to his home
after a day at the office.

By reducing the representation of people's bags to iconic forms, the schematics of BAGviewer emphasize differences of structure over differences of surface appearance, and thereby afford investigations into, and comparisons of, the subjects' strategies for designing and managing their portable architecture. The BAGviewer was implemented by Golan Levin, Yin Yin Wong, Baldo Faieta and Jonathan Cohen.

excellent the design, there is always an element of inducing people to have needs, persuading them to consume, dispose, and consume again.

Both Apple and Interval, who sponsored the *Portable Effects* project, regarded it as research in the service of design. And yet the staff designers who were inventing and prototyping wearable devices—the very colleagues whom I regarded as my accomplices—seemed to apprehend something paradoxical and potentially hazardous about attempting to reconcile design insights gleaned from non-professionals with any prescription for how to build the ultimate electronic handbag. For underlying *Portable Effects* is an understanding of culture which assumes that design is not limited to the province of specialists who have formal training in such disciplines as architecture, graphics and industrial design. Rather, design behavior is a fundamental element of our species adaptation—key to humans' survival strategies.

Can Cinema Be Construed as Research?
Actualities, Spontaneities, and Digitals

Reluctant to pick at a sore, the writer is nonetheless obliged to acknowledge that the status of motion pictures as a tool of scientific recording—as a method for gathering evidence—has been profoundly disturbed, along with our faith in representation, during the hundred years or so since cinema asserted itself as the bold new media technology.

Once upon a time lens-based recordings of reality were deemed irrefutable in their evidentiary authority, and the movie camera was heralded as the latest instrument for scientific data acquisition, joining the ranks of thermometer, telescope, and microscope [Winston 1995, 127—129]. Even in the realm of entertainment, "actualities" was the name that was given to short single-scene snippets of everyday life that were filmed outside the studio in actual locations. Mounted by the Lumière brothers in Paris in 1895, the first public cinema programs featured a selection of field recordings that depicted workers departing from a factory, the baby's lunch, a rowboat leaving the harbor. Predating all the moral pretensions and epistemological complications that have encumbered the development of documentary film since then, this term "actualities" restores to imagination one early and unspoiled idea of cinema that may reserve curious potential for the new digital media of our own day.

Filmmaker Dai Vaughan has suggested that what astonished and delighted the Lumière audiences was not the staggering technological feat of motion photography, but rather the ability of this apparatus to portray spontaneities that could not occur in the theater. More remarkable than the movements of living people, whom early moviegoers perceived as performers, was the participation of inanimate phenomena—such as rustling leaves, locomotive steam, or the dust of a demolished brick wall—in making their own inscriptions. As representations of events, actuality films were engaged in the unpredictability of the events themselves—such as a sudden swell of waves that takes the oarsmen, camera operator, and viewers by surprise. This interjection of the spontaneous into media arts defied that premise of willful and precisely controlled communication which had previously been taken for granted [Vaughan 1999, 3—6].

For purposes of entertainment, the sensational novelty that attracted audiences to these primitive experiments in observational cinema was soon eclipsed by the allure of fiction, and the documentary form became relegated thereafter to a grim life in public education and news reportage. Hollywood studios proceeded to apply industrial manufacturing techniques to the mass fabrication of fantasy. The introduction of editing, which depended on multiple camera setups, and the subsequent addition of sound, which required bulky camera blimps and cumbersome audio gear for location recording, tended to annihilate any glimmer of spontaneity. Explorations in the grammar of observation by early avant-garde filmmakers such as Dziga Vertov notwithstanding, the evolution of cinematic construction has been dominated for the rest of its history by models of realist fiction.

Although the spontaneous motive in cinema had asserted itself at the very outset, it did not resurface until many years later, with the introduction of light-weight cameras and synchronous audio recorders in the 1960s. Vaughan notes that this technological development happened to coincide with a time in history when artists in many fields were incorporating chance and improvisation in their work—"seeking to overthrow established grammars which had begun to seem complicit with political oppression" [206]. The new observational technology provided the basis for a rebellion against the codes of Hollywood, as well as against a regime of non-fiction films that amounted to illustrated lectures about general themes, in favor of a more personal and direct approach that embodied the perspectives of actual observers. "In place of a camera that resembled an omniscient, floating eye which could at any moment be anywhere in the room (with a close-up, an over-the-shoulder shot, a reverse angle), there was to be a camera clearly tied to the person of an individual filmmaker" [MacDougall 1998, 86]. Instead of expounding abstract ideas and universal human conditions, practitioners of this new observational approach turned their attention to exploring idiosyncratic particulars of everyday life and the behavior of individuals in specific environments and social situations.

In the waning years of the 20th century, postmodern theory overturned the old idea of a world whose existence is independent of our representations of it, and thereby invalidated that economy of truth and representation that had constituted the very basis of documentary filmmaking. But even before we ceased to believe in reality, the evolution of the actuality strain of cinema had long been troubled by the paradoxical nature of cinema—that it is at once both a record and a language. The difference between film and reality, says Vaughan, is "that film is about something, whereas reality is not." Social scientists' various prescriptions for neutralizing the filmmaker's intervention, such as the elimination of camera movement and the minimization of editing, have approximately the same effect as burying one's head in the sand in hopes of becoming invisible. For minimum of structuring does not yield maximum of truth. "The antithesis of the structured is not the truthful, or even the objective, but quite simply the random" [Vaughan, 57].

Is it science or is it entertainment? MacDougall attributes the resistance of social science to incorporate cinema in its research practice to an incompatibility between the respective modes of description and discourse that belong to writing and moviemaking. "Inevitably, the extraordinary precision of the camera-eye as a descriptive aid has influenced conceptions of the use to which film should be put, with the result that for years anthropologists have considered film preeminently a tool for gathering data, And because film deals so overwhelmingly with the specific rather than the abstract, it is often considered incapable of serious intellectual articulation" [MacDougall, 131].

Plowman's "Ethnography and Critical Design Practice" chapter shares a participant observer's methods and his experience working in the design field ⊙30 PLOWMAN.

Do You Mean What You See?

Beneath the many styles in which documentary has historically mani-fested itself may be discerned a common purpose: to enable the charac-ter of film as a record to survive, so far as possible, its metamorphosis into language [Vaughan, 55].

What can we specify about the language of observational cinema? Cinema mani-fests itself through perspectives of embodied sensory experience that are com-mon to moviemaker and audience, as well as to people (whose perspectives may be represented) in the movie. Vivian Sobchack has observed that the substance of cinematic language consists in acts of seeing being seen, acts of hearing being heard, acts of moving on the part of people and objects, and on the part of the camera in response to people and objects. In the experience of a film, perception and its expression are the same thing [Sobchack 1992]. Cinema is essentially not a verbal language, "neither lexical nor grammatical in a linguistic sense" [MacDougall, 192], although words—both spoken and inscribed as text—are among the objects it records and incorporates in its construction. It is essentially a manner of revealing rather than a language of telling. It reveals relationships of things in time and space. It also employs a uniquely cinematic system of relation-ships, commonly called montage, for joining shots and for coordinating disparate media types, such as images and sounds. Jean-Luc Godard has said that "the only big problem in cinema seems to me to be where and why to start a shot and where and why to end it" [Godard 1999]. Like oral and written languages, the language of cinema encompasses an enormous range of usages and styles.

As for stylistic indices that have been uniquely identified with documen-tary—the wobbly camera, poor exposure, temporary lapses of focus and imper-fect continuity—these have most always been dictated by technical and budget-ary limitations. Indeed, the observational form of documentary has generally striven to approximate structures of realist fiction, including character develop-ment, dramatic conflict and resolution, the logic of cause and effect [Nichols 1991, 6; Vaughan 1999, 64]. It might be said that the language gap between documen-tary and fiction has narrowed in recent years. Or at least that the advent of small, silent cameras capable of producing crisp images in dim light has enabled far more subtle and intimate approaches to the recording of real people and actual loca-tions, executed with a fluency of camerawork and naturalness of action that rival the most polished of studio productions. By eliminating many of those practical impediments that had heretofore stunted and flawed the grammar of observa-tional cinema, such enhancements in the apparatus of field recording endow research videographers with unprecedented freedom of expression.

If we agree that the "cinema of observation" must proceed to evolve by articulating a language of its own, then what will be the rules of practice, codes of representation, principles of structure and elements of style?

One hallmark of observational cinema, and perhaps the essence of its claim to authenticity, is an inexhaustible attention to the minutiae of everyday. Outside the regime of fiction where an economy of signification prevails, the details availed to observation are under no obligation to advance a story or contribute any particular meaning, but simply emerge from the rhythms and textures of everyday life—either of no particular interest or only of interest for their own sake. Because the prevailing sense of time in such a movie clings to the moment of filming, Bill Nichols characterizes it as "a particularly vivid form of present-tense representation" [Nichols, 39—40]. The moviemaker's process of awareness while looking through a viewfinder is not so much directed at the people who may be regarded as subjects as it is engaged in attending to the environment she shares with them and mutual experience of unfolding events. What is the verb for what one does with a movie camera? Most of the time this camera is not even running. Without a script or shopping list to furnish clues, it is not a matter of aiming and firing, but rather a question of finding and selecting. The personal space-time that is expressed in observational cinema—corresponding to the drift of cameraperson's attention—is of a different order from the supposed Euclidean space and causal chronology of realist fiction. Whereas narrative cinema has conventionally employed multiple camera positions with dollies and cranes to simulate the perspectives of characters and to synthesize an omniscient view of continuous action in a space re-constituted from fragments, observational films have favored prolonged sequence shots and camera movements that represent the viewpoint of a lone pedestrian observer looking through the viewfinder with starts and stops. Rather than regard the shot as one of various ingredients in a recipe whose flavor will be imparted by the cumulative effect of single-note ingredients that are introduced in a linear series, the challenge is to achieve fully developed self-contained sequences in continuous takes.

It is a possibility of cinema to call attention to things—through the use of techniques such as framing, focus, and narration. It is equally a possibility of cinema not to call attention to particular things and parts of things, but rather, as film historian Stanley Cavell commented, "to let the world happen, to let its parts draw attention to themselves according to their natural weight" [Cavell 1971, 25]. Practitioners of cinéma vérité have shared the latter propensity, wanting to enlist viewers' participation in the act of selection, discovery and interpretation. Yet until recently, any film or video experience—regardless of its content, recording approach, or the producer's intention—needed to be once-and-for-all monolithically constructed for one way linear playback on a single screen. In practice, there was no way that filmmakers could tailor movies to address the curiosities of individual viewers. The encoding of cinematic media in digital form interjects some twists that could transform cinematic construction into a process influenced by the interests and attentions of individual viewers. Today's technology enables, for example, synchronized polylinear display of multiple video streams in virtual 3D space or on multiple screens distributed in a physical space.

Lev Manovich's analysis of *The Language of New Media* acknowledged two formative developments that seem particularly relevant to observational cinema. One is the transition from narrative structure as the predominant principle of organization, to that of a collection (or database). "Many new media objects do not tell stories; they do not have a beginning or end; in fact they do not have any development, thematically, formally, or otherwise that would organize their elements into a sequence" [Manovich 2001, 218]. I do not mean to signal that the status of storytelling as a cultural form is in any jeopardy. Rather, in Manovich's words, "narrative becomes just one method of accessing data among many." A collection is by nature open-ended. The connections between its terms are not limited to cause and effect, and the trajectory of experience is susceptible to a viewer's input.

The second feature in Manovich's scheme of digital things that deserves mention here is a new way of conceiving space, whose precedents can be found not only in videogames and motion simulators, but also in interfaces for interaction with any kind of computer data. Asserting "navigable space" as nothing short of a new symbolic form or media type, he also identifies its aesthetic challenge: "Rather than considering only the topology, geometry and logic of a static space, we need to take into account the new way in which space functions in computer culture—as something traversed by a subject, as a trajectory rather than an area" [Manovich, 279]. A related trend is "spatial montage," prefigured in the multiple windows of GUI and in object-oriented programming. "The logic of replacement, characteristic of [traditional] cinema, gives way to the logic of addition and coexistence. Time becomes spatialized, distributed over the surface of the screen. In spatial montage, nothing needs to be forgotten, nothing is erased .... In contrast to the cinema's screen, which primarily functions as a record of perception, here the computer screen functions as a record of memory" [Manovich, 325].

Video editing tools have yet to become useful for shaping media with Seamless Expansions, or for visualizing, aligning, and keeping track of simultaneous streams. So-called nonlinear editing systems are still designed to produce linear results. Meanwhile the Internet has collected our imaginations in a display environment for a movie with many channels. Polylinear construction, enabled by digital technology, holds promise for fulfilling a desire that was only partially expressed in the idiom of *cinéma vérité*—to create a kind of motion picture that lets the world reveal itself and permits discovery on the part of viewers.

Game Forms
for New Outcomes

EMMA WESTECOTT

> *Only that which can change can continue: this is the principle by which*
> *infinite players live.*— James P. Carse

A recent anomaly in modern media evolution is the concept of interactive media, primarily typified by the digital game form. Our concept of game form continues to widen and deepen. The game has become a lens to look afresh at the world, a research tool to better understand the transition from analysis to praxis, a method to unify experience within context and a fulcrum from which to express a practitioner's philosophy. As a form of activity present in human life at least since the beginning of recorded history, the game is deeply embedded in the human psyche. Contemporary digital games do not even begin to scratch the surface of how the game form might influence every aspect of human culture and behavior.

To paraphrase my old boss Douglas Adams, we are only just realizing the potential of the personal computer; at various points in history we have thought it was a typewriter, television and a brochure. Douglas said:

> *Of course, the computer isn't any of these things. These are all things*
> *we were previously familiar with from the real world which we have*
> *modeled in the computer, so that we can use the damn thing. Which*
> *should tell us something interesting. The computer is actually a model-*
> *ing device. Once we see that, we ought to realize that we can model any-*
> *thing in it. Not just things we are used to doing in the real world, but the*
> *things the real world actually prevents us from doing* [Adams 1997].

I work at one of The Interactive Institute's applied research studios in Sweden, Zero-Game, where our work focuses on game form. Digital games are powerful as research tools in two ways: as a medium made for modeling and as a framework for focus. At Zero-Game our approach is to wrap applied research around specific projects. Our objective is to produce and communicate new knowledge via game demos, software demonstrations, academic papers and documented methodologies.

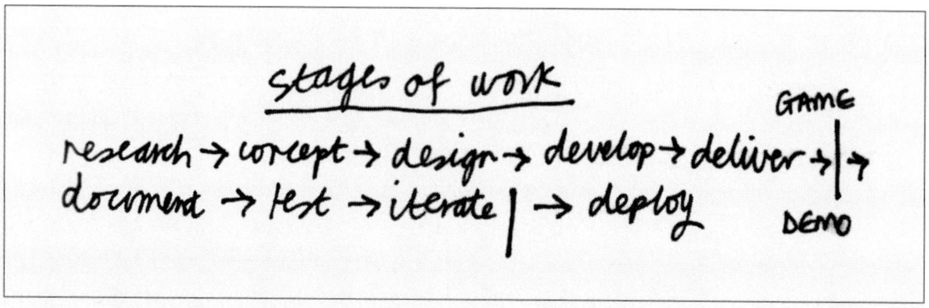

stages of work

research → concept → design → develop → deliver → | → GAME

document → test → iterate | → deploy   DEMO

Working notes showing the
iterative software development
process.

Our chosen method is via an iterative software development process. The magic of manifestation gives the designer opportunities to realize and review research thinking before moving into production. We consider our design research to be successful when it triggers further interest and development in a range of different channels.

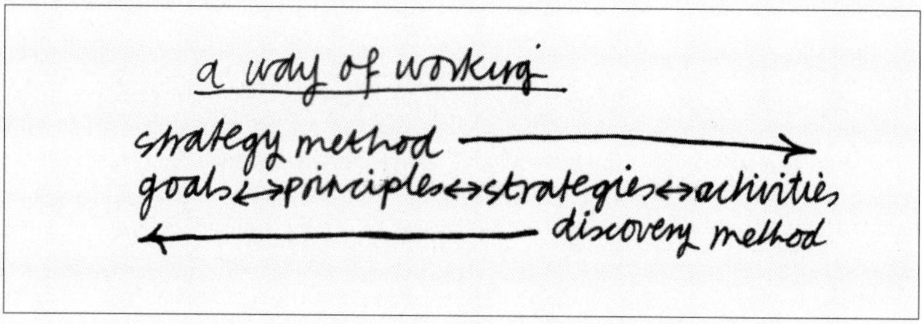

a way of working

strategy method ─────────────→

goals ⇄ principles ⇄ strategies ⇄ activities

←───────── discovery method

Westecott's diagram of
alternate ways of working.

At Zero-Game we started with a simple definition of games as "a set of rules played over time to be won or lost." The process of designing a game is itself a research tool available to designers to more closely understand their own design process and potential outcomes as well as the audiences for their work.

Each of the following points provide a jumping-off place for the designer when it comes to exploring specific themes and motivations for game development:

ACTION

The key interest of game form is its active nature. When this is viewed in the context of a consumer service, game form seems a natural candidate for guiding research.

FRAMING FOR EXPERIENCE

Each game experience has its own narrative style; for example, the intimate physical nature of using a mobile device calls for a more personally directed style of narrative. Broadly speaking, each game can be mapped against a particular type of narrative experience—intimate, public, social or spectacular. The point of view and situated background that a player brings to interaction (where and how they are playing) and type of player (why they are playing) determines the relevant mapping.

CONSEQUENCE

The active nature of games has the potential to change the dynamic embodied in existing cultural media—that media supports distance from culpability. Games have the potential to positively affect our culture of remoteness by involving players in the interplay between action and consequence. This is one of the most exciting aspects of game form and points to possibilities for individuals, societies and cultures in building and communicating ethical values. It is important to note that the designer should not make the moral decision for the player; rather the designer provides a tool set for decision-making and feedback regarding the associated outcome ○256 WRIGHT.

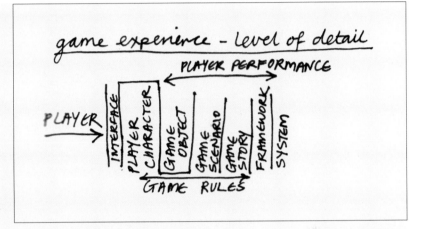

Westecott's notes regarding the player as performer.

PLAYER AS PERFORMER

Game pattern analysis looks at the bottom level of game activity necessary to build a pattern of behavior to "progress" the game. Carrying out this pattern of activity to progress the game can be regarded as a performance on the behalf of the player. At Zero-Game we coined the game genre "first-person actor" where we put the player in the role of a character in scenarios that emphasize dramatic interaction between players. Our practical design work looks to support different acting styles and modes of characterization within a game context.

SOCIAL CONSTRUCTION

By transposing social structures into a simulated game space it is possible to model and explore different forms of social structure and community construction that are extremely relevant to the designer's task of more closely understanding their audience.

CULTURAL HEALING

On a recent trip to Australia I was fascinated to find that games are being used to 'heal' communities in crisis. Within the aboriginal community in Alice Springs, games have found a use as a discussion driver around the issues of violence and abuse. By talking about in-game behavior it has proved possible to provide enough emotive distance from the real-life situation to enable productive discussion of the issues at hand. As Darion Rapoza argues in this volume, game designs may be targeted to address and make interventions with specific types of at-risk players ⊙260 RAPOZA. The potential of game design as a tool for healing extends from individuals to national and global culture, from specific game-play features to overarching themes and forms.

NEW BUSINESS

Games are drivers for new business opportunities. Whether using location-based gaming for tourism activities or product placement and branding opportunities with entertainment, games drive high-tech skill acquisition. As explorations of game form lead to new outcomes, the market for games will grow from the entertainment sector into other domains, including education, health, citizenship, ethics and policy. At Zero-Game we are exploring the game form to encourage and facilitate this expansion and to more fully utilize the power of the game.

We feel that the greatest challenge of effective research is to find the right questions to ask. In any field of investigation that looks to explore radically new concepts, it is important to enter into a design process that refines and focuses direction in an open and playful way. To explore concepts that are truly new, it is often more productive to build on what we understand about people, form and design process than to aim for technology-based solutions. We have found game form to be an exceptionally generative framework for such explorations.

The Zero-Game Manifesto

Part I / Critique

Games are too powerful to be regarded as merely entertainment.

Games have the potential to change society.

Current games obsessed with supremacy are only one amongst many possible forms of game experience.

Part II / The Nature of The Game

Games should be regarded as an opportunity to inspire our realities.

Games represent a form of reality.

Playing games is a creative activity.

Playing games frees human awareness from the everyday.

Games are a form of ritual.

Games are art.

The game player, by playing, completes the piece.

Games are a form of magic.

The Game is the Great Work.

Part III / Praxis

Our games will not be dictated by the market.

Our games will be art.

Our games will break boundaries.

We will introduce gameplay as a virus into the concept of story.

We will use and reuse the shadow ideologies of history as a catalyst for new visions.

We will not be limited to articulations within a dogmatic language.

We are architects of the third place.

We will celebrate the universal dialectic of the binary code.

We will be shamans of the post-human age.

We will walk the path of the trickster.

Strategy, Tactics and Heuristics for Research
A Structuralist Approach

ROB TOW

Grand Strategy, Strategies and Tactics

Deciding "What to Do Next" (and How to Do It) is a problem I've faced repeatedly in my career. Over time, I've developed an approach that has a definite structure. Much of it is inspired by the thought of several historians of military history, combined with a wry appreciation of some of the valid points of deconstructionist philosophers. I combine these tropes into a method for conducting research for inventive design—that is, the design of that which is novel.

Liddell Hart, the military historian, wrote of a three-level top-down structure to the struggles between nations. He called the top level "grand strategy." It is the single overarching high-level end goal; for example, to defeat the Axis, or to eradicate Carthage. An example in design would be Microsoft's desire to dominate the desktop. The next level down is that of "strategies." Liddell Hart described strategy as "the art of distributing and applying military means to fulfill the ends of the war." The bottom level is "tactics" [Hart 1991].

A grand strategy is typically supported by more than one strategy (the second level down). Strategies are distinct patterns of action. Examples in war are daylight strategic bombing, guerrilla warfare and blitzkrieg combined-arms maneuver. In research, examples are Edison's strategy of methodically testing thousands of substances for the filament of the incandescent light-bulb [Schivelbusch 1995], or Goodall's careful observations of chimp behavior [McGrew 1992]. Both of these latter are "dialogues with Nature," where previous understandings lead to a choice of observations and measurements, with expectations that may be contradicted by what Nature actually does. In business, Microsoft's "embrace and enfold" is a powerful strategy. In design, think of Nokia's targeting of the teen market.

Strategies are supported by tactics. These are the details in the small of battles, the day-to-day struggles. They change rapidly. Examples are the infantry assaults on pillboxes on Omaha Beach and the use of MP3 as a format by Rio to sell music hardware. Nokia's downloadable ring tones and swappable covers are tactics supporting their strategic focus on the teen market.

Many workers in research and in design start their efforts by falling in love with a whizzy strategy—or worse yet a mere tactic—and then try to dream up something grand to do with it. This is like the Polish obsession with the glory of horse calvary tactics at the eve of WWII, doomed to failure in competition against Guderian's panzer divisions.

Let's take these three levels—grand strategy, strategies, and tactics—as a given structure, and observe that starting from the top level and working down is a powerful way to proceed with an economy of effort. Nothing at the lower levels is accepted except that which supports the next level up.

Finding the Void

Sun Tzu observed that direct assault on fortified cities was the most costly and dangerous strategy. It is more effective to appear where one is not expected [Sun Tzu 1971]. What is the corresponding maneuver in research and design? It is to find the "void"—the unpopulated area where nothing yet exists.

This observation sets a meta-requirement for strategic thinking: to find the void. I approach this in a structuralist manner, describing the essential qualities of an existing design space, technology or user experience and then imagining inverting a small number of its specific qualities. In a way, this is akin to the deconstructionist creation of the "other" by knowing the "self," or to inferring the nature of a lost text by inverting its triumphant Hegelian opponent [Culler 1983]. For example, consider a conversation between two people. In days ancient and now forgotten conversations were all face-to-face. The opposite (inversion) of this is to have bodies separated in space. Let's think of describing this structurally as a number line, with face-to-face at the left end at (0), a shouted conversation across a canyon a little to the right (0.3)—and a telephone conversation at the far right (1). We now have three points along an axis. One could imagine building something to populate the unoccupied point at (0.6)—perhaps a super-mega-phone?

We can imagine a new axis, at right angles (the "y" axis) to the first (call the first axis "space"), and call this new axis "time". What would excursions along it be like? Well, face-to-face is at the origin and a recording is at the top of the y-axis. We now have a Cartesian grid, with tape recorders at (0,1), face-to-face conversations at (0,0) and telephony at (1,0). And there is a void—an unoccupied locus—on the grid at (1,1). Clearly, its "nature" would be a recorded conversation between two people far apart in space and separated in time.

In other words, voicemail.

Can we add a third axis? Perhaps that of other media types? This rapidly takes us into what is now the domain of instant messaging services, which are all populating new loci in "conversation space." Perhaps we can even add a fourth axis: the number of people involved.

Notice that many of the loci exposed by such a structuralist analysis are dependent on having technologies to create capabilities to support their intent. Often such capabilities are logistical in nature, as in the telephone network—but they can be re-purposed to support a new intent revealed as part of a structuralist design process—just as the telephone network was re-purposed to be used by the first computer modems to transport digital data over analog voice lines by the

Strategic Air Command's SAGE network in the 1950s [Edwards 1997]. Cleverly re-purposing existing logistics is an important heuristic for design. But sometimes there is no way to create the capability that can populate the void—we call this "unobtanium."

Nonetheless, we now have a powerful analytic tool for design. We describe experiences and affordances, creating a Cartesian multispace, and note where existing things cluster. Then we observe where the unpopulated loci are and describe their nature in terms of experience and affordances. Then we analyze the technology needed to support their existence and proceed to actual engineering.

Resource constraints and social factors can cause problems in engineering. I'll examine these and illustrate them with some examples from my own experience. First, let's look at resource constraints.

The Russian Sleigh Ride

Years ago I saw a painting of a horse-drawn sleigh racing across the Russian steppes, chased by wolves. The people in the sleigh were throwing cargo out, lightening the load to escape. In my memory a woman was holding a baby and looked to be desperately thinking of tossing the infant to the wolves.

This painting provides a metaphor for what to do when you have a design with many features—a lot of cargo—and you are being chased by constraints in resources—time, money, staffing, etc. You have to lighten the load.

In what order do you throw things out?

This problem arose in a project that I worked on with two brilliant designers, Brenda Laurel and Rachel Strickland: the *Placeholder* virtual reality project at the Banff Centre for Arts. We had planned an elegant and ambitious design for a multi-person and multi-world virtual reality installation, with 3D spatialized audio, manipulable virtual objects, field recording of visual and audio real-world locations, elaborate avatars as petroglyphic spirit animals that would transform the participants' "bodily" appearance, a rich multisensory environment and trans-formations of participants' spoken voices. Due to a scheduling collision at the Banff Centre, we found ourselves with six weeks to do six months' worth of work. The chief programmer had a nervous breakdown, and the head of the program panicked and demanded that we build something much simpler—one person, one world, no spatialized audio, no fancy avatars.

I thought hard about this, and for the first time did an explicit structural analysis of a design. He wanted one person; we wanted a social experience. He wanted one world; we wanted multiple worlds. He wanted no avatars; we wanted "smart costumes" where people could be embodied as Spider, Fish, Snake and Crow. We wanted to let people record snippets of narrative to leave behind in the virtual worlds and to let them fly like birds when they were embodied as Crow; he wanted a simple walk past a landscape, with no shared history.

I made it my goal to make a plan that preserved as large a space as possible—

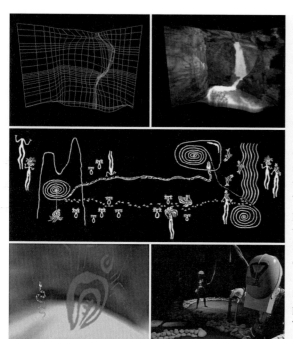

Placeholder virtual reality
project.
Top: The wireframe virtual relief
projection of the waterfall and
its ultimate appearance.
Middle: A graphical-narrative
"map" of the Placeholder
worlds.
Bottom: Snake and Spider in the
cave environment, as the participants are seen from inside
and outside of the virtual world.

a volume within the multiple axes of social experience, multiple worlds, affordances and sensory
experience. I tossed out elements that did not
increase the enveloped volume within the design
space—for example, we got rid of the mosquito that
I had programmed to pester participants by buzzing
around their heads—and we abandoned an effort to
map bodily movements to "wriggles" in the bit-maps
of the petroglyphic avatars. We did not implement
sensory transformation models for the special qualities of vision for the Crow avatar, or for the Spider.
Working with the programming and design staff, a
plan was made that conserved the excursions along
the structural axes, preserving the volume in the
hyperspace of the design elements. We tossed a lot
of stuff out of the sleigh.

We met our performance date. It was a
Russian Sleigh Ride exercise of desperate order that
preserved the baby. And yes, people did fly through the
Three Worlds when they were Crow [Laurel et al. 1997].

Action in the Polis (1)—Hail Imperator

Some of the problems in design, and in expressing design in engineering, are
social. Action can be hard to achieve.

The fighter pilot, designer and strategist John Boyd did the first thermo-
dynamic analysis of air-to-air combat. He translated his mathematics into the
design of the F-16 and the A-10 "Warthog"—machines designed for very different
roles. He also originated a cognitive and social model called the OODA loop—
"Observation-Orientation-Decision-Action." Individuals (fighter pilots) and organizations (companies) both iterate this loop in their behavior. Boyd observed the
importance of actually performing each step of this loop, and in shortening its
standard delay. "Getting inside your opponents loop" (e.g., acting faster on similar
data) is an important heuristic for a fighter pilot—or a design team [Coram 2002].

An organization has to be able to actually perform each step of this loop.
Sometimes the hardest part is the "decision" part—particularly in organizations
that profess to operate by consensus. Committees have a hard time making decisions. When decisions can't be made explicitly, according to the social contract,
they will be made covertly, and the confidence of the group in its process—and
therefore its will to succeed—will be lost.

This problem also arose in *Placeholder*. There were two co-directors with
very different artistic aesthetics. There were weekly design meetings. At the time
of the crisis, there was no agreement between the co-directors. A *coup d'état*

eventuated, in which the technical staff (the sergeants) threw its support behind one of the directors (a captain), resulting in fast action on a unified design. The problem was the original structure of command and control—it was not unitary.

Designing the social structure of a design team should be done in such a way as to make the OODA loop work. This is best done by a hierarchical tree, with local autonomy residing in one person at every level. This should funnel to one person at the top. Discussion and feedback, both public dialogue and Japanese-style back-channel conversation to preserve face, are important—but so is the ability for decisions to actually be made and acted on. The wise leader listens to her subordinates, and also is not afraid to do what she decides is correct—and to expect to be followed.

At the banquet at the end of the *Placeholder* project I rose to my feet, and toasted the triumphant director with the ancient salute of the Roman legions to a commander they felt was worthy to lead them into battle—hail Imperator!

Action in the Polis (2)—The Laurel Maneuver

I am indebted to Brenda Laurel for the following insight concerning strategy and grand strategy.

Brenda is a *Star Trek* fan of great enthusiasm. Her favorite character is James T. Kirk. Kirk is famous in the grand narrative of *Star Trek* for finding "the third alternative" in win-lose situations. Brenda has been heard to challenge her staff to "find me that third alternative!"

A problem facing many designers is an ethical one. How can you work for a company that has a grand strategy that is problematic for you? Brenda's insight is that a designer can sign up to work on a specific strategy that can serve two different grand strategies—one grand strategy that the company desires, and a different one that the designer desires.

Consider a feminist working for Nike. Nike wishes to sell more shoes than anyone else. The feminist wishes for certain oppressed groups to increase their well-being in the world. These are different grand strategies. However, the strategy of designing an ad campaign to enhance selling running shoes to women can be enthusiastically shared by both—because it sells more shoes, and because it increases the physical well being of women to run.

I call Brenda's insight the Laurel Maneuver.

Action in the Polis (3)—Sanjuro: The Ronin Leaves Town

My first really good design inversion came to me when I was working at Xerox PARC in the late 1980s. I had spent several years working on color printing, digital halftoning, image processing—pushing pixels. One day at lunchtime I was sitting in the cafeteria, reading Jacques Vallee's book on the sociology of belief in UFOs as one of my co-researchers excitedly exclaimed "... and we can hyper-link all the pages by putting a barcode on the bottom of every page!"

Now, I had designed digital typefaces. Good type and the aesthetics of page design are important to me. So I looked up from my book, and said: "That would be *fugly*!!!"

Suddenly it flashed on me that there was an alternative—one that not only would not be ugly, but also could achieve a much higher data density.

The insight came from my knowledge that halftoned pictures are made up of dots of various sizes—dots that are usually shaped as ellipses, oriented at 45 degrees. This is done digitally in a way that apes the way it has been done photographically for 150 years. The key was that in the analog world the dots all line up in the same direction, but in the digital world—with control over every dot in ways not possible with an analog halftone screen—one could make the ellipses tilt to the left and denote a zero—and tilt to the right to denote a one. This could embed information within an ordinary picture, at rather high densities, in a two-dimensional grid [Tow 1994].

The technology was the easy part. Getting a gigacorp to actually use it was the hard part. I also discovered that a senior researcher was stealing credit for my idea. Fortunately, I had documented my insight, and got the basic patents nailed down. But I grew dispirited. I was in love with the beauty and elegance of the idea, and had struggled hard to find marketing reasons why Xerox should use it (this was my "Polish Calvary" experience).

Finally I left.

But what I soon discovered was that it was not my last good idea—and that there were other places where the sword of my mind was valued. I joined Interval Research, where we were challenged to "do the next thing."

The lesson is that, like Kurasowa's wandering ronin Sanjuro, you can leave town, and it's OK to do that. It's important to be passionate about your work, and be true to yourself—and sometimes the best way to do that is to walk away from an employer. You always have to have a customer for your work—one that values it.

Shoot your own Dog

When Interval Research was founded the original 24 members of the research staff were challenged by David Liddle to "create something as different from the personal computer as it was from the mainframe."

I thought about this, in a structural manner, and concluded that the right way to proceed was by systematically inverting a number of the media theoretic elements of what a personal computer (or workstation) was (circa 1993). Doing structural inversion on these elements, with the added heuristic to design to human qualities and abilities that had been "left out" of the user experience of computer use, led to some interesting contrasts, as shown at right.

I properly noticed that this design exercise, carried through to its logical extreme, results in a crowd of unruly puppies. Since I didn't think Paul Allen wanted Interval Research to be a puppy farm, I backed off a little, and decided to explore building mobile robots that communicated emotionally with people and each

SYSTEMATIC INVERSION: AN EXAMPLE

WORK STATION MODEL:	INVERSION:
• Communicates to people via a two-and-a-half dimensional grid of semantic relations (i.e., the desktop metaphor).	• Communicate emotionally–facial expressions, affective sound, bodily gestures.
• Has a paucity of input senses–a keyboard and mouse.	• Use multiple sensory modalities that are shared by humans–including vision, touch and hearing.
• Is fixed in space–it sits on a desk.	• Make something that can move around independently.
• Constrains the body of the user to a cramped posture and limited set of gestures.	• Have it move/experience/act through the same physical and social spaces as people do.
• There is one workstation per user.	• Make lots of them–and have them exhibit flocking behavior.

other, and which existed in the same realm of the senses as people did. This was my entry into what is now known as affective computing.

I argued against simulation of such, because people would inevitably react differently to something on a screen than they would to an entity with a body in space. Building real physical robots was therefore essential in order to create a joined system where people were the environment for the robots and vice versa, and where we could ask such questions of people as, "What is the robot feeling?"

When the project was started, it was in uncharted territory; no one else was doing anything similar. The patent search for the background intellectual property uncovered only a few remotely relevant pieces of intellectual property— a flocking patent, a game patent, and a few others.

My grand strategic goal for the project was to make a strong design statement that would produce design heuristics that others could emulate. Such a strong design statement could be subsequently relaxed from its initial purity of expression to find use in other areas, such as adding affective communication into workstations—in other words, one would not have to always make a full-up robot to take advantage of the understandings produced by first building an emotionally communicating robot.

We started by identifying what were the minimal elements needed to make a face that people would experience as having expressive emotions. We decided not attempt realism, but to aim for what amounted to a line drawing in aluminum and steel. Mark Scheeff built what we called the Mark One "Severed Head"—a cube with six degrees of freedom for two lips, eyes, and eyelids, each driven by computer controlled servos. The Interval "Aquarium" staff (our experimental psychologists) did user testing with naïve subjects who were directed to use a computer keyboard to drive the face to achieve various emotions—happy, sad, angry, afraid, etc. A surprise occurred when we observed the test subjects miming the

facial expressions they created on the robot's face with their own faces! We used the resulting settings for the servos to build a database of emotional control points.

Then we proceeded to build a full-up robot. The end result, four years later, was a prototype robot that had an expressive face; a mobile body with a articulated neck and head; gestures that emulated the ballistic motions of animal gestures; a sense of touch that differentiated between a caress, a light contact, and a blow (using sub-modalities of an accelerometer and a capacitive sensor); stereo color vision that located peoples bodies in space and tracked them via 3D blob analysis; a voice that could be expressively gendered male or female—and implemented an internal emotional state machine that emulated the seven basic expressive emotions described by Charles Darwin in *The Expression of the Emotions in Man and Animals* [1872].

By 1998 others had started to work in the same general area. Some of these poured far more resources into their engineering—notably Sony with the "Aibo" robotic dog. In the annual project review I argued that we should either spin the project out of Interval as a development effort aimed at real products in the toy market with enough resources to succeed, or we should kill the project. In the end, I killed my own dog—the project was ended.

Mark Scheeff, the member of the research staff who did the mechanical design for the robot, followed on with a six-month "cremator project." He ripped all of the AI out of the system and turned the robot into a tele-operated puppet. His goal was to explore what people perceived about the robot without knowing what it was "under the hood"—i.e., what they projected onto the media surface. He exhibited it at the Tech Museum in San Jose, and members of the project under his leadership published a paper summarizing the results from this exploration of projective intelligence [Scheeff et al. 2000].

The other tangible result from the project was a very broad patent (and a subsequent improvement patent with the same title) covering emotional communication of real, embodied robots with each other and with people, where the major prior art cited was Charles Darwin [Tow 1998].

The lesson from this is don't be afraid to shoot your own dog, if that's the right thing to do. A failed project can be a research success—its influence on inventors and designer can long outlive its original context.

The Wandering Ronin School of Research

sharp sword for hire
jobs behind, and jobs ahead
the ronin walks on

Top: John Pinto in the Interval "Aquarium" user research lab controlling the Mark One "Severed Head."
Second: "Shy" robot.
Third: "Angry" robot.
Fourth: Robot, with skin removed.

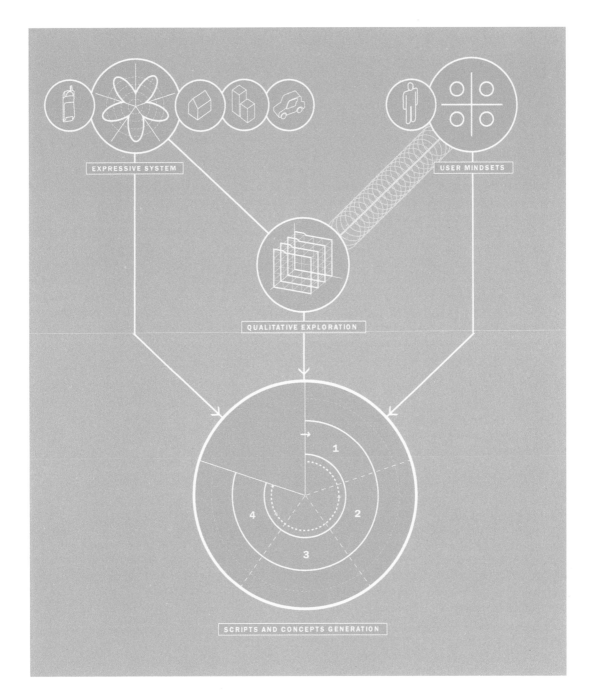

Test Pilots

BRENDA LAUREL

"What is to be done?" is an excellent question in the context of Design Research. The sections on People and Form have offered a variety of well-considered answers to that question. So far, so good. But the answer to the question, "How?" is often much messier. Reality intrudes in new and often excruciating ways. Resource issues, power hierarchies, turf battles and communication glitches can create complex turbulence in the Design Researcher's journey.

The "how" of Design Research is intimately bound up in its context, and it can be approached in many ways. Some of the following chapters offer clear procedural models and well-articulated techniques for deploying Design Research successfully ⊙143 RHEA, ⊙153 SHEDROFF, ⊙193 SVENNSON. Some authors in this section offer heuristics rather than procedures for keeping oneself and one's work on track in the midst of organizational and operational complexity ⊙172 DEASY, ⊙234 CANAAN. Some offer visions of environments and practices that predispose designers to think productively in exploratory ways ⊙175 ZIMMERMAN, ⊙225 MOON. Some focus on techniques for effective communication ⊙201 FOGG, ⊙221 KIM. Others approach the process from within, teasing out the often covert structures of power, communication and belief from a position "on the ground" ⊙212 LOCH, ⊙164 DON-AHUE. These "embedded" approaches help us to see clearly despite—or perhaps because of—the situational factors that color our view.

Each of the approaches described in this section can fail; that's why it's good to have more than one of them in your back pocket. The research we conducted in the formation of Purple Moon provides an excessively rich example. We employed literature searches, expert interviews, quantitative surveys, dyad interviews, applied ethnography, user testing and a variety of branding and identity explorations. We represented our findings in reports, prototypes and presentations. But the organizational contexts in which we were embedded eventually brought us to our knees. If I had known then what I know now,

based upon both my personal experience and the wisdom of the authors in this section, I believe that we could have succeeded in achieving all our goals.

Rob Tow often parodies the design researcher's process as that of a test pilot whose experimental plane is plunging toward the desert floor—"I'm trying A, I'm trying B, I'm trying C …" The goal is not to crash the plane, and hopefully not to have to eject. Things rarely get quite so dire in the Design Research process. But in both cases it is true that the "test pilot" had better be informed about the situation and the alternative courses of action that are available. The flight is almost never smooth, but there are ways to keep plane, pilot and project alive to continue the exploration, and to express findings in ways that inform the process and lead to fulfillment of the mission.

Bringing Clarity to the "Fuzzy Front End"

A Predictable Process for Innovation

DARREL RHEA

What's so Fuzzy?

The early stages of product development are routinely described as the "fuzzy front end" of development. This is when businesses go through the process of discovering what to make, deciding whom to make it for, understanding why to make it, and defining the attributes for success. While Design Research can make contributions throughout the many stages of business activity, the processes and tools of Design Research are central to developing the necessary insights for answering these very strategic questions.

The fact that the business community uses the term "fuzzy front end" to describe how corporate strategy for development is generated is quite revealing. Management perceives the process as ill-defined, random and mysterious; the impetus for new products often comes from a wide array of sources, and the way these products get manifested is not considered predictable. While the processes for incremental improvements and evolution are taken for granted in most companies, achieving "significant innovation" is considered a high-risk venture depending on individual genius and luck.

While the tools of Design Research are regularly employed to create new products, our profession has not done a good job of presenting a coherent framework to describe how Design Research can actually drive an organization's innovation strategy. Customer-focused innovation processes can be highly effective at producing breakthrough products, but researchers need to articulate how their work can turn the "fuzzy front end" into a predictable process for inventing the future of the organization, and advocate its value to senior management.

What Senior Management Really Wants

25 years of dealing with senior-most management have taught me that most care more about the results that successful new products produce (increased revenues, higher margins, distribution clout, etc.) and less about the processes and tools that generate innovative products and services. That makes sense when you look at how they are evaluated and compensated. There are always exceptions — passionate CEOs that are deeply involved with the design of their products. But it's a lot more likely to find CEOs focused on their stock price or other financial metrics than on the processes of research or design.

As we advocate for the use of Design Research and describe what it is we do, we need to connect to those results that senior management cares about. Senior management funds development initiatives while making trade-offs with competing organizational needs. What are the results they want?

Management needs to preserve the core of the enterprise by maintaining and growing it in a way that limits risk and maximizes return. Design Research provides the means to optimize product performance and appeal, while reducing risk. But they also need to identify the path for new growth. Design Research can help identify the next new platform for generating revenue, or "The Next Big Thing" through customer-based innovation processes. Design Research processes can actually lead to breakthrough discoveries capable of transforming the future of the organization. In this article, I'll focus on defining the role of Design Research in the front-end innovation process.

Be Humble

While customer-based innovation is an excellent way to manage innovation, it is not the only effective way. Many companies have been extremely successful without ever studying a customer or hiring a designer. Some of my clients have generated literally hundreds of billions of dollars in revenue without this competency. For many, the traditional sources of inspiration for innovation have been technology or a focus on operational excellence. These sources emphasize an inwardly-focused "inside-out" approach to development, and are capable of generating competitive advantage.

Design Research emphasizes the user or customer as a source of inspiration for innovation. It also uses design thinking, design processes and creative design expression as means to discover new, effective ways to compete. By focusing on satisfying customers' needs, we look externally and take an "outside-in" approach. Many of us believe this is the most efficient and sustainable way to invent solutions that customers care about.

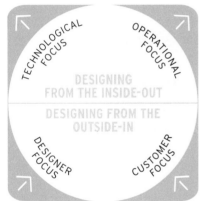

Where does design come from?

Without technology, the product won't work. Without operational excellence, the product won't be profitable. Without design, the product won't evoke desire. And without consumer relevance, the product won't sell. Some perspective from each area is required to make a successful product. Design researchers should value the contributions of other disciplines and be humble about their own. The point is to develop great breakthrough products and inspire others to help you get them to market—not to be dogmatic and win the debate over how to do it.

IDEA CLOUD

ADVANCED
DEVELOPMENT
FUNNEL

! A VIABLE CONCEPT

↓ STAGE GATE PROCESS

1 — 2 — 3

Typical "Fuzzy Front End"

The Plumbing Metaphors

The common view of the fuzzy front end looks like a cloud raining on a funnel. Some vague mixture of ideas, trends, user requirements, etc., swirl around in a cloud. Some of these ideas and influences drop into a funnel and get reduced into a product that (magically) emerges out of the end of the funnel. From there it enters the new product pipeline, passing through what is commonly known as a "stage gate process" that allows management to review the product's progress periodically and determine if it meets their criteria for additional development resources.

No wonder people call it "the fuzzy front end!" There is no model here for how information and insight can lead us to reliably positive outcomes. Versions of the funnel metaphor have been used for years. It may be useful for describing the increasing focus and refinement that ideas go through, but it is clearly inadequate to describe a logical process—the elements that go into the funnel are too random and its inner workings are obscure.

What typically goes into the advanced development funnel in most companies today? The reality of business tends to force inputs into the funnel that are reactive and tactical; e.g., the demands of your biggest retail customer for a specific SKU, the favorite half-baked technology of the hour, the rush program needed by sales, a vague notion of a product concept, finished working prototypes submitted by others, actual products on the market from a corporate acquisition, and of course, the CEO's pet project. There is nothing wrong with these inputs, but they are not likely to lead to a real innovative solution because they are so internally focused. The outcomes of these inputs tend to be incremental improvements rather than breakthrough products. I characterize the mindset that produces them a "fire, ready, aim" approach.

The Goal of Advanced Development

There are many possible objectives for an innovation program, but most companies have expectations that go beyond the tactical improvement or evolution of existing products. They desire real invention—the development of transformative products that disrupt the rules of the current marketplace. While these new products create discontinuities that allow for significant competitive advantage, breakthrough products are not easy to achieve. They require us to take an approach to advanced development that allows us to understand what others don't.

In applying Design Research to innovation, our goal is to develop a unique, proprietary understanding of who the customers are and what they want and

DIVERGENT THINKING

CONVERGENT THINKING

Innovation requires divergent thinking before convergent thinking

need, to identify the right problems to solve, and to identify the right questions to ask. This won't happen without a systematic and rigorous approach to defining the inputs to the funnel.

Diverge Before You Converge

Rather than simply responding to the inputs that are thrust upon the development group, we need to create the process, time and budget to do divergent thinking before we start filtering and prioritizing ideas and designing solutions. This is the "ready, aim, fire" philosophy. We must allow the time to think more deeply and broadly about our business and products than we normally do.

Deeper inquiry into our product category is critical. Typical market research initiatives tend to broadly characterize the market behavior and be more focused on tactical issues. We aren't looking for "low-hanging fruit"; we are looking to find what everyone before us has looked for and missed. Research needs to be designed for discovery, not to track existing conditions and assumptions.

Broader thinking also helps us to break out of the current mindset. Looking at contiguous categories can reveal new opportunities. When we are focused on the existing business, it can be difficult to plan and fund explorative research that looks toward the fringes. But discovery research is about finding new frontiers. We often use expert interviews when studying a category, and we find that our most productive and enlightening experts are outside the category. Their perspective and frame of reference are unique—exactly what we need to challenge more entrenched thinking.

Understanding what others don't involves original thinking. It is unlikely we will develop a proprietary perspective by rushing through routine data collection methods and analysis. Using new methodologies can make it clear to management and the development team that the purpose is new learning and insights.

This early phase of development involves contextual research. Contextual research involves any data that help us assess the internal business context, the external market environment, or the definition of the customer. It can include a wide range of traditional and non-traditional research methods. Business context information usually includes corporate strategy, business unit input, alliances and partnerships, technology roadmaps and product roadmaps. The market environment deals with social/cultural trends, political trends, regulatory trends, competitive trends and design trends. Defining the customer is done via segmentation studies, lifestage segmentation, subject explorations, attitude and usage studies, ethnographic studies, and psychographics and demographics.

Many large organizations routinely collect such information, but it is often dispersed throughout the company and not easily accessible to advanced development. For example, business context information might reside in a central

DIVERGENT THINKING
EMPHASIZES BROADER, DEEPER, MORE ORIGINAL EXPLORATION THAN TYPICAL DEVELOPMENT. FOCUS IS ON IDENTIFYING SIGNIFICANT NEW CUSTOMER PROBLEMS AND OPPORTUNITIES.

CONVERGENT THINKING
PRIORITIZES OPPORTUNITIES AND EMPHASIZES CUSTOMER NEEDS AND DESIRES. FOCUS IS ON CREATING COMPELLING CONCEPTS WITH HIGH PROBABILITY OF SUCCESS-IN A TIME- AND COST-EFFICIENT PROCESS.

DIVERGENT THINKING
- DISCOVERY & OBSERVATIONS
- FORECASTING POV
- IDENTIFY OPPORTUNITIES

Initial Process Steps

strategic planning group, or more likely, it exists at the divisional level and spread out among several individuals in product or marketing groups ○70 DON AND PETRICK. The challenge is to collect this information in order to enable the development team to get a holistic view of the business. I advocate having advanced development groups be responsible for collecting these data, and if necessary, generate data through primary research activities. This creates situational awareness where it is needed most: with the people responsible for inventing the future of the company.

It's Not the Pixels, It's the Picture
Having the information isn't enough to make much of a difference. Advanced development should (but rarely does) take the contextual information and synthesize a clear point of view about what the future will look like. This can be a fuzzy generalization. It is an honest attempt to forecast the forces of change and articulate how our company, our market and our customers will be different. From this work, we should be able to identify what is important, and perhaps what aspects might be missing.

Design researchers should be equipped to lead the development of the POV. With our training and analytical capabilities, we should be able to understand the context and communicate these using frameworks as well as narrative and visual tools.

Time to Get Expansive
Once a clear POV is established, the development team should generate a list of significant opportunities. Opportunities are not product concepts or solutions at this stage; they identify potential problem areas to focus on. They should identify customer or market needs that we can choose to pursue. A wide range of opportunities that extend or expand the current business activities should be examined. This is the phase to encourage expansive thinking, out-of-the-box thinking, dangerous thinking, with the willingness to revisit previously considered and rejected opportunities. Remember, the objective is to innovate and create breakthroughs. There is usually plenty of pressure to produce incremental evolutionary ideas during the normal course of business. This is where Design Researchers can help the company stretch.

At the end of this process, the team and management are presented with a range of opportunities that can now be assessed in terms of how they align with the core competences, assets and strategic interests of the company.

Start the Convergence

At this point we should have 30 to 40 new opportunities identified in our innovation portfolio. (If we have only identified 5 opportunities, it usually means we haven't dug deep enough to get beyond the obvious, close-in ones.) These become inputs into the development funnel, joining the more immediate tactical opportunities that are thrust upon us by the existing business environment.

It is now time to prioritize the opportunities so we can determine which ones to focus our limited resources on. The criteria for evaluating and selecting opportunities will differ for every company. Obviously, we want to select opportunities that play to our strengths and to choose battles we can win. We must have the necessary competencies and resources to succeed, and we need to balance a range of competing priorities to support the needs of the enterprise.

- PRIORITIZE OPPORTUNITIES
- MODEL THE BENEFITS
- GENERATE CONCEPTS
- CREATE MODELS
- REFINE CONCEPTS
- BUILD PROTOTYPES

CONVERGENT THINKING

Convergent Process Steps

This is when the organization must deal with risk. It is critical to get buy-in from senior management at this point and to make sure we connect to their strategic issues and aspirations. If advanced design activities are not linked directly to senior-most management (usually the only people in a large organization willing and capable to accept risk-taking), the only opportunities that will move forward will be safe, close-in, easy to execute ideas.

Real innovation is inherently risky and involves change. Design Research provides the rationale for the organization to understand why considering a change is worth the risk. Almost all people and organizations resist change, only embracing it when required to for survival. Innovation is threatening, requiring new ways of thinking, working, manufacturing, distributing, communicating and selling. This creates discomfort for people, and generates internal "corporate antibodies" that fight innovative ideas ⊙212 LOCH. Groups tend to seek stasis or a status quo, not reinvention. This means senior management must intervene to overcome these tendencies. It also has implications for how much autonomy and distance advanced design groups should have from the core business.

One of the factors that limits the success of companies' innovation initiatives is they either don't declare which areas of opportunity are critical priorities to be focused on, or they take on too many opportunity areas. Innovation requires significant resources, and focus is essential. There may be hundreds of innovation initiatives going on simultaneously across a large organization, each one siphoning off scarce resources. When we manage innovation as a portfolio of opportunities, we can assure that there are a few big ideas capable of sustaining the future growth of the company. The role of Design Research in this phase is to facilitate management's declaration of the development risks they want to take on. The biggest contribution we can make is to help the company discover their next big thing—the next platform for growth.

Model the Experience

Once we have defined areas of opportunity that are aligned with the business and have management's support, we should define the benefits that are expected and desirable in the product category. Research that explores the emotional benefits and psychological satisfactions of a product or service can start to define the necessary ingredients of a successful user experience. We are looking for which parts of the user experience to focus on and enhance (to delight users), and which aspects we can minimize (to reduce irritation or inconvenience).

Critical attributes and benefits should be explored before solutions are generated. If we launch into a creative phase assuming we know what the essential ingredients of a successful product are, there is a good chance we will get it wrong. There is even a bigger chance that we will frame the problem/opportunity in the same way it has been approached before, limiting the possibility for an innovative solution. If we are just cranking out the next improvement or subtle evolution of an existing product, it is likely that we, in fact, do know enough to start designing. Nothing can be more blinding than the assumption that "we already know" the answer—it can almost eliminate the possibility of a breakthrough concept.

Modeling the benefits helps us to identify the principles for design success and the appropriate metrics for assessing the quality of the product concepts and designs that follow. This will provide the development team with guardrails to keep them solving the right problem.

Facilitate Creative Concept Generation

Now we know what problem we want to solve and the basic criteria for success. It is time to start envisioning possible solutions. Design researchers can support the creative process by helping define the product with conceptual tools and research stimuli.

One of the most efficient and effective ways to generate concepts is to create user scenarios ○70 DON AND PETRICK. Such scenarios create a script of the user experience that defines examples of who is using it, what there are using it for, why they are using it, when they are using it, and how they are using it. This can be done quickly with simple text and illustrations. User scenarios provide excellent stimuli for Design Research. They focus the respondent on what the product will do for them, what it will feel like, how it might fit into their life.

Concepts can also be articulated in positioning statements. These statements typically are comprised of a couple of sentences that capture the premise of product and are used as marketing shorthand. Testing positioning statements at this early stage of design can help determine if the innovation will be easily understood and communicated—another important component of successful innovations.

Help Create Models

Now is the time to get physical fast. Designers should be translating the concept into physical or experiential models at this point in the process. Design Research can provide critical input by conducting evaluative research on the product experience during design.

We don't have to wait for final prototypes to test. The experience of the product can be simulated in discrete components. For example, we can separately model the interaction with a control panel for usability testing, and create different models for product appearance or handling issues. By being closely integrated with the development team, design researchers can provide real-time input to help expand the creativity of the whole team.

Refine the Models

By providing continuous customer input, Design Research can help arbitrate between alternative concepts and guide refinements. Remember, this is advanced development—we are generating viable product concepts, not commercializing them yet. Research needs to be scaled appropriately with the anticipation that additional testing for refinements and validation likely will follow during the commercialization phase.

Our biggest contribution in this phase is to help kill bad or mediocre ideas. Initial descriptions of concepts and scenarios that elicit enthusiasm from customers in early stages have a way of becoming compromised. The realities of what is technically feasible chip away at the appeal of the concepts. One of the responsibilities of a design researcher is to help the team realistically assess how the concept is performing, and to take a stand when it is time to on to more promising products. Few things are as expensive to a company as developing and commercializing mediocre products. Don't wait until a doggy concept takes on a life of its own; have the courage to kill it early.

Build Prototypes

At the final stage of the advanced design process, prototypes are developed to embody the concept. How refined do they need to be? Only refined enough to enable management, internal audiences in the business units, and strategic partners understand what the concept is and why it is worthy of commercialization. Going too far this early in development can waste resources; not going far enough may keep people from grasping the potential.

Advanced development teams often underestimate the importance of selling the innovation to the organization because they have been living with the concept and consumer's response to it for several months or more. The bigger the innovation, the more selling is required for company to accept it. Remember, most innovation is threatening, requires change and business risks ○212 LOCH.

The design researcher can play a critical role in helping the team lay out a coherent and compelling story. We can communicate the source of the inspiration for the idea, what needs and desires it fulfills for customers, and why customers think it is exciting and valuable. Just as we are responsible for killing bad ideas, we need to be responsible for making sure great ideas get just consideration, even when they are controversial as breakthrough products always are.

The Innovation Process in Action

How could a company use this approach? Let's take a real example from a company that manufactures windows.

Discovery Phase We might start by making a few simple observations about consumer or customer behavior; for example: *"Builders don't put on window screens on our windows until the house is sold because they detract from the aesthetics of the home."*

Forecast Phase We would write our POV to predict what we believe will be important to customers in the future based on our trend information. A small excerpt might include: *"People will increasingly want to bring the outside into their homes, and will place greater value on the quality of natural light and the view that windows provide."*

DIVERGENT THINKING
- DISCOVERY & OBSERVATIONS
- FORECASTING POV
- IDENTIFY OPPORTUNITIES

- PRIORITIZE OPPORTUNITIES
- MODEL THE BENEFITS
- GENERATE CONCEPTS
- CREATE MODELS
- REFINE CONCEPTS
- BUILD PROTOTYPES

CONVERGENT THINKING

Identify Opportunities Searching for problem areas and "empty quadrants" that offer the potential for novel ideas ○136 TOW. Our goal is to generate a large number of possibilities beyond the normal scope unusually considered. One such opportunity might be: *"We could make insect screens for windows less offensive (or more attractive) by decreasing their visibility and allowing in more natural light."*

Prioritize the Opportunities We assess the potential of the full range of opportunities we might focus on. *"We sell many millions of window screen units a year within our existing distribution system, and have an installed base of many hundreds of millions . . . yet window screens are an undifferentiated commodity that is seen as a necessary evil. If we could capture a higher margin by offering a differentiated product, this could generate significant revenue and would certainly be a problem worth solving."*

Model the Benefits Knowing that this is an opportunity with business potential, we can then model the benefits. Based on research, what are the compelling attributes and benefits we should be trying to deliver? *"For any user of any window, the benefits should be a less visible screen, allowing in more light, more ventilation, fewer bugs, with less need to remove screens for winter seasons, etc."*

Generate a Product Concept Now we have the basics to generate a product concept. *"Let's create an invisible insect screen! We can describe it in a positioning statement and test it."*

Create Models Now design starts to accelerate. We create models of product configurations that deliver the desired attributes and benefits. *"We identify more than 15 ways to apply technology to accomplish the desired result. We simulate a few of the best and test with a range of audiences like builders, architects, designers, consumers."*

Refine the Concept We continue to support the team to refine the concept. *"We focus on the 'science of invisibility,' material science, IP opportunities, supply chain issues, mounting systems, category analysis, etc., making sure that the concept still delivers the attributes."*

Prototype Finally, the team builds a prototype. *"We create prototypes and test them. The result? We achieve magic! An invisible window screen that is differentiated, has a high volume potential, high margin potential, is proprietary with valuable IP, and is exciting to customers, the company, and the channel too. This product is disruptive and has the potential to transform the category. Design Research is used to tell the story to senior management who considers commercializing it. The prototypes are held up to the industry, the press and the shareholders as proof of the company's leadership in innovation."*

Conclusion

While success can be generated by exploiting new technologies and or creating new operational efficiencies, deriving our inspiration from a focus on customers is more efficient and predictable. The practices of Design Research and the unique skill sets of Design Researchers are invaluable in uncovering big innovation opportunities, and for leading the efforts of advanced development teams. With the customer as our guide, there is no need for "the fuzzy front end" to remain fuzzy. Design Research might be the key for reinventing the future of the business.

Research Methods for Designing Effective Experiences

NATHAN SHEDROFF

Because Experience Design encompasses so much new territory for designers (such as social issues, business strategy, the senses, emotions, and the creation of value), designers need to learn new ways of understanding their audiences in order to better prepare for their needs. Some would argue that it's a designer's responsibility to understand user needs such as fulfillment of desire, pleasure and enhanced capability, as well as business needs such as viability, sustainability and (usually) profitability. Unfortunately, designers are seldom taught tools for these explorations. This chapter discusses some of the emerging issues for designing experience and explains practical methods designers can use to expand their research repertoire in order to rise to these new challenges.

The techniques outlined in this chapter are neither foolproof nor applicable in every circumstance. They are merely tools to add to the toolbox of design research and user-centered design. Mostly, they apply to the conceptual stages of the design process and not the evaluation stages (such as user testing). By no means are these complete, exhaustive or universal. However, they are unique and imaginative and can be quite useful when employed in appropriate ways and at appropriate times in the development process.

Why New Methods are Needed

"In the field of Human-Computer Interaction, the measure of a tool or application's success is most often based on whether its intended users can perform their task objectives easily and efficiently. Traditional user-centered design approaches and techniques work in service to these objectives, but in a cultural product whose task is to address issues of self-definition or expression, this may be the wrong mind-set" [Miller].

Interfaces are becoming increasingly social as they as they mediate more social activities (such as conversations) in more sophisticated ways. This makes them cultural products. We already attribute social behaviors to our interfaces, and this trend is growing. Design research must help us understand our audiences and their interfaces on a social level if we aim to make them happy or successful. It is not enough for interfaces or designs to be merely usable. They also must be desirable, useful, needed, understandable and appropriate. They also need to be human, which implies vast diversity. If we are merely designing for ourselves and our own needs, then we should just dispense with the pretense, money, and time involved in so-called "user-centric" models.

Method One: Taxonomies

One way to approach the discovery of both uses and experiences is to analyze situations and opportunities systematically. By deconstructing a situation into component parts and analyzing its aspects either one-by-one or in combination, it is possible to flesh out a much more complete understanding of experiences and your opportunities to design them. Often, it isn't even terribly important to do a thorough job. Merely enlarging the design terrain a bit can lead to new insights and innovative approaches.

In my classes at Stanford several years ago, I used several methods to derive taxonomies of experiences. One exercise was to investigate life 100 years ago and looking for meaningful activities and values (since looking 100 years into the future isn't possible). This gave us insight into universal human values and goals. All of these were added to the taxonomy. Another technique was to deconstruct strong memories, termed "takeaways" by writer Douglas Coupland in his book, *Generation* X [1992], for components that made them memorable and important. This, too, gave us more attributes to integrate into the taxonomy. Still another approach was to deconstruct media in order to derive an understanding of what made interactive media unique [Shedroff 1]. These generated a few more attributes. What we ended up with was a taxonomy of experiences that is still growing [Shedroff 2].

This taxonomy has become a tool for developing new experiences. It is part of the process I use to conceive of new opportunities to make successful and innovative experiences. Although it is by nature incomplete and will always evolve, the strongest attributes within it are the ones that address persistent human values and emotions. It has also served as the basis of an interactivity chart that I've used for over a decade to help differentiate appropriate uses of interactive media in different situations. These 6 attributes are merely a synthesis of the most important attributes in the Experience Taxonomy (the ones that seem to be the most influential).

Taxonomies can be built for any situation. They're not particularly time-consuming, but they must address attributes of a problem from many dimensions—especially those representing human, social attributes rather than merely technological ones.

MOBILE EMBODIMENTS

One project that made extensive use of taxonomies when generating new solutions in mobile contexts was completed in the Fall or 2000 at the Interaction Design Institute Ivrea. This exploration by Giulio Ceppi, Analia Cervini, Juan Kayser and Mack Thomas identified axes and attributes of technologies, needs

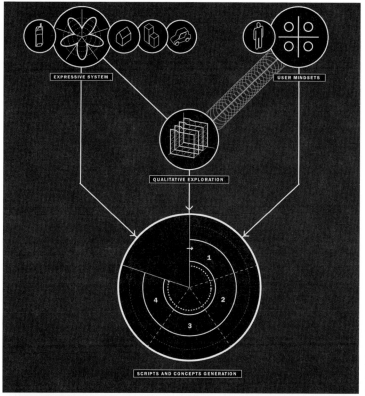

A process diagram from the
Mobile Embodiments team.

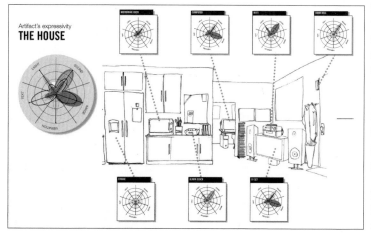

Another example diagram from
the *Mobile Embodiments* team.

and contexts for mobile communications. While it was a formal, well-documented system, it was also exploratory and allowed for a great deal of interesting investigation [Ceppi et al.].

The *Mobile Embodiments* team explored questions such as: How can we enhance the qualities of expression in an object that by definition should be small, light and portable? What sensorial means does the designer have to express the richness of these potential new services? What new types of service could these new devices offer?

To facilitate their explorations, the team used axes such as 3G technologies, environmental context (body, home, and work), activities, emotions and different modes of meaning (heraldic, juxtaposed, dense, synthetic and ethereal). They devised a chart to plot these findings in each context in order to visually compare the differences. The chart also provided an impressive array of presentation types to describe, in detail, their analyses. They built scenarios that addressed interactions and experiences along a range of solutions. Thus the scenarios could address a range of behaviors and emotions that truly reflected a wide spectrum, not only with the variation of people, but within the behavior of a single person at different times.

Each proposed design solution is expressed in not only descriptive but also emotional terms. Although the design evaluations appear quite technical and substantial (the charts alone suggest scientific data more than design sketches), the data communicated is actually more experiential and human than merely technological. This is an important innovation that allows designers to communicate to clients (and others) the importance of experiential, social and other human values in ways that can be evaluated and addressed by engineers and businesspeople who might otherwise tend to ignore such ethereal concerns. It gives designers a way to not only evaluate their concepts but a way to communicate them to others in quantitative ways.

Method Two: Dreams

Another approach to understanding users and other audiences on emotional and social levels is to use dreams as a way of allowing them to indirectly disclose issues important to them. The indirection is critical because, when dealing with social and personal issues, too much attention paid to the process (or direct inquiries) often leads to phony results. The classic story of research subjects describing their behavior in ideal terms rather than actual ones in questionnaires regarding issues such as television viewing is a case in point. Research subjects often give researchers exactly "what they're asking for" if they sense judgmental reactions from the researchers or overlay their own judgments and aspirations onto their own responses.

Instead, asking them indirect questions that focus on issues or situations that are tangential to those being surveyed often exposes useful information that isn't contaminated by second-guessing. Using subjects' dreams is one way of doing this. Instead of asking a person what their hopes or goals are, or what issues are most important to them, asking them to share their dreams, in detail, often exposes these desires, needs and aspirations.

WEARABLE DREAMS

This is exactly how Stijn Ossevoort approached the beginning of his project, *Wearable Dreams,* when researching wearable design solutions at Interaction Design Institute Ivrea [Ossevort]. His intention was to identify existing relationships between people and their favorite clothes. He began by building questionnaires that asked his subjects to share personal stories about themselves in indirect ways. He built a process for administering these questionnaires as well as evaluating them to pull out meaningful details that he could use in his design process.

Stijn's questionnaires start with a simple inventory of clothing and its uses. He asks about favorite pieces and how people feel about them. This set the context for some less direct inquires, specifically: "If your favorite wearable object was a person, how would you describe his/her personality (name, gender, shy, angry, existing person, fantasy figure, place of birth, profession etc.)?" This is clearly an attempt to get people thinking in non-traditional ways about their clothes—specifically, in emotional and social ways. Conceiving of an object or interface as a person is actually more helpful than it may seem at first. Stanford Professors Cliff Nass and Byron Reeves have already shown clearly how we layer human values and personality traits onto inanimate objects—especially, but not limited to, computers and interactive devices. In their book, *The Media Equation: How People Treat Computers, Television, and New Media like Real People and Places* [1996], they describe their research in detail and explain why we react to non-human experiences in distinctly human ways, including having expectations of human-like responses from devices and experiences and interpreting machine behavior from human social perspectives.

Naming interfaces, devices and experiences—or characterizing them as people—is a method for embodying emotional and social reactions in a way we can interpret and understand quickly and easily. It is a shorthand that designers can use to understand people's relationships to things so that we can design suitable experiences that have the effects we intend. You could easily start naming the software applications you use on your computer, for example, and the names you choose would tell a great deal about how you feel about the experiences they offer you. In user testing, this technique might help designers understand the less tangible aspects of the things they create; specifically, the social, human values and meanings conveyed through the things and experiences we design, as well as their understandability and their usability.

Stijn's questionnaire, then, continues into the realm of dreams:

The person that resembles your favorite object gets lost in a difficult situation. Luckily this person has an amazing quality/power that saves him/her.

First make a list of situations that you wouldn't want to get lost in yourself. Pick one of these situations in which your person is to be the main character. How does the environment look, are there more people or certain objects around?

Write a short story/part of a story in which your person uses his/her qualities to get around the difficult situation. Don't be too critical about what is and isn't possible and use drawings wherever needed. Don't worry too much about the precise length, quality, depth, etc. of the fantasy as I will use them as the starting point for my own work.

The final two projects that Stijn created came from the many experiences his test subjects shared via their questionnaires. His product designs (the devices and his users' interaction with them) were directly inspired by the feelings conveyed

Compass Coat

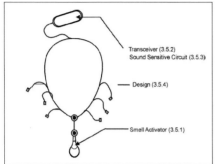

Thoughts of Love

through the questionnaires. The first is *Compass Coat*, a jacket with embedded EL wire (around the entire coat) that shines as a compass to indicate which direction is North. The second is *Thoughts of Love*, interactive jewelry pieces that use smell to signal their remote activation (and reminds the wearer that their loved one is thinking of them). For sure, the questionnaires didn't short-circuit the design process, reducing the designer to merely imple-ment others' ideas. Instead, they served as a source of inspiration and insight into the emotional and social lives enabled by the things people wear.

Stijn's dream questionnaires reflect a recognition of the need to address desire and meaning in the design process as real parameters. His philosophy is that objects need to fill our emotional needs as well as our physical or rational ones. Stories are one of the best ways to express this level of meaning and stories are a common and comfortable way for people to share such informa-tion. This is what makes this technique so simple and powerful.

Method Three: Games

Sometimes, questionnaires are too formal, too textual or too much like a test. One alternative is to present the questions and interactions as games. These might be physical games—kinesthetic, visual, aural or merely cognitive. Games have a way of making people feel more comfortable and less judged. They can be used to initiate activities and prompt thinking and responses through stimulation of the senses.

Games can be solitary or involve interaction with others. The more they prompt responses, the more data collected and the more there is to learn about people's reactions and feelings. Games are sometimes judged too frivolous by researchers and design-ers, but research subjects tend to have a higher tolerance for novel approaches.

FARAWAY

A great example of how games can form the core of a design research project was also completed at the Interaction Design Institute Ivrea, by Kristina Andersen, Margot Jacobs, and Laura Polazzi [Andersen et al. 2003]. These designers creat-ed an extensive number of "games" as a series of exploratory tools

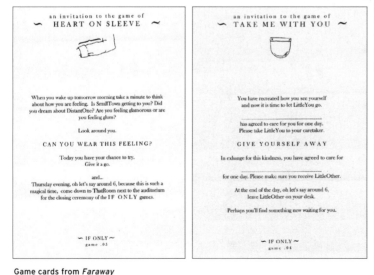

Game cards from *Faraway*

designed to test different ways of embodying access and communication in the emotional space between two people. Their questionnaires took days or weeks to conclude instead of only minutes. The games were designed to evoke emotional responses along a variety of axes in order to better understand the audience in general and specifically, the nature of relationships between distant friends, family members or lovers.

Their processes are well documented on their website Andersen et al. and include samples of each game, some of which are shown here.

One example, *Faraway*, was focused on exploring long-distance communication between loved ones. While *Faraway* didn't extend into the design process of creating new solutions, the set of games and other methods it utilized represent a valuable approach that can be used for the creation of any product, service, event or experience. In addition, it provides valuable insight into the nature of presence, emotional distance and emotional communication. In the creators' own words, the value of these games is in looking for emergence and evolution of the following:

- Suspension of disbelief
- Projection of presence
- Levels of ownership and affection
- Language
- Behavioral patterns
- Rituals
- Interaction with other means of communication
- Re-definition of functionality
- Emotional qualities about form
- Exploration of content
- Level of identification

These are exactly the kinds of issues that designers need to address more and more often and exactly the kinds of issues we are least prepared to investigate. The methods and processes we learn in design school and on the job are usually adequate for training us to think of the entire process and to work well in teams that incorporate many skill sets. However, most designers are ill prepared neither to understand people beyond simple issues of usability (if at all) nor to address human needs from emotional and social perspectives. Games like the ones created for Faraway are fairly easy to employ (thanks to their excellent design) and can speed designers to the kind of understanding that can lead to more meaningful, valuable and appropriate design solutions.

Experience Design Cards

An example that combines aspects of games, questionnaires and taxonomies are the *Experience Design Cards* I've created to accompany my *Experience Design* books as a design and teaching aid. While these cards are not yet sold publicly, the

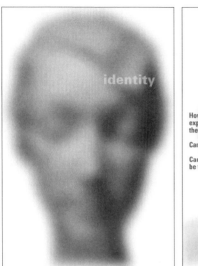

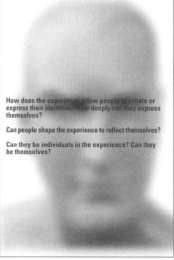

How does the experience allow people to create or express their identities? How deeply can they express themselves?

Can people shape the experience to reflect themselves?

Can they be individuals in the experience? Can they be themselves?

One of the *Experience Design Cards*

few people who have used them, including myself, find them another useful tool in our design toolbox.

The idea of the cards is simple. Each of the 50 topics of the *Experience Design 1* and *2* books introduces and discusses an important design issue for creating all kinds of experience. Each is also accompanied by an example of this issue well addressed to design in both real and digital worlds. As instruction and inspiration, the books are somewhat successful; however, they are difficult for some designers to use in their design processes.

The cards address each of the topics in the form of questions posed directly to the designer. Simply shuffling through the cards and posing the questions creates an opportunity for designers to remember to address more issues than might be in the initial project brief. The innovation consists primarily in convenience, and designers, of course, can create their own cards that address their own issues and processes. The cards can be used alone (and moving through each deck can actually go pretty quickly) or they can be used as an aid to brainstorming sessions. The idea isn't to design a solution for each question, but to evaluate whether the question is appropriate to the project context and only then address the issue in the design process.

If nothing more, these cards serve as mnemonics for designers, who are often too busy to introduce potentially distracting methods into their process, to remember to address questions of a wider context for the design of solutions. For example, every experience happens in time and 3-space, if only because the user or audience exists somewhere in the world. We often forget such simple facts as we focus on technologies or projects that are often narrowly defined in the beginning. Even experiences with websites have physical aspects (since people will be somewhere physically when accessing them). As long as interfaces, products, services, and events are created for people (and not machines), then these are, necessarily, experiences with emotional, social, sensory and other human aspects. Tools such as the *Experience Design Cards*, or those developed in the projects described above, are ways that designers can begin to address these issues regularly and (somewhat) thoroughly.

Full-Spectrum Research

Designers regularly do themselves (and their intended audiences) a disservice by not addressing the full spectrum of experience when designing solutions. Experiences (and, by default, products, services, events, etc.) are much richer than most design processes reflect. We are only now developing tools that can help us address these wider issues in order to build better solutions.

Of course, this adds time to most processes and designers are already painfully aware that there is never enough time to do everything they intend on a project. Too often, we are required to jettison user testing, evaluations, descriptions and other ways of extending and deepening our understandings of our users and their contexts. Adding yet another set of dimensions to address doesn't, at first, seem like an aid. However, these approaches are critical—perhaps even more critical than other accepted aspects of user-centered design. If we aren't addressing social context, for example, applying technology may, in fact, create a worse solution (or situation) than designing nothing at all ⊙164 DONAHUE, ⊙41 DISHMAN. Certainly, this has been shown to be the case in many instances of twentieth Century "design" in industry, health, nutrition, food and materials science. We can't afford to be blind to human social contexts when applying technology to the solving of problems, partly because technologies may introduce new (and worse) problems, and partly because technologies are rarely the important part of a solution. Usually, various forms of human behavior have a bigger influence on a design's impact or acceptance.

All good design processes acknowledge the need for reflection time, to process our knowledge gained and to understand what we've already come to create ⊙83 GROCOTT. Too often, we move from one step to another without even considering what was learned and what effects it might have on the final solution.

Finally, it is important for designers to take the time to develop their own methods and codify them into reproducible processes and artifacts. Too often, knowledge gained on a design project is lost forever and cannot be reliably employed on other projects. The time it takes to consider and document our design experiences and evolve them continuously into our design processes can make the difference between success and failure on a project. Certainly, well-documented methods improve consistency within organizations and greatly reduce training time. They can also help us create better solutions. But, most important, they make us better designers because they reorient our attention, focus and concerns in meaningful ways.

Enabling Design

SEAN DONAHUE

For nine months I was blind. Part of that blindness included having "no vision." Other parts included dealing with family relationships and learning to navigate and exist in a sighted society. I surrounded myself with available resources in order to be able to connect with the world, establish relationships, and contribute to family, community and culture. Ultimately, my blindness gave way to "low-vision." Partial vision and degenerative vision is diagnosed as "low vision," making it a space uncomfortably situated between "vision" and "no vision" but nonetheless considered "blind." Those with low vision do not possess the full faculties of vision but have enough sight to function uncomfortably with the tools developed for seeing. Having this partial ability is exactly what makes low vision so difficult to deal with. Even though those diagnosed with it indeed have sight, they are unquestioningly identified as "blind." This is the core issue: there is a significant difference between the concept of blindness and the tangible realities of having low vision. The Design Research I've conducted with the low-vision community made it clear that the imposition of the concept of blindness and all the physical preconceptions associated with it onto the low-vision community was the heart of the issue. Those with low vision and those who have been dealing intensely with the subject, and the community understand that having low vision is exactly that. Their lives require us to rethink how society perceives and addresses the realities of having partial sight.

To be honest, I was only blind figuratively, in that I was unaware of the realities and perceptions that result from actually being visually impaired or "blind." Acknowledging this is a major part of a dimensional research process. For instance, I could blindfold others or myself in order to understand the physical realities of not having vision. What I could not do with the majority of the existing models of design research was build empathy for understanding the psychological effects and ramifications of being associated with "blindness."

Why is this project important to the discussion of Design Research? It brings to the foreground a significant difference between designing artifacts that establish their role and designing a role for an already established artifact. A major part of the investigations done in the low-vision project mentioned above were conducted as a way of identifying the appropriate questions to ask in order to begin. They were not about repacking content or positioning or about the designer as curator of surface. They did not rely on existing briefs to set project parameters or preconceived design objects. Rather, my investigations involved stepping back and reposing questions through Design Research so that the final design contribution could be developed with a renewed formal investigation and from an established design position. Placing emphasis on the front end of the design process brings collaboration and creativity to bear at an earlier stage than most commercial practice allows.

Dimensional Research, a Practice

The low-vision project relied upon methods that provide opportunities for designers to move beyond what could be viewed as their traditional role of bringing context to concepts through form. Instead, these methods allow the design researcher to identify concepts through form making and an understanding of context. This expanded mode of investigation transitions the designer's role away from the modernist notion of the designer as reactive problem solver and towards the idea of the designer as proactive leader, able to identify areas of contribution through Design Research. It erodes the idea of a predetermined problem that the designer must "solve." In this model, design and the designer are integral to the project from its inception. The model utilizes designers' command of form and communication to develop direction and focus.

I initially began my project with investigations into how typographic expression could inform the language of Braille. Could the application of the principles of typography to Braille communication enhance the tactile language? Those initial investigations were based on the assumption that Braille was the major form of communicating for the blind community. In reality, it was not. Only read by 20% of the no-vision community, Braille was not easily adopted. This is particularly troubling because in instances were Braille is learned, literacy rates, secondary educational and professional job acquisition skyrocket. My initial investigations were supplemented by later findings that showed Braille literacy percentages to be even smaller among low-vision readers. The design question became focused on how to enable low-vision readers to take advantage of the guarantees that the Americans for Disabilities act provides Braille readers. A majority of low-vision service providers and educators take the point of view that low-vision communities need to assume a position of blindness. If we had adopted this perspective, our investigations would have been limited to only exploring tactile communication. The reality, however, is that low-vision communities are not blind, and they desire specific tactile and graphic communications that meet them halfway as they transition from having vision to having no vision. This is especially important because the population of the low-vision community is expected exceed 20 million over the next 10 years in the Untied States alone.

Thus my initial investigations into the blind community led me to the final project focus on the low-vision community. This exploration of different and overlapping areas provided foundation research that proved later to be integral to understanding the issues surrounding low-vision and no-vision communities. The hybrid graphic and tactile communications I developed were appreciated by low-vision communities but also provided budget relief for educational facilities that instructed students with no vision. Because this hybrid material established a one-to-one coloration between tactile language and the printed word, it could be used to create learning materials that allowed non-Braille reading aids to assist blind students in reading, spelling and grammar with the same materials. These contributions flew in the face of what many of the established institutions considered appropriate or effective. But if I had limited my scope to questions formulated and posed by one point of view I would never have achieved effective results.

Dimensional Research, a Process

Expanding the breadth of the design inquiry and the position of the design contribution requires a more holistic understanding of the subjects being engaged with. It necessitates that the designer avoid marginalizing any aspect of the elements that make up their world. The dimensional investigation outlines and visualizes a process by which traditional design exercises are conducted within an expanded scope of inquiry. This process aids design in that it identifies the multiple factors that contribute to the issues or topics at hand.

Dimensional research allows the designer to begin establishing relationships and perspectives between areas of investigation conducted around any given subject. In doing so, it gives designers the ability to make grounded design decisions that are informed by juxtapositional observations. Designers' ability to interpret and identify complex relationship between perception, representation, form, function and utility provide them the unique ability to transition from micro to macro, understanding how the multiple facets of their subjects' lives converge in the whole person.

My engagements with the no-vision and low-vision communities included meetings and personal interviews with program directors, families and members of the low-vision community. I was looking for insight into points of view and issues of utility. It was as important to understand the perceptual issues as well as the physical ones. I observed not only how a person first diagnosed with low vision is educated in tactile language but also why those programs are decided upon and how people react to participating in them.

While investigating no- and low-vision communities I intentionally visited community centers that aided each specifically, but not both. Then I investigated situations were the two communities were encouraged to interact. This provided opportunities to find common ground and to identify areas where each group engages with communication equally.

Immersive Investigation

Immersive investigation utilizes direct engagements with subjects in order to work past the designers' own misconceptions and to establish an intimate understanding of the complex relationships between provider, subject, budget, infrastructure and community.

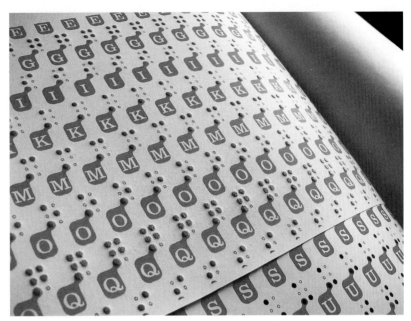

Graphic/tactile aids created as a way to self-educate Braille.

Immersive process is at the core of my own design practice. An intense immersion in the realities of the subjects being investigated is a cornerstone of the dimensional process. Spending time observing, interviewing and participating in the multiple facets of a subject's life builds understanding and allows the designer to establish empathy ○34 PLOWMAN. Immersion is not singularly about the observation of physical inabilities in order to establish products that better fit handicaps. Rather, it's about understanding the complex effects of being outside the cultural norm—as low-vision people are—on individuals, their family members, friends or colleagues, as well as effects on relationships, self-esteem and the sense of one's potential.

I had the fortunate opportunity to spend time with several families to do exactly that. While conducting the low-vision project, I visited with families in their homes, sharing meals and receiving visitors. These experiences supplemented the insight garnered from observing institutional settings where educational and other resources are procured by establishing local and personal relationships. Experiencing both areas allowed me to come to the understanding that the very resources available to low-vision individuals are one of the major items that isolate them and further add to their depression. For instance, corrective devices generally supplement the vision inadequacies of those with low vision and books on tape provide access to storytelling. As vision degenerates these magnification devices become obsolete quickly and rise in cost, resulting in a stronger dependence on verbal communication. As a result, the most frequent complaint of low-vision individuals is that they miss reading from a book and looking at pictures. This again emphasizes the need to have flexible modes of communication that flow between graphic and tactile. Such hybrid modes provide those with limited budgets and decreasing vision the ability to maintain written communication. This makes an even stronger argument for the encouragement of low-vision readers to learn tactile languages based on Braille and form. However, foundation Braille books that would just as easily function as children's bedtime readers create uncomfortable learning scenarios, to say the least. For a 55-year-old adult, it is somewhat humiliating and non-motivational to have grandchildren and peers watch them attempt to read from such a book. Additionally, the rest of the family is unable to participate or share the reading or learning experience even if they wanted to.

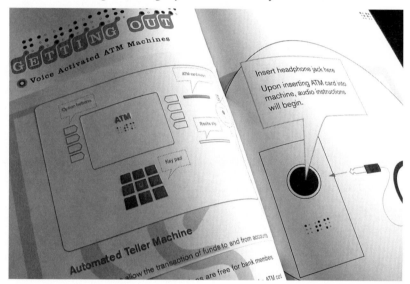

Hybrid tactile/graphic diagram
of physical interface.

The Braille book was a deterrent rather than a resource—only the cover is illustrated and set in traditional printed type, just enough to let people know what a person is attempting to read. The expanded families' inability to understand Braille has a negative impact on family dynamics. The inability for sighted family members to relate or connect to tactile communication material fosters an uncomfortable and awkward environment. Through my explorations in hybrid content, intermixing graphic and tactile form and language, I was able not only to address the specific visual requirements of the low-vision reader but also to allow the entire family, sighted and non-, to share and react to the same communication material. My hybrid publication was a bridge that addressed both the physical and physiological needs of the community, and it did so with a level of sophistication and maturity that was in line with the spirit of the reader. I was not just designing for the "user." I was using design to address the concurrent situations that make up that individual's life, physiological and otherwise.

This research process requires the designer to believe that their creative and observational contributions can add value to the collaborative engagement. The resulting design artifacts are informed by the observations and research investigations. These must be executed through the constant generation of form and active communication and interpretation. My interactions with the low-vision community were accompanied by rapid design sketches. These prototypes were also used as conversation catalysts. I introduced ideas into households and low-vision community centers to garner reaction and to provide ways for people to envision what I was doing during conversation. Interestingly enough, these also

 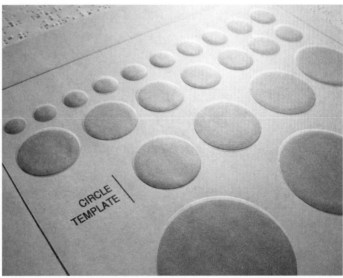

Left: Braille Exploration into layout and typographic expression. Right: Older readers Inability to feel traditional-sized Braille dots prompted me to explore scaled Braille studies, providing older readers the ability to learn Braille from larger dots.

provided opportunities to test the physical success of the work. Were the tactile marks readable? Did the reader understand what was being communicated?

These investigations exhibit many of the qualities that differentiate Design Research from marketing research. Interviewees are preconditioned to relate only to what they have already been exposed to. For instance, if a person has only been exposed to Braille, then they are not going to know how to discuss "print" communication except in terms of what they've heard form others, if at all. By utilizing design prototypes you allow the interviewee to envision—you expose them to alternatives and options that they had no concept of. Then the discussion is able to move past the familiar and into a conversation about possibilities and alternatives.

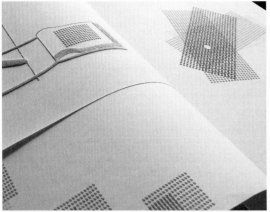

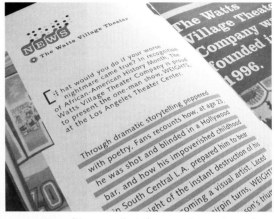

Top Left: Introducing readers to the hybrid graphic and tactile material through form and experience.
Top Right: Universal design guidelines were used as an asset, embracing graphic structures that aid reading while also providing visual interest
Bottom: Tactile lines aid readers in following written content

By making sure that these prototype investigations resurface in the final artifacts, you are developing a language and practice that derive directly from the abilities unique to the design profession. Design Research is not represented as ethnography, sociology or marketing research but rather as the process of design. Design Research acknowledges that the form of designed objects have taken in the past does not pre-define what we are able to create in the present or future. What we incorporate into our practice inevitably presents itself in what we craft, but it does not singularly define what we do or create.

That point of view allowed the low-vision project to offer a plethora of formal insights that went on to inform the work of designers, sociologists, vision researchers and policy-makers. It additionally resulted in the creation of a transmedia system that provides access, content and self-publishing resources to those identified as members of or associated with low-vision communities, involving multiple forms of communication that work across communities associated with sighted, low-vision and no-vision individuals. Text, Braille, tactile and graphic forms provide a hybrid communication medium geared specifically for the low-vision reader. The design of the publication creates function out of form. It uses the design and the hybrid language both to introduce its readers to some of the options available to them (by literally engaging with the publication) and to educate them through reading merged tactile and visual language and form. The design embraces the potentialities of low-vision experience.

Taking into account that a reader most likely will have access to a magnification device, the publication's design communicates on multiple levels, cre-

Top and Bottom: Tactile photo essays provide the opportunity to feel and see spaces, further reinforcing the idea of utilizing touch and sight as a way of receiving communication.

ating sophisticated communication and narrative material. Instead of simply transcribing each article into separate forms of reading material, the publications are designed with multiple communication devices. Taken together, they form a "universal" medium that speaks in sophisticated and diverse ways to meet the complex needs and desires of a sky-rocketing demographic. Most important, the hybrid publications address the needs of the low-vision community to interact with and function within a sighted world.

Conclusion

The approach to design research as presented above is intended to broaden the designer's conceptual and creative scope in order to directly inform their form making. These expanded relationships and perspectives on the role, use and position of design have become the foundations for establishing a practice that I describe as Research-Centered Design. The design contribution moves beyond the repositioning of style and towards an emphasis on the designer as mediator, facilitating questions and formalizing inquiries. It is the goal of the Research-Centered Designer to expand the scope of their inquiries and to hold the resulting formalizations in higher regard. This is practice, not just discussion. We need to establish methods for extending the findings of situated inquiries into the discourse and practice of design.

Such an expanded design pursuit requires that designers begin to establish methods, languages and a body of ethics surrounding our practice. As a discipline what is the designers' role? As a profession, what is it that design aspires to? Form making is unquestionably part of our practice, but to say that it is that by which we singularly define ourselves is limiting. It is as simplistic as saying architects only make buildings. Design is a discipline that has room for a depth and breadth of practice and education beyond what is acknowledge by most designers and by society at large. We give form to ideas, craft delight, create thought, raise questions and encourage debate. But most important, we "communicate though inquiry." It is the scope of that inquiry that we need to expand and it is the value that we place on the resulting formalizations that we need to hold in higher regard. When we do that, we will cause society and our associative professions to reevaluate the role of design in their collaborations. In short, we will "enable design."

Non-Assumptive Research

Beginning the Process

Begin the process of Design Research with a blank slate. While this sounds easy, a common pitfall of much Design Research is that it is based on faulty underlying assumptions, for example:

- You know who will be using the product or taking part in the experience
- You know what the person using the product or enjoying the experience needs and wants
- You know the way a product or experience will be used or valued as the designer intended it to be
- You have the solution before you've fully defined the challenge
- You can begin with a prototype or form factor rather than beginning with an understanding of the customer's underlying motivations

The antidote to assumptive thinking is to be on the lookout for assumptions that may be built into the research at each of the key milestone areas: planning, methodology design, execution and analysis.

Planning

At this critical stage, examine the assumptions that are being made about both the object of the research (e.g. product development, graphic development, experience design) and the research itself.

STEP 1 GET A FRESH PERSPECTIVE

Involve a multidisciplinary or cross-functional team. Even if people from other groups are not on the core team, a brainstorming session with a variety of people (for example, people from design, engineering, distribution, marketing or systems) can help you check out the underlying assumptions that may have already become "givens." Include people who are not close to the project. This will help you to examine assumptions by forcing you to think about how to explain the project and the history of the team. New people will not have the same bias as those on the team and will help you ferret out assumptions.

STEP 2 MAKE A LIST OF ALL HYPOTHESES

Write down what is assumed to be the reason for the design and the appropriate way to conduct the research. Any time you or a colleague says, "We know that..." whatever follows is a good candidate for the hypothesis list.

STEP 3 PREDICT THE OUTCOMES FOR YOUR HYPOTHESES

For each item on the list of hypotheses, predict what you would expect the outcome to be. This is an exercise in owning your bias. It may be done alone or with the team, openly or privately, depending upon the culture. The goal is to get a feel for what you think you already know so you can be sure to include ways to test each hypothesis in research design and execution.

STEP 4 BECOME A LEARNER

Seek input from as many different avenues as possible as they relate to the topic at hand. Read poetry on the subject, watch movies, search the Web, talk to experts. The more broadly you think about a topic, the more likely you are to be struck by insight. Follow tangents and allow the broad scope learning to be fun.

Methodology Design

The language of design is experiential, visual and contextual. It is critical to not depend solely on verbal or written data to inform the process.

STEP 1 SEEK EXPERT ADVICE

Before you decide on your methodology, talk to a handful of experts who know the category and the people who are likely to use the design. Pick their brains to learn what they perceive to be the important issues to study. Be broad in your definition of expert; for example, teens make great experts when you are investigating instant messaging.

STEP 2 INCLUDE ETHNOGRAPHIC METHODS

Nothing can replace direct observation for providing context. During a study of rapidly growing companies, one company founder related the importance of freedom from distraction. Moments later, there was a loud cracking sound from the next cubicle and a sweet, woodsy fragrance filled the air. Someone was chopping wood to make *ad hoc* monitor stands. No one in the office seemed the least bit fazed, including the person we were interviewing. This gave us a better understanding of what "freedom from distraction" meant for that culture.

STEP 3 BUILD IN TIME AND BUDGET FOR AN ITERATIVE PROCESS

Most good research uncovers additional questions or areas of inquiry. Be sure that the team has time to absorb their learning experience. Make the process flexible enough to accommodate changes to your initial hypotheses. Rapid-response iteration can be accomplished with field notes, shared websites or weblogs.

STEP 4 QUANTIFY CRITICAL HYPOTHESES

Qualitative methods should be used heavily to provide the greatest experiential, visual and contextual information, but they may not provide an adequate field of view. A minority opinion in qualitative research may turn out to be an important segment when quantified. Quantification allows you test the scope of your learning from qualitative rounds.

STEP 5 REVIEW YOUR METHODOLOGY PLAN AGAINST LIST OF HYPOTHESES

Before finalizing the methodology plan, check it against the list of critical hypotheses. Make sure that the chosen methods address all areas that need to be verified.

Research Execution

No matter what questions you ask, you will get answers. The key is in asking the right questions, and capturing the answers in meaningful ways.

STEP 1 USE VIDEO AND STILL PHOTOGRAPHY AS MUCH AS POSSIBLE

If the designers are not going out in the field with the research team, you need to make the data engaging and relevant. Video and still photography can help bring the work to life. Video does not need to be broadcast quality; it simply needs to be able to convey what is being learned in the field. Sending clips after a day's interviews helps to create excitement and involvement in the process.

STEP 2 USE A MIX OF OBSERVATION AND DIRECT QUESTIONING

Both observation and interviewing are important. Observation will allow you to "see" the answers, and questioning that follows up may help you understand what you observed. If there is a conflict between what you observed and what someone says, trust the observation.

STEP 3 USE EXPLORATORY QUESTIONING

Questioning should be as open-ended as possible. Rather than looking for "yes/no" answers, seek to learn. For example, if one hypothesis is "speed is important," then the question should be phrased as "what are the aspects that are important to you?" Questions that are exploratory often begin with "what," "in what way," "tell me about," or "why."

STEP 4 LISTENING IS KEY

Avoiding assumptions is as much about the listening as it is about the questioning. Listen to what has been said and notice whether or not it answered the question you asked. Listen for what is important to the person answering. Also, listen for what is not being said. If you hypothesized one set of outcomes and those issues are not talked about, seek to understand what is underneath the response.

STEP 5 INCLUDE PARTICIPANTS IN THE ANALYSIS

Check out some of your hypotheses with the people whom you're interviewing. Share a little of the learning and ask them for their opinion or to respond to your theories. For example, "We're hearing several people, just as you just did, say _____. What is that about?" or "It seems people need _____. What do you think about that?" Be genuine in your inquiry and be open to hearing a perspective different than what you expected to hear.

Analysis

See if your key findings pass the "hindsight test." Those nuggets that are "truthful" may stand out as obvious in hindsight. While a particular finding may be counter-intuitive, the overall analysis should make sense and have addressed all critical assumptions.

STEP 1 LOOK FOR PATTERNS

The results of the research shouldn't be so much about finding answers as about identifying patterns of behavior, motivation, needs and desires. The patterns that describe a majority of people are important, but understanding the exceptions to the dominant patterns provides more insight.

STEP 2 SEGMENTATION

If you are finding contradictory information in the learning, it is a good indication that there is segmentation in the population you're studying. Look for unique groupings of people, not just for the patterns that describe the whole. Segmentation is likely to be more by attitudinal or behavioral than demographic. Look beyond the obvious dividers.

STEP 3 MULTI-DISCIPLINARY ADVISORS

Take the data and initial analysis back to the multidisciplinary group. Share your learning and host an informal discussion on the meaning of the findings. Get others' perspectives and interpretations.

STEP 4 BE AWARE OF BIAS DURING ANALYSIS

Break the findings into three main groupings:

- State what was observed or learned with as little interpretation as possible, for example, "Most people eat a snack about 10 minutes before dinner is served."
- For the key findings or learning, examine the meaning of the observation. Expect that there will be some bias in the interpretation and use team members to check out the assumptions you make.
- For each interpretation, what are the actions or recommendations implied? This is the area of analysis where bias is most likely to exist and it should be flagged or "owned" as such.
- Assumptions disturb truth by distorting the questions, the answers, the findings and the analysis. Learning how to identify and segregate them is critical to successful research.

Play as Research
The Iterative Design Process
ERIC ZIMMERMAN

Needs and Pleasures

Design is a way to ask questions. Design *Research*, when it occurs through the practice of design itself, is a way to ask larger questions beyond the limited scope of a particular design problem. When Design Research is integrated into the design process, new and unexpected questions emerge directly from the act of design. This chapter outlines one such research design methodology—the iterative design process—using three recent game projects with which I have been involved.

The creation of games is particularly well suited to provide a model of research through design. In this book's conclusion, Brenda Laurel alludes to the difference between designing to meet needs and designing "for delight" ○316 LAUREL. While all forms of design partake of both of these categories in some measure, game design is particularly skewed toward the creation of delightful experience, rather then the fulfillment of utilitarian needs. Although it is true that we can create and play games for a particular function (for exercise, to meet people, to learn about a topic), by and large, games are played for the intrinsic pleasures they provide.

As a form of designed "delight," the process of interacting with a game is not a means to an end, but an end in and of itself. It is this curious quality of games that makes them wonderful case studies for Design Research through the process of design. As a game evolves (through the *iterative process* outlined below), it defines and redefines its own form, the experiences it can provide for players, and the very questions about design that it can ask. Through this play of design itself, new questions come into being, present themselves to the designers, and sometimes are even answered.

Iteration Iteration

Iterative design is a design methodology based on a cyclic process of prototyping, testing, analyzing and refining a work in progress. In iterative design, interaction with the designed system is used as a form of research for informing and evolving a project as successive versions or *iterations* of a design are implemented.

Test; analyze; refine. And repeat. Because the experience of a viewer/user/player cannot ever be completely predicted, in an iterative process design decisions are based on the experience of the prototype in progress. The prototype is tested, revisions are made, and the project is tested once more. In this way, the project develops through an ongoing dialogue between the designers, the design, and the testing audience.

DESIGN

ANALYZE

TEST

The iterative design process

In the case of games, iterative design means playtesting. Throughout the entire process of design and development, your game is played. You play it. The rest of the development team plays it. Other people in the office play it. People *visiting* your office play it. You organize groups of testers that match your target audience. You have as many people as possible play the game. In each case, you observe them, ask them questions, then adjust your design and playtest again.

This iterative process of design is radically different than typical retail game development. More often than not, at the start of the design process for a computer or console title, a game designer will think up a finished concept and then write an exhaustive design document that outlines every possible aspect of the game in minute detail. Invariably, the final game never resembles the carefully conceived original. A more iterative design process, on the other hand, will not only conserve development resources, but will also result in a more robust and successful final product.

Case Study 1: SiSSYFiGHT 2000

> Summary: SiSSYFiGHT 2000 is a multiplayer online game in which players create a schoolgirl avatar and then take part in games where 3 to 6 players vie for dominance of the playground. Each turn a player selects one of six actions to take, ranging from teasing and tattling to cowering and licking a lolly. The outcome of an action is dependent on other players' decisions, making for highly social gameplay. SiSSYFiGHT 2000 is also a robust online community. You can play the game at www.sissyfight.com.

In the summer of 1999, I was hired by Word.com to help them create their first game. We initially worked to identify the project's *play values*: the abstract principles that the game design would embody. The list of play values we created included designing for a broad audience of non-gamers; a low technology barrier; a game that was easy to learn and play but deep and complex; gameplay that was intrinsically social; and finally, something that was in concert with the smart and ironic Word.com sensibility.

These play values were the parameters for a series of brainstorming sessions, interspersed with group play of computer-based and non-computer games. Eventually, a game concept emerged: little girls in social conflict on a playground. While every game embodies some kind of conflict, we were drawn towards modeling a conflict that we hadn't seen depicted previously in a game. Technology and production limitations meant that the game would be turn-based, although it could involve real-time chat.

Once these basic formal and conceptual questions had begun to be mapped out, the shape of the initial prototype became clear. The very first version of SiSSYFiGHT was played with post-it-notes around a conference table. I designed a handful of basic actions each player could take, and acting as the program, I "processed" the actions each turn and reported the results back to the players, keeping score on a piece of paper.

Designing a first prototype requires strategic thinking about how to most quickly implement a playable version that can begin to address the project's chief uncertainties in a meaningful way. Can you create a paper version of your digital game? Can you design a short version of a game that will last much longer in its final form? Can you test the interaction pattern of a massively multiplayer game with just a handful of players?

In the iterative design process, the most detailed thinking you need at any moment is that which will get you to your next prototype. It is, of course, important to understand the big picture as well—the larger conceptual, technical and design questions that drive the project as a whole. Just be sure not to let your design get ahead of your iterative research. Keep your eye on the prize, but leave room for play in your design, for the potential to change as you learn from your playtesting, accepting the fact that some of your assumptions will undoubtedly be wrong.

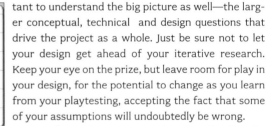

SiSSYFiGHT 2000
early prototype

The project team continued to develop the paper prototype, seeking the balance between cooperation and competition that would become the heart of the final gameplay. We refined the base ruleset—the actions a player can take each turn and the outcomes that result. These rules were turned into a spec for the first digital prototype: a text-only version on IRC, which we played hotseat-style, taking turns sitting at the same computer. Constructing that early, text-only prototype allowed us to focus on the complexities of the game logic without worrying about implementing interactivity, visual and audio aesthetics, and other aspects of the game.

While we tested gameplay via the text-only iteration, programming for the final version began in Director, and the core game logic we had developed for the IRC prototype was recycled into the Director code with little alteration. Parallel to the game design, the project's visual designers had begun to develop the graphic language of the game and chart out possible screen layouts. These early drafts of the visuals (revised many times over the course of the entire development) were dropped into the Director version of the game, and the first rough-hewn iteration of SiSSYFiGHT as a multiplayer online game took shape, inspired by Henry Darger's outsider art and retro game graphics.

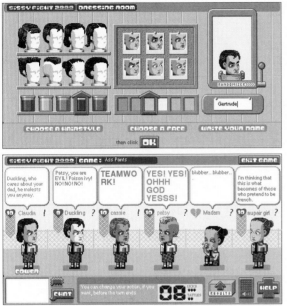

Top and bottom: SiSSYFiGHT 2000 final version

As soon as the web version was playable, the development team played it. And as our ugly duckling grew more refined, the rest of the Word.com staff was roped into playing as well. As the game grew more stable, we descended on our friends' dotcom companies after the workday had ended, sitting them down cold in front of the game and letting them play. All of this testing and feedback helped us refine the game logic, aesthetics and interface. The biggest challenge turned out to be clearly articulating the relationship between player action and game outcome: because the results of each turn are interdependent on every player's action, early versions of the game felt frustratingly arbitrary. Only through many design revisions and dialogue with our testers did we manage to structure the results of each turn to communicate unambiguously what had happened that round and why.

When the server infrastructure was completed, we launched the game to an invitation-only beta-tester community that slowly grew in the weeks leading up to public release. Certain time slots were scheduled as official testing events, but our beta users could come online anytime and play. We made it very easy for the beta testers to contact us and email in bug reports.

Even with this small sample of a few dozen participants, larger play patterns emerged. For example, as with many multiplayer games, it was highly advantageous to play defensively, leading to standstill matches. In response, we tweaked the game logic to discourage this play style: any player that "cowered" twice in a row was penalized for acting like a chicken! When the game did launch, our loyal beta testers became the core of the game community, easing new players into the game's social space.

In the case of SiSSYFiGHT 2000, the testing and prototyping cycle of iterative design was successful because at each stage, we clarified exactly what we wanted to test and how. We used written and online questionnaires. We debriefed after each testing session. And we strategized about how each version of the game would incorporate the aesthetic, game design, and technical elements of the previous versions, while also laying a foundation for the final form of the experience.

Case Study 2: LOOP

Summary: LOOP is a singleplayer game in which the player uses the mouse to catch flittering, colored butterflies. The player draws loops around groups of butterflies of the same color, or of groups in which each butterfly is a different color (the more butterflies in a loop, the more points). To finish a level, the player must capture a certain number of butterflies before the sun sets. The game includes three species of butterflies and a variety of hazardous bugs, all with different behaviors. LOOP was created by gameLab and is available for play at www.shockwave.com.

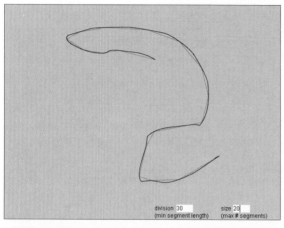

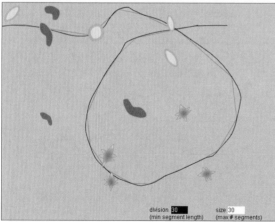

Top and Bottom: LOOP early prototypes

Initial prototypes are usually quite ugly. Game prototypes do not emphasize aesthetics or narrative content; they emphasize the game rules, which manifest as the internal logic of the game, tied to the player's interaction. Visuals, audio and story are important aspects of a game, but the core uncertainties of game design, the questions that a prototype should address, lie in the more fundamental elements of rules and play.

Another way of framing this problem is to ask, what is the *activity* of the game? Rather than asking what the game *is about*, ask what the player is *actually doing* from moment to moment as they play. Virtually all games have a core mechanic, an action or set of actions that players will repeat over and over as they move through the designed system of a game. The prototype should help you understand what this core mechanic is and how the activity becomes meaningful over time. Asking questions about your game's core mechanic can guide the creation of your first prototype, as well as successive iterations. Ideally, initial prototypes model this core mechanic and begin to test it through play.

LOOP grew out of a desire at gameLab to invent a new core mechanic. There are ultimately not very many ways to interact with a computer game: the player can express herself through the mouse and keyboard, and the game can express itself through the screen and speakers. Deciding to intervene on the level of player input, we had a notion to cast aside point-and-click or click-and-drag mouse interaction in favor of sweeping, fluid gestures.

The first prototype tested only this core interaction, allowing the player to draw lines, but nothing else. Our next step was to have the program detect a closed loop and add objects that would shrink and disappear when caught in a loop.

Each of these prototypes had parameters adjustable by the person playing the game. The length of line and detail on the curve could be tweaked, as well as the number of objects, their speed and behavior, and several other variables. As we played the game, we could try out different parameters and immediately see how they affected the experience, adjusting the rules to arrive at a different sort of play. This programming approach of building accessible game design tools into a game prototype is a technical strategy that takes iterative design into account.

As the butterfly content of the game emerged, so did debate about the game's overall structure and victory and loss conditions. Did the entire screen need to be cleared of butterflies or did the player just have to catch a certain number of them? Did the butterflies gradually fill up the screen or did their number remain constant? Were there discrete levels or did the game just go on until the loss conditions were met? Was there some kind of time-pressure element? These fundamental questions, which grew out of our core mechanic prototyping, were only answered by actually trying out possibilities and coming to a conclusion through play.

As the game code solidified, the many adjustable parameters of the game were placed in a text file that was read into the application when it ran. These parameters controlled everything from the behavior of game creatures to points scored for different numbers of butterflies in a loop to the progression of the game's escalating difficulty. Thus the game designers could focus on refining game variables and designing levels, while the rest of the program—screen transitions and help functionality, the high score system and integration with the host site—was under construction.

Top and Bottom: LOOP final version

LOOP followed a testing pattern similar to that of SiSSYFiGHT, moving outward from the game creators to include a larger circle of players. During the development of LOOP, gameLab created the gameLab Rats, our official playtesting "club," to facilitate the process of testing and feedback. In the end, LOOP managed to achieve the fluid interaction we had first envisioned. An entire game evolved from a simple idea about mouse control. That is the power of iterative design.

Case Study 3: LEGO Junkbot

Summary: LEGO Junkbot is a singleplayer game in which the player helps the robot character Junkbot empty trash cans throughout a factory. The player doesn't control Junkbot directly but instead uses the mouse to move LEGO bricks around the screen, deconstructing and reconstructing his environment brick by brick, building stairways and bridges that help Junkbot get where he needs to go. A variety of helpful and hazardous objects and robots add variety and complication to the game's 60 levels. Junkbot levels can be solved in multiple ways and the game structure encourages players to go back to previously solved levels and complete them using a different method.

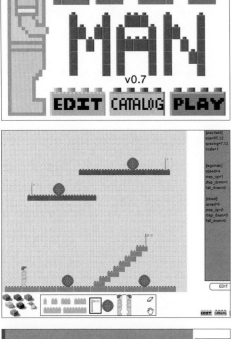

The conceptual starting point for the creation of LEGO Junkbot came from gameLab's client, LEGO.com. LEGO wanted a game about brick construction with a target audience of 8- to 12-year-old boys that that could also be played and enjoyed by adults. Here was our challenge: gameLab had been tasked with creating a web game in which real-world LEGO play was the clear referent. Yet in no way could we ever hope to recreate the sublime interactivity of plastic LEGO bricks. How could we translate LEGO play into a digital game?

Our first step was to purchase and play with a whole mess of LEGO bricks, as a way of analyzing and understanding the subtleties of LEGO play. Then, as with most gameLab projects, we began to design by identifying the project's play values. These values, which embodied the material and experiential qualities of LEGO as well as the cultural ethos of the LEGO play philosophy, included concepts like modularity, open-ended construction, design creativity, multiple-solution problem-solving, imaginative play and engineering. Using these play values as our limiting parameters, we brainstormed a number of game concepts.

The concept LEGO selected was called LEGOman (the character and storyline of Junkbot had not yet emerged) and it centered around moving bricks to indirectly help a character move through an environment. The first playable prototype was the simplest possible iteration of the core interactive idea: the player could use the mouse to drag bricks on the screen; there was a single, autonomously-moving protagonist character, there were goal flags to touch, and there were rolling wheel hazards to avoid.

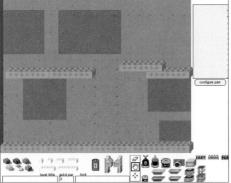

All: LEGO Junkbot early prototype

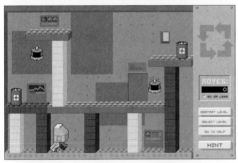

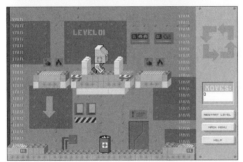

Top and Middle: LEGO Junkbot
level editor tool
Bottom: LEGO Junkbot

We played the prototype. And it was not very fun. Because gameLab projects often try to invent new forms of gameplay, we sometimes find that our initial prototypes are just not that enjoyable to play. At such an early juncture in the iterative design process, we could have scrapped the design altogether and started fresh, building on insights learned from the unsuccessful prototype, or we could dig in and push on through. We chose the latter. Gradually we added elements to the game, refining the interaction, expanding the level possibilities, putting in new kinds of special bricks and robot hazards.

Each new element addressed something that was lacking in the experience of the previous prototype: it was monotonous to move bricks one by one, so we implemented code that let players stack bricks and move them as a group. We needed a way to move the main character vertically on the screen, so we added fan bricks, which float Junkbot upwards. The game obstacles all felt too deterministic, so we introduced robot hazards that responded to Junkbot in real time. And as these interactive embellishments deepened the game (which was actually becoming fun to play), the character and storyline of Junkbot emerged.

Throughout the process, we utilized a level editor, a visual design tool that let the game designers create and save levels. The editor allowed them to experiment with game elements and level designs, refining the overall experience and planning features for the next iteration of the prototype.

Playtesting continued with the gameLab Rats, using a web-based form to collect and collate testing data about the difficulty and enjoyment of each level. However, our main concern was whether the basic brick-construction core mechanic would be understood by our target audience, so we visited an elementary school computer classroom, sat kids down in front of the game, and let them play cold. This testing was invaluable, and confirmed our fears: too many of the testers had trouble picking up basic game concepts, such as how to make a stairway for Junkbot out of bricks. This testing directly influenced the design of the game, and we slowed down the overall learning curve, designing the first several game levels to more clearly communicate the essential interactive ideas.

A good rule of thumb for iterative testing is to err on the side of observation rather than guidance. While it may be difficult to keep your hands off the tester's mouse, sit back and see what your audience actually does, rather than telling them how it is supposed to work. What you observe can sometimes be painful to watch, but it will help you design more successful play. Part of iterative design is simply learning how to listen.

Conclusion

Iterative design is a process-based design methodology, but it is also a form of Design Research. In each of these three case studies, questions emerged out of the process of design—questions that were not part of the initial problem but that were nevertheless answered through iterative design and play.

To design a game is to construct a set of rules. But the point of game design is not to have players experience rules—it is to have players experience *play*. Game design is therefore a second-order design problem, in which designers craft play, but only indirectly. Play arises out of the rules as they are inhabited and enacted by players, creating emergent patterns of behavior, sensation and interaction. Thus the necessity of the interactive design process. The delicate interaction of rule and play is something too complex and emergent to script out in advance, requiring the improvisational balancing that only testing and prototyping can provide.

The principles of this process are clearly applicable beyond the limited domain of games. Rules and play are just game design terms for structure and experience: a designer creates some kind of structured system (a typeface, a building, a car), and people encounter, inhabit, explore and manipulate the system, using it, experiencing it, playing with it.

In iterative design, there is a blending of designer and user, creator and player. It is a form of design through the reinvention of play. Through iterative design, designers create systems and play with them, but only in order to question them, bend them, break them and re-fashion them into something new. This process of iteration, of design through play, of discovering the answers to questions you didn't even know were there, is just another form of what this book is about: Design Research.

CREATING A CULTURE OF DESIGN RESEARCH

ERIC ZIMMERMAN

As this book abundantly demonstrates, Design Research can come in many forms, from quantitative market research to personal interviews to experimental design explorations. But Design Research is more than a set of strategies and procedures. It also represents a particular attitude about design, a willingness to look beyond the immediate concerns of crafting a specific project, an openness to integrating ideas and insights from the outside world into the design process itself. Successful Design Research in a commercial firm requires a company culture that embraces research in concert with design.

This demo outlines some of the strategies taken at gameLab, a game development studio founded by myself and Peter Lee, to foster a culture of Design Research. At the heart of the way we run gameLab is a relentless drive to connect the experience of working at our company to larger cultural spheres. Whatever it is that your firm designs, emphasize the links between your daily design practice and related cultures outside the company walls.

1. Create a space that encourages design research

gameLab designs and develops computer games, and the office space we inhabit is filled to bursting with games, toys, and other play objects. Company staff are encouraged to spend time playing every day, whether that means surfing online games, spending lunchtime playing a boardgame, or taking work breaks interacting with one of the many game consoles in the office. Work tasks always take precedence over this kind of play research, but generally staff end up spending several hours a week just playing. This activity serves many purposes for us, including competitive market analysis, technological research and general design inspiration.

Any office is a nexus for the exchange of ideas, and at gameLab we encourage staff to share the insights from their informal play research. A section of our intranet is reserved for posting links and thoughts about new games and game sites. Furthermore, the open physical layout of our office lets us see what is happening on each others' screens, reducing the potential stigma of "playing at work" and encouraging discussions about games even as they are being played.

2. Build a design research library

One concrete strategy we've undertaken at gameLab is the development of a research library. Our library includes retail game titles, books and graphic novels, DVDs and videotapes, magazines (we have many subscriptions), board and card games, and toys of all kinds.

While some of our research library has come from the research needs of specific projects, most of it has evolved over time through staff purchases. Every month, each gameLab staff is encouraged to contribute to the research library by spending up to $50 (reimbursed, of course) to buy something for the office. Thus the library is a reflection of the tastes and interests of the staff, giving them a way to express themselves and to shape the mindspace of the company as a whole.

The library fosters research by encouraging gameLab staff to seek out cultural objects and bring them into the company from the outside world. And of course the library itself is an ever-present opportunity for formal or informal research investigations as well. A sign-out sheet lets staff check out items from the library for use outside the office.

3. Attend and create events

Be on the lookout for cultural events relevant to your company's design work. In the past, gameLab has attended films, exhibits, conferences, and other events connected to games, design and popular culture. These group activities (always optional and always paid for by the company) serve double-duty as research opportunities and as occasions for team-building. We keep outside field trips somewhat infrequent, so that they maintain their status as special events.

In addition, we host our own Design Research affairs. Approximately once per month, game developers in the New York City area come to the gameLab offices for an evening of beer, pizza and boardgames. These get-togethers not only let our staff learn about fundamental game design principles through non-computer game play, but also help foster the local game development community, giving us an opportunity to network, share industry gossip, discuss technical dilemmas, and even show off game prototypes—all forms of Design Research.

4. Let them teach

A majority of gameLab staff teach. Peter and I encourage them to teach courses, attend critiques, participate on panels, and give talks and workshops. Teaching is a profoundly challenging and effective form of research, and gameLab staff have taught everything from game design and game programming to Masters thesis seminars and interactive narrative design.

Having your staff teach also builds bridges between your company and the local academic community. Teaching creates contact with students and faculty. As a result, gameLab has constant access to qualified interns and freelancers, potential new staff hires, and legions of enthusiastic student game testers. Our academic relationships have also fostered unique project opportunities as well, such as a studio class at Parsons School of Design in which students work with gameLab to research, design and implement an experimental game.

create a space

build a design research library
that encourages design research

create contexts for experimentation

5. Encourage side projects

We encourage our staff to pursue personal projects. These can take the form of articles, essays, and books (many of our staff are published writers); experimental design projects (our Director of Technology Ranjit Bhatnagar regularly exhibits his robot artwork); and the creation of non-computer games (such as gameLab Game Designer Nick Fortugno's self-published role-playing game).

As long as the side projects of full-time workers do not compete directly with gameLab's core business of making commercial computer games, Peter and I urge our staff to have creatively rich lives outside their work at the company, and we celebrate their accomplishments in such endeavors. Games are culture, and the success of our collective work at gameLab is dependent on the cultural sophistication of our staff. By engaging with culture productively on their own terms outside gameLab, our staff bring insight into the projects they complete within the company.

6. Create contexts for experimentation

Although gameLab is a commercial studio, from time to time we create opportunities for our staff to undertake experimental, noncommercial projects as a form of design research. For example, over the last three years, gameLab has designed and implemented a large-scale social game for our annual industry gathering, the Game Developers Conference. These massively multiplayer off-line games are events played by thousands of players, and they vary in form from year to year.

Although the primary purpose of our conference games is to research forms of social game play, they have a number of side benefits as well. The games serve as potent publicity stunts for our industry peers, game publishers and the game press, highlighting our profile as an innovative game company. The games also feed other research efforts: some of our staff are currently writing a paper about the design insights we have gained from these conference projects.

In sum, there are innumerable ways of incorporating Design Research into the everyday experience of your firm, thereby fostering a company culture that embraces research. The informal guidelines outlined above are not meant to replace more formalized research techniques, but instead to foster a company context in which Design Research is tightly integrated into design practice. A company that engages in Design Research on a daily basis will be much more open to bring research into specific design projects when the opportunity arises.

While all of these Design Research activities may seem like a drain on your company resources, in fact the benefits of fostering a Design Research culture far outweigh the costs. gameLab is a small design studio of about a dozen staff, and if we can do it, you can too. All that is required is a willingness to open your company to the world beyond its walls, to imaginatively mix cultures and contexts inside and outside the company. Design shapes the world: shouldn't we let the world shape our design?

Interdisciplinary Design Research

PATRIK SVENSSON

Intersections

It is becoming increasingly critical to be able to relate ideas and experience from many different fields. The world is not neatly categorized, and this chapter is about intersections of thinking and doing that you will not find shelved in a bookshop or distinctly pigeonholed by search engines. Being at the forefront of any kind of field means that you have to have a sense of what is going on, and where new ideas, products and research emerge. For designers this is particularly important, and in this chapter we will consider interdisciplinary Design Research as a process and tool.

Let us use a fairly concrete example to illustrate the concept of interdisciplinary research. I am a frequent bookshop visitor, and have often reflected on how bookshops in fact reflect some kind of categorization of the world. Over time you might observe changes in the way books are shelved and categorized; for instance, how new fields slowly make their way into the established scheme of categorization. An example would be the field of cognitive science, established in the late 1980s in the form we now know it. It encompasses research in areas such as linguistics, biology, neuroscience, computing science and philosophy. For a long time, the relevant literature was spread out all over bookshops, and the field might best have been described as multidisciplinary. Over the last decade, many academic bookshops have introduced cognitive science sections. This development has been accompanied by growth of cognitive science journals, conferences and professional organizations [Klein 1996, 57]. At least in some parts of the world, cognitive science has not only moved from being multidisciplinary to interdisciplinary, but is also on its way to become a new discipline in its own right. In the following, we will mostly be concerned with exactly the stage at which something new is coming into being, and indeed, how we as designers can both benefit from and contribute to such processes.

Being truly interdisciplinary is rarely easy, as it is all about fuzzy boundaries and being in between established categories [Nissani 1997]. First of all, we have to be willing to break out of discipline-specific structures; as we all know, walls between disciplines or departments do not exist only in the academic world. Second, we need to be open to the ideas and language of people who have different backgrounds and ideas about the world (for example, the different "languages" used in the first and second sections of this book). As a consequence, we need to be willing to change the way we think about the world and what we do. Third, in order to be open to new possibilities we also need to know something about current themes, relevant fields and people in relation to our own field. Fourth, we need to maintain a strong sense of who we are and where we come from. Interdisciplinary work sometimes has a tendency to be shallow as it brings together people who know a bit about many things—we should take care not to lose ourselves in the interdisciplinary process. But what is absolutely vital is being passionate about exploring new arenas and not giving in to standard solutions.

The process of carrying out interdisciplinary design research and using it is probably best described through examples, and I will discuss the field of digital culture as well as two case studies set within this field. The examples focus on technology and its cultural context, but many of the basic ideas apply to other fields and contexts as well.

Many of us spend much time on the computer, on the mobile phone, and engaged with new kinds of activities emerging in computer games, online forums and text messaging. Technology here serves not so much as a tool as an arena and our world is to some extent "technologically textured" [Ihde 1990, 1]. The cultural, societal and commercial potential of this arena is enormous. The two case studies focus on specific aspects of digital culture; namely, innovative learning environments and the interrupt culture. We will look at a project where students have created graphical virtual worlds instead of traditional paper essays as learning environments. Graphical virtual environments have a great potential as collaborative and creative spaces that can be used, for instance, in supporting life-long learning in industry. The second case study, the Interrupt Culture Project, deals with increasing information flows and time fragmentation. How do we as humans with our evolutionary past manage multiple information flows such as email, pagers, PDAs and blogs? And how can we design new products and thinking that make it easier for humans to mange the emerging interrupt culture?

Digital Culture

A very clear example of intense interdisciplinary activity today is the area that might be called digital culture. In the western world, and increasingly elsewhere, we are becoming more and more digitized. This is true of processes, activities and communication. Many of us find that we spend a fair share of our lives on the computer, and that computers are also moving out of the gray boxes and into our everyday lives in the form of PDAs, mobile technology and wireless networks. Some aspects of our lives are becoming virtualized. Clearly, this is an area that is inherently multidisciplinary as it involves so many different academic disciplines, industries and competencies. In the past, much industrial activity has been technology-based, but increasingly, there is a common acceptance of the necessity for teams with multiple competencies and interdisciplinary knowledge. Design competence is especially relevant to interaction design, participatory design and experience design and, in this context, it makes good sense to have an overview of the field. How can we achieve that?

First of all, it is a good idea to identify some of the salient aspects of digital culture. My personal list would probably include cyberspace, spatial design, virtual reality, online communication, virtual communities, online environments, social aspects of online life, embodiment (or its converse), socialization, identity, reputation, immersion, interfaces, hypertext, narratives, blogs, digital art, computer games and emergence. This is a long list that at first might seem a bit cluttered, but it does help us to approach the field. Looking at just one or two of these aspects will not be enough for a real understanding of what we are dealing with here. If you are involved in designing computer games you need to know about social aspects of gaming worlds, reputation systems, identity and immersion (among other things). Even though these issues might seem new and particular to digital media, we rarely find that is the case. Sociologists have been concerned with social behavior for a long time now; anthropologists work with reputation and social structures; and researchers in literary reception studies have thought about how young people get immersed in the worlds that are created through texts.

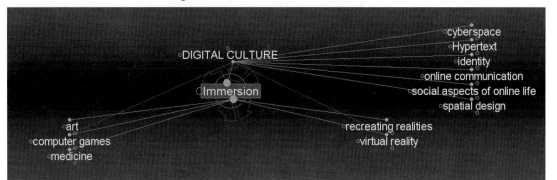

Digital culture brain

We are usually not equally interested in all the nodes in an interdisciplinary network. We tend to have a theme, project or question that provides a starting point or focus. The nature of interdisciplinary work requires us to follow connections and relate things in unexpected ways. This is not something that is easily learned, but having a holistic understanding and being open to "cross-thinking" certainly help. There are also tools that allow you to visualize thought structures and links, and these might be useful in laying out a network. In the illustration above the field of digital culture is represented on one such platform, and here the focus is on "immersion." The full network can be found at www.hum-lab.umu.se/brain/, where you can investigate my personal interpretation of digital culture in an associative, interactive way.

Let us look at the immersion node a bit more carefully. In techno-industry, immersion has become closely associated with expensive technology that gives you a wide visual field filled with computer-generated graphics, sometimes

Scott McCloud on immersion
[McCloud 1990, 30]

employing spatialized sound, through CAVE environments or head-mounted displays. There is much focus on the visual environment. People who work with 3D graphics design frequently seem to be concerned with recreating reality in the computer. I know many people who work with 3D graphics and animation who are obsessed about recreating "real" water in the computer—a particularly difficult challenge ⊙268 DAVIS ET AL. Computer games are becoming increasingly photorealistic, and an important design concern relates to how we best create immersive environments. Naimark states that entire industries work with these issues, and that "[t]he goal is less about creating metaphor and poetry as about not creating headaches" ⊙109 NAIMARK. It could be argued that creating immersion has become far too involved with high-end graphics at the expensive of social and narrative depth ⊙276 DAMER. Also, humans are very good at detecting faults with visual presentation that is highly photorealistic. Such representations tend to be non-symbolic in nature as the audience is given such a "filled out" presentation. Immersion is not only visual, of course, and people may be perfectly well immersed in text environments (such as MUDs) and literature.

From the point of view of design, this is an interesting and highly relevant area. How do we create truly immersive environments? What features are important? How much should we rely on photorealistic graphics? Can we create real social depth? Evidence and research come from many different spheres. One such sphere is admirably represented by cartoonist Scott McCloud in the illustration on this page.

For someone concerned with the creation of immersive environments it certainly makes sense to listen to experts on visual communication like McCloud. Other sources would probably include literature on 3D graphics, presence, online communities and interaction design. It would probably also be worthwhile looking at literature concerned with representation and magical realism in literature [Walton 1990] and immersion in art [Grau 2003]. Moreover, we might be helped by

Langer's book *Envisioning Literature* [1995] in which she discusses building worlds in our minds with particular focus on literary understanding and literature construction. There are many other possible materials and competencies, of course, but we cannot go into greater depth here. The main point is simply that we need to consider a broad range of perspectives, and that one thing often leads to another. Unexpected connections are rarer, but potentially more useful and eye-opening. When I recently visited the Virtual Reality Medical Center in San Diego, I had not expected immersion to be the primary topic of discussion, but it turns out that in using virtual reality technology for treating phobias, Dr. Brenda K. Wiederhold and her team have made an important observation. Their whole concept works much better with medium-detailed graphics which allow patients to fill in the rest themselves [Wiederhold and Wiederhold 2000]. Again, the symbolic level of immersion proves to be significant.

In real-world production situations, there might not be time and money for extensive background research, and a key issue is making the best use of the time that is available. At the same time, we must work to increase the perceived value of interdisciplinary design research in organizations. We need to make the case that the cost is small in relation to the potential gain, that we are often concerned with possible order-of-magnitude return [Moore 2002 35], and that it is the responsibility of forward-looking industry to invest in research. Commercial projects should be focused, of course, but it is also vital to bring in overall perspectives, links across boundaries, and to allow for interdisciplinary gains early in the process.

Virtual Worlds as Learning Spaces

Interdisciplinary work is about people and ideas meeting in creative ways, and we will now look briefly at an educational project where students work intensively in a virtual meeting place with interdisciplinary themes. The students are English students, and traditionally they write a third-term degree paper (the equivalent of ten weeks' work). They choose between linguistics, cultural studies and literature, and the papers are text-based and usually individually rather than collaboratively authored. In the project described here, students work with themes that bridge the disciplines, and instead of writing a traditional "paper" essay, they create a multi-modal representation in a graphical virtual world. The work is both individual and collaborative, and people from the outside are brought into the process. Here the interdisciplinary process mostly takes place in the virtual world ("in-world").

Education is an interesting arena for new design. Over the last few years, there has been an increased emphasis on flexible learning and the use of new technology, but the result is often a digitalization of the classroom—moving it into the computer—instead of exploring ways to promote student empowerment, intercultural meetings, interdisciplinary work, constructivist learning [Fosnot 1996] and play. In fact, web learning platforms are creating a new classroom that in some ways is startlingly close to the old-type traditional classroom. Teachers become producers of information, and students become recipients. The creative aspects of new media are employed more by teachers and programmers than by students. There is much to say about this, but it is clear that educational technology is a field that is both interdisciplinary and in need of design research ○244 JENKINS.

The world that is used for the project belongs to the students. It is theirs to explore and fill with content and critical analysis. It is a cumulative space that provides a very different kind of archive. Among the interdisciplinary themes employed so far are "the city" and "recreating realities." Student work results in a graphical representation, a rich set of hypertext pages, a virtual manifestation with

Virtual student presentation

an international crowd, and in extensive linking between students and between hypertext papers and the world. This project is basically about developing an interdisciplinary arena where students are encouraged to express themselves creatively. It is also about bringing other people into a creative process at an early stage. In many ways, distributed virtual environments of this kind are ideal for managing complex interdisciplinary processes.

In the figure we see one of the in-world student presentations. There were about 30 people present from all over the world, and to the left we can see the students presenting their work below a couple of self-representing pillars. In designing environments like this one we need to take many aspects into account. For instance, how does a real-world presentation translate to an in-world event? What do we know about social behavior in virtual environments? How can theory about constructivist learning help us to design creative learning spaces? What is the in-world equivalent of a traditional argumentative text? What level of graphical detail is necessary? Would it be useful to construct non-realistic spaces? How do online chat conversations relate to traditional spoken and written language? What factors create a feeling of presence?

In the project, ethnographic studies have been employed for evaluation as well as analyses of the learning experience and the argumentative structure of the student work. In general we have found that working in virtual arenas gives us ways of collecting data that are very useful to the design process. For instance, there are ways of tracking all movement in a virtual world, and analyzing usage patterns [Börner et al. 2002]. This would be useful, not only for studying how people move about in the world during a presentation, but also for collecting long-term data about the learning, building and collaboration processes. We need to know more about design in virtual space, and how to create spaces and processes that facilitate new kinds of interaction and learning.

The Interrupt Culture

There is no simple way of predicting where new, interesting things will emerge (see Gladwell 2000 for a useful discussion). Most often, however, it is a matter of intertwining thoughts and ideas coming together, and people communicating. If we imagine the kind of visualized networks we were looking at earlier (on a larger scale), we would probably notice a few nodes here and there rapidly attracting new connections. These would be points of intersection and potential innovation. In my own network, one such "hot" node is currently the "Interrupt Culture" [Damer 2001].

The "Interrupt Culture" is a consequence of increasing access to communication technology and the basic communicative need of humans. When text messaging was launched in the early 1990s in Europe it was not meant to facilitate consumer-consumer communication [Wray 2002], and no one could have anticipated

the explosion in usage with 1.3 billion messages being sent every year in Sweden alone (with a population of 9 million people). With multiple information and communication channels, we have less uninterrupted time than ever, and managing phones, PDAs, text messaging, instant messaging, email, blogs, virtual worlds, chat, caller ID and the web puts new demands on us. This development coincides with an immense increase in stress-related illness. In Sweden this has been identified as a major health problem. Moreover, the communication tools that we use are often not coordinated and not necessarily innovative. Email management, for instance, is very much based on the mailbox paradigm, and has not really changed in any significant qualitative fashion.

This would seem to be a good time for new thinking and new design. We are facing a complex situation and any kind of serious attempt at designing new tools or interaction possibilities would have to involve multiple fields. There is a growing literature on information overload, anthropological aspects of time management, medical consequences of the "Interrupt Culture,"

The Interrupt Culture.
HUMlab/Linda Bergkvist

interaction design, evolution, information visualization and sociology that would seem relevant. The field is certainly not neatly categorized in bookshops, but there are various connections between different aspects of the phenomenon. We would also have to take into account new technologies; for instance, augmented reality, software agents and aggregation tools. The results of this kind of Design Research could have a substantial impact on our future lives, and it is also a way of taking responsibility for the technology that we as humans have developed. I dream about integrated interfaces to large amounts of multiplex data, thematic and social views in my email program, real-world documents seamlessly linked to electronic documents, and the right amount of filtered information projected onto my retina.

Conclusion

As I pointed out at the beginning of this chapter, interdisciplinarity is rather elusive and difficult to get down on paper. It is clearly an experience-based activity, and this chapter has attempted to explore interdisciplinary design research through a number of examples and observations. I would like to finish with another list: this time a list of suggested strategies for interdisciplinary work. It is also personal, but hopefully helpful:

- Open yourself up to neighboring fields.
- Map the relevant conceptual territory.
- Be prepared to find unexpected connections.
- Communicate with people unlike yourself.
- Think across boundaries.
- Make sure to introduce interdisciplinary strategies early in the process.
- Use interdisciplinary design research to convince the people in charge that. interdisciplinarity research is crucial for creating well-thought out and innovative design.
- Most important, be passionate about reaching out.

Conceptual Designs
The Fastest Way to Capture and Share your Idea
BJ FOGG

Brainstorming Is Not Enough

Brainstorming can be pure pleasure. With a good creative team, new ideas can keep rolling in like waves to a shore, one right after the other, offering endless variations on a theme. Being in the creative flow and having so many ideas wash over you can be invigorating. But like waves dissipating on the beach, the energy of simple ideas—even excellent ideas—usually gets lost after the brainstorm is over. There's a problem in the process of invention: Designers lack an efficient method for capturing and communicating the power of their best ideas.

In this chapter, I hope to solve that problem by showing you how to create what I call a "conceptual design." The process I describe can help you develop your idea to the point where you can actually envision it becoming a reality.

The process of creating a conceptual design is simple and quick. In less than three hours, you can develop a first draft, ready for sharing with your target users, colleagues or boss.

Conceptual Designs Let You Share and Improve Your Idea

Sharing ideas early and often is one key to success for designers of end-user products and services. Sharing with target users gives you feedback to help you improve your concept. Sharing with colleagues helps to ensure that everyone on the team has a similar vision. Sharing with your boss enables you to enlist her support and feedback early-and if she hates the concept, to turn your attention to something with more potential for your organization.

I've been developing the format for conceptual designs since 1996, when I worked at Interval Research. Since then I've taken the method with me to my professional work, inventing new products and services at Sun Microsystems, Casio Research, and for a variety of clients. I've also taught the method to about 150 students over the past seven years at Stanford University. Over this time I've improved the format, distilling the formula down to the essential parts in the right sequence, and have created a series of slides as a template for conceptual design.

Like most conceptual designs, these slides share lots of information in a logical sequence. What you don't see at first is how much the framework for conceptual designs help to identify what designers needed to do to make their concept understandable. By the end of this chapter, I hope you will recognize the role that conceptual designs can play in your own work.

Elements of a Conceptual Design

The standard conceptual design has twelve parts:

1. title page
2. overview
3. user description
4. storyboard of user experience
5. prototype
6. features/functionality
7. justifications for design (theoretical and practical)
8. results of user testing
9. shortcomings of design
10. expansion—what else is possible
11. next steps in design process
12. summary

As I've evolved the formula for conceptual designs over the years, I've modified elements along the way. As the formula stands now, these twelve elements serve most purposes, though at times teams may need to add some elements to describe market landscape or revenue models.

Over the years, I've also found that it's simplest to create conceptual designs in PowerPoint or other types of presentation software. Word processing programs aren't as effective because they don't have powerful visual capabilities. I've created a template (available at www.bjfogg.info/cd.html) to help you develop your conceptual designs. With this template in hand, you won't have to think about the order of ideas or formatting issues. Instead, you can stay focused on the particulars of your user group, concept and audience.

The easiest way to demonstrate how this template works is to show an example. In the pages that follow, you'll find my template next to a student team's final concept, each slide side-by-side. I'll provide explanations along the way, but you should also note how the students worked from the template to create their deliverable. This two-person team spent 10 hours on this project, start to finish.

1. THE TITLE PAGE

In the conceptual design formula, the title page launches the concept quickly and clearly. The concept name and creators are listed prominently, and the graphic generates visual interest. Both of these elements set expectations about what's to come.

Because the template in this example is geared toward design challenges, the title page includes a summary of the design brief and the project time limit. In a corporate setting, designers should instead say what they are trying to accomplish with their concept (for example, "Project Goal: To win back our market share in the digital camera space") and list how much time they've invested in the project so far. Explicitly stating the goal and time investment helps the design team and executives decide whether it's worthwhile to continue the project.

2. THE OVERVIEW

The overview restates the project name and expands on the purpose. It's worth repeating these elements, since the concept may be new to your audience. The most important element on this slide is the visual of the industrial design, whether it's a physical device or an interface. Getting this visual into people's heads early helps them start thinking about your concept in concrete ways.

Note that at the bottom of each slide there is a footer that contains information about the project, date, designers, and so on. If someone arrives at the presentation late, these elements help orient the latecomer to the concept. Also, in many corporate settings presenters hand out paper slides for participants to take away. These pages can easily become separated down the road, so it's good practice to put all this information on each slide.

3. THE USER DESCRIPTION

The user description should not be overlooked, although it sometimes is, when designers assume that everyone knows the target user. In fact, those who are new to your concept may not know the target user unless you define the user for them.

At this point in your design process you may not have much information about your target user, but you can put something down on this slide, ideally including photos of people to help your listener envision the target user. If the project expands, this area in the conceptual design will expand dramatically as you gain more understanding about your target audience.

4. THE STORYBOARD OF USER EXPERIENCE

Note: The team created four more pages of prototype material, which is not shown here.

The most effective way to share your concept is to tell a story about how a particular user would experience what you propose. Of all the slides in a conceptual design, the storyboard slide has the potential to communicate best—and to win people over. If you have time to share only one slide from your conceptual design, this is the one to share.

Of course, executives will want to see hard numbers to make a business decision, but I've found they can't easily say no to a good story. In the early stages of design, you don't have time to round up all the market data or technical requirements, but you should take the time to invent a story and create some visuals. When you show a storyboard to executives and decision-makers, they will understand your idea quickly. And if your story is compelling, you buy yourself more time to round up the data that management will need down the road.

Storyboards are also a great way to share a concept with target users. Showing a storyboard slide starts a productive discussion in focus groups and interviews. A storyboard can give you the same type of high-level feedback as a rapid prototype.

Storyboarding is also an effective strategy for cross-cultural innovation. During the three years I worked with Japanese executives who had marginal English abilities, I found that sharing storyboards was key to making my concepts clear. Carefully scripted pictures can overcome language barriers.

5. THE PROTOTYPE

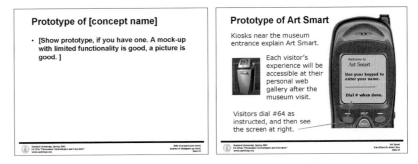

I define "prototype" broadly. A prototype can be a visual that suggests functionality, as the example above illustrates. It can be photographs of a paper prototype. Or it can be a rapid digital prototype created in just a few minutes. In these conceptual designs, the level of prototype depends on how much time you have given the project. Even if you have just three hours to produce the conceptual design, you can at least sketch a prototype. Often a sketch at this early stage is superior to something that appears to be high resolution, since a sketch will evoke comments about the overall concept, while a high-resolutions version can distract users or executives who might focus on pixel-level details.

When sharing a new concept, some people jump right into presenting the prototype before they establish the project purpose, the target user and the context of use (shown in the storyboard). Rushing to show the prototype is a mistake. Without knowing the other elements, your audience won't be able to think accurately about your concept or how to evaluate your prototype. They'll make guesses about the purpose, the user and the context of use, which you don't want them to do.

In my year-long stint as a VC just before the dot-com crash, I listened to dozens of presentations where entrepreneurs proudly showed off their prototypes while my team and I sat in the dark, scratching our heads. Sometimes we had little idea what the entrepreneurs were showing us. It was frustrating. I eventually learned to stop the entrepreneurs so they didn't waste everyone's time; I would ask them to back up and tell us a story about someone using their innovation, whether it was another company using their video compression technology or an end-user wearing a new type of fitness device.

6. FEATURES/FUNCTIONALITY

Features/Functionality	Features/Functionality
• [What does this do? Outline the features and functions.]	• Visitor comes to museum and uses his/her own cell phone (free minutes are co-sponsored by museum and phone company) • Dial number to access museum system • "Phone guide" helps visitors through exhibit • Visitor makes choices about what to see • Visitors can hear narrative about artwork, critique artwork as memo, save activities to their gallery and access the gallery online • Online gallery is accessible two weeks

This features/functionality slide gives you an opportunity to outline details of the concept, including those that the storyboard and prototype could not convey. At this point your audience understands the big picture and should be ready to deal with more details. But don't include everything on this slide. One of the hardest things about creating a conceptual design knows what to include in your concept and what to exclude. The temptation is to include lots of features and functionality. Don't do it!

To help myself and others resist the temptation to overload the features/functionality slide, I ended up adding a new slide toward the end of the template (#10—What Else is Possible). This is where you can put ideas you really like but which don't fit into the streamlined vision. (More on slide #10 later.)

In an industry setting, after the sections on the prototype and the features/functionality, you'll eventually want to include an overview of technical requirements or a systems diagram. When I work on industry projects, I farm this part out to engineers.

7. JUSTIFICATIONS FOR DESIGN

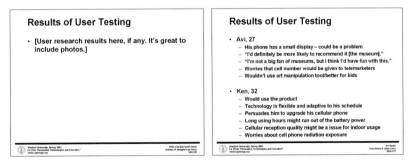

The justification section allows you to explain the rationale behind your design decisions. In the example above, the designers justified their concept by drawing on academic theories of persuasion and compliance, which was fitting for a project in my persuasive technology class.

But in an industry setting you've got to be more practical, since people who control the purse strings are rarely impressed by academic theories. While theoretical underpinnings might strengthen your case in the corporate world, executives want to see practical types of justification, such as the value proposition; market size, timing, and positioning; and the fit with company goals, risk profile and competencies. If you understand a company's market and goals, these bullet points are fairly easy to outline in a few minutes. In my experience, the real benefit of this slide is to start a discussion—both inside the innovation team and with decision-makers—about whether or not it makes sense to pursue a concept further.

8. USER TESTING

I'm always pleased when designers manage to complete some user studies as part of a 10-hour project. It's true that having just a handful of studies may not reveal much (though at times it does), but I think it's good discipline to perform some.

I include this slide in the standard template to make a point: user studies are important. In reality, this slide often ends up empty, and with good reason. It takes time to prepare materials and conduct user studies. If your time is limited, you won't be able to fill this slide with substantive results or user feedback. But don't leave this slide blank (or worse, just delete it). In my own work, when I don't have results to share, I use this slide to outline a rough plan for conducting future studies with users. This takes only a few minutes and shows you're serious about moving ahead with the project.

9. SHORTCOMINGS

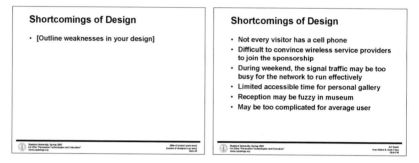

While all the other elements in the conceptual design formula point out the positives, this section on shortcomings points out the problems, both in the concept and the work done so far. Beginning designers find this step counterintuitive. But in an industry setting, it's vital to make weaknesses clear. And it doesn't hurt. Really.

Paradoxically, the positive elements in your conceptual design become more positive when you point out key shortcomings; when you include shortcomings, the concept you're proposing will seem more realistic and less like hype. You also build your own credibility by showing an awareness of why your concept may not work.

If you do not point out the shortcomings of your design to executives, they will do it for you. In fact, this is likely to be an executive's first response: outlining all the reasons why your idea won't work. When you point out the weaknesses before executives have a chance, you focus the subsequent discussion on the overall project, not just the problems.

When sharing shortcomings with target users, they will agree with some of your points, but they sometimes may argue back, saying that certain things aren't really weaknesses. For example, the first shortcoming listed for the ArtSmart concept is that not everyone has a mobile phone. If you share this shortcoming with users, you may hear them saying you're wrong: pretty much everyone has a mobile phone these days—or they will—so this isn't really a shortcoming.

Sharing shortcomings with your target audience is a way to figure out if users perceive the same shortcomings or not—a helpful perspective.

10. EXPANSION—WHAT ELSE IS POSSIBLE

Expansion - What else is possible?

- Other form factors or ID possibilities
  - [expand here]

- Other features and interactions
  - [expand here]

Expansion - What else is possible?

- Museum visitors' chat room
- Use phone to vote for favorite artwork
- Color star system for recognizing return visitors (shows up on website)
- Allows return users to access old critiques/art
- After two weeks, website displays a link to the museum calendar
- Based on Art Smart choices, phone alerts you to museum events of particular interest to you

The section on expansion allows you to capture and share a wide range of ideas you had for the concept. Of course, not every form factor or feature can go into a single concept; you've got to make decisions about what ideas to cut. But some of these ideas may be good, and cutting them can be painful; some of the ideas may be part of "Plan B" or a future project. For these reasons I've found it important to include a section on "what else is possible" in the standard conceptual design template.

When an innovation team reaches a sticking point about what to include and what to cut, being able to put someone's pet idea into this slide (rather than making it a key feature) helps the work move forward.

When sharing a conceptual design with executives, you might find that they love an idea you've listed in the expansion section. In the more typical case, showing executives "what else is possible" lets them see you have considered and ruled out competing alternatives.

Sharing the expansion points with users allows them to give you quick feedback about ideas you're cutting from the project. You may find that one of the ideas on the chopping block is actually the secret sauce for your entire concept.

11. THE NEXT STEPS IN THE DESIGN PROCESS

Next Steps in Design Process

- [Outline what you'd do next if you were to continue working on this project.]

Next Steps in Design Process

- Build rapid prototype of Art Smart
- User test in a museum with our target audience (Is the phone is distracting? Other major concerns?)
- Get programmers to consider feasibility of technology
- Iterate
- Focus groups with different target users
- Build more technical prototype
- Usability and learner studies

The last new piece of information in a conceptual design is a list of next steps in the design process.

In an industry setting, the section on "next steps" gives the innovation team a chance to discuss and identify what they should do next. This keeps people coordinated around a plan, even if the plan is tentative and outlined in just a few bullet points. As the conceptual design becomes more fully developed, this section will start looking more like a project plan, with a work schedule and deliverables.

I've found that many students are unrealistic (or naïve) about what their next steps would be. Even now, after the dot-com crash, some student teams still list the same next step: "get funding." This gives me a chance to help them understand what steps would come after the first draft of a conceptual design—and it's not fundraising.

12. THE SUMMARY

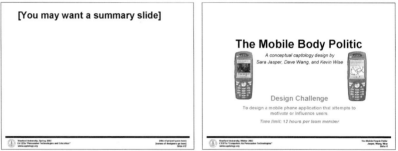

Note: This team did not include a summary slide.

The final section in a conceptual design can take on different forms. The default mode is to provide a summary of the project. Or you can simply cut the summary and focus your conclusion around the "next steps," as discussed in the previous section. Either approach works.

When presenting a conceptual design to decision-makers in an industry setting, I almost always use the summary section for action items: "This is what I want from you now." I typically list bullet points asking for immediate feedback, for support (including money or talent resources), and for a decision about the next deliverables and deadlines. I like to discuss and decide right on the spot, not in some future meeting. This keeps a project moving.

If decision makers decide to kill the project, it doesn't hurt so bad, because you have not spent weeks or months putting your heart and soul into the concept; you've invested only a handful of hours. And if the decision-makers like your concept, you can move forward with confidence and with some preliminary feedback. Getting team and executive feedback early boosts your efficiency and, in all likelihood, your work satisfaction.

What Comes after the First Conceptual Design?

After you've created the first version of a conceptual design, you can build on it to develop expanded versions.

You can complete the first draft of a conceptual design in about 3 hours. Once you have the first draft, you can continue to expand the document as the project moves forward. For example, in one innovation project about digital imaging my team expanded and refined our conceptual design for over 6 months. At that point many other parts of the organization were involved. They started creating their own documents (such as technical requirements or spreadsheets with revenue models), but the central artifact of the project was still in the conceptual design format. We eventually had about 70 pages of content. When we had a presentation to give, we would select the pieces we needed for our audience and purpose—one set of slides for a meeting with a potential strategic partner, for example, and another set for a meeting with technical people inside the company. No matter what audience or purpose, we almost always included user descriptions and storyboards as part of the mix.

As you start to use the conceptual design format, you'll find it's both easy and powerful. A few words of warning, though: First, unless you have a compelling reason, don't change the order of the ideas in a conceptual design. I've created and evaluated over 300 conceptual designs, and I've found that when people change the order of the ideas, they usually weaken their document.

Next, depending on the breadth of your job, you may need to add slides to the conceptual design that deal with business or technical issues. This won't be true for all designers and innovators, but I've found that "blue sky" ideas don't go far in most companies without something more concrete behind them.

Another caution: Realize that when you present a conceptual design, most people will assume you're farther down the development path than you really are; the conceptual design framework creates the illusion of lots of work. That's one reason I like to include the time investment on the title page. If your listeners guess you've invested 180 hours into the project, they will expect excellent answers to tough questions. When they know you've invested only eight hours, they'll have different expectations.

Finally, I want to ask for your help. As you use this method and find ways to improve it, I invite you to share your innovations with me so I can update and refine the template (again, the template is freely available at www.bjfogg.info/cd.html). The template as it stands now incorporates insights from dozens of people. I hope to continually improve this approach to design research. By soliciting ongoing feedback, incorporating the best ideas, and sharing the conceptual design template widely, I believe we can increase the quality, efficiency and enjoyment of our work as innovators and designers.

Moving Your Idea Through Your Organization

Beauty Is in the Eye of the Beholder

CHRISTOPH LOCH

You have just come up with the most beautiful design ever devised. You know it will dazzle the product engineers, factory managers, salespeople and customers alike. But when you present your design to management, you are devastated by a cacophony of hostile reactions: "This is goofy! And it doesn't even fit the product line—is it a strategic priority to fill this tiny market niche? Who told you to mess with this product area anyway, that is the responsibility of department XYZ!"

You are not alone—history is filled with brilliant product ideas that did not go anywhere in the organization. It is not always objectively clear what the best design is—that depends on the evaluation criteria. And even if the "best" design exists, it does not always win. If you want your design idea to be heard, you have to understand who the "players" are in the organization and what their objectives are, and you need to give them the feeling that they are involved. This element of "politics" is not necessarily a sign of a dysfunction, but reflects the inherent ambiguity and fuzziness of important product decisions.

Introduction: An Example

It sounds pessimistic to say that good designs do not always win in the organization. Well, of course it helps to have a good design, but it is not enough. Let's look at an example and then discuss the lessons of what a designer can do to be heard by the decision makers. The example describes a brilliant but ultimately rejected design at a car company, Lemond Automobiles [Loch and Sommer 2003].

One gray winter morning in 2000, a private inventor stood on the doorstep of Antoine Alsace, the new business innovation manager at Lemond Automobiles. The man brought along drawings of his idea: a flying car. This idea connected to something Alsace had long (although unconsciously) been looking for. He was hooked right away. "Imagine you're in a gigantic traffic jam, and you put your wings on and simply fly over the traffic jam! We ought to do something like that!" Everyone who later saw Alsace's concept drawings reacted first with incredulity and then with enthusiasm.

Alsace assembled an extraordinary group of experts who were competent, stubborn, and linked by a shared enthusiasm for the project. With their combined expertise and a lot of help from external partners, they transformed the half-baked idea into workable concepts of vehicles with attachable wings and propellers. Working on a shoestring budget with several small outside partners, and with everyone (including the outside partners) putting in their private time, they at first pursued three concepts in parallel. After a year, the most promising of these concepts was chosen to continue, while the other two were stopped. The final concept was the DuoSport, based on an experimental three-wheel curve-tilting fun-sport vehicle that existed already. A 1:2.5 scale prototype successfully flew in August 2001, and the maiden flight of the final prototype took place on June 2, 2002. The final budget ran to 2.5 million Euros.

The DuoSport Prototype. The picture is disguised in order to protect the confidentiality of the design and the company. The real design is much more elegant than this disguised version.

In addition to the creation of a new market niche, which, although potentially huge in the long run, was very risky, the DuoSport concept offered several strategic benefits to Lemond. First, there was PR value in being the first to credibly develop this breakthrough concept (which had impressed everyone who had seen it). Second, regardless of market success, a technology transfer into car development was virtually guaranteed as the DuoSport incorporated three new technologies: cost-effective light-weight carbon fibers, fly-by-wire technology (eliminating wire harnesses), and a new 3D graphical human-machine interface, which allowed instant switching between car mode controls and flight controls. Third, the DuoSport fit Lemond's new technology strategy of moving from a leader in accessories to a core technology leader with greater ability to collaborate with external partners.

However, the company found itself in a general climate of scarce resources. An ambitious investment and restructuring program forced everyone to stretch to the limit to reach operational goals. In this climate, the project met resistance in the organization. Marketing saw the whole thing as a distraction. The chief designer had been given the mission to establish a "common recognizable design language" for Lemond, and thus he saw this project as an unauthorized design effort that should have gone through him. Moreover, the Advanced Development Department had overrun its budget that year. On the defensive and facing resistance from the side and from above, they became worried about the reaction of others who said: "There is no money left to get all our new car introductions ready on time, and you have money for something like *that*?" Skepticism became prevalent, although the total cost of the project was extremely low.

The final blow came when the External Communications department joined the act. They proceeded without further coordination with Alsace, calling several newspapers to reserve a full page for "a big announcement" in June 2001. Upper R&D management heard about this plan, and feeling bypassed and overrun by events, slammed on the brakes. In a last-minute effort, the letters to the newspapers, containing the press release, had to be hand-picked from the outgoing mail baskets. The project team ended up being blamed for not keeping upper management properly informed. On the following Monday, all communication was called off. DuoSport development was barely allowed to continue until the successful maiden flight (it had to be kept secret even from other departments in order to protect it), and then it had to be shelved.

The team members became very frustrated, and at the same time ever more determined to make the DuoSport fly. To give the reader an impression of the personal initiative and risks that the team members were willing to take, here are excerpts of an April 2002 interview with Jean-Pierre Breton, core team member and original developer of the fun three-wheel fun-sport vehicle:

I'm running into quite a bit of headwind even with my three-wheel fun vehicle, because I contracted with an external free-lance designer after our head designer refused to work on it. People get crucified around here for going around the head designer, and he has already written memos to all department heads to block any presentation of my prototype (with the excuse that the engine is supposed to be presented to the public only in 2005).

For the survival of the DuoSport, I have now started to lie and to hide info from other departments, to prevent them from killing it. Last week I made a stupid mistake, I went to our in-house insurance agency for the [legally required] prototype testing insurance. So, I call them, and they send me an official letter (I hate official letters!) admonishing me about the risks and telling me this must be coordinated with legal, and that they need all legal contracts with our external partner who builds the physical prototype. So I dutifully send the documents, and the next thing I know is they want a detailed project report with all background and history. At this point, I realize I have made a mistake. I stall for time and schedule a meeting, but I tell the caseworker he would not get a written report from me, so he cancels the meeting.

OK, so I went to my boss and told him what happened. He asked whether there wasn't an alternative insurance available outside, as our in-house colleagues didn't seem to like our project too much. I say, sure, I get the insurance outside! Half an hour later I pass by the in-house insurance department and get all my documents back (they looked pretty stumped!). The rest was easy: a call to AXA, I fax a one page risk description to them, one more phone call to clarify questions, and the following Monday my boss signs an airplane owner and operator insurance policy. We send it to the FAA, and one week later we have our official permit for the prototype tests.

But now it's getting interesting: just today, I received an official letter from legal, warning me to not buy insurance outside, and ending like this: "We hereby send you in writing the demand to send us complete information about your project." I immediately called the caseworker and said, there wouldn't be any tests, and therefore no insurance and no need for their services. Of course, he didn't believe me and said he would send me one last official demand before taking additional action. I had to control myself to not tell him he could kiss my … I said, "Do what you have to," and hung up.

But the permit is the last barrier before we fly this baby in June. The DuoSport will fly, you can bet on that. If the company refuses to pay the insurance, well fine, my colleague and I pay the 880 Euros ourselves, we can just about afford that. I'll keep my boss out of this to protect him. That's the only way to get the DuoSport to fly, without armies of bureaucrats and know-it-alls from corporate running our project into the ground.

Why Good Designs May Not Be Accepted In The Organization

Why did the innovative design project of the DuoSport fail to win support and funding at Lemond, although it had many good arguments going for it? Let's analyze what stood in the way. A designer trying to get a feeling for the chances of his/her project must keep in mind four levels of decision influences, each of which may cause resistance strong enough to kill the project.

At the top level is the strategic fit of the project with the business priorities of the organization. Most people are aware of this level—business and economic arguments have their place here. But below are three more levels that are often overlooked: the political interest constellations of the players involved, the culture of the organization, which (often implicitly and almost unconsciously) defines "how things are done around here" and punishes deviators, and the emotional reactions of the players, who hate the feeling of being diminished in their egos, of a breach of loyalty, or of being outside the "in-group." They are often willing to put their foot down (if necessary with fake arguments) if they feel aggravated.

STRATEGY
- A fit with the business needs ("maximizing payoffs")

POLITICS
- Interests of the decision makers (e.g. turf, control)
- Network of relationships and influences

CULTURE
- "This is how things are done here" (e.g., legitimacy, appropriateness)

EMOTIONS
- How have the players been approached, in terms of ego, reciprocity and group identification?

Four Levels of Influences on the Acceptance of an Idea in an Organization. See [Ancona et al. 1999] for the first three levels and [Loch et al. 2000] for the fourth.

Strategy and Economic Reasoning

An organization has a legitimate interest in pursuing projects only if they support the organizations' priorities. The difficulty with that lies in the fact that strategic priorities can never be "proven"; they always involve judgment calls. In other words, reasonable people can disagree about what the strategy really requires, and a dialog among the decision-makers is required to come to a common judgment [Loch and Tapper 2002] ⊙145 RHEA.

That did not happen for the DuoSport project. Although very good strategic arguments for the project existed (they are listed in the description of the story), these were not shared. Marketing saw the project as a distraction (thinking that the current product line needed strengthening rather than starting a new business), and the car-body people didn't yet see the potential of carbon fibers (except for a few advanced body development designers, who weren't being heard by the mainstream of their department). But the debate never really took place— for example, Marketing dismissed the project after hearing a short description, without ever becoming fully informed.

However, it is important to realize that Lemond may have been right in shelving the project. Perhaps there really were not enough resources to pursue the project further without endangering the current business and its restructuring (the pity is that the dialog did not take place, for political reasons—see below. The levels of acceptance interact!). Shelving projects is legitimate and necessary for organizations to maintain focus, and designers must realize and accept that, without taking it too personally ○145 RHEA.

For example, it is commonplace practice in car companies to stage concept design competitions, in which up to a half dozen elaborate vehicle designs are developed in parallel (for example, in clay or wood, looking like the real things), and then top management chooses the most promising to go into engineering. This is necessary because one cannot judge a concept design from drawings beforehand; it's too complex. The designers whose concepts are not chosen are often depressed for months [Bangle 2001]. But really, all of the designs are necessary to be sure of having a promising one at the end, and no one's effort is wasted (although it feels that way). This is part of designing in a business.

Politics and Influence: Differing Interests and Network Structure

The strategic view of an organization pretends that the organization acts like a unit—a single entity that makes decisions to maximize its success. But that is, of course, only true in special cases (for example, when the organization undergoes an existential crisis). Most of the time, an organization is a coalition of partially conflicting interests. Every department manager looks out for his career, his resources and his influence, and there always exist multiple and shifting alliances, which can help you if you piggyback on them and can destroy you if you get in their way.

This insight has two important implications for the designer who tries to get an idea accepted: 1.Be informed about who has what interests, and how your project affects the various "interest turfs." 2.The organization is a network, in which power and influence are not completely mapped by the official hierarchy. Know who is allied with whom, so you can approach key players who then do your work and convince others for you.

INTEREST TURFS

At Lemond, the head designer felt threatened by the project, because if it succeeded, it would diminish his monopoly on design expertise. Marketing also felt threatened because they claimed to be the experts on the judgment of market niches, and if the project succeeded, it would imply they had overlooked something. Moreover, all other departments were interested in limiting the power of Engineering, and were happy to use the budget overrun in Advanced Engineering (where the DuoSport was located) to score a victory. Knowing the "turfs" is critical in predicting where resistance comes from, and what arguments can diffuse that resistance as much as possible (for example, by letting Marketing share the credit for identifying a new and promising market).

INFLUENCE NETWORKS

Managers do not make decisions in a social vacuum, but look for guidance and advice from their superiors, their peers and often also from subordinates. When other people rely on you for information and advice, you have informal power. Informal power is often dispersed in ways that are different from the official hierarchy—yes, you have to listen to the boss, but you may go to a peer for the kind of information that drives your decision-making. This kind of influencing power resides in the social network structure of an organization. While a few people are "naturals," most people do not pay enough attention to the social networks. It is worthwhile to understand who is central in the network, who is always informed, and whom others listen to. If you get those people on your side, their support tends to amplify [Ancona et al. 1999, Gladwell 2000].

For example, at Lemond, the head of Advanced Engineering had little informal power—the organization was used to him peddling gadgets and paid little attention. The heads of Marketing, Design, and Manufacturing were well-regarded and listened to in upper management circles. The Manufacturing head might have been won as a natural ally—the carbon-fiber technology was something relevant to him, and he had the reputation of being open and reasonable. A special presentation to him might have been a good investment.

Culture

Culture defines, both explicitly and implicitly, "how things are done around here." It defines appropriateness and legitimacy. The sociologist Edgar Schein discovered in the 1970s that cultures are powerful organizational memories of intelligent rules [Schein 1985]—if every employee had to make a conscious decision at every turn (rather than just following a feeling of what's "naturally" legitimate and appropriate), mistakes would abound and chaos reign. Chris Bangle, the chief designer of BMW, appeals to the culture of designing the sleekest performance cars when communicating with the organization at large [Bangle 2001].

As the cultural rules are "automated" and no longer reflected upon, they carry the danger of becoming obsolete when the environment changes. This is well captured by an example in a biography of Thomas Watson Sr., the first CEO of IBM [Maney 2003]. In the 1920s he instituted a policy that IBM salespeople should be dressed like their customers, mainly banks and large conservative companies (to fit in and to foster trust). Three CEO generations later, in the 1980s, this rule had fossilized into the famous "blue suit and yellow tie" stereotype, which made IBM salespeople look entirely out of place when they were together with high-tech clients in slacks and sandals. And yet, when Lou Gerstner scrapped the blue-suit rule in 1994 (in effect going back to Watson's original philosophy), traditionalists howled that this threatened the very core of IBM's culture!

Legitimacy and appropriateness affected the DuoSport project at Lemond: who had the right of doing a "far-out" project like this? Antoine Alsace's New Business Development department had developed strategies and made presentations before, but never gone all the way to functional prototypes. In fact, Breton officially belonged to a sister department, not to Alsace; he just worked on this project part time. No one in the organization expected such a breakthrough firecracker to come out of this department, and it scared people. Prototypes usually came out of another department, Advanced Technology. Perhaps an "adoption" of the project by Advanced Technology might have helped (but of course, that raises turf questions of who gets the credit!).

The second important cultural issue affecting the DuoSport was related to the path of presentation and successive authorization. The project was *de facto* run like a "skunk work" (industry jargon for a project running in isolation and secrecy from the rest of the organization) [Rich 1994]. The habit of the organization was relatively quick to run them when projects became tangible, by upper R&D management, then an investment council, and then the CEO. But the DuoSport had missed that window, having run too far ahead without the CEO being informed (partially driven by the perceived turf conflicts and resistance in the organization). The CEO was rumored to have made a remark, when seeing some pictures—"I thought we don't do these cowboy projects any more!" (but this was just a rumor; the DuoSport team did not really know whether it was true). The team was now trapped, not daring to show further progress to the CEO, for fear of officially being forbidden to continue. Until the end, they hoped for the "revelation" at the maiden flight.

Egos and Emotions in the Approach of Individuals

Apart from strategy, political alliances and cultural habits, people commonly (not only in business organizations!) exhibit three emotional needs that you neglect at your peril: friendship and reciprocity, group identification ("are you one of us?"), and ego. Whether or not you consider them in the way you approach decision makers or supporters may make the difference between support and indifference, between neutrality and hostility.

The first emotion is friendship and reciprocity. On the positive side, investing in people by paying attention to them, being sympathetic, coming across as fair and reasonable, or helping out, do carry benefits that can be "called in." Just put yourself in the situation of being approached with a design by a colleague with whom you have had a positive relationship for a long time. It will be emotionally very difficult for you to tell that person that this is really stupid, incompetent and inappropriate for the organization! Your natural bias will be to look for strengths in what your colleague does, to be negative only if you can't avoid it, and even then to be nice about it. On the negative side, friendship can turn into active hostility if someone feels crossed by a person who was supposed to be trusted. Friendship opens possibilities, but it also constrains you in order to keep the relationships positive.

The DuoSport team was too weakly connected with the rest of the organization to use friendship ties. Upper R&D management, two levels higher, could have done so, but these managers were either cautious (because of the turf issues) or had not been sufficiently mobilized. This lack of emotional involvement made it easier for the rest of the organization to dismiss the concept.

The second emotion is the feeling of loyalty and solidarity of "Us" against "Them." In some situations, one might be able to mobilize a manager by telling him: "Look, Chrysler just presented the Dodge Tomahawk 400-horsepower motorcycle at the Detroit Auto Show, and it's just a gimmick but they get lots of press. Do you think we should let them look more innovative than we are? We could steal their fire by showing the DuoSport!"

Third, people crave the stroking of their egos: getting credit for what they have done, receiving compliments for their competencies, being asked for their opinion, and having an influence on events. They absolutely hate the feeling of being bypassed, wrong or insignificant. The higher they are in the hierarchy, the more pronounced the ego becomes [Loch et al. 2000]. Can you harness this energy by giving someone the chance to feel significant by helping you? A humorous example was told to me by the Mexico country manager of a different car company. He needed to coax the Mexico City dealers into upgrading their facilities (which required a significant investment). He called them together and told them: "Only one dealer, Mr. X, is allowed to participate in our upgrading program, because this is only for the best. The others are not allowed to participate for now, and I'll keep you posted." Now the other dealers actively fought to be awarded the right to participate (and invest a lot of money) because they could not stand to not be among "the best."

Lessons: Map the Decision Influence Levels to Sell Your Design

If you are trying to get a design idea accepted in a large organization, you can perform a *mapping exercise* to identify the selling points and the potential points of resistance that you are facing. Each organization is, obviously, different in terms of the precise criteria at each level and in the relative emphasis placed on the levels, but the levels of decisions influences are stable categories to consider. The first two parts of the mapping are about the content of your arguments.

LEVEL ONE: STRATEGY

Understand the business priorities of the organization, and map with respect to them what your project can/cannot contribute (this may include monetary numbers, or qualitative contributions, as long as you can explain them). For example, the DuoSport team at Lemond started working on a "mobility strategy," which might later convince the company to revive the project.

LEVEL TWO: POLITICS

Map the key players, what their interests are, how the design project in question relates each one of them (who will find it helpful, who will find it threatening or distracting?), and who are the influential people who might help to influence others. This will suggest an approach for garnering support for your project. The DuoSport project had some natural enemies, while failing to rally the natural allies. This was very costly in terms of momentum.

Parts 3 and 4 of the mapping exercise are about the approach of "selling" the design idea to the organization.

LEVEL THREE: CULTURE

What is the "appropriate" way of introducing such a project into the organization? Who are natural sources, what are the accepted channels of communication, what does authority rest on? What in the proposed approach feels "funny," and why? The DuoSport team was an unexpected source of a design innovation of this type, and it was trapped in communication expectations that contradicted the looming political minefield. At the same time, the company Lemond had a proud history of innovations and initiative-taking by teams at a low hierarchical level; the team might have appealed to other people's consciousness of that history.

LEVEL FOUR: EMOTIONAL NEEDS

What are the emotional "hot buttons" of the players and intermediaries? Again, everyone is different, but the types of hot buttons are always the same: the desire for personal loyalty, the emphasis on a common group identity against a shared outsider group, and the needs of ego acknowledgment. This level, like the third, worked against the DuoSport team: they were *de facto* outsiders (a general problems that skunk-work teams often have) and had weak friendship ties to the network of decision makers. The levels of decision influences interacted—the team's upper management preferred to lie low for reasons of political turf, and so the pull of personal relationships was missing as a supporting force.

    The DuoSport example shows how a good design idea—with solid arguments for it at the "strategy" level—failed because it was weaker at the other three decision influence levels. Mapping the levels helps you to diagnose where your strengths and weaknesses are and to devise an action plan that will maximize the former while minimizing the latter. Recognizing the four decision influence levels is the necessary preparation to navigate the organizational jungle.

VIBE HUNTING
Soft Data and Sharp Insights
A Perspective on Qualitative Research

SOMI KIM

We all tend to draw upon our own experiences when evaluating a product or user experience. It's easy to construct composites of consumer segments based on how we feel or who we know. But we're missing opportunities if we convince ourselves that what we invent or imagine or believe on our own can lead the population at large, especially if a target audience is outside our own cultural space.

ReVerb has expanded its services beyond design to include conducting international and regional qualitative research for clients such as Hewlett-Packard and Sony Electronics. Our research augments and complements larger usability, purchase process or segmentation research initiatives. We look specifically at cultural context and its implications for message and experience creation.

We dive into in-depth interviews with templates that focus on emotions and everyday experiences. Then we flesh out consumer profiles through a process we call segment illumination and package our findings so that the client's creative agencies or product teams can sink their teeth into the insights and act on them. Again and again we are inspired and surprised by the individuals within the stereotypes: the things people dream about, the words they utter, the ways they spend time.

CONT'D ON P. 224

sometimes I dream of being a pilot

we are Super Deformed Sumo Wrestlers

junior high school students, 14

CONTEXT OF THE WORLD AT THIS MOMENT

CULTURAL UNDERSTANDING

but as a mom I don't want to be in a
until it's time for dinner

technological independence + personal dependence

or riding the space shuttle
housewife, 38

touchpoints: user interfaces, marketing messages, environments, experiences, corporate identity, product names, packaging, distribution channels

as in physics, the vibe of a company is most effective when more of these factors synch up

emotional connection

rational connection

tangible experience

products/services

CORPORATE UNDERSTANDING

personal independence + technological dependence
situation where I can't answer the phone

We value emotional intelligence and seek to knit together the soft drivers of behavior and needs with communications that speak to the drivers (emotions, feelings). These insights can be an effective springboard for the design of touchpoints—experiences, products, packaging and communications—thus minimizing the gap that often exists between marketing and product divisions within companies. The tangible results will be more grounded in the intersection between a company's offer of products or services and an end-user's realities.

Research confirms or debunks hypotheses and uncovers patterns, fissures or entry points. It captures emotional relevance of products and services and successes or failures of existing products, messages, services from the perspective of end users.

Research helps us process the textures and fabrics that make up individual and collective experiences. Understanding the symbols, artifacts, transactions, memories that resonate—and why—shows us how life transforms technology, and vice versa.

Living Proof

TRACY MOON

Unveiling the Value of Pre-Search

I always knew I wanted to be somebody. I see now that I should have been more specific.—Lily Tomlin

In today's multi-media extravaganza of a world sometimes the haystack is so big you need an arsenal of tools to find the proverbial needle.

While there are many ways to conduct Design Research, the goal of any "scholarly or scientific investigation or inquiry" should be to yield more valuable knowledge than you started with. I have found that, especially in the early stages of discovery, training yourself to listen to and learn from your own experiences and observations can be an invaluable information-gathering tool. No matter what subject you're studying, this "pre-search" activity can help arm you with the kind of powerful and personal ammunition that makes finding ways to outwit, outlast and outplay the competition a legitimate labor of love.

After many years of observing and participating in both quantitative and qualitative studies by some of the largest design firms in the world, I have seen how well-orchestrated research can play an important role in the creative process. In some cases traditional research on a creative product functions as an insurance policy as well as a measure of success. The more linear process that classic research methodologies afford can provide those who don't understand, or give credence to, less conventional approaches (i.e., many clients and account executives) added comfort that due diligence has taken place. In the immortal (albeit quite recent) words of Buffy Shutt, fellow author: "I don't believe…the findings. But I understand the allure of believing them. I understand the attraction to numbers, to columns of figures that can sort out this complicated world which teems with choices…" ◐293 SHUTT.

In my decades of experience as a designer and creative strategist I have utilized a myriad of different approaches to help clients research their company, product or service. Amazingly, many clients were ready and willing to build on quicksand—anxious to promote themselves to carefully screened audiences, but rarely armed with any real self-knowledge.

In the face of this obvious need to help with the groundwork that should come before more traditional methods of research, what evolved was my own visual identity firm. Visual Identity, as I practice it, is helping clients align perception and reality by discovering their reason for being and translating that into terms which can be seen, understood and appreciated by others; in short, helping companies figure out who they are first, and how to get credit for it second.

My professional approach to this preparatory phase is highly personal and almost entirely qualitative, relying heavily on the instinct and intuition innate to my client and myself. By viewing a company in much the same way as you might view a person you can do the soul-searching necessary to result in more visceral, more intimate and, therefore, more unique solutions. As such, the careful balancing of observation and intuition becomes both a valid and valuable, albeit less traditional, form of Design Research in and of itself.

What we feel can be a lot more important than what we know, especially in the seminal stages of information gathering. In a world where every potato chip and car tire is studied and analyzed and disaster-checked to death to make sure it pleases us in just the right way, at just the right time, in just the right color, I find it natural to spit into the wind and ask whether or not we need potato chips at all. The art, as I see it, is in helping clients learn to do the same.

Explaining how this is done is tricky. It is an intimate process, likely to differ in detail from person to person. The only common thread would be the absence of numbers, charts, spreadsheets, Venn diagrams or PowerPoint presentations. Just observation, intuition, instinct, perception and a risk-free environment. (At its purest, this type of experiential research may well be the original "reality show," minus the smarmy host.)

As a Baby teetering on the outer cusp of the Boom I feel inordinately fortunate to have had a graphic design career spanning 50% pre- and 50% post-computer, making me as comfortable with kerning as I am with Quark, and as stimulated by DeStijl as I am by diffusion dither. Combine that with an upbringing that reads like a dime store novel (and I mean novel) and you get a perspective that, while a tad warped, seems to work in my favor—especially when it comes to outing truths. Here are just a few of the ways I research the world around me for the benefit (and sometimes amusement) of my clients:

HINT 1 LISTEN UP

The only thing you can truly own, that is truly unique, is you—so trust your instincts. When I am trying to get to the heart of what matters I listen to the little voice in my head that talks to me in Woody-Allen-like fashion all day long…telling me to magnify minutiae, seek out strange, unearth odd, obliterate obvious and assemble the puzzle from the inside out. It gives me permission to look at things from as many angles as possible. Question authority. Make enemies. Interrogate suspects. Take no prisoners. Because anyone who has ever tried to create something from nothing knows that while the shortest route from A to B may well be a straight line, that doesn't mean it will be the most scenic. Alas, the quest for answers is anything but linear ○145 RHEA.

HINT 2 WASTE TIME

Unlike those who listen intently to every word a client says, taking copious notes and preparing early to offer intelligent feedback, I am often doodling. Scribbling words. Planning solutions, right then, right there. It's brilliant! It's the answer! I am a genius! It's usually drivel.

But—and here's the bonus part—I am hooked, right from the beginning. By ignoring what I've been taught just long enough to do what feels right I create things that excite me in a way that more politically correct approaches don't. Most of the really Big Ideas I've had originated from those primitive musings when I was supposed to be furrowing my brow in a combination of fascination and respect. I encourage my clients to do the same—spend time at the big Dry-Erase® board in the sky asking "What if?" and "Why not?" Trained to make every minute count, I think the value of wasting time is grossly underestimated ▶94 GONZALES CRISP.

HINT 3 SHOOT THE BREEZE

Speaking casually with long-time employees at all levels within a company will help you get to know the company from a more human perspective. If you want to hear the kind of adjectives you won't hear in the boardroom or during an Official Executive Interview, talk to a secretary who has been there 20-plus years. Finding out what causes an employee's eyes to light up when they talk about their (seemingly mundane) product illuminates the truly amazing fact that virtually everything is fascinating to someone. Once you find what ignited the initial passion, then, and only then, do you have seeds worth sowing.

HINT 4 GET OVER YOURSELF

At the core of my belief system about how creativity happens is a veritable dearth of beliefs. In fact, I could argue that my only real belief is not to have beliefs. Creativity is the first casualty when beliefs are allowed to get in the way. If I find myself believing a certain thing to be "good" or "bad" or "not for me" I instinctively take the opposing position. Play devil's advocate. Become impossibly and persuasively perverse. In so doing I expose myself, sometimes uncomfortably, to the widest possible view. The knee-jerk desire to know and declare what I stand for is replaced by a hunger to know what there is to stand for instead. By vowing to stay open to all possibilities for as long as possible you can outwit Creativity's killer nemesis: Narrow-Mindedness. By listening to our intuition we are forced, in the inimitable words of Dr. Phil, to get real. This willingness to forego artifice makes us more open creative vessels: ones more likely to be half-full rather than half-empty, and ones with a higher likelihood of combining seemingly disparate elements to form something genuinely new.

HINT 5 MIX IT UP

Although people in my profession are often perceived as "arbiters of taste," I'm no design snob (and don't play well with ones who are). I don't have better or worse taste than anyone else, just personal preferences and a point of view that I am both compelled and excited to share. (David Canaan defines creativity as, among other things, "tolerance for ambiguity over time") ▶234 CANAAN.

An avid "multi-media" devotee, I immerse myself in virtually every kind of communication available. I have a thirst for information and a broad, eclectic range in taste. My studio CD collection ranges from DEL the Funky Homosapien (a brilliant rap lyricist) to ColdPlay (seriously cool pop) to Jaio Gilberto (haunting chords and vocals) to Donna Summer (dance dance dance to the beat) to Windham Hill (new age ambrosia) to Sigur Ros (icelandic Bjork-like suicide ballads). Last month I saw "The Core," "The Pianist," and a theatre production of the hilarious and poignant transgender hit "Hedwig and the Angry Inch." I am a regular viewer of "American Idol," "Biography," The Discovery Channel, "The West Wing," "Sixty Minutes," "Entertainment Tonight" and CNN. I listen to NPR (public radio), KFRC (oldies) and 101.3 (house music). I have subscriptions to about 10 magazines, including *Scientific American*, *People*, *The NY Times Book Review*, *Esquire*, *W*, *Martha Stewart Living*, *TV Guide* and *Cosmopolitan*. My dogs are mutts; my cats are purebred.

My point? There are a lot of ways to conduct research. Somewhere early on I just started living it.

Big Ideas in the Real World

Finding out who a company or product is, and conveying that information to the outside world are two very different activities, each fraught with peril and potential reward.

The following pages offer some real-world examples of how the discipline of pre-search has served my firm and my clients well over the years. In each case traditional design research probably should have occurred, but didn't, and I think the result was the better for it.

THE PACIFIC BELL CALLING CARD *CLEARLY THE BEST CALL*

Pacific Bell calling card

Whether it's lack of time, lack of money, lack of understanding, or all of the above, sometimes great results are born of situations where research isn't even an option.

Such was the case for Pacific Bell back in the late 80s. AT&T had all but cornered the market on plastic telephone calling cards, while PacBell still offered a dog-eared, old-fashioned paper alternative. Giving us about $10,000 and two weeks to create a "hard card" for them, our client clearly wasn't focused on design—they just wanted a physical object, fast, to both save face and play catch-up.

As a new Design Director this first assignment wasn't exactly inspiring. An apathetic client. No money. No time. And a new design staff that there wasn't really budget to use. What I did have was an insightful superior who knew that this was a task best handled by a designer whose first words wouldn't be "shouldn't we conduct some design research?"—it simply wasn't in the cards (or budget) ⊙234 CANAAN. I was the perfect tool—fresh, naïve and ready for action. If the client wasn't going to get excited about the project, I would get the project to excite the client. It was here that the process of "strategy through design" gelled for me: sometimes strategy just isn't visible, let alone viable, until design reveals it.

I set out to create a card which was so new, so hip, so head-turningly unusual that people would have to keep it—they simply wouldn't be able to throw it away. What was born was the first completely transparent credit card ever. With limited wallet slots and so many competing cards the modern consumer had some excruciating choices to make about what to keep: My Blockbuster Card? My United Mileage Plus card? My Awesome and Impressive New Phone Card? Screw utility—the card is a chick magnet, a real conversation starter—it stays.

With nothing to lose, our client threw the proverbial dice and went for the Big Win. Requests for the card increased 80%. Customers wanted to know how to get one and what to do with it, and there was nothing else to attribute interest to except design. It was a direct mail dream.

The PacBell clear card didn't earn its "share of wallet" by being useful (it wasn't). It earned its slot by being cool.

EPILOGUE

NOTE 1 Three years later, when a new Product Manager took over the Calling Card program for Pacific Bell, his first executive decision was to add pigment to the card making it white (without altering the design) because he said it was easier to find in his wallet. I'd like to see guys like him researched sometime.

NOTE 2 I am filled with a mixture of pride and envy when, more than thirteen years after the clear card project, I drive around the Bay Area and see that American Express has recently introduced "the world's first clear credit card"—and did it the right way—with large acrylic billboards all over town. Pacific Bell was way ahead of its time, but way too bureaucratic to do anything about it. I predict research would have loved this one. But, even in the absence of research, intuition (and an apathetic client) told me that this was a big idea whose time had come.

PG&E *LET THERE BE LIGHT*

In 1987, when the second largest public utility in the country finally decided to take a look at their corporate identity they weren't at all ready to give up the trusted (albeit rusted) logotype they'd used and abused for 68 years. Although they were a regulated utility (and had no say about the price of their services), they were constantly under fire and had become both annoyingly apologetic and a sad, sad case of hiding your light (pun intended) under a bushel (no pun at all).

As a tall, blonde girl presenting to a cadre of shrinking, silver-haired septuagenarians I was naïve enough to tell them what I truly believed: Come out of the closet and stop apologizing. Go for it. Just Do it. *Carpe Diem*. (Fish of the Day? Seize the Fish?) As I saw it, there were only a few genuine miracles on the planet: garbage collectors, the water and sewage people, the phone company (there was only one then), the mail system (there was only one then, and it was still relative-

ly earthbound), and a few others. These were the people providing things we couldn't easily provide for our-selves—these were the people we needed to worship— not Macy's. Not only did PG&E provide literal miracles (light, heat, security) every minute of every day, but they did so under adverse conditions they couldn't control. It was time to step up to the plate, take a swing, and start being proud of their accomplishments.

After presenting solutions for a bold new look to bring them out of the dark ages and into the light, they approved the most radical of all the concepts presented.

PG&E Truck

Without a single minute of post-design research they followed that internal voice that said yes, by golly, we do deserve something shiny, proud, proactive and new— and they adopted the PG&E "Spotlight" symbol we see today.

Love 'em or hate 'em, I believe PG&E is still around because they had the courage to trust their instincts and bolster their image long before the current cli-mate of cutthroat competition. I think research would have squashed this solution in favor of a less risky approach. It was a bold leap from their existing identity and not at all what people would expect from such a large, conservative organization.

It was one of the most courageous decisions I have seen a client make in my career, and I salute them for it.

LENOX ROOM RESTAURANT *TIP WELL AND PROSPER*

If you're a restaurant in Manhattan it's not enough to have great food and a hip atmosphere, you need a hook, a "buzz"—something to make you stand out from the culinary crowd. Renowned restaurateur-slash-chef Charlie Palmer left the

task of seeing that his newest restaurant venture opened with a bang to me and his partner Tony Fortuna (a classic upper-east-side New Yorker who, rumor has it, never ventured below 58th Street).

Charlie's great food and Tony's neurotic, only-in-New-York management style would surely succeed—if the restaurant could get noticed. What they needed was an over-the-top tagline that could walk the fine line between confident and smug with true New York style.

The tagline, "Tip Well and Prosper" was part tongue-in-cheek Trekkie trivia and part homage to my (desperate) belief that what goes around really will come

Lenox Room Restaurant graphics

around. First used as a placeholder line (thinking it too cheeky, even for me, to actually print), when it came time to put ink on paper I took another look and—yes, it said it all: feisty, irreverent, appropriately trendy, buzz-worthy and, best of all—true. "Tip Well and Prosper" was a keeper.

I predict research would have killed this one in a New York minute.

But upper-east-siders ate it up.

Physician, Heal Thyself

When I made the decision to start my own firm twelve years ago, it was when I sensed that, in certain instances, my instincts could be as valuable as other people's facts. It was when I realized that, for many people, quantifying things wasn't necessarily the best (or at least not the first) path to enlightenment.

At our 10-year anniversary I decided to create a new identity for my own firm, changing the name and visual look we had used since Day One. I first examined my feelings about my company, including my company name, offering and plans for the future, from both a personal and professional perspective. Too often I saw clients try to be what they thought others wanted, clearly afraid to be themselves first. Confident that my instincts had served me well so far, I looked closely at our successes and failures and tried to divine (as opposed to determine) what the next best step in my company's evolution might be.

Aerial Pushpins, one of 15 photographic business cards, each depicting an aerial view of something, or something "airborne."

While the original company name, "Aerial," had served us well, it had outlived its usefulness. Named to reflect an overview perspective on the identity process, we no longer needed the name as a segue to explain our reason for being. Even our original series of whimsical, aerial photograph business cards which had created a stir for many years had run their course and now seemed somehow both a vestige of the 90s and not authentic enough for the looming New Millennium.

(Add to that a growing frustration with spelling "Aerial" and explaining that, no, it wasn't named after Disney's Little Mermaid, I was confident it was time for a change.)

In searching for a new professional name and visual image I faced several very personal realizations:

My original desire to have my own firm be about "more than just me" had been proven somewhat naïve and, basically, false. "Aerial" was, regardless of its original charter, all about me—my philosophy, my perspective, my skills. At the ten-year mark I found that I was finally comfortable with this idea. Naming the firm after myself no longer seemed self-indulgent; it seemed appropriate.

My skills as a manager had improved considerably over the first decade.

Reflecting that in a new name and identity change would be a positive step for everyone—me, my employees, and my clients. No longer nervous about dealing with the myriad of personalities a small business must juggle (oops, manage), I had become much more adept at Managing without Fear. A new name and identity would serve as a signal of this important rite of passage. I had grown up (again!), was more seasoned, and felt more comfortable in my own skin.

Although I counseled my clients on a daily basis to take the plunge and navigate the sometimes-difficult waters a new identity presents, I had never experienced that particular process myself. I felt the urge, even the obligation, to experience the journey firsthand and walk a mile in their moccasins. I conducted the ultimate research experiment an identity designer can undertake and embarked on my own identity project.

StudioMoon business card

After building strong positive equity in our original identity it could be argued that it was an unnecessary risk to rock the boat. However, with the decided advantage of being judge and jury, I was free to move forward with less second-guessing. I had taken the time to get to know myself and, therefore, had a solid foundation to build from (not to mention an omnipresent and vaguely nauseous feeling—the truest indicator that you're onto something big).

The result was more than a visual change—it was a more seasoned firm in every respect. It reflected me better as a person, and it represented the more mature offering I was now able to provide my clients. While research might have told me what clients wanted, only I could tell people who I was, and why that would benefit them. StudioMoon is proof positive that identity comes from within.

A New Point of You

No matter what kind conduct, good research is inevitably worth the trip. In my company I encourage clients to come along for the ride, especially at the beginning.

Hopefully we find answers to their truly meaningful questions, like "Why do we bother every day?" "What is it that floats our boat about this venture?" and "What would it look like if everyone could see what we already see?" There are few numbers or percentages in the answers to these questions. But there is a far greater chance of finding a small smile hidden inside, one that can blossom into a full-blown grin over time.

It's not an approach without inherent risk. Knowing where the line is between pre-search and traditional research methodologies is critical. Counseling a client to make major decisions about their identity, company, product or service based on intuition alone might qualify as design malpractice. At the very least it's just plain dumb.

That the subject of Design Research elicits such rich and broad commentary illuminates the fact that we now live in a world where a singular approach to inquiry is not only insufficient, it's old hat.

That some of the most valuable research, especially on identity, should emanate from within seems like a no-brainer to me. Rather than trying to determine who and what others want them to be, companies—just like people—need to focus on finding out who they are first, and then be that in a big way. If you build it, they will come—and they'll pay more for the ticket.

It can be a more difficult path because there are fewer road maps, but I believe it can also be a more rewarding one. And, just like life, it ought to be the going, not just the getting there, that's good.

Take-Aways

- Be the Research: There are all kinds of ways to conduct Design Research. Get to know and appreciate every one of them, especially the one where you and your client's opinions count.
- Practice What You Pre-search: Working with clients in a more personal way before traditional research takes place helps them start with a strong foundation, know where they're headed, and ask the right questions.
- Listen Up: Follow your instincts, you're probably way smarter than you look.
- Waste Time: Be willing to. Creativity isn't linear.
- Shoot the Breeze: Make friends with people behind the scenes. They're easier to get to, know the really good stuff, and aren't afraid to talk.
- Get Over Yourself: Don't take yourself too seriously, or no one else will either.
- Mix it Up: Be genuinely willing to explore and "think outside box." Hell, think outside the box the box came in if you have to.
- Big Ideas in the Real World: Have the courage of your convictions. New ideas are rare. Work hard not to let the real world (and its many helpers) squash them.
- Live fast, have fun, and leave a good-looking logo.

Research to Fuel
the Creative Process

DAVID CANAAN

Design as a Commodity

In the past, design professions were somewhat protected by a limited availability of people with the skills to get their ideas on paper or into production. Technical skills were required and most colleges concentrated on training "artsy types" in typography, production, drawing, model-making, print-making and layout. Jobs for graduates were apprenticeships to hone commercially usable skills and, once a passable level of technical skill was achieved, designers could differentiate themselves by excelling in a certain "look" or technique. If they had a client (or patron) willing to pay and able to leverage the uniqueness of a design style as a profitable differentiator for their own business or product, the designer could make a living based on creative capabilities only.

Over the last 20 years, computers have revolutionized the design industry by lowering the need for the technical, production and drawing skills formerly used to differentiate designers. As the barriers to entry into the field have dropped, clients can find almost unlimited resources to provide excellent visual materials for their communications needs and the economics of design are rapidly moving toward commodity pricing.

The economics of design could be modeled like this:

$$\textbf{SUCCESS} = \frac{\text{CONTRIBUTION TO PROFIT} \times \text{CLIENTS ABILITY TO PAY}}{\text{AVAILABILITY OF RESOURCES}}$$

Contribution to Profit is the measure of a design to successfully impact the profit of an enterprise. Cases where this is true abound: Diet Coke saw a $200 million increase in sales the first year following the introduction of new global packaging; Williams-Sonoma saw 400% sales increases when they redesigned their private label pasta packaging; and average checks at Denny's increased 15% when they changed their outdated signs.

Client's Ability to Pay defines the potential in a design program. The impact of design is limited by factors like distribution, audience, profit margins and financial resources. Design, while a powerful tool, has finite limits and programs with untapped design capacity are most likely to benefit from great work. Programs with other inherent problems, including under-funding, poor management or insufficient confidence that design success would deliver adequate profits to fund the project are likely doomed to failure.

Availability of Capable Resources is the divisor in the design success formula. As the availability of good resources grows, fees for creative services drop. Design compensation and project budgets fall. Competitive design pressures force designers to look at their ability to affect the economics of the industry and conclude that they must enlarge the "contribution to profit" factor if they desire future success. This means understanding the business implications of creativity—knowing how to motivate sales, influence brand loyalty, support commercial goals, and appeal to specific audiences.

This recognition is already in evidence as traditional identity/packaging/brand design firms are becoming more "consultancies" than "studios" and traditional management consultancies like McKinsey, Bain, and Arthur Anderson are developing creative communications practices employing creatives within their exclusive MBA brotherhoods. The line between the "suits" and the "creatives" is being blurred as truly successful creative experts are as much analytic in their thinking as they are inventive.

Taking all these factors into consideration, research is an enormously important tool to inform the creative process. As a designer, I've always been personally intrigued by the power of research to help me understand people who don't share my outlook on life. I want to understand what values are communicated visually or verbally, but more important, I want to understand the priority customers put on those values and which buttons need to be pushed to stimulate their actions. I'm not so interested in their opinion of a design or layout—I assume the aesthetic responsibility is mine (and I am passionate about doing things that are visually pleasing)—but I must understand how their behavior is influenced by what I do if I'm going to affect the "contribution to profit" factor in the formula.

Enlightened researchers understand that this type of research differs from mere opinion-gathering. Louis Cheskin was a pioneer in it. He kept his head above the tactical opinion gathering and focused on the behavior assessment with indirect research methodologies for evaluating creative work. "Sensation Transference," the crown jewel in Cheskin's practice, is a fundamental concept for evaluation. I firmly resist having creative work "analyzed" with techniques like focus groups with people discussing opinions of creative work as a group. The dynamics of groups usually uncovers opinion (i.e., "Television's greatest problem is that there's too much sex and violence") but rarely measure behavior (it's the sex and violence that is being watched). Instead, I push for monadic studies (one person sees one exhibit) with multiple participants (quantitative samples) independently responding to the same questions and the only variable being a change in the creative stimuli—studies where specific behavioral characteristics of designs can be compared and informed decisions can drive creative executions.

Hallmarks of Creativity

Creativity is an instinctive urge; a powerful drive that fights logic; an activity that gives creators an unusual euphoria and generates an unmatched sense of satisfaction. Creativity is the core of new ideas. It's the source for new products, new designs, and vision to see the world in a renewed way.

Creativity is also enormously misunderstood. It is thought to be a gift randomly bestowed at birth, an unpredictable trait and a mystical talent. Parents with underachieving children frequently make the excuse, "this is the creative one in the family." The stereotypical "artsy" type is drawn to drama, music or art classes, dresses strangely, is a loner and does poorly in academic courses. Professional "creatives" are considered unconventional, unruly and unpredictable. They work in a "bullpen" or "the back" and are separated from the "suits." Client contact with creatives is carefully monitored and expectations for businesslike behaviors are low. "All-nighters" are thought to be standard and unusual hours are casually tolerated.

Most people do not consider themselves "creative." If asked, they shrink back with hands up and claim they can't draw a straight line or have a single new idea. In reality, everyone has extraordinary creative resources unique to themselves. Tapping those resources is a process that can be learned with practice and beefed-up resistance to the lifelong programming that discourages use of those abilities.

The apparent logic and precision of the research process seems at odds with creativity. Designers are leery of research where their experience has been observing focus groups from behind the glass and listening mutely as some schmuck without taste shreds their creations. Discouraged, some designers limit their creative exploration on the assumption that good ideas will be rejected by research. Understanding the creative process and structuring research to encourage new thinking is key to achieving breakthrough ideas.

Creative people share 3 common traits: 1. the ability to make new associations from unrelated elements, 2. willingness to pursue an idea they know they will ultimately reject, and 3. tolerance for ambiguity over time. How research can support these traits is the purpose of this chapter.

Making New Associations from Unrelated Elements

No one ever "creates" anything; they reorganize existing elements—heresy to the creatives, but true. Creating means seeing a relationship between new information and a previous experience and developing a fresh combination. Creativity is an attitude, not a mysterious gift. Individuals successful at making new associations from unrelated elements tend to have unusual access to their subconscious memories and conscious access to the potential in new input.

Creativity is available to everyone in an equal dose because everyone has a completely unique set of past experiences to draw from. The menu of ingredients to make new relationships with is proprietary for each individual. The ability to access those ingredients is what characterizes those thought to be creative. This part of creativity can be learned. However, readily accessing our subconscious to gain new insights while on a deadline is difficult.

Without a detailed treatment of brain function including descriptions of "right brain" and "left brain" differences, suffice it to say that our minds are complex structures. Authorities agree that the human brain has enormous storage capacity and uses only a portion of its processing ability to manage physical actions in the body. The remaining capacity is used for "higher" processes including imagination, self-awareness and abstract imagery.

In my experience, conscious access to these processes appear to be blocked occasionally and predictable use of my higher capacities is the exception. Often, "bolts of insight" seem to strike my conscious mind when I am not deliberately thinking about a problem. This makes creativity on demand a challenge. The spontaneous creativity of fine artists frequently allows them to "wait for inspiration" or "get in the mood." For example, accessing the catalog of personal experience with diapers because an assignment to promote them is due right away is not easy. Turning on the spigot of new ideas from the subconscious can be done with drugs (as occasionally it is), but the quality of insights drops off quickly. Hypnosis does bypass nature's blockage, but that puts a second person in control of the outcome and is generally ineffective.

Experience confirms that anxiety is a consistent and effective chemical to stimulate creativity on demand. The greater the anxiety ("you'll be fired if the presentation isn't ready by tomorrow morning"), the more effective it is at bringing out creative energy (thus, common "all-nighters" by creative staffs everywhere). However, frequent abuse of anxiety can result in paranoia, fear and discouragement. My best clients and coworkers are those I respect enough that I fear disappointing them, but trust enough to take creative risks with them.

Breakthrough creativity happens when the quality of elements for seeing new relationships is relevant to the opportunity at hand, but not so restrictive that meandering thoughts cannot be explored.

How to Structure Research so New Associations Can Be Made

Because my own creativity is based on creating visual relationships, I learn more by seeing than hearing. A picture is indeed worth a thousand words. A written report of how people feel about a product pales compared to seeing a competitor's products, advertising and collateral materials. Completely new products may not have obvious direct competitors; but all products—real or imagined—carry expectations for where they'll be used, when they'll be needed and the characteristics of people who might use them. Photos of prospective audiences, shopping aisles, living rooms, and other products possibly used when or where the new product is planned are helpful tools for discovering new associations and feeding the creative process.

In every project, preliminary assumptions about outcomes must be made. Comparisons, analogies, objectives, scenarios and business plans are the vocabulary to describe a project while the outcome evolves through the creative process. Involving creative thinkers early provides a resource for developing the comparisons and analogies. Seeking input on what might compete for share of mind with an upcoming product or what brands might be analogous to the desired outcome before launching a formal research study is invaluable in finding the "unrelated" elements that make up the basic menu for identifying new relationships.

Experiencing a shopping event or using the software or driving the car are high-speed programming tools for the mind. Fact and figures, while useful at the intellectual level, are poor substitutes for intuitive input into the creative process. Researchers who add visual communications to their findings get significantly higher value from their insights. Project leaders desiring breakthrough thinking should partner with their creative colleagues to collect background information from visual, factual and emotional data points to supplement qualitative and quantitative insights.

The resources from which to draw the unrelated elements are the subconscious (with the proper environment, group "brainstorming" can be a harvesting of this resource), past experience (industry expertise is valuable here), new input (relevant original data collection and sharing), and conscious goals (specific objectives for the outcome of the assignment). Since everyone has a unique subconscious resource from which to draw, everyone can (and should) contribute to the "databank" of ideas. All too frequently, the perceived distance between the creatives and everyone else prevents fully leveraging that uniqueness. Establishing a non-judgmental environment for freely sharing thoughts from all sources is essential. Organizations who have mastered that skill (such as the Disney "Imagineer" culture) have made giant leaps in generating ideas with broad appeal.

Willingness to Pursue an Idea You Know You'll Ultimately Reject

The goal of creativity is not to find the right answer, but to explore the range of possibilities. The broader the range of ideas that are explored, the more likely it is that one can discover breakthrough concepts.

Most of the best ideas start with the phrase like, "This is a dumb idea, but…." A conscious recognition that the idea about to be presented won't work opens the door to creative exploration. Editing ideas before they have a chance to be expressed stifles breakthroughs because when only "safe" concepts are considered, new ideas have little chance to happen. Creative outcomes require exploring the range of possible answers to a problem, not finding the "right" one.

Throughout life we are taught to find right answers. "What does the cow say?" "What does c-a-t spell?" "What is 2 plus 2?" "Who was the 12th President?" "What country is immediately East of Belgium?" We are programmed from early age to learn facts and to report them accurately. Coming up with correct answers is rewarded. Wrong answers are discouraged. Early schooling provides little incentive for exploration out of the box. Children who would rather daydream than listen or prefer to draw rather than study are disciplined, counseled, held back or isolated. It should be no surprise that creative geniuses like Edison and Ford lacked formal education or painters like Monet and Van Gogh left school early to pursue their creative talents.

The creative process is more like play than like study. It requires speculation, humor, tangents and dead-ends. For breakthrough ideas, creative exploration needs to generate as broad a range of possibilities as possible before editing or selecting final candidates. Supporting "failures" with the same enthusiasm as successes is where creative cultures begin.

How Research Can Support Ideas that Will Ultimately Be Rejected

Researchers who enjoy the mathematical exactness of quantitative research can have a hard time balancing the efforts of creative teams to pursue concepts that seem to fly in the face of their work. When they understand the necessity of sustaining unpredictable ideas through the incubation process, their ability to contribute grows. Rigid parameters cause premature editing of ideas and will cut off productive creativity. Establishing "creative targets" rather than "project mandates" encourages broad exploration. Enthusiastically adding insights and accepting the apparent inefficiency of speculation contribute to an environment that will be more likely to discover new ideas from established facts.

The ability to pursue an idea you know you'll ultimately reject is counterintuitive to efficiency, but it's essential to breakthrough ideas. Organizations who support "playing" with an idea that doesn't appear to have merit are rare. 3M and Sony do it as a regular part of their business. The auto industry has canonized the practice by showcasing "concept cars" at auto shows. Experimental theater, themed art exhibits and independent films occasionally deliver exceptional ideas, but usually not with profit goals in mind. A differentiator of the creative types is their willingness to start a comment with the phrase, "This is a dumb idea, but..." Suits don't get many organizational points for doing that. Creatives are condescendingly tolerated when they do. Using research to define avenues to pursue as creative targets can recast the traditional efficiency measures by widening the breath of exploration possibilities without the premature limitations of practicalities.

Tolerance for Ambiguity over Time

A characteristic of creativity that can be frustrating to others is the need to let fragile ideas distill before finalizing them. Time gives the subconscious space to process insights and work on problems that have moved from the conscious mind. A noted designer once told me that when he was in college he would tape his design concepts on the back of his dorm room door so when he came in and closed the door the idea would surprise him. That split second of unexpected observation was one of the few ways he could see his own ideas with fresh eyes. Then he made refinements.

Getting completely away from a project before it is finished delivers improvements and inspiration for breakthrough ideas. In the quest for competitive ideas, time is always at a premium. Project plans identify tangible deliverables at specific times. There seems to be little room for breaks while answers are unresolved. However, project environments where creative developers are not encouraged to present ideas with unanswered questions inevitably fail to produce breakthrough ideas because ambiguities need to linger in order to be resolved. Trusting in the mental resources of team members to find successful new thoughts while not appearing to be working on the project requires great patience and confidence. But it is essential to a successful creative culture.

Research shares a similar need. The practice of providing a top-line brief of a field study before presenting a full report is an excellent way to let findings distill. Getting away and coming back to information is critical to understanding it in a broad context. Even then, re-interpretation should be encouraged as unexpected insights along the creative path reveal different ways to see the data or require additional examination of findings that were previously thought to be irrelevant.

Having the right answer is a false goal when seeking breakthrough creative ideas. Having the right *range* of ideas is a better way to seek innovative solutions. Enlightened companies evaluate multiple prototypes before landing on final executions. Efficiency seems to cry out against letting unresolved ideas remain in limbo for any length of time, but it's that very ambiguity that stimulates energetic solutions. Research on the impact of the range of ideas can be very helpful, but it must be done with care to identify symptoms, not solutions.

Creative professionals wishing to affect the business goals of their clients and stand out above the competitive mass of "artsy" practitioners see the necessity of research to encourage companies to invest in new ideas. However, many fear the crippling effect of poorly conceived studies that threaten the energy and "freshness" of their work. By understanding the creative process and sharing methods at each step to make research a dynamic tool to support invention, more effective, satisfying and impactful solutions will result.

And just maybe, the traditional adversarial relationship between the "suits" and the "creatives" might become a partnership of respect and fun.

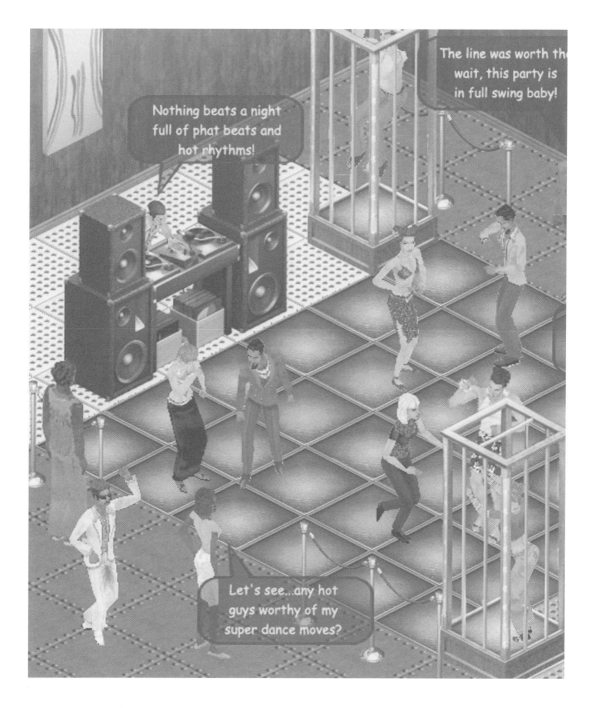

Reports from the Field

BRENDA LAUREL

In the section on Form, the authors' work necessarily represents both process and outcome, as the two are fundamentally inseparable in that context. Although many of the chapters in previous sections have incorporated examples having to do with the design of products and services, this book would not be complete without a few focused case studies. How is the execution and application of Design Research experienced by its practitioners in the context of products, services, brands or audiences? How do methods produce outcomes, and how do we measure their effectiveness? At the end of the day, what worked and what didn't? How do we deal with failure and how can we achieve success?

It takes quite a bit of courage, dedication and resilience to actually employ the methods we've been examining, especially within a commercial context ●83 GROCOTT, ●234 CANAAN. Every design context has its own set of obstacles and limiting factors. The market (or the management) seems always to be breathing down one's neck. Design Research intends to encounter the unknown—an uncomfortable journey for an executive with an eye on the bottom line or a marketer who wishes simply to shore up an established brand ●212 LOCH, ●145 RHEA, ●225 MOON. As with manned space flight, failures of all stripes serve to amplify resistance to the risk, time and expense involved in research. Lack of predictability can drive executives crazy. But for the design researcher, each step of the way is informed by the one that precedes it. Even with the best maps and compasses, they must be both cautious and nimble as they navigate new terrain. Design researchers learn by doing. Their experiences and reflections prepare us for our own close encounters.

Many of the chapters in this section deal with the design and development of computer games ●244 JENKINS ET AL, ●253 WRIGHT, ●268 DAVIS ET AL., ●260 RAPOZA. The reasons for this focus are many: games are currently the most exuberant region of the recently flat-lined technology sector.

Games must incorporate knowledge about both people and form in exquisitely intertwined ways. The emerging form of the massively multi-player online game (MMOG) is not coded and shoved into a box like the single-player games of yore. MMOGs cannot be said to be "finished" until someone literally pulls them off the Internet; they are always evolving in response to players' behaviors and the changing tropes of popular culture. Because of their technological nature, MMOGs offer the unique opportunity to incorporate technological methods for conducting ongoing design research and making use of findings throughout their life spans.

A word about voice and values. The chapter entitled "Researching *America's Army*" chronicles the development of a product intended to function both as a game and as an educational tool about the United States Army ●268 DAVIS ET AL. As such, it incorporates the language and attitudes of the Army—attitudes that are also strongly held by the game's developers. As with any other designed object, some may disagree with the intent, tone, values or goals of the project, but it is important that we know what they are. I chose to feature this game primarily because of the unique challenge of designing a multi-layered representation of something that exists in the real world. I also chose it because, within the domain of design, it represents an extreme excursion into the realms of values and politics. My hope is that it serves to remind us that values are implicit in everything we do. *America's Army* gives us a rare opportunity to study a case where values are explicitly expressed by both the designers and the design. In Damer's chapter, "A Virtual Walk on the Moon," you will encounter a different set of values—"spacer" values, for want of a better word—that are employed just as passionately ●276 DAMER.

Movies and television also make an appearance in this section ●293 SHUTT, ●301 SINGER. I remind those critical theorists who eschew popular culture that it is relevant to them precisely because it is designed, and that its quality may be as much a measure of designers' willingness to engage it as it is of the public's tastes. As the soup in which all swim, popular culture lends itself to design interventions that can have massive effects. Popular media demonstrate a particular cultural feedback mechanism: they must be sensitive to shifts in public tastes, but they also have a role in shaping those tastes. Games, movies, television and other elements of popular culture provide familiar, accessible examples of design research in action.

The museum experience designed by Jin Hyun Park (and touched upon by BJ Fogg in the People section) is another kind of encounter with the public ⊙201 FOGG, ⊙285 PARK. Here, the design problem is to make objects of elevated cultural significance accessible to the general public. The designer encounters the challenge, not only of making the museum's contents meaningful to unique individuals with different goals, but also of designing, albeit indirectly, the movements of people through real space. As new technological capabilities continue to emerge, the intersection of media design and environmental design will become increasingly fertile ground for creative exploration.

Finally, the design of identities and brands are examples of designing ways to communicate the value of other designed objects to their intended customers and audiences ⊙301 SINGER, ⊙309 MASTEN. Brand/identity design incorporates another sort of cultural feedback loop, where the brand both represents and influences the design of products, services and properties. The section's final chapter may be understood as a meta-field report wherein the author condenses a lifetime of encounters with brand and identity design into a pattern that can be seen as both descriptive and prescriptive ⊙309 MASTEN. I place it as the concluding chapter of the book because, beneath the conversational tone, Davis Masten brings extraordinary experience and wisdom to his description of where the rubber meets the road.

"You Can't Bring That Game to School!"

Designing *Supercharged!*

HENRY JENKINS, KURT SQUIRE, & PHILIP TAN

In the mid-1990s, The Doonesbury franchise commissioned a campaign simulation game which allowed players to choose a slate of candidates from more than a hundred actual political figures, map their campaign strategy day-by-day and state-by-state, make ad buys, schedule debates and interviews, manage scandals and determine the outcome based on the electoral college. And when the son of one of our researchers played the game, he instantly made the connection to what his parents were watching on CNN, explaining why Dole and Clinton had scheduled stops in key electoral states. When he took the game to school to play during lunch, the school librarian refused, citing a school policy permitting the use of educational software but not games. Her determination that "you can't bring this game to school" was a shocking reminder of the uneasy relationship between education and popular culture.

Within the games industry, edutainment has become a bad word, suggesting an earnest aesthetic, derivative game play and poor production values. Common wisdom is that educational games fail both commercially and creatively. Most simply try to make drill-and-practice feel more palatable. It's a little bit like serving a spinach sundae: the results are not very good for you and not particularly tasty. The only people who disdain such edutainment as much as gamers are learning scientists. Such games embody theories of learning and knowing—based primarily on rote memorization and behaviorist conditioning—that are at least thirty years out of date. The learning sciences now see learning as occurring in social and cultural contexts and as depending on active processes of investigation, experimentation and interpretation.

If traditional edutainment products have been uninspiring and simplistic, James Paul Gee argues in his book *What Video Games Have to Teach Us About Learning* [2003] that educators might benefit from studying how game players learn through game play. As he explains, "When kids play videogames they experience a much more powerful form of learning than when they're in the classroom .... Each level dances around the outer limits of the player's abilities, seeking at every point to be hard enough to be just doable." To achieve this effect, game designers must be thoughtful about sequencing tasks so that players master what they need to do well step-by-step along the way. The designers also have to make these tasks fun in their own right, so that there is no point where playing ends and learning begins.

The Games-to-Teach Project, a joint effort of MIT and Microsoft, has developed a series of conceptual models of games that bring together what we currently know about pedagogical uses of new media with what we know about games as popular culture. We see tremendous opportunities for, say, using simulation and construction games to engage students in engineering or architectural design processes, using role-playing games to immerse students in the roles of doctors, anthropologists or scientists, or multiplayer games to encourage students to think about what life might be like in Colonial America. Few examples of such explicitly educational games exist today, although we can learn a lot by closing examining games already on the market, such as *Sid Meier's Pirates* or the *Civilization* series, which allow students to experiment with "what if" questions about history or to learn geography through mastering contested spaces [Jenkins and Squire 2002, Squire 2000].

Our design work cuts across different game genres, different academic fields, different pedagogical models, and different strategies for integrating games into the classroom [Games-to-Teach Team, in press; Holland, Jenkins, & Squire, 2003]. In a few cases, we have begun to develop playable prototypes to illustrate and test our ideas. This is a case study of one such prototype, *Supercharged!,* describing our design research and how this process has led us to continually rethink our assumptions about gaming, education, research and popular culture.

Research Approach: Design Experiments

We are, in effect, studying educational games that do not yet and may never exist. Through this process, we hope to learn more about games' pedagogical potentials, factors driving or inhibiting their adoption, their effectiveness, and the kinds of classroom activities needed to support them. Within learning sciences, design experiments enable us to investigate how complex learning occurs within rich social settings when using innovative materials [Brown 1992, Collins 1992]. Whereas naturalistic research creates better understandings of the world and experimental research builds models of specific variables, experiment-based design research strives to develop an underlying theory and create changes in social practices [Cobb et al., 2003]. These complex research goals often require researchers to employ a variety of research techniques (theoretical, humanistic, historical, qualitative, quantitative, naturalistic, or experimental methodologies).

First Prototype: *Supercharged!*

"Have you seen *Halo*? The real-time Physics are incredible," ranted John Belcher, Professor in Astrophysics at MIT and winner of two NASA Exceptional Scientific Achievement Medals. Belcher creates animations to help students learn Physics and thought that games might make his animations more interactive. Digital visualizations can allow students to see and interact with the normally invisible electromagnetic forces around everyday objects. Yet, as Belcher explained it, students had few compelling reasons—apart from passing the test—for studying his visualizations. A game would allow them not simply to observe the laws of electromagnetism at work, but to interact with them to solve puzzles or overcome obstacles. An electromagnetism game might teach players new ways of thinking about their physical surroundings. Gamers are increasingly experiencing games that distort our perception, helping us to see the world through different lenses [Poole 2001]. Could we use shifts in perception to help students learn to see field lines so that they would anticipate their effects even if, as is normally the case, they are invisible?

A sample of field line visualization from John Belcher.

In our first pass, we imagined a college student, Alina, seated in the back of a classroom. Alina looks under her seat and notices a comic book. Flipping through its colorful pages, she learns about a superhero whose special goggles allow her to see electrostatic forces. Alina flips over the comic and notices a pair of cardboard glasses on the back of the comic. Using these glasses, she assumes the powers of the comic book's protagonist and flies off to explore the wacky world of electromagnetism. Such a frame story offered a rationale for why Alina could sometimes see field lines, and we hoped a female superhero who has mastered the rules of physics could help us combat gender stereotypes that often disadvantage girls in the science classroom. Adding to the drama, the superhero could battle her evil physics professor who manipulates electromagnetic forces to his diabolical ends. We imagined the player doing a series of environmental puzzles (ala *Half-Life*), using electromagnetic principles to solve puzzles.

We encountered several problems: rendering all of the electric or magnetic fields operating in any given scenario—from the Earth's magnetic core to local currents—would tax any computer and ultimately be confusing to the student. The alternative would be to develop a "special-case, single instantiation" game that would be extremely hard-railed; that is, the player's actions would be severely constrained and goals narrowly defined. However, if part of the educational allure of games is their capacity to be sandboxes for players to experiment with ideas, we didn't want our first prototype to be a "point and click adventure on Physics!"

Shortly after we reached this painful realization, we met with Alex Rigopulous, MIT alumnus and CEO of Harmonix Music Systems, developers of Playstation 2 games, *Frequency* and *Amplitude*. Rigopulous suggested that we embrace a more stylized approach to the game. Graduate student Walter Holland noted that most of the Electromagnetism syllabus could be boiled down to a handful of laws (Maxwell's equations) that expressed electromagnetism as simple mathematical equations describing forces that would, in turn, lead to motion. A rapid brainstorming discussion ensued where we discussed a relatively simple, abstract game—like *Frequency* or *Rez*—where the player was a charged particle flying through abstract electromagnetic worlds. We imagined a fast-paced game

much like first person pinball where the player flew through mazes changing her charge, placing charges and avoiding obstacles.

Over the next month, three graduate students (Walter Holland, Elliot Targum and Robin Hauck) reinvented *Supercharged!* Starting with the Xbox controller, we imagined that players could use the triggers to place positive and negative charges, and then the XY buttons to flip their own charge. We

Supercharged! concept art

designed levels that forced players to confront important ideas in electromagnetism, such as the inverse relationship of electromagnetic force over distances. We adapted the back-story accordingly, imagining the player as the same plucky college student, but this time sucked into a surrealistic world of electrostatic forces through a science experiment gone awry. We imagined this world as populated by a race of small creatures called Fizzgigs that the player would collect as power-ups as she raced through levels. Undergraduates from The Gibbs School developed concept art for the project, and MIT Undergraduate Deborah Lui developed screenshots and storyboards to communicate basic game ideas.

The End of Pre-Production

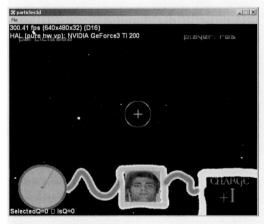

Once the original game design document was approved for production, we gathered a team of one graduate and four undergraduate students that would develop the game engine over the summer of 2002. *Supercharged!* was expected to be the flagship undertaking of the Games-to-Teach project complete with a fully 3D engine, quality animation, narration and music. On the surface, we wanted *Supercharged!* to look and function as if it might belong in the window of a typical videogame store, not on the back-room "edutainment" shelves of preschool suppliers.

These expectations posed enormous challenges. Commercial games require multimillion-dollar budgets and production timelines of two years or more. We had

p3dmouse demo of
moving particles

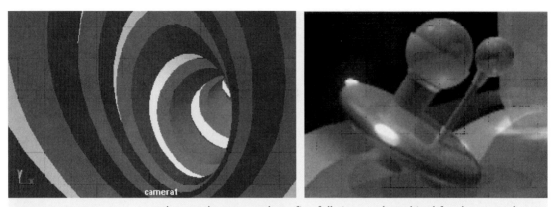

Left: 3D Concept Art for
Supercharged!
Right: Concept Art of the Ship
in *Supercharged!*

only enough money to keep five full-time students hired for three months. We recruited undergraduates (Robert Figueiredo, Timothy Heidel, Thomas Wilson and Megan Ginter) and graduate student (Philip Tan) with diverse tastes, skill sets and game preferences. Most members were avid gamers and had appreciable programming experience but had never worked together before nor written a 3D game.

In weeks, the undergraduates created a working technical demo (called "p3dmouse") that featured dozens of charged dots in 3D space, exerting forces on each other and moving in a real-time, wire-frame 3D engine. This rudimentary code demonstrated a 3D engine running an electrostatic simulation and what charged particles might look on screen (and what the world might look like if you were a charged particle).

Next we revisited Harmonix, where Eran Egozy, an MIT alumnus and co-founder of Harmonix, suggested that we examine *middleware* tools, which are collections of code designed to facilitate the implementation of commercial games. Criterion Software gave us free access to their RenderWare Graphics libraries and ongoing online support in exchange for publicity. However, RenderWare's technology still required a significant amount of exploration. There were no third-party "RenderWare for Dummies" books and, our tight production schedule (60 days to develop a 3D simulation game) meant that losing even a day to undocumented changes in RenderWare could derail our efforts.

Although RenderWare helped bridge the technological divide between the artists and the programmers, there were other obstacles. Physical distance between artists in Boston and programmers in Cambridge slowed production. Ambiguities in the original design document left the student programmers coding the project to make up parts of the game as they went along. Not surprisingly, the undergraduate programmers prioritized development tasks according to their own personal tastes. After a few weeks, the game lost much of its story and the game mechanic of saving Fizzgigs, but irretrievably inherited a first person-shooter style interface. Ultimately the music (a playfully retro soundtrack by composer

Left: An early build of
Supercharged! showing dynamically drawn field lines.
Right: A screenshot from a
typical "tunnel" level in
Supercharged! designed to
focus players' attention on
the goal.

Jerome Rosen) and script helped restore some of the mood and narrative focus
envisioned by the original design document.

Despite these conflicts, the summer came to a close with a playable and
extensible game engine. Additional levels were added to extend the playability
and challenge of the game throughout the subsequent fall semester. The combination of flight-simulator-like game play with first-person-shooter camera controls resulted in a visceral sense of the forces buffeting charged particles while in
continuous motion, which we believed to be a significant achievement in getting
physics students to think of electrostatics as an actual physical phenomenon
rather than a collection of formulae.

Initial Play Testing

Throughout the fall of 2002, we brought in college and high-school students see if
players could understand the basic game premise and objectives, learn the controls and navigate their ship. We were particularly concerned that students would
be able to grasp the game premise within a few minutes, given that the game was
intended to be used in classroom settings. We also wanted to ensure that the color
palette and interface would not alienate non-gamers or non-science-fiction fans.

We brought 12 college and high-school age students into the lab, exposing
each to a random order of our three level types (mazes, tunnels and open flying).
The players all preferred the first-person shooter style, maze-like interface, which
most clearly communicated the objective of the game (get out of the room successfully). The first-person controls were also the most intuitive. Few, if any, of
the players had actually played flying games, and most players found the tunnel
levels confining. The players who had already studied electromagnetism quickly
made links between the game and Physics concepts.

Although all of the players could navigate through the levels and were able
to communicate the basic game controls to the testers, most players had difficulty
finding their orientation and the exit. To ameliorate this, we added an introduction

Left: A "tunnel" level in
Supercharged! focuses players'
attention on the goal.
Right: Mazelike *Supercharged!*
level inspired by *Doom*.

cut scene for each level where the camera would preview the goalpost and the game characters would explain scientific concepts. We also added digital indicator, which would always be pointed in the direction of the goal and indicate its relative distance from the player's vehicle.

Controlled Experiments

In the spring of 2003 eight MIT students enrolled in an electromagnetism course participated in controlled laboratory exercises playing *Supercharged!* We found that participants had many misconceptions about electrostatic forces. Students who could recite Coulumb's Law would fail to predict how charged particles would

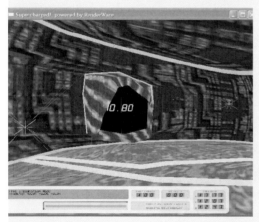

Supercharged! level
designed to combat
students' misconceptions

interact, particularly over varying distances. We designed new levels specifically to address these beliefs. In level 4, we surrounded the goal with two charged particles so that students could experience how their ship would be sucked to the closer charge instead of flying straight into the goal. In pre-test problems similar to this level, roughly half of the players believed that their ship, if negatively charged, would fly straight between the two charged particles into the goal. In reality, the ship would probably travel in a curved line toward the closest charged particle. From these controlled studies, we learned that levels designed to address students' current conceptions about electrostatics could help produce conceptual changes. Students would apply these new understandings to subsequent problems.

Moving into Schools: Field Work

Next, we tested how students played *Supercharged!* within high school contexts. Our first test site was an urban math and science magnet school. Whereas in the lab settings most students patiently sat through cut scenes and deliberately explored the control schemes, these students rushed through the game. Competitive groups formed as students shouted across the room announcing whenever they beat a level. Post-interviews with students revealed that few students made connections between the game play and Physics content. Clearly, more instructional supports were necessary for *Supercharged!* to be a viable instructional tool.

Our second set of field studies occurred with 125 middle school students at South Waltham Middle School. We developed a two week curriculum that combined playing *Supercharged!*, doing guided inquiry activities, and discussing electromagnetic concepts. Students reacted to the game much as in the first trial. The boys continued being engaged until they had "beat the game." Girls were generally less interested in the activity, although the 4 to 5 girls in each class who were engaged with the game played it even more purposefully and longer than the boys. Interviews revealed that girls enjoyed the exploring levels, playing with different ideas and trying different approaches.

Each day the class began with the teacher reviewing game concepts with a video project and setting 2 to 3 goals for students. The teacher created reflection sheets which required students to set goals, devise plans, hypothesize how their charged ship would move and monitor the results. The teacher moved from group to group, observing play and asking students thought questions. The teacher ended class by displaying a game level for discussion.

This study highlights how the game-play experience is only partially determined by the game; it is also a function of the students playing it and the social context that they construct. The "laboratory" milieu frames activity differently than the classroom. In the lab, students worked through the game in very methodical ways, making connections between the game and pre-post exercises. Even when we had students play the game in pairs, we did not see overt competition. Students knew they were testing a game and behaved accordingly. In contrast, bringing the game into school also brought with it the discourse of gamers. Many boys were competitive against the game and against themselves, challenging one another to see who completed the game the quickest or had mastered the controls. Most of the girls who embraced the game explored its boundaries in non-directed ways.

Teacher draws descriptions of Electrostatic concepts on the board.

The final site where we used *Supercharged!* suggests how participants might shape this social milieu to encourage educationally valuable play. By guiding activity, providing scaffolding in the form of worksheets, and encouraging individual and group reflection, the teacher was able to shape the experience so that the game was a useful tool to support learning. Making a meaningful educational intervention isn't simply a matter of designing educational games; it involves mapping strategies for deploying those games in the classroom, recognizing that every classroom has its own social milieu and that each teacher will adapt the game for their own teaching style.

Conclusions

Now that *Supercharged!* v1.0 is making its tour across test sites, our research has shown several different directions that future iterations can take. We have already begun testing simple prototypes of other game genres, such as side-scrolling shooters, that could demonstrate electrostatics ways that are accessible to broad audiences. Early design considerations assumed that the fast-paced game would be played on home computers, but integrating the game into a classroom setting has pushed us towards a slower-paced, more cerebral puzzle game that would provide teachers with more opportunities for instructional intervention.

Watching game-play change across contexts reminds us that educational materials and interventions are not simply adopted by educators, but remade in order to meet local needs. In *Understanding Popular Culture*, John Fiske draws a distinction between mass culture, which is made by media companies, and popular culture, which emerges as consumers adapt those contents for their own purposes, negotiating their meanings in relation to our identities, social structures and existing semiotic patterns [Fiske 1989]. Similarly, designing an educational game involves the negotiation of designers' identities, existing genres, tropes, and pedagogical assumptions. As the game moves into the classroom, further negotiations occur as teachers and students contest over the meanings of games: are they entertainment or education? Are they a fantasy environment or do their rules apply to real world spaces? Can we stop playing long enough to think through the implications of our actions?

As we move forward, we are building teacher support materials and support communities so that teachers have models of how to use the game effectively in class, have peers to learn with, and engage in the critical reflection of their teaching practice [Barab, Barnett and Squire 2002]. Our hope, however, is that this research will do more than just provide interesting insights but also result in products, processes, and social networks that will transform the social practices of schooling. Building on the work of John Dewey, we argue that the best design research is transformative, its value and validity are tested in social settings where its innovations will have an immediate and tangible impact. We hope to not only develop games that can be brought into the classroom but to also develop teachers who know what to do with them when they get there.

SimSmarts

An Interview with Will Wright

BRENDA LAUREL

Brenda Laurel Over the years as I've played the games you've designed, it seems to be that there is a big quantum leap in terms of usability between *Sim City* and *The Sims*, and I'm wondering how you got to that. It seems like breakthrough.

Will Wright It's more procedural than anything else. Also, we have the luxury now of sitting back, taking some time. Almost a year before we put a new game on the shelf, we start a process called Kleenex testing, which is about once a week.

BL Why do you call it Kleenex testing?

WW Because we never use the people again; we use them once and then we throw them away.

BL Got it.

WW We bring in people who have never seen the game, never touched it; we usually bring in couples, whether they are roommates or friends, or married. We put two of them at the front of the computer, boot the game up, and then give them the least amount of instruction. We give them some minor tasks, like "see if you can get this guy to do that", or "see if you can get to that spot on the game." And then we just sit back and observe them for like two hours.

BL Do they talk to each other?

WW Yeah, that's the reason we bring in two. One person would sit there and just get frustrated, but two people will start verbalizing their theories about the way it works. "No don't click that, that'll make this happen." "No, I think it'll work that way." So you hear them verbalizing their internal models of the mechanism. And it's incredibly frustrating as a designer, because you think it's so obvious to go click on that to do that. But when you sit back and watch someone struggling with the button, not knowing what it does, it's totally clear what needs to be done. There's no argument from that point. And so every week we try to get on a cycle where we can iterate what we've learned from the week before.

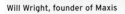
Will Wright, founder of Maxis

BL When you did *The Sims* originally, had you changed your target audience from the audience for *SimCity*?

WW Not a lot, although I think at the end it became more apparent that we were shooting for a more gender-balanced audience. We always were shooting for a pretty broad age range. I think more recently we started thinking more in terms of more casual players, which kind of matches the females demographic, but not directly.

BL What did you learn about female players and how did it influence the design?

WW In the testing we found that when women played the game there were certain points where they had a lot of comfort. And not to be overtly sexist, but they were very comfortable with the shopping part, mainly because there was not time pressure. I find that in general women tend to be less comfortable in any game where there is the time pressure. They'd much rather sit back and think about what they're about to do, plan it out, run thing through their minds, and then do it at their own rate—as opposed to, "Do something right now or you're going to die." This also maps a little bit more to games that are based on creativity and a little less around performance. In *The Sims*, there's live mode, build mode, buy mode and so on, and in the live mode women are just kind of clicking, watching characters do things, things happening, every interaction is a fun new surprise. Once they get to the buy mode, they totally understand it, and that becomes their structure for understanding the rest of the game. They work their way to the underlying game structure from that end.

BL So do you think most players have model of the underlying game structure?

WW Yeah, I think it's crucial.

BL Do they think if it as a program or do they think of it in some other way?

WW I think that they are reverse-engineering the model at all stages—even when they first see the box, because it's a really low-resolution model of the game. When you look at the box, you're running that low-resolution game in your head. When you go pick up the box and turn it over, and then your model gets more detailed. And if that model is still the imaginary model you play in your head and it's still fun, you might actually buy the game. A lot of times it's good to bring in a metaphor that people are comfortable with, that they can overlay on the game.

BL Sort of like the desktop interface metaphor...

WW Yeah—with something like *SimCity*, it's kind of like a train set, and *The Sims* is like a dollhouse. That automatically gives people a set of associations and expectations they can map, some of which will be correct, some of which wont be. If you can figure out what their initial metaphor is, you can leverage that to bootstrap understanding deeper and deeper into the game. So one of the things I find that I do every game now is I design a box, fairly early on, that is initially used inside the team. "Here's my model of what the game is going to be."

BL So your box is your spec in a way?

WW Yeah, it's the lowest resolution model.

BL How did you make the decision to do *Living Large*?

WW That was more of an experiment really, to see if we could sell expansions for *The Sims*. At the time there was a lot of user-generated content you could download for free, and because we understand how to program theses things to a deeper level we could add wholly new dynamics to the game.

BL Why did you pick that particular extension as the first one you did?

WW All the expansions have largely been driven by the players—by what we've seen them doing on *The Sims Exchange*, which is where they tell the stories of the game. We look at a lot of the stories and we look at where they're hitting brick walls. In their imaginations they want to be able to see the Sim do X or Y, and the game doesn't support it for whatever reason: there aren't the right dynamics or objects. So we looked at what players were telling in their stories on the website

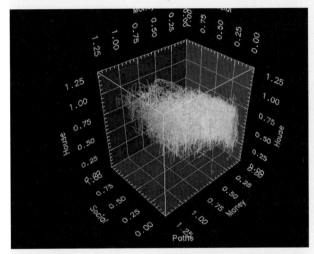

A 3-D representation of captured player data

and we found that early on that lot of people were pushing the game towards more of a fantasy world. They wanted to see kind of magical things or spooky things—popular genres like what we see in television. And so that was kind of the theme of *Living Large*.

BL Your design was driven by your fan community.

WW Yes, the direction of the expansion package. And in fact even the next version of *The Sims*.

BL Was the purpose of *The Sims Exchange* precisely to gather information from players that would inform future design?

WW Not really, that wasn't apparent until later. Again, that was kind of experimental, the whole storytelling aspect. People pair up with people

from another game, and they're telling stories to each other as they are playing the game, and the stories are hilarious.

BL And then you discovered that it was a resource for you?

WW Yeah, in a couple of ways actually. There's a point where players have had enough of the game and they want to go to the next level, so there's a meta-game they can play—they can compete on our website. They can rate stories, and there are competitions among the stories for each genre. We have about 50,000 stories now. Huge amounts! And some of them are amazingly detailed and really well written. They are like small novels, they aren't tiny little comic books—well, some of them are, but a lot of them are really deep, and certain people have a reputation for doing ongoing series.

BL So how does *Sims Online* relate to all this?

WW With *Sims Online*, we're trying to take a lot of the community dynamics that we've learned from *The Sims* off-line and reinterpret them in an online world. And we study the online community all the time. It's a very interesting community—it's over half female, which for an online game is totally different. And it turns out that a community of 55% females behaves very differently than a community that's 75% males. It's ongoing and we're still learning—we're capturing huge amounts of metrics in terms of the way people are playing the game. In fact, we're capturing very detailed information. I can tell you how many people are kissing more today than they were yesterday, or how that's correlated to other things.

On the story site, embedded in every story is the same game that the player created that story in, so anybody can read a story if they like the characters or the
house, whatever, you can download it and play it as a game. Embedded in every
saved game is a history file of how they played every Sim day, or certain key factors: how may friends, how many people in the house, how much money they
have, where they were focusing their efforts on. And so I've had interns studying
that data.

BL It's amazing that you can do that.

WW It turned out to be pretty easy. We have actually found some interesting
game-play patterns in *The Sims* just by looking at thousands of players and the

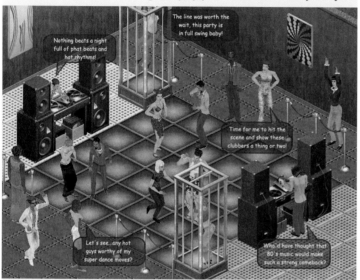

way they traverse the game space.
And so that's something that I think
is going to be critical to us going forward, the fact that we have these
endless tools that are fairly cheap to
embed. We need to bring down the
cost of that data mining and
increase the relevance of it. But still
the fact that we have analytical
design tools available to us now that
we didn't have five of ten years ago,
its tremendous.

BL Do you see yourself as putting
values into your games?

WW I'm actually much more interested in building a vessel that players put their own values in. With *Sim
City*, a lot of people on the message
boards would attack our liberal bias on the transportation level, and I thought that
was great, not because they didn't like the way our assumptions worked, but
because they had to be very clear about what their assumptions were. And *Sim
City* became a point of reference, a landmark, that they could then discuss: "Oh I
think this city is too liberal in the way taxes are done." Or "I don't think so, I think
it's realistic compared to where I live." Someone who's at odds with you model has
to crystalize what their own assumptions are. Then it becomes a forum where
people can come together and talk about what the issues are and how they feel
about them, how they relate to where they live and how their lives are experienced. Players can use the game as a tool for communicating with other people.

BL What else do you learn from these conversations?

WW You know, one thing that has been kind of ironic about *The Sims* is that a lot
of people play it for a while, like 4 to 6 hours, and they walk away thinking it's
very materialistic. But the ones that have played it for 20 hours realize that it's

the opposite. If you buy stuff in *The Sims*—every object has some sort of traits—it can go bad, or break, need maintenance, need to be watered. If you sit there and build a big mansion that's all full of stuff, without cheating, you realize that all these objects end up sucking up all you time, when all these objects had been promising to save you time. So they are all kind of time-bombs in a literal sense. And it's actually kind of a parody of consumerism, in which at some point your stuff takes over your life. But because it's fairly subtle, and you have to play the game for that long—half the player don't even see it's a parody. They think, "oh it's so consumerist."

BL That must be really interesting for you to watch people have their little light-bulb come on.

WW Yeah, and there are a couple of spots in the game where I've seen people have interesting revelations. One that a lot of people have where they're playing *The Sims* is, their Sim is sitting there—maybe he's playing on the computer and staying up too late—and they realize that he has to go to bed early or he will not do well at his job tomorrow. They're very concerned in getting the Sim to bed, and he's trying to stay up late, and they suddenly realize they're up at three in the morning to play this game, and that's when they realize they are taking better care of their Sim than they are of themselves. Some of the players have had that epiphany.

BL Before we stop I want you to tell me a story about your adventures on dating boards, why you did that and what you learned from it.

WW We do that stuff all the time. We were doing research for the *Sims Online*, and one thing we were very curious about was how people liked to build representation of themselves in their online space. Just by looking at all the different dating sites, it was interesting the different dimensions in which they have you describe yourself. There's something very compelling about glorifying yourself, period.

I've seen a lot of different dating sites, and some of them use different levels. My favorite one is *Hyper Match*—it has variable resolution descriptions, and it's actually very cool. First you can say where you are and then where your ideal spouse is, on each slider, and then also how you feel about it. So it's kind of multi-dimensional, with a cool little interface. They have kind of a first pass, which is maybe 20 questions—very first-level things—and then they have a second level that's much more detailed, and then they have a third level that's incredibly detailed. You go down to "hobbies" and one of the things on there is "I play *The Sims*." So you can go on there and make a very quick profile of yourself in five minutes, but you can come back there and every day add a little more detail on yourself. You get this very impressionistic sketch to begin with, and then the next day it becomes more of an illustration instead of just a charcoal sketch.

BL So did you meet any interesting women?

WW Well it got to the point where they were sending me these matches, and at that point I didn't want to lead anybody on...

BL Was your research on the dating boards really valuable in designing player profiles?

WW Yeah, and what it basically told us is that we wanted the players to be in control of how much information about themselves they put up. We didn't want to force them to use a fixed form. They can either go with our template, or go with whatever they want. Some people go with a poem they wrote, or their favorite quote. The very first thing you see when you open these profiles, and this turns out to be one of the largest degrees of segregation for the game, is age. It has a lot to do with Internet talk—are they spelling words out or are they writing "2U"? That immediately tells you whether they are under 25. The next level is what are they talking about. Some people want to have relationships, and then there are intelligent people who are wanting to have fun and role-play. You can tell that stuff very easily by reading their profiles. A couple of other things are interesting. They crystallize around certain alpha-numeric symbols that they use for sorting each other. The strongest early community that we had in the game, even before we had many communities forming, was gays and lesbians. And they were scattered all over the world, and they all sort of clicked "rainbow" for the type of symbol. So it was the "Rainbow Club" or the "Rainbow Casino." And eventually they ended up moving their lots and forming their own neighborhoods.

BL Some journalist called me a couple of days ago and asked me about *Sims Online* and what I thought of it, and I said I hadn't played it that much, but I wish players had made the Castro, and you're telling me they did. That's so cool.

WW Yeah, and it became the largest neighborhood we had in the game.

BL Are you ever present in the game as a player?

WW I was until just recently when I deleted that character because every time I logged on too many people knew who I was, but I had like 10 characters.

BL So you take a walk down the street in disguise every now and then?

WW All the time now.

BL Are you a girl?

WW I have one girl; I have about four males.

BL Do you think that's a really robust form of research, to be in there as a player?

WW I have about 10 close friends that I've made in the game, that know who I am. A lot of these people have a lot of visibility in some aspect of the community, and so they're kind of like my spies, and I can go in and ask them how it's going, what are the players like and what are they doing? In the metrics we have totally dispassionate statistics, and that's very different than going in and asking someone, "What have people really gotten into now?" What's the hot spot, or what's the cool activity, or what's the exciting thing to play or be talking about, or what's the thing people are really annoyed with? That's the type of thing you can't really get from metrics.

BL So there are three levels of research that happen. You've got your personal experience, communication with other players of the game, and then you've got the metrics.

WW Yeah, I think the metrics are giving us the very raw, formal description of the system, things that we can measure. How long are they spending where doing what? Going around talking to people and playing the game is where you actually get the motivation. Why did somebody do that? Why are they spending all their time here? Then you go up and talk to them and they'll explain their motivation."I really like doing this because of X, Y and Z," or "I really like going there because of that." What is the current flavor or mood? What is the collective interaction of all these people and their motivation? What does that add up to?

BL Do you get very involved in secondary research?

WW I start by thinking about what other fields have faced the design problem before, or what insights are going to come from psychology, or another design field, or even things like summer trends. How do you build a game out of that? What are the things that are actually turning over in the player's head? What type of mind-space is the player going to be in? Are they going to be dealing with the dynamics of shopping, or dating and flirting, or constructivism, and then what can inform me about that? The players, their mind-set, what motivates them—how cane we leverage every click the player makes in the game to something that they will find valuable? Are there some surprising things that happen? Or some creative things they make? There are so many different ways you can look at any single problem. Each of our design staff will take a central problem and try to look at it from five totally different perspectives. You're triangulating your design problem with all these different perspectives. So for the designer, the greatest skill I can imagine having is to take any single thing and look at it from as many different perspectives as you can.

Social Impact by Design
Tailoring Game Play for the Play-Styles of At-Risk Players
DARION RAPOZA

When my wife left me alone too long with her college roommate's husband and some video games, we decided to found a game company and build a game of our own. I'd use my background in drug abuse research to get the government to pay for our development of a drug abuse prevention game! When my daughter was born and I promised her I would make the world a better place for her to live in, the game became my life's mission, and the work began in earnest.

STEP ONE PURPOSE. CHECK.

STEP TWO BACKGROUND RESEARCH, STARTING IN THE LIBRARY.

Standing on the shoulders of giants beats re-inventing the wheel every time. I found that researchers had identified a number of empirically based, research-derived principles of effective interventions that were directly applicable to the design of a video game-based intervention. These included:

- Interventions should be "theory-based." Those designers who paid attention to the lessons learned by others who came before them were the most successful in preventing drug use.
- Effective interventions are delivered in an engaging, interactive format, rather than didactic one. To be effective as an intervention, a videogame must be fun!
- Changing attitudes (not just knowledge) should be an objective of the intervention.
- Developmentally appropriate information should be delivered. Children and adolescents are more interested in concrete information on current experience than they are in information about possible consequences in the distant future. Older adolescents and young adults may be less responsive to authoritative approaches than their younger counterparts, and show an increased reliance on trusted information from which they can draw their own conclusions and make their own behavior choices.
- Social resistance skills training should be employed.
- Concepts of self-efficacy should be reinforced. Self-efficacy for a specific health behavior is the belief that one is capable of carrying out the behavior successfully.
- Players should learn by doing, as opposed to learning by instruction or observation.
- "Scaffolding" should be used to build new skill sets to be acquired within the game. Learning is enhanced when recently acquired knowledge must

be applied as part of the performance of the immediately subsequent
learning experience.

• Games should include adequate coverage of the intervention material incorporated in the game, and ideally, provide for subsequent follow-up. Designing
socially beneficial games for re-playability permits the player to rehearse the
skills acquired in the game, and apply them in different situations. Planning
the release of game sequels would directly address the established need
for social interventions to have sufficient follow-up a year or more after the
initial intervention.

• The principles of operant psychology should be applied, particularly with
attention to conditioned reinforcement, conditioned avoidance, and generalization. Briefly, desired behaviors displayed in-game should be reinforced
with in-game rewards. For prevention efforts, engaging in targeted risky
behaviors should hamper progress towards meeting game objectives, conditioning future avoidance of these behaviors. Closely modeling situations the
player will be likely to face in real life increases the likelihood that lessons
learned in the game will generalize to real life and impact real-life behavior.
The implication is that truthfulness and integrity are critical.

• Avoid reliance on instructional learning. With instructional learning, first-
person experience is replaced with instructions (e.g., subjects learn vicari-
ously through direct observation, or by verbal, written, or some other form
of symbolic communication). Combining instruction in program content with
playing essentially unrelated game material could actually distract the user
from the material the intervention intends to convey [Malone 1980].

• The characters played by the user should be attractive and similar to the user.
Studies have shown that children are highly attentive to characters that are
very similar to them, and they feel validated to see those characters represented in mass media [Johnston and Ettema 1986, McDermott and Greenberg
1985]. Furthermore, children are more likely to imitate a model they perceive
as similar to themselves if the model is attractive [Oei and Baldwin 1992].
Examples include having avatars available that match the user's gender, race
and ethnic background, and are appealing but not improbable.

• Multi-component approaches should be used. The efficacy of the intervention
will be greater if the videogame intervention is an integral part of a larger
program; for example, the game could be supported with links to informa-
tional websites, "ask the experts" bulletin boards and monitored chat rooms,
or linked to materials and exercises for the classroom or at home, to be completed with parental involvement.

My library research also found a number of reports of theory-based
games having profoundly beneficial effects. For example, health behaviors in

childhood were significantly affected by computer games concerning asthma [Rubin et al. 1986, Yawn et al. 2000, Bartholomew et al. 2000, Homer et al. 2000] and diabetes [Grossman 1987, Lieberman 1998]. In each case the studies reported as much as a 70% reduction in emergency room visits when comparing the videogame plus-physician instruction to physician instruction alone.

To fill in the gaps that I was certain couldn't be filled in by reading the literature I did some first-hand research. I played games. Many, many games, from all the different genres I could identify. Finally, I asked a lot of questions, talking to gamers, game designers, venture capitalists, publishers, parents, teachers and preventionists. The take-home messages I got were that:

- If the game were too "in your face" or "preachy" about drugs, it would be rejected by teens and fail, period.
- There needs to be a "game reason" to use drugs, or the intervention portion of the game design would be avoided.
- The game could not require players to use drugs. Forcing a player to use drugs would be antithetical to the objective of the intervention as well as bad game design.
- Gamers and publishers (among others) were skeptical that a drug prevention game would sell, and wondered how it could be marketed.
- Interventionists were concerned that knowing that the game was intended as an intervention could lead to reactance (rejection of the message).

STEP THREE CONCEPTUALIZE A MODEL.

I saw that to date, all the video-game-based interventions had been single-player games. One particularly promising area is the design of socially beneficial, massively multiplayer online role-playing games (MMORPGs). MMORPGs permit the application of theories relating to social influences on behavior, which is impossible in single-player games because they lack player-player interaction. Using MMORPGs enables the design of interventions based on social learning theory (which holds most behavior is determined by learning from peers), social control theory (behavior is controlled by peer leaders and social norms), and peer cluster theory (behavior is most heavily influenced by one's closest associates; i.e., friends). Furthermore, with their large player bases, MMORPGs would enable intervention designs intended to reach specific player sub-populations. Similar approaches have proven to be effective in the drug rehabilitation clinic, suggesting they may also prove effective in the videogame milieu [Conrod et al. 2000].

I decided to use a stealth approach in delivering the drug intervention content because: publishers had tended to balk at the idea of a "drug intervention game," but had no concerns about a game with drugs in it that (bonus!) casts them in a negative light. Interventionists felt that being too direct might invoke resistance, and players and game designers agreed that drug use had to be optional anyway. Therefore, to keep the drug intervention profile to a minimum, my objectives were to differentially deliver intervention content to those players at greatest risk for substance abuse, and to tailor intervention content for and selectively deliver it to specific player sub-populations, based on their personality characteristics.

The stealth part was easy. I arrived at a design in which I crafted the classic RPG (Role-Playing Game) Attributes and Skills system to model human attributes for which the biological bases are well understood, and game-relevant skills that are performed at a level which is in-part dependent upon the current level of the appropriate attribute(s). For example, I replaced the standard "intelligence" and "wisdom" attributes with short-term memory, long-term memory, memory consolidation, focus and emotional intelligence; and I discarded "charisma," introducing instead confidence and physical attractiveness. Drug effects are realistically portrayed within the game, directly impacting the attributes/physiological systems in a dose-dependent manner and consequently affecting skill performance level just as they do in real life. For instance, performance of one's "computer hacking" skill, which relies, in part, on short-term memory and focus, would be impaired under the influence of marijuana. Where human physiology is modeled more directly through the user interface (UI), appropriate drug effects are illustrated through the UI as well (e.g., loss of motor control due to alcohol intoxication is modeled by impairing the user's control of their character's movement through the game environment, etc.). Where drug effects were not easily modeled through the standard user interface or the attributes and skills system, new game mechanics were designed. For example, to model compulsive drug seeking in addiction, pop-up messages appear (e.g., "You sure could use a cigarette about now") and must be responded to in order to continue game play. To model the chance of stroke (etc.) with stimulant (etc.) use, there's a small chance of death (also modeled on real-life data) with each use of the drug.

Since scare tactics or a one-sided "preachy" approach would be ineffective, positive effects of drug use are also illustrated, such as the suppression of natural hand tremor by low doses of alcohol improving accuracy with long-range hand held weapons, or the modest increase in stamina obtained with stimulants (which is really only useful in marathons). I included a "psyche meter" in the display to indicate the mood altering effects of drugs, which also reflects success or failure in reaching game objectives. This permits the realistic representation of the positive mood-altering effects of drugs without providing an unnatural "game reward" for their use, as well as the illustration of negative mood swings during recovery.

I felt that the game mechanics I had created could fully support a typical MMORPG design while transparently providing the player who learns them with a framework for understanding the short-term effects and long-term consequences of drug abuse.

When I turned to content design, some design choices were simpler than others. The genre had to be current day science fiction. Crack and roofies just don't fit in a fantasy realm with elves and goblins. Today's street drugs would be

out of context in the past, and probably in the future as well. As a socially conscious game, current concerns about videogame-induced violence had to be taken
into account. The sci-fi genre permits the inclusion of non-human (robotic) com-
batants for lethal combat, and the design of a variety of non-lethal combat
weapons for combat with humanoids. The player-characters are cadets, hand-
picked for the space academy—achievers, just a bit older and more accomplished
than the target audience, credible role models in the game's sci-fi setting. Game
advancement comes through study, with courses (and later, posts, apprenticeships, etc.) selected in advance by the player. Skills are gained over time, and
advancement is influenced by intervening game play (anything from ongoing
alcohol use impairing memory consolidation and learning to earning and securing
the services of a tutor to speed skill acquisition). Initial drug offers come not from
seedy strangers hanging out on the corner, but peers—other cadets—such as on
the occasion of events to be celebrated: a cigar to commemorate graduation, a
few beers to celebrate a well-played prank, a joint after the successful completion
of a mission, etc. Peer pressure in these circumstances *is* a real game concern, as
non-player characters remember how you respond to them and adjust their
future interactions with you accordingly. So far, so good. But how would I selectively target those players most at risk for substance abuse, and what types of
game design would work best for them?

The answers were not yet in the literature, but there was sufficient background to base a rationale for a research study on. I drew on Bartle's classic analysis of player types, Yee's factor analysis of why people play MMORPGs, and
Zukerman's Sensation Seeking Scale. Richard Bartle analyzed the behavior of
players within multi-user games, and concluded that play-styles cluster into four
characteristic types: achiever, explorer, socializer, and imposer or "player-killer"
[Bartle 2003]. Achievers set themselves in game-related goals and vigorously set
out to achieve them. Explorers set out to learn everything they can about the virtual world, from mapping out the virtual geography, to un-masking the algorithms
that control interactions with objects within the game (i.e., "physics"). Socializers
make maximum use of the game's communication facilities, and apply the role-
playing that the game engenders as a context in which to converse (and otherwise
interact) with their fellow players. Imposers, or Player Killers (PKers), to quote
Bartle, "…use the tools provided by the game to cause distress to (or, in rare circumstances, to help) other players. Where permitted, this usually involves acquir-
ing some weapon and applying it enthusiastically to the persona of another player
in the game world." The game developer community at-large has widely embraced
this terminology (although the nomenclature remains fluid), but has sub-divided
the player-killer category to include "Player-Killers" (unfortunately there was no
change in terminology), who add to the enjoyment of the game by the player community at-large by taking on the roles of villains or who simply enjoy brawling
with each other, and "Grief Players" (as the term will be used in this chapter),

whose apparent motivation is to cause as much distress and frustration in other *players* as possible, harassing and killing characters that are no match for them, spewing taunts and vituperations targeting players (as opposed to the character), and generally making it difficult for others to enjoy or play the game.

While Bartle's model was derived from observation and speculation, Nicholas Yee used empirical data to build a model of the different motivations of why people play MMORPGs [Yee 1, Yee 2 2002]. Yee's findings supported the hypothesis that the different play-style motivation factors (Relationship, Immersion, Grief, Achievement, and Leadership) correlate with different real-life personality traits, as assessed using validated measures of personality constructs. These personality traits include: Neuroticism, Extraversion, Openness, Agreeableness and Conscientiousness. Yee also found support for the existence of three of Bartle's four player types (PKr/grief, achiever/achievement, and socializer/relationship), albeit with some modification, and if the "explorer" type is defined as exploring the game environment (as opposed to rule sets), it may be validated by the immersion factor Yee identified. Among his other findings, Yee reported that players who scored high on his "grief" motivation scale also scored low on the Agreeableness personality scale and tended to be younger players.

When taken into account, each of these putative play-styles has different implications for the optimal design of a game. Achievers might best be reached by clear demonstrations that drug use by themselves, their companions, or members of a community to which they belong hinders their advancement within the game. Socializers may constitute one population that *would* respond well to observational learning. Renowned characters within the game suffering negative consequences from substance abuse could provide "the grist for the mill" for the socializers. Designing the game to encourage the formation of play groups, guilds, clans, etc., and ensuring that the group's stature can be impacted by the drug use of any individual member might facilitate drug-avoidance learning for achievers and socializers. Explorers might be particularly interested in learning about the medical consequences of drug abuse, and with proper in-game prompts, might be motivated to "read-up" on these effects in the game manual or in in-game facilities, such as a medical library or computer. They could then apply their knowledge when, by design, the situation arises, such as by recognizing and seeking medical attention for another character who has overdosed. On the other hand, players who express a high degree of immersion motivation in Yee's analysis (who might also be termed "explorers") may be particularly responsive to "learning by doing": the preferred approach under the theory of reasoned action—and the *opposite* of the approach theory would have suggested for Bartle's explorer type. Player Killers turned out to be the population of greatest interest. I found good reason in the research literature to hypothesize that they were the players the intervention should target most, as well as empirical evidence that led me to predict what type of designs would work best with them.

Certain personality traits have been demonstrated to be risk factors for or protective factors against a variety of real-life risky behaviors. The Sensation Seeking Scale (SSS) is an extremely well validated survey instrument the constructs of which have been cross-validated with multiple other personality measurement scales. Sensation seekers need varied, novel and complex sensations and experiences to maintain an optimal level of arousal. They are presumed to have optimal arousal levels that are greater than that of non-sensation seekers, to become bored and nonresponsive more quickly than most other persons when faced with repetitive experiences, and to be more sensitive to internal sensations and less conforming to external constraints than others. High SSS individuals tend to be dominant, impulsive, nonconforming type extroverts, as opposed to good-natured, cooperative, adaptable, attentive, trustful, warm-hearted extroverts. Sensation seeking scores correlate negatively with age. There appears to be a biological basis for sensation seeking [see Harrington and Donohew 1997]. High sensation seekers have lower levels of platelet MAO and higher levels of testosterone. Polymorphism in exon III for the Dopamine D4 neurotransmitter receptor is associated with the SSS-related personality trait of novelty seeking. Not surprisingly, sensation seekers have been found to prefer complex over simple designs, and prefer and pay greater attention to commercial messages with high sensation value-message characteristics defined as novelty, complexity, intensity, ambiguity, unconventionality, suspense, fast pace and emotionality. The SSS as well as 3 of its 4 sub-scales correlates strongly with substance abuse.

A number of similarities are apparent between high sensation seekers, PKs, and players with high "Grief Motivations." The "desire to engage in...activities with elements of speed or danger," the "gravitation to an unconventional lifestyle and a resistance to irrational authority and conformity," and the "dominant, impulsive, nonconforming type of extroversion"—validated characterizations of high sensation seekers would all seem to be an equally apt description of Bartle's PKs, particularly of the subset of "grief players" as defined in this chapter. Also, it's possible that grief players are particularly susceptible to boredom in the game, leading them to generate their own excitement through PKing activity. In a similar vein, grief motivation correlated negatively with agreeableness in Yee's factor analysis. While sensation seeking is higher in younger individuals, Yee found grief motivation to be higher in younger players, who also were more likely to report wanting to be thought of as "more powerful," or "evil."

Based upon the observation of multiple similarities between sensation-seekers and PKs, I hypothesize that PKs are high sensation-seekers. Furthermore, I propose that as sensation seeking is a known, powerful predictive indicator for future experimentation with drugs [Zukerman et al. 1972], PKs may be the most appropriate targets for drug interventions embedded in a game. Targeting PKs might be done geographically, in game designs where PKing is only permitted in certain areas. It should also be done by PK specific design, where PKs that necessarily have to interact with to proceed in the game (now that they are outlaws) will have more, targeted drug intervention-related design. It should be done user control, where players must identify themselves to the system as PKs before they can kill and be killed (and in so doing the world might respond differently to them, including being approached more often by drug users, dealers, etc.), or even operationally (their "conscience" won't allow them to attack another human except in self-defense, except under the influence of drugs)—a model with actual medical validity, giving PKs, and only PKs, a "game reason" to use drugs. High sensation seekers respond more positively to drug abuse prevention messages designed specifically for them [Harrington and Donohew 1997], suggesting that they might also respond more positively to game design created specifically for them. As with other messages that speak well to high sensation seekers, a game design that targets them should be novel, fast-paced, non-repeating, complex, intense and unconventional; incorporate ambiguity & suspense; and be emotional.

STEP FOUR FORMULATE AND TEST HYPOTHESES.

I'm currently developing a grant proposal to empirically study whether sensation seeking correlates with a preference for PK/Grief play-styles. I'm also building a prototype of the intervention game that includes each of the approaches I've discussed. I'll start the iterative design process by surveying play testers and correlating their play-styles with how well they liked each intervention approach I incorporated into the game. Two experimental groups will either be informed or uninformed as to the game's purpose to prevent drug use, to test the publisher's and interventionist's fears about being too forthright. With solid research and a little luck, I may just make good on a certain promise I plan to keep.

Researching
America's Army

MARGARET DAVIS, RUSSELL SHILLING, ALEX MAYBERRY,
PHILLIP BOSSANT, JESSE MCCREE, SCOTT DOSSETT,
CHRISTIAN BUHL, CHRISTOPHER CHANG, EVAN CHAMPLIN,
TRAVIS WIGLESWORTH AND MICHAEL ZYDA

During the Vietnam war, the U.S. military suffered a loss of prestige among youth from which they could never quite recover. A generation that had grown up admiring WWII heroes had begun to see the armed services as, at best, an embarrassment, and at worst, the enemy. Although recruiters tried on a number of appeals over the last thirty years "Be All You Can Be," "Get an Edge on Life," "An Army of One," etc.), these campaigns failed to resonate with their audience because they no longer spoke the language of the young. Until recently, enlistment fell short of annual goals.

The horrors of the 9/11 attack raised national consciousness that there really are bad guys and they really are out to get us. The liberation of Iraq, with its kick-ass technology and compassionate commandos, did much to prick curiosity about the work and ethos of national defense. The videogame *America's Army* (*AA*) was constructed to field such curiosity. While work on the game began well before 9/11, its timing as a mediator of Army culture to game-playing teens has been ideal. The integrity displayed by American soldiers in the deserts and cities of Iraq is explicated in the game (and indeed is central to the plot), and the dangerous missions and cool gear so beloved of young men are represented with authority and gusto. With *AA*, the Army again speaks to teens in their native tongue.

The project seemed unlikely. That the Army would issue a videogame offering free, networked, no-cookies play online for all comers was dubious; but if so, one could only expect—face it—a stodgy misfire, outdated months, if not years, before release. So when *AA* debuted as a world-class contender at E3 2002—sharp, immersive, informative, exciting—it was dissonance inducing. *America's Army's* was a surprise attack worthy of any mission in the game.

As a product of the behemoth that brought you thousand-dollar toilet seats, it might be supposed that *AA* was researched exhaustively in conception and choked with money and personnel in gestation, and struggles today against zealous over-protectionism. Not so. The idea came to a West Point instructor, Colonel Casey Wardynski, at a cocktail party: why not build a video game to help recruitment? Kids don't know beans about the Army anymore; why not educate them in a way they'll enjoy, allowing those who might be interested to identify themselves?

At the Naval Postgraduate School in Monterey, California, a computer scientist was thinking the same thing. Professor Michael Zyda (zyda@movesinstitute.org) had been up to his elbows in digital graphics for a couple of decades, knew everyone in the military, industry and academia. He had organized the MOVES Institute for modeling, virtual environments and simulation in response to a National Research Council call to arms and was avid for worthy projects. An NPS graduate connected them, the two agreed it could (and should) be done, and they found funding.

Was it hard to convince the brass? Not really. Nor was much demographic research required. Everyone knows young men ages 18 to 24 play videogames and that they have to learn a lot in order to play them successfully. Use of the military as a gaming premise was tried and true, having been explored by industry for years. No need to reinvent the wheel, but only to hire master wheelwrights.

The Army did have a requirement: that the game be played absolutely straight, as an honest representation of the service, especially regarding ethics, codes of conduct, and professional expectations, and extending to accurate depiction of hierarchy, missions, weapons, equipment, uniforms, settings, discipline, tactics, procedure—in short, this was to be a game a platoon sergeant could play without wincing.

Drop your weapons. A combat brigade bursts from a Stryker in the AA online game.

This square shooting obviated the usual marketing flurries. For one thing, the goal was modest: not persuasion, but education; the game didn't have to part a fool and his money, it had merely to be played. Second, *AA* was self-defining—that is, if a game were to give the player the experience of performing an infantryman's job, it would be a first-person shooter with team play based on real missions (themselves inherently dramatic and easily adaptable), in which the primary design constraints are training prerequisites, the Army's code of conduct (including consequences for infraction), and a teen rating.

All parties understood that setting the right tone was key to avoiding public-relations disaster. The Army could not be perceived as celebrating trigger-happy Rambos, nor, by downplaying lethal force, be guilty of deceit and hypocrisy; must not pander to the testosterone of the demographic, yet must keep teens engaged; must avoid charges of jingoism, mesmerism, cynicism, cliché, exploitation of vulnerable youth, incitement to violence, or a hundred other incorrectnesses. In light of these constraints, the Army, having stated their objectives, had to invest a great deal of trust in the sincerity and comprehension of the ragtag crew building *AA*. One postmodern excess and the game was up.

The technical front was assigned to Zyda, and a team was scouted. Here *AA* hit on very good fortune. Alex Mayberry, tapped for creative director (and subsequently executive producer), was the disaffected veteran of eight years in the industry. He knew how games were built and wanted to build them better; towards that end he handpicked a team as much for collaborative attitude as competency (see the roster at www.movesinstitute.org/team). The Army supplied Lt. Colonel George Juntiff as design consultant, an onsite proofreader for both particulars and look and feel, and made soldiers available for interview. The MOVES Institute contributed a raft of master's and doctoral students (all of them military officers), whose emergent research, including streamlined graphics algorithms and analysis of the psychological dynamics of immersion, was piped into the game.

Work began as Wardynski and the designers roughed out the contents of the levels. The activities agreed upon were at once authentic, technically feasible and fun—or made fun. Take the radio-tower mission: yes, rangers would disable the tower in real life, but they might do that by blowing it up—which would be over too quickly in a game. Instead *AA* requires the player to find friendlies, take down terrorists, and safeguard foreign-aid workers till the communications people can effect a takeover.

Missions the gamers thought exciting but the Army judged irregular were rejected, and elements the Army wanted but the team couldn't build to their own satisfaction were shelved for later. For example, while a parachute jump is in the game, a beach landing is not, because recreating water's splash and flow is extremely hardware-intensive. Similarly, ropes used dynamically in knotting and casting are currently more trouble than they're worth. But *AA* is continually under improvement and expansion. As the game engine evolves and consumer equipment improves, it will be possible to animate the Strykers and other vehicles that players can presently climb into and sight and shoot from; for now, they would move too slowly, look too crude, and require too vast a background.

Top: Special forces soldier on CSAR (combat search and rescue) mission.
Bottom: Medic training–all play and no work makes Jack a bad soldier.

The triumph of *AA* is that it manages to grip an action-oriented audience while insisting on a formal, educative structure. As every general started with boot camp, so also in *AA* you earn access to online play by paying your dues in basic training (thus experiencing the Army's merit-based promotion) and qualify for good stuff like marksman, airborne and medic through advanced classes. Basic teaches you to think Army-style (forget shooting your drill instructor) and provides a handy space for learning how to maneuver before joining online play. The very pace of play, which is deliberate compared with other shooters, reminds the player that the Army proper is *not* a game.

Rifle-range production progresses from photograph to screen.
Top: Not just any rifle range: the prepared fighting position for firing-point nine on red-range one at Ft. Benning, Georgia.
Middle: The same view reconstructed in the game editor. The firing position is modeled with foxhole cover removed.
Bottom: The model imported into the editor and skinned. The white arrowheads are movie projector icons, used to cast shadows for trees. They are invisible during play.

To convey Army core values (loyalty, duty, respect, selfless service, honor, integrity and personal courage), *AA* rewards soldierly behavior and penalizes rotten eggs. This works out in practical ways. In basic training, for example, you can opt to become a combat lifesaver. Doing so reflects duty and selfless service, so you get points and expanded opportunities for going through training. Out on mission, your buddy collapses in front of you. You can attend him, which earns points for loyalty and honor, or keep running, which scrubs points. If you do stop, you become a target yourself, which takes courage, and if you're hit, your health will suffer, so you need the integrity to inform your actions with sound judgment. Doing your duty *and* saving both your lives wins the most points. Just like in combat.

For the first release (July 2002), 10 levels were agreed on and a shopping list drawn. Over the two years beginning in May 2000, the team visited nineteen Army posts, including Ft. Benning (for the rifle range), Ft. Lewis (weapons), and Ft. Polk (vehicles and house-clearing operations). Besides photographing modeling and texture referents, shooting motion-capture video for animations, and recording thousands of sound effects, the team jumped from towers, submitted to dog attacks, even rode a Blackhawk helicopter at 3 a.m., watching the fireworks as live shells barraged the terrain below. These first-person encounters gave the team an enthusiasm and surefootedness that mere stock footage and cold data could not provide.

Back home, the artists sorted through stills and b-roll, posting the likeliest to the network for perusal by the modelers and level designers. Virtual sets, consisting both of Army-post reproductions and fabricated hamlets and landscapes—together with hundreds of common and military assets—were built to translate reality into gaming levels.

Character modeling began with the assumption that the player will always see himself and his team as American soldiers and his opponents as terrorists. He can choose from three skin tones (with vaguely concomitant facial features), but otherwise he's a young, midsized man, as is his generic and randomly-complexioned enemy. As roles for women are added to the game, so also will female avatars. Players distinguish each other by dress, gear and weapons: the Americans in regulation uniforms, rucksacks, and helmets, the terrorists in black, drab, or tiger stripe, with perhaps bandannas or caps. Both sides wear the paraphernalia appropriate to their weapons and combat roles—detail that is lost on many players, but which adds depth for the observant.

Extensive, continually updated weaponry is an *AA* distinction. Modeled from high-res orthographic shots with as much refinement as a 2,000-polygon budget permits, weapons are employed logically and strategically; a grenadier who tried to conduct himself like a sniper would suffer decreased combat effectiveness, as would a sniper shooting on the run. To ensure equal advantage, much investigation went into matching up rival weapons. Where the Americans employ M-16 assault rifles, for example, the enemy carries AK-47s, the nearest real-world equivalent, with the AK-47's higher caliber and firing rate duly reflected. You can capture and fire enemy weapons, which results in twisty visuals: if you drop your M-16, the other side sees you drop an AK-47, and if they pick up your weapon, they see it as an AK-47 and you see it as an M-16 that fires like an AK-47. This isn't a bug, but a conundrum proceeding from the premise that though you've captured a weapon with a faster firing rate, all your weapons will look American to you.

For animations, soldiers were rigged with motion-capture sensors and filmed enacting common operations. Procedures such as erecting a bipod or pulling and throwing grenades were performed strictly according to doctrine. The resulting sequences are truly tutorial—in fact, they've been used as such at West Point. Where absolute adherence to reality would bog down the game (e.g., if running or jam-clearing were depicted at true speed), animators relied on cropping and streamlining to reconcile veracity with the need to sustain excitement, stepping frame-by-frame through motion-capture video to identify key postures and weed out intermediate movement, allowing the eye to jump as with a flipbook. Artificial limitations on avatar range of motion were sometimes imposed to keep actions onscreen. In a reloading animation, for instance, the weapon is held at chest level (rather than dropping to midsection) and the hands stay clear of the player's view. In such cases, the illusion of free and fluid sweep depends on confinement and restraint.

Top: The range as seen in the game. Note that in the previous screenshots the red targets were lying behind black mounds. The script pops them up at the appropriate time. Bottom: Raw motion-capture video of a soldier stalking with an M-16.

Augmenting his MOVES research in auditory psychophysics with extensive consultation with entertainment's top audio designers and engineers, *AA* sound designer (and Navy lieutenant commander) Russell Shilling engineered the complex, multilayered sound that supports the game's immersive punch.

To determine the importance of audio in evoking emotion within videogames and simulations, Shilling's graduate students conducted research in three areas, with measures relying on objective rather than subject observations of performance enhancement. First, to ascertain the direct role of sound in creating presence and emotion, physiological responses (heart rate, respiration, electrodermal response, etc.) were measured [Scorgie and Sanders 2002]. Auditory task analyses determined what sounds were requisite in the videogame for a realistic experience to occur [Greenwald 2002]. Finally, it was shown that by heightening emotional aspects of game play, performance on memory tasks is enhanced [Ulate 2002]. To determine both the role audio plays in evoking emotion within videogames and the relationship of emotional arousal to memory and learning, Shilling's master's students measured adrenaline levels and temperature response during gameplay with and without sound, and studied house-clearing experts as they conducted virtual clearings in *AA*, noting their evaluations of the game's auditory cues as compared to to those in real-world execution of the task and determining which sounds and utterances were key.

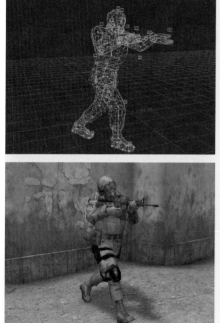

Top: Editing the data in the motion-capture editor. Bottom: All dressed up and somewhere to go: skinned, equipped, and animated online.

Professional techniques for sound mixing and enhancement were brought to bear, with sound effects, weapons foley, and ambient sounds custom recorded or obtained from professional libraries. Weapons animations, for example, are accompanied by detailed and accurate audio representations enhanced for visceral impact and perceived realism. Footsteps, bullet impacts, particle effects, grenades and shell casings are accorded texture-specific impact noises and room acoustics are represented using Creative Lab's EAX 3.0 technology.

In a typical *AA* firefight, bullets whiz and crack by the player's ear, slam into the wall behind, and tinkle concrete and glass fragments at his feet. The player hears his shell casings thunk off the wooden door-frame behind him and ping the concrete floor. Meanwhile, to the clatter of a nearby reload, the enemy creaks across a steel catwalk overhead. The player hears a flash-bang grenade scud off the floor behind him just before being incapacitated by the roar and ring of tinnitus in his ears. This scrupulous audio won the game prestigious Dolby Digital 5.1 Surround Certification and approbation from industry reviewers.

In the realm of programming, realism was pursued through careful attention to game physics. When shooting, for example, the weapon sways slightly with the avatar's breathing, recoils on discharge, and occasionally jams. Bullets penetrate or ricochet depending on the makeup of the target (e.g., wood, adobe, dirt, glass or steel), distance from target, and the weapon's caliber, type and firing velocity. The target's composition also determines depth of penetration and distance and angle of reflection. For naturalism, the spray patterns produced by multiple shots are randomized within a logical ambit so as to spread believably.

Realistic physics inevitably influence players' decision-making. For instance, because ricochets tend to travel along vertical surfaces, players learn to resist hugging walls if they want to stay healthy and combat-effective, and they don't detonate a blinding, deafening flashbang at close range if they value seeing and hearing. While it's faster and more fun to charge around shooting from the hip, *AA* gives big points for zooming in and aiming through the sights and rewards shooting from stable postures such as crouched and prone. As on the battlefield, friendly fire is an inevitable reality, and you can't escape its penalties.

Mortal flesh can expire quickly in *AA*. If you're shot, 50% of your health is at risk: 25% up front plus another 25% that will drain away without medical help. If you are patched up, your combat effectiveness rises, because presumably you can still shoot.

Where reality is compromised, it's generally where literalness would give poor returns next to the engineering and byte-grinding involved. For example, straight vectors substitute for accurate ballistics in the case of fast-firing weapons like the M-16, where the eye can't follow bullet trajectories anyway; but for grenade launchers and other big, slow ammo, virtual gravity is switched on to create accurate flight paths, and shooters must aim accordingly. Similarly, sound fidelity loses out in the case of shellfire from a Stryker: whereas from inside the real thing you can't hear the gun's report, in the game, a big bang is just plain obligatory, and therefore dubbed in.

Because terrain datasets in the game were larger than normally supported by the Epic engine, extensive research relating to terrain-rendering algorithms was conducted—but these algorithms were found unsuitable for the system due to hardware requirements, task limitation or inefficient memory management [Greenwald 2002]. These limitations were addressed by modifying the original terrain algorithm to include multiple levels of detail for complex terrain. This method raised new issues with projected textures, transparent textures and multi-resolution rendering; to address these concerns, the implementation technique includes resolutions to address them specifically. The Epic world editor was also modified to give world designers control of these details.

Performance tests showed that this terrain level of detail system significantly improved display times, allowing greater terrain complexity while maintaining interactive frame rates. Rendering times in environments with small terrains improved almost forty percent, while large complex terrain environments (km2 at 1m resolution) fared even better.

As the project progressed, the Army realized the game had the potential for a much larger scope than originally conceived, including use of helicopters. Unfortunately, third-person perspective helicopter physics were not included in the game engine nor *AA*'s initial design. MOVES thesis students employed Unrealscript to design a physics system that interfaces with the Unreal engine and interpolates smoothly among physics states within the bounds of helicopter capabilities and the appearance of realism [Perkins 2002]. In testing, 53% of subjects thought the helicopter physics were very or totally realistic, and 72% found them better than those on commercial graphics systems. In a follow-up study, 86% of participants found the helicopter physics equal to or better than those of a high-quality commercial 3D helicopter.

Like all games, *AA* suffers its share of soreheads and hackers among the players. To deal with bad behavior, the Army contracts HomeLan for round-the-clock server-administration coverage, through which users can file complaints and call server admins to enforce civility. Within the game, major offenses such as shooting civilian targets or your own team, or in some cases destroying an objective you are charged to defend, trigger a non-negotiable sentence to Ft. Leavenworth. The *AA* programmers originally combatted hackers and cheaters themselves, but the next update will unleash Punkbusters software to continuously detect hacked game files and lock offenders out.

AA's insistence on getting the Army right implies unlimited potential for expansion as the game evolves and occupations and missions accumulate. The game's fan sites [www.americasArmy.com/community.php] reveal diverse interest in both the game per se and as it relates to the real Army, an encouraging sign that an ever-wider range of individuals will sign on in future releases. The online community *AA* has achieved will provide future opportunities for social scientists to explore dimensions of individual and social behavior characteristic of games like *AA* and to study correlations between play, recruitment and Army career success; but note that such studies are subject to widely accepted ethical safeguards to privacy. *AA* sets no cookies and doesn't pry.

Respect

Talk to the team, and you'll soon uncover their deep respect for the men they encountered in making the game. As art director Phillip Bossant put it, "I got to know these guys. More and more my motivation for excellence is to honor them and the job they do. Guys helped us, gave us their time, who are now dead. The game is our tribute to them."

Besides adrenalinated reviews and features, *America's Army: Operations* continues to collect trophies, including Action Vault's *Debut Game of the Year*, *Surprise of the Year*, and honorable-mention *Multiplayer Game of the Year*; Frictionless Insight's *Best Business Model (Developer) at E3;* IGN *Editors' Choice Award* for first-person shooters; IGN's *Biggest Surprise of E3;* Gamespy's *Best PC Action Game* runner-up; Penny Arcade's *Best Misappropriation of Taxpayer Dollars Ever;* Wargamers *Best of Show*, first-person/tactical shooters; Well-Rounded Entertainment's *Best of E3 2002;* DoubleClick's Insight Awards, honorable mention, *Best Multi-Channel Marketing Campaign;* Academy of Interactive Arts and Sciences, finalist, *PC First Person Action Game of the Year;* and Computer Gaming World's *Editors' Choice*.

A Virtual Walk on the Moon

Cyberspace meets Outerspace:

Experimental Design Research in a New Medium

BRUCE DAMER

When a new medium is born, there is a period of *ad hoc* research carried out as a series of experiments that fill the medium's available creative envelope. Following the invention of the movie camera, for example, the group of experimentalists in that medium included entrepreneurs, artists, hobbyists, industrialists and scientists [Robinson 1997]. When we look back on the film projects of the 1890s to early 1900s we are surprised by the variety and often the naïveté of the efforts.

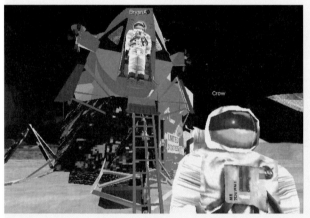

In the 1970s through the 1990s successive generations of computer workstations brought the concept of real time 2D and then 3D graphical interfaces to reality [Daimaru 2001]. Then, in May 1992, the game *Wolfenstein 3D* showed that 3D real-time graphics could bring immersive spaces to an ordinary consumer computer. In May of 1995 a San Francisco startup company, Worlds Incorporated, introduced a networked 3D world featuring a space station with players moving about in digital personae called "avatars" [Damer 1997]. Thus began a veritable "Cambrian explosion" of experimentation within the medium of networked virtual worlds. Around this time I co-founded a not-for-profit community organization called the Contact Consortium to be a home for that experimentation.

A prime directive of the Consortium was to establish a series of best practices for the creation of successful and engaging online events in graphical cyberspaces. A full recounting of the Consortium members' experiments can be found at the organization's web site www.ccon.org, but here we will recount the tale of just one of these events, the Virtual Walk on the Moon, held on July 20th, 1999, precisely thirty years after Neil Armstrong's first steps on the moon. The reason that this particular event merits a book chapter is that I felt that for the first time we had achieved a truly engaging online event and finally understood the best practices behind that success. Given the popularity of multiplayer online gaming and other virtual worlds in Cyberspace, these practices are increasingly important to understand.

Computers as Low-Resolution Theater, Virtual Worlds in the 1990s

Question: How do you re-create one of the most inspiring events in human history within the rough-hewn medium of polygonal low-resolution worlds delivered through tenuous net connections onto a small screen? The answer: Make up for all the shortcomings by having a powerful actor tell a good story. Of course, there is more to it than that, as Brenda Laurel points out in *Computers as Theatre* [Laurel 1991]. In the keyhole reality of the first online virtual worlds, how can a true sense of "being there" be achieved? Read on!

STEP 1 SEEKING THE PERFECT ACTOR

It is March 1st, 1999 and I rose at dawn from my sleeping spot amongst the scrub in the desert of the Rosamond Dry Lake near Edwards Air Force Base, the legendary proving grounds of the first supersonic jets. I had made it to the rollout of the Rotary Rocket, a private enterprise effort to create an affordable pathway to space. I had come to the desert to find an astronaut to be an actor in a pioneering online event, a synthesis of Cyberspace and Outerspace, a Virtual Walk on the Moon.

I was brought here through the hard work of University of Cincinnati professor Benjamin Britton and his team who built the Moon world, an online "mutual reality" art installation, which is fully described at the CERHAS Moon web site www.moon.uc.edu/. Ben needed an event to be held in his virtual world installa-

tion at the exact moment of the anniversary, July 20th 1999 and I had taken up his challenge.

Now back to the desert, where speeches were made and the prototype rocket rolled out of the hanger to the sounds of Also Sprach Zarathustra. In the crowd I was introduced to Lee Weaver and just as he was telling me how he worked with Pete Conrad to effect the rescue of the Skylab space station in 1973 up walked the very man, Pete Conrad.

Pete's handshake held the strength and sureness of a man who had piloted Apollo XII's Lunar Module (LM) to a pinpoint landing in late 1969. After he finished describing how he had set down the Apollo XII LM "like a baby" I interjected that a group of us hoped to reenact the moon landing come July 20th—in Cyberspace—and did he know of anyone from the Apollo corps who would like to be the guiding figure for the event? Pete was quick to beg off the job, claiming a low level of nerdliness, while saying "Neil probably wouldn't do that, he's too private." He thought for a second

Left: Crowds gather around the Rocket.
Right: Pete Conrad prior to Apollo IX mission, Photo courtesy NASA.

more and then said "Rusty, Rusty Schweickart, he would do that kind of thing." I thanked Pete and he moved off into the crowd.

Russell Schweickart, was born in 1935 in Neptune, New Jersey and had a career as a fighter pilot and research scientist before being selected by NASA in 1963. Rusty, as he was known all his life (his name fitting well his shock of red hair), served as lunar module pilot for Apollo IX, logging 241 hours in space on March 3-13, 1969. Rusty's job on this flight was to help validate the Lunar Module, and life-support backpack that was to be used in the exploration of the Moon's surface. Rusty tested the suit by exiting the LM hatch on a 46-minute EVA (Extra Vehicular Activity) while orbiting high above the Earth.

After a brief meeting Rusty agreed to be our guide for the July 20th event. We had our actor!

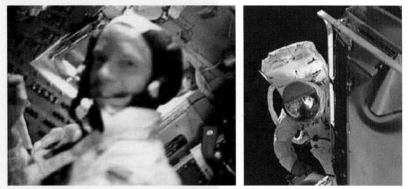

Left: Apollo IX astronaut Russell Schweickart during the Apollo IX flight, March 1969. Photo courtesy NASA.
Right: Russell Schweickart emerging from the Lunar Module "Spider" on the Apollo IX flight. Photo courtesy NASA.

STEP 2 TRAINING AN ASTRONAUT TO FLY IN CYBERSPACE

The Moon world team had re-created an Apollo IX mission, complete with red-helmeted Rusty coming out of a hatch. They had also set up a reconstruction of an Apollo Lunar Module sitting on the surface of the moon. With these props I scripted a simple three-act play.

True to Pete's word, Rusty was adept at the keyboard, and highly versed in the subtle protocols of chat-room dialogue. I pushed his envelope by giving him training in navigation within a 3D online space. We worked entirely remotely during the training and the event.

One poignant moment came when we were out in Booster Park at the top of the model of the Saturn V and where Rusty, Jim McDivitt and Dave Scot had sat in their seats awaiting launch. Suddenly Rusty jumped off and let the virtual worlds' artificial gravity carry his avatar down the side of the Rocket. He said, "Look, this is like seeing the liftoff of the vehicle." It was then apparent that Rusty had internalized the aspects of the medium applying his pilot's Einsteinian way of viewing the world: everything is relative.

Next I introduced Rusty to the reconstruction of his Apollo IX mission and beckoned him to follow me into the spacecraft, testing his ability to accurately navigate his avatar. He kept using astronaut and pilot terms, asking for example, if his "attitude" was correct. I then proclaimed that he was Cyberspace-flight certified and commented with some irony: "Hey Rusty, do you realize how strange this is, I am training you to navigate through space, but you did this for real in orbit thirty years ago?"

Lastly, the choreography was worked out: "We will start in the lobby of the museum, greet people, then float up to your mission area, where you will float by the Apollo IX reconstruction and talk about your mission, then we will go out to the Lunar Landing site."

At one point I came up behind his avatar and noted he was floating and looking at the LM below. Rusty had been the first person to experience a real debilitating case of space sickness. I can only conjecture that this affected his selection for the Apollo lunar landing missions.

Left: Bruce Damer and Rusty Schweickart floating their avatars by the Saturn V in Booster Park.
Right: Rusty viewing the Apollo IX reconstruction in the Moon Museum upstairs gallery.

I frankly didn't have a plan for what we would do at the Lunar Landing site, only that Troy and Ben had requested us to be there to somehow re-enact the first walk on the moon at the precise minute 30 years to the day after it happened.

STEP 3 DRESSING THE SET, TRAINING THE STAFF

With the event only days away, it was time to begin finalizing the set and training staff. As the space built by Ben and his team was so superbly constructed and navigational aids, such as maps, signage and "teleporters" (kind of "phantom tollbooths" that allow you to move your avatar some distance to a set spot in the world) already present, we did not have much set dressing to attend to. I found an image of Rusty on the web and we had that placed inside the world on a prominent surface. This personalization of the space would help to orient the online guests as they "teleported" into the digital space.

A volunteer staff calling themselves "gatekeepers" agreed to help train guests as they first arrived and another group known as "the Peacekeepers" agreed to help deal with the usual set of disruptive users who might show up. Staff assigned private whisper channels and granted bold-text public speaker rights to Rusty to help us get above the textual din of a typical online chat event.

STEP 4 PROMOTING THE EVENT

Ben and his team had already produced a full website (www.moon.uc.edu/) and to add to this, I documented both the Apollo IX and XI missions and my training time with Rusty. We then built awareness and excitement with mass e-mailing promoting the event to a wide public in the fashion of a movie studio using a trailer to publicize a film.

STEP 5 PARTICIPANTS ONLY, NO SPECTATORS THROUGH AVATAR FASHION FUN

Ben and his team had developed a number of "stock" avatars for the event to evoke the times, including costumed bodies resembling such 1960s notables as Richard Nixon, John Lennon, General Secretary Khrushchev, Yoko Ono, Dalek and Robbie the Robot. Like any great costume party, dressing up enhanced guests' feelings of involvement.

STEP 6 ALL SYSTEMS GO... NERVOUSLY LAUNCHING A NEW MEDIUM

At the cusp of the emergence of the Internet as a medium for human expression we had just enough technology, art and design in place to create a compelling experience re-enacting the cusp of space flight 30 years before. Rusty Schweickart's Apollo IX mission in March of 1969 was all about testing and proving brand new systems: kicking the tires on the Saturn V, and operating Command/Service Module and Lunar Module (LM) all as a single package on-orbit. At the same time, three decades on, this online event would test the four-year-old medium of online virtual world platforms under the load of an open, public event within a space conceived as both art and accurate historical reconstruction of perhaps the boldest human endeavor.

Top: Rusty in his avatar navigating toward a hatch in the virtual Apollo IX spacecraft.
Bottom: Rusty regarding the LM.

STEP 7 BEFORE THE CURTAIN RISES, AMAZING HISTORIC CONVERGENCES

Just before we opened, Rusty typed that he had just returned from attending Pete Conrad's funeral at Arlington National Cemetery in Washington DC. Pete had lost his life two months after I had shook his hand in the Mojave Desert. In another twist of historic fate, Gus Grissom's sunken Mercury capsule had been recovered from three miles below the Atlantic Ocean. Both men were contemporaries of Rusty and gave us the sense that we were blessed to have the presence of this man from the dwindling corps of 1960s pioneers of space travel.

And Let the Show Begin!

With the curtains about to go up, I positioned myself, Rusty and our staff in the Moon museum foyer to greet the early arrivals.

WARMING UP THE AUDIENCE

One very important component of any online event where the focus is a "celebrity" or other central actor is for that person to quickly establish his or her authenticity and authority. Rusty set the stage by introducing himself ("...Yes...I was the Apollo 9 Lunar Module Pilot") and telling a few stories. Story is a key to immersion and Rusty's "immersion" story centered around riding the Saturn V, then the most powerful vehicle ever to carry human beings:

> *Rusty1: Actually riding the Saturn V was quite a thrill. It was noisy right after lift off but smoothed out within a few seconds and you couldn't hear the rocket at all after that. The main surprise was the first stage cutoff ... it threw us forward almost to the instrument panel, no one knew about the impact of the sudden cutoff ... and we aggravated it by loosening our shoulder harnesses to give more mobility.*

Guests of the event accumulating in the Moon museum foyer

Next we did a set change by "floating" the crowd upstairs into the more open missions gallery. Once there, our rehearsal and choreography with Rusty paid off. Rusty positioned himself close to the reconstruction of Apollo IX in flight and talked about the mission.

FINAL ACT AND NOW TO THE MOON

We arrived at the Lunar landing site, close to the exact time of the 30th anniversary of the Apollo XI's moon walk. Then, spontaneously, a guest who said she was a ten-year-old named "Julie" sent me a private message asking if she could actually try to re-enact the walk on the moon herself. Rusty then instructed her that if she piloted her avatar up to and then inside the LM its polygons would simply "melt away" and she would then find herself inside a gray, boxy space with the hatch on one side. Moving forward through that hatch, Rusty said she could then look down and she would be at the top of the ladder and then could simply slide down to the surface until making contact.

When Julie's avatar started to emerge from the LM when Rusty messaged "stop, Julie, you are doing it wrong...you have to come out backwards...you see, with the moon suit, we couldn't come out head first, we came out rear-end first."

At this moment Rusty made a wry comment to me about something to do with the fact it was a good thing that the camera broadcasting the moonwalk was pointed at the ladder and not the hatch.

Having gotten into the correct "attitude" Julie then slid down the ladder to the surface of the virtual moon and was witnessed by the group with one attendee declaring "one small step for...an avatar!"

Left: Rusty guides the attendees to the mockup of his mission where he describes what happened to him 30 years before.
Right: Rusty and his virtual reconstructed self on EVA from the hatch of the Apollo IX Command Module.

After witnessing this, many of the attendees also wanted to re-enact the first steps on the moon, and so ensued a rush on the LM. Rusty and the organizers moved to have folks line up and experience their own re-enactments in an orderly fashion. At this point, Julie had her avatar parked right at the LM and so when Rusty moved forward to aid in directing the crowd, he came right up to her and then his avatar passed through hers, his polygons melting away on-screen in front of her. At this instant I received a private message from Julie proclaiming: "I have been touched by an Apollo astronaut!" I responded: "No you haven't Julie, his avatar just passed through your avatar." And she came back to me with: "No, you are wrong, I feel it in my body, I have been touched by an Apollo astronaut and I will never forget this!"

It was at this point that I caught myself and realized that in this moment after years of experimentation we had finally achieved what we had sought: a profound sense of contact and presence experienced in an online virtual space. All of the work of the Moon world team, Rusty's training and skills in telling the story, the magical mix of attendees and their actions, and historical events had come together to give us one of the first truly engaging events held in a virtual world on the Internet.

Mining the Best Practices

To create a compelling event in this space you must borrow heavily from other media and employ the following practices:

THE PERFORMERS

You need one or more good actors, otherwise online events are about as interesting as bus stop conversations (Forrest Gump excepted). As in improvisational theater or stand-up comedy, the actors must convince the audience of their authenticity and merit. These actors must be skilled in the new medium, word-smithing on their feet to handle the intense two-way dialogue and accommodating audience members as they become visible actors.

Left: Event attendees move over to the Lunar Landing site for the finale.
Right: Sliding down the ladder to the surface of the virtual moon.

THE SET

You must build an attention-grabbing visual virtual world setting while understanding that everyone will be walking around freely and creating their own moving point of view within your installation. Unlike a museum or theme park, overly realistic or animated visuals will distract from the focus of the event, which is people and their dialogue. Code enough realism—even cartoon representations are good enough—and leave something to the imagination.

THE STORY

The story is implied by the set of the virtual world, but carried by the words (and to a limited extent avatar "body" movement and gesture). A long lecture will fall victim to the Internet user's notoriously short attention span, so story is best presented in an interruptible stream with the audience participating. In order to create online theater of the long attention span variety, dialogue must be inclusive. In Shakespeare's Globe Theater, skeptical audience members interjected their own dialogue into the script and even joined the actors on the stage.

SOCIAL ENGINEERING

Virtual world events require the careful training of event staff in the conversational skills of a carnival barker or bouncer, and use many other techniques to herd the crowd around and keep them listening.

CROWD FLOW DESIGN AND CONTROL

Like the imagineer designing a theme park ride, very visible wayfinding techniques (teleporters, signage) should allow guests to self-guide through the event space.

EVENT CHOREOGRAPHY

Moving the audience between locations (3 to 5 maximum) accomplishes a theater-style set change. Things for the audience to do at each location will sustain their engagement (but don't include that virtual waterslide ride if you want to keep them in your event). Rehearsals with actors and staff are extremely important to constantly tell the audience where they are and what they are doing. A school field trip of sixth graders is a good analogy here.

MAKING ROOM FOR IMPROVISATIONAL OR SPONTANEOUS ACTS

Permitting a spontaneous volunteer actor to "steal the show" is very important. Like Burning Man, the best virtual events promote the idea of audience as participants over passive spectators.

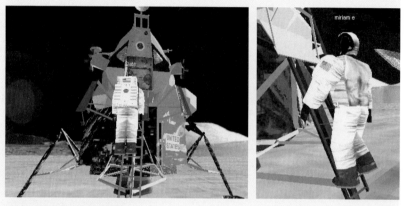

Left: Moon walk re-enactment by another member of the cast. Right: Final view of the Virtual Walk on the Moon.

RECOUNTING THE STORY

Assigning someone to capture screen images and event chat logs and sharing these like "trip reports" helps to cement the meaning and memory of the event, which likely was perceived very differently from each participants' point of view. The Moon event was captured in this way and is presented on the web at www.digitalspace.com/worlds/apollo/index.html.

THE CURTAIN FALLS

The Virtual Walk on the Moon event helped us to understand that by skillfully applying the practices above, compelling audience participation theater can be created inside virtual world Cyberspace. As with the birth of film a century ago, I sense that we can now look forward with anticipation to some blockbuster virtual events in the near future.

MOBIUM
The Museum as Storyteller

JIN HYUN PARK

"Once upon a time, a long, long time ago . . . " On long winter nights, armed with warm rice cakes, I traveled as a child on fascinating adventures which were my grandmother's stories.

With this in mind I created *Mobium*, a system that uses digital technology to tell stories that are as complex and exciting as my grandmother's used to be. *Mobium* is a transmedia design system that tells these stories by creating intergrated museum experiences. During my research process, I asked the question, "how can media design transform a museum that was well established before the digital revolution?'" Could I create system to organize museum's collection and deliver an innovative and engaging experience to its visitors at the same time? *Mobium* integrates the museum's collections with the use of media ranging from wireless tags to object-based information panels, from site-specific information kiosks to handheld devices (PDAs), from customized print-outs to websites available from both within and away from the museum. The *Mobium* experience should not be complicated, despite the 3 years of research, process and planning that it took to create it.

I explored various research areas related to people, spaces and information which included human psychology and behavior, architecture, experience design, information architecture, database structure, content building, storytelling and current mobile technology. *Mobium* is the result of these varied research methods. The key design research innovation is the way in which *Mobium* uses narrative as the organizing principle behind the visitor's experience. The transmedia system becomes a personalized tour guide, creating a customized museum tour based on the story the museum visitor chooses. *Mobium* stitches the visitor into a narrative experience of the museum and the history of a people.

How *Mobium* Started

When I first started graduate school at Art Center College of Design, I did not know exactly what I wanted to do. It was a coincidence actually, that I started the museum project. My work with the Onyang Museum began as a branding project taken on outside of my studies. The museum's administration brought me in as a graphic designer to redo their logo, signage, stationery and business cards. In the course of re-branding, I then started to think about using the graphic palette I developed within a broader, more ambitious thesis project. I tried various research approaches during the process. I went to many museums and collected museum publications, interviewed museum professionals and professors of Korean Studies, and read old and new books about Korea and Korean culture. During the process, I answered many of the questions that I was initially curious about. Through developing branding strategies, I conceived of the overall concept of the museum system. It was a rather organic approach to the problem.

The system is flexible and adaptable. The concept is drawn from the Yin and Yang theory and the idea of the five elements (water, fire, tree, gold and earth). The interactions of these five elements create a basic structure and organization of the museum. It is not only applicable to physical parts of the museum but also carries over to the digital applications.

Mobium evolved from the research process of re-branding the Onyang Museum. At that time, my personal interest was mobile communication. I began that work by thinking through the interface issues around hand-held PDAs for museum use. It was at that point that I saw the opportunity not simply to repurpose the existing museum information infrastructure, but to create a new narrative base around which to build a transmedia system and to transform visitors' experiences. For me, that is the very nature of design research: to focus more deeply than the surface of the page or the screen, to discover new territories for design, and to develop categories of experience rather than simply catalogues of products.

Rethinking the Onyang Museum of Cultural History

Mobium reshapes Korea's Onyang Museum of Cultural History, which was founded in 1978. It has over 20,000 artifacts, three permanent exhibition halls, one special exhibition hall, a temporary exhibition hall, and outdoor exhibits as well. The Onyang Museum presents the country's cultural heritage to local and international visitors and preserves the past for future generations of Koreans. But in the quarter century between its founding and my decision to reinvent this museum as a thesis project, the Korean people's connection to this folk culture had grown even more distant. I discovered from my own visits that the experience of the museum was not that different from my trips as a child, even though the environment around the institution had transformed and modernized completely. Although the museum had many interesting artifacts, the displays felt extremely outdated and unexciting. I began to wonder if there was a way that I could solve these problems through concepts I had been exploring in media design.

The contents of the Museum are organized around the individual objects themselves. When the museum was established in 1978, visitors could relate to the artifacts because their parents and grandparents used many of these objects in their daily lives. Elders helped children to make linkages between themselves and the exhibits they were seeing. More recent visitors, especially school-aged children, the urbanized generation after the Korean economic revolution, do not have any context with which to view these objects. For example, the average school child spent 15 to 30 minutes on museum trip. In contrast, children with parents or grandparents spent more than 2 hours touring the museum.

For me, that is
the very nature of design research:
to discover new

MOBIUM
Mobile Museum Information System

Above: Mobium logo
Right center, top: Old museum logo
Right center, bottom: New museum logo
Far right: Museum, outdoor exhibition

온양민속박물관
ONYANG MUSEUM of
CULTURAL HISTORY

new categories of experience . . .

Mobium is a media design system that aims to contextualize the museum's artifacts through a personalized and connected digitally-enabled narrative experience. This integrated transmedia design system allows for strategic planning on how museum content can be delivered to an audience efficiently and uniquely through the use of information technology. By orchestrating digital, wireless communication technologies within a rigorous transmedia design strategy, *Mobium* draws more out of the permanent exhibitions to give museum visitors a customized narrative experience. To use a digital metaphor, the visitors become hyperlinks themselves, as the system provides storytelling based on their interests as they evolve and manifest during their visit.

territories for design and to develop

Above: Museum exhibition hall
Right: Museum exhibition hall, re-creation of Yangban
(upper class) woman's room

Mobium Media Types

Mobium is an experience. My first interest in creating the system was focused on mobile devices such as PDAs and Cellular phones with wireless networking. I met with various experts who answered most of my technical questions about how *Mobium* could integrate current mobile technology into visitors' experiences. However, a mobile device has its limits. I envisioned providing content and story in specific locations at a larger viewing size than a PDA screen. This concept required a more complicated media structure. The *Mobium* database incorporates many media types such as Radio Frequency Identification (RFID) tags, information panels, information kiosks, handheld devices (PDA), customized print outs and Web sites. *Mobium* supports its central purpose, the development of a narrative for the museum visitor, with the systematic and integrated interaction of various

CONT'D ON P. 292

THE MOBIUM SYSTEM

MEDIA SYSTEM

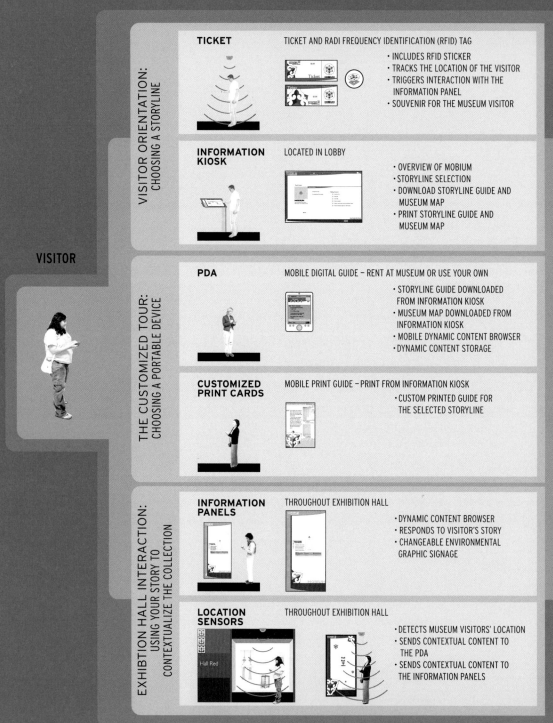

VISITOR ORIENTATION: CHOOSING A STORYLINE

VISITOR

TICKET
TICKET AND RADI FREQUENCY IDENTIFICATION (RFID) TAG

- INCLUDES RFID STICKER
- TRACKS THE LOCATION OF THE VISITOR
- TRIGGERS INTERACTION WITH THE INFORMATION PANEL
- SOUVENIR FOR THE MUSEUM VISITOR

INFORMATION KIOSK
LOCATED IN LOBBY

- OVERVIEW OF MOBIUM
- STORYLINE SELECTION
- DOWNLOAD STORYLINE GUIDE AND MUSEUM MAP
- PRINT STORYLINE GUIDE AND MUSEUM MAP

THE CUSTOMIZED TOUR: CHOOSING A PORTABLE DEVICE

PDA
MOBILE DIGITAL GUIDE – RENT AT MUSEUM OR USE YOUR OWN

- STORYLINE GUIDE DOWNLOADED FROM INFORMATION KIOSK
- MUSEUM MAP DOWNLOADED FROM INFORMATION KIOSK
- MOBILE DYNAMIC CONTENT BROWSER
- DYNAMIC CONTENT STORAGE

CUSTOMIZED PRINT CARDS
MOBILE PRINT GUIDE – PRINT FROM INFORMATION KIOSK

- CUSTOM PRINTED GUIDE FOR THE SELECTED STORYLINE

EXHIBTION HALL INTERACTION: USING YOUR STORY TO CONTEXTUALIZE THE COLLECTION

INFORMATION PANELS
THROUGHOUT EXHIBITION HALL

- DYNAMIC CONTENT BROWSER
- RESPONDS TO VISITOR'S STORY
- CHANGEABLE ENVIRONMENTAL GRAPHIC SIGNAGE

LOCATION SENSORS
THROUGHOUT EXHIBITION HALL

Hall Red

- DETECTS MUSEUM VISITORS' LOCATION
- SENDS CONTEXTUAL CONTENT TO THE PDA
- SENDS CONTEXTUAL CONTENT TO THE INFORMATION PANELS

ARTIFACTS

CONTENT AND CONTEXT

PERSONALIZED NARRATIVE EXPERIENCE

THE VISITOR SELECTS A STORYLINE TO LEAD THEM THROUGH THE COLLECTION. THE STORYLINE SERVES AS BOTH A MAP AND A GUIDE TO THE EXHIBITION. THE VISITOR FOLLOWS EITHER A PRINTED GUIDE OR A PDA INTERFACE WHICH THEY DOWNLOAD UPON ENTRY. THE STORY ALLOWS THE VISITOR TO MAKE MEANINGFUL CONNECTIONS BETWEEN THE ARTIFACTS ACCORDING TO THE NARRATIVE THEY HAVE CHOSEN.

COMMUNICATION SYSTEM

THE SYSTEM TRACKS THE VISITOR'S LOCATION. INFORMATION PANELS PLACED THROUGHOUT THE EXHIBITION HALL DYNAMICALLY PROVIDE CONTENT BASED ON THE VISITOR'S CHOSEN STORYLINE AND LOCATION.

media types. Location sensors track the visitor's RFID tags, the museum database streams suitable content to the PDA or information panels based on the visitor's location, and all ancillary print materials relate directly to the museum goer's central narrative, and the website allows visitors to get more information at home. All of these are controlled by and contribute to the museum database. *Mobium* seamlessly integrates a transmedia system to tell a story appropriate to the interests and expectations of the visitor.

Conclusion

Mobium is a digital storyteller. It cannot replace the stories of grandparents, but it could be the second best thing in a museum setting. I believe that *Mobium's* design research methods and results are applicable across a range of other areas and disciplines. The narrative focus of *Mobium* could serve to organize other museums, libraries and cultural repositories. This integrated transmedia approach could be applied to everything from high-end retail to location-based entertainment. The design research that generated *Mobium* is flexible enough to handle a range of different situations and robust enough to produce distinct solutions dependent on the context in which they would be deployed.

Research and the Movies

BUFFY SHUTT

On May 14, 2003, the *Los Angeles Times* reported that a British academic had found the formula for making motion picture box office hits. According to Ms. Sue Clayton's research, the following is an outline for a successful movie: 30% action, 17% comedy, 13% good vs. evil, 12% sex/romance, 10% special effects, 10% plot and 8 % music. I was stunned by this research. I quickly began to run down some of my favorite films to see if they fit her formula: *Notorious, Singing in the Rain, The Godfather, The Seven Samurai, The Best Years of Our Lives, Bringing Up Baby, Schindler's List, Klute, Notting Hill*.

Did these movies properly add up, or perhaps, more accurately properly breakdown? Was there, after all, a formula, a magic bullet, a guide to making hit movies and, if so, was 10% plot all that was really necessary to connect to a large audience? Was the narrative really 20 points less important than action? Did it make sense that plot and special effects were equal in importance? While this seemed like a pleasurable research project—screening a lot of movies and closely monitoring them for seven specific attributes—I don't trust her findings. But I understand the allure of believing them. I understand the attraction to numbers, to columns of figures that can sort out this complicated world that teems with choices; numbers that can transform the delicate into the substantial; numbers that promise to protect our financial investment while seeming to cater to artistic demands.

Research and movies have an old alliance. In recent times—the last 25 years—it is often viewed as a bit of a dirty little secret, but Hollywood has always looked to research—testing the product (preview screenings) and polling—for advice in making key decisions about movie making and movie marketing.

In the so-called Golden Age of movies in the 1930s and '40s, studios routinely previewed their movies to gauge audience reaction and to make changes to the film if they were dictated. In fact, MGM previewed so many movies so many times, Thomas Schatz tells us in his wonderful book *The Genius of the System* that the Pacific Electric Company cut a track right onto the MGM lot so executives could be taken by private car to a Los Angeles suburb to view the rough cut of the movie with an audience. If the movie played well, they would play cards or have a few drinks on the way home; if the movie played poorly, everyone was silent [Schatz 1988,118]. Today, executives go on private planes to other suburbs, but the joy and silence are the same. Frank Capra reportedly filmed four different endings for *Meet John Doe* and tested them all. The great Gary Cooper movie we know today has the fifth and final ending [Sklar 1994, 211]. Today, filmmakers and executives would be reluctant (though it happens) to shoot four different endings for a film and then test that many times because of the potential for bad press or bad

Internet buzz. Hollywood today creates and refines its movies pretty much in public. Old Hollywood worked behind a screen—a porous one maybe, but they understood how to control information about their stars and their movies with a ferocity that today's executives cannot approach.

Perhaps a lesser-known fact about old Hollywood was its use of audience surveys to help cast movies and, in some cases, to determine which genres audiences wanted to see.

In the late 1940s, Hollywood underwent a significant change in how movies were made and, with this change, came doubt about what movies to make. According to Robert Sklar in *Movie Made America*, a fascinating and informative social critique of film, MGM surveyed audiences to see what genres they wanted to see. The resurgence of the musical comedy was one result of these surveys. Westerns, however, fared rather badly and were judged to be the least popular genre. Still two major Westerns were produced, *High Noon* and *Shane*, which tells us the kind of relationship the movie studios had with their research findings [Sklar, 282].

Mr. Schatz also tells us that David O. Selznick, one of the most successful producers ever, asked the Gallop Company's polling company ARI in 1942 to test various star combinations when he was in the process of casting *Jane Eyre*. David Ogilvy, who worked for Gallop, sent Selznick a report detailing which stars were most liked by which audience members. For example, Walter Pidgeon was said to be on a "rising market" particularly with male viewers under the age of eighteen. There were combinations that did well if the respondents knew the Bronte book, combinations if they didn't know the book, but liked the synopsis. And if they didn't know the book and didn't like the synopsis, they wanted Ronald Coleman and Olivia DeHavilland. In the end, the movie was made with Joan Fontaine and Orson Welles, though Mr. Welles had been the very weakest candidate [Schatz, 329]. And it seems that Mr. Welles who went on not only to star in, but also to co-write and co-direct (albeit uncredited) the feature, did not get the 17% comedy memo.

The use of research in the marketing of movies began soon after the profound shift in the early 1970s of how movies were released—in many theatres simultaneously—and how they were advertised—on television: network television, *expensive* network television. Gradually, movie marketers looked to research to determine how well their advertising tested, a question not unfamiliar to other executives in different industries who were also advertising on television. Of course, the differences among the advertised products were stark. Movies were a product, but they were also an art form.

Most movies lose money. Again, most movies lose money. The average cost to make and market a major studio release in 2002 was, according to the MPAA, $89.4 million, an average of $58.7 million to produce (up 3.3% from 2001) and $30.6 million to market (down a bit from 2001) [MPAA 2003]. Now perhaps you will be a bit gentler when bashing a movie as you exit the theater. $89.4 million is an average. Many movies cost less (mini-major releases, independent movies, and art house movies) and many cost more (the so-called franchise movies based on book characters, comic book heroes, television properties). It becomes crucial to determine with laser precision what will drive the biggest audience to the theater opening weekend. The opening weekend (the Friday, Saturday, and Sunday gross) determines the success or failure of studio movies. And part of that answer is derived through research. Given these numbers, you might think research would be the queen of the studio. But, research is more of a sentry—a good looking, articulate sentry with special gold braid on his uniform—but a sentry nonetheless.

Filmmakers know this sentry either to nod at him in passing or sometimes to converse in a more intimate and often emotionally wrenching way, and other times their encounters with research are satisfying and agreeable. Most filmmakers have a love-hate relationship with research. Though they may not know it, that makes them pretty much like the rest of us. We love research when it says we are right, we are smart, we are on the same wavelength with the audience. We hate research when it says anything unflattering, anything that suggests the movie is less than perfect. Filmmakers understand and, for the most part, have embraced the screening process. After all many of the most beloved movies from the golden age of Hollywood were screened.

Where it gets a bit more complicated is in the world of marketing research. Marketing research: it actually sounds unfriendly to artists, more Madison Avenue than Hollywood Boulevard, more Armani suits and columns of numbers than black t-shirts and vision. But it's all in the communication. Or it's mostly in the communication. Some filmmakers will always suspect that some number on a page made the decision to cut the budget or reduce the number of screens, but most filmmakers will allow that research has a place in the daunting task of successfully designing the marketing campaign for a movie.

Here then, very briefly and elementally, are the research tools most studios use during the development of the marketing campaign. Many of these tools are numbers-driven. Industry norms have been developed over many years using many films. Marketers are trying to reach and possibly exceed these norms. The basic research tools are: historical and comparative research, tracking, on-line surveys, positioning surveys, ad material testing and focus groups.

HISTORICAL AND COMPARATIVE RESEARCH

Historical and comparative data are an important, but rather low-tech compilation of available information from the large universe of all films from the major studios. You determine what old movie is your new movie most like in terms of such factors as release date and pattern, rating, genre, target audience, and the perhaps the single most telling statistic: box office performance. Then, using a smaller pool of your studio's own movies, you cross-reference the scores of your movie's ad materials with the scores of similar movies. (Clearly, each studio does not have access to each other's confidential ad testing scores.) And finally, you cross-reference with the tracking of those movies you have deemed comparable, and you have something to aspire to. It is this kind of research that can say to you—again all in numbers, all orderly, some nicely graphed, others ranked—that your new movie cannot outperform the other movies you have chosen as comparable. The marketing campaign for *Babe*, a Universal movie, was a challenge from the outset. Based on the historical data that said no live action movie where animals played key roles had ever grossed more than $30 million unless it had a *Disney* logo, it seemed there was a ceiling on how well *Babe* could perform. *Babe* beat the odds. The movie grossed $64 million. These data will assist in the creation of the marketing campaign and four weeks before opening, the movie will go on tracking, an industry-wide polling survey usually conducted by NRG, the company that pioneered movie research.

TRACKING

Tracking tells executives and filmmakers how well your marketing is working and how well your competition's marketing is working. One senior executive believes each of the four main indicators on the tracking is the responsibility of a particular department within the marketing group. *Awareness*: media. *Definite Interest*: creative advertising (this number should bear some resemblance to the scores achieved when the spots were first tested). *First choice*: distribution (picking the right release date vs. competitive movies). *Unaided awareness*: publicity. Has the movie (or its advertising) entered the ever-changing lexicon of the movie-goer with no prompting?

ON-LINE SURVEYS

Audiences are surveyed as they exit the theatre to determine their movie experience satisfaction and to gauge which media vehicles had the most influence on their decision to purchase.

POSITIONING SURVEYS

Using a paragraph to describe a movie for which probably no frame of film has yet been shot, this survey is designed to elicit from your projected audience the positioning's strengths and weaknesses. You may along the way find some weaknesses of the film's idea itself, but that is not the purpose of this survey. Research for product development, if done at all, is done strictly confidentially. Josh Goldstine, Executive Vice President, Creative Advertising for Sony (Columbia and TriStar) believes the reason people go to movies is "because an idea draws them in. Successful marketing is about an idea that eventually permeates and drives every aspect of the overall marketing campaign" [personal conversation]. Can an idea be tested ❯225 MOON?

In the winter of 1998 when movie-goers were read a paragraph about *The Mummy,* a Universal Picture, their reactions were so negative—one of the ten worst concepts ever tested—that executives alternately "wanted to reach for a razor blade, abandon ship, find a financial partner to share the risk. Or just pray" [personal conversation, Shmuger]. *The Mummy* was conceived as a "tent pole" movie, a franchise movie with sequel and cross business potential. And it was in pre-production. All movie-goers knew the title. It was, as the studio suspected, a brand of sorts. Only it was a negative brand. Marc Shmuger, Vice Chairman, Universal has said "the value of the early positioning research was to understand the baggage surrounding the title and it helped to clarify the challenges before us. We did not process the information in a strict, literal way. We saw that movie-goers needed a completely new and different set of associations both emotionally and intellectually than the ones that had grown up around the title during last sixty years" [personal conversation].

Still no matter how many times the report was read or how many times the survey was conducted, there was no indication of how to solve the problem that had been so forcefully laid before them. But it gave Mr. Shmuger and his associates this much: "everything about our campaign—from creating the image, the iconography for the film—every choice from shape, color, width, length, typeface—in every way we understood we had to make a radical departure from its history, a complete rebranding, not a modest re-styling. We confidently embraced what we knew we were capable of communicating about this brand and once we re-imagined the property just as the filmmakers were so spectacularly re-imaging it on film, we unlocked an unbelievable reservoir of good will and interest" [personal conversation]. *The Mummy* shattered May box office records, opening in 1999 to $45 million and spawned one of the most successful franchises in the business.

AD MATERIAL TESTING

The meat and potatoes of research for the studios is testing trailers—the previews that precede a movie—and television commercials, usually thirty-second spots. Studios spend approximately 60% of their media dollars on television, in all its forms—TV shows with big audiences and TV shows with audiences so small they barely register rating points but which reach a constituency that might be crucial. Research respondents continually cite television as the primary driver that made them come to the movie. *Made them* is important. Marketers must create a visceral, nearly tribal need to attend one movie over the three or four other new movies opening on a specific Friday; over the five or six holdover movies from two to four weeks earlier, one specific movie over all other entertainment choices—renting a DVD, going to a concert, staying in to watch *The Sopranos*, choosing to attend one specific movie over everything else in life they could be doing. Again, a lot of money is at stake and a movie can only be launched once theatrically. Once. There are no do-overs in movie marketing.

Understandably, we do not test ads on people who do not regularly go to the movies. Some of the people who saw *My Big Fat Greek Wedding* hadn't been in a multiplex in months, if not years. And it wasn't the TV spots that got them there. It was word of mouth at its most powerful.

The TV spots are tested either in focus groups or more likely in large, geographically dispersed quantitative surveys through the mall intercept method. The report comes back telling the marketer which spots appealed to which quadrant though clearly Hollywood caters to very specific and sometimes somewhat narrow targets, there are the four main gender age splits we tend to live and die for: men over and under 25; women over and under 25. Sadly, a woman who may have just celebrated her 26th birthday is an older female.

The respondents typically view the spots twice and then answer a series of questions designed to understand the appeal of the spot (overall impression and nearly an edit-by-edit reaction) and how motivating it is to this potential movie-goer. This process will tell the marketer how well the spot is performing. And say, if it's 55 to 60% (i.e., 55% of our respondents say they are definitely interested in seeing the movie based on this commercial) or 15 or 20 points above the norm, the marketer will feel pretty good about the campaign. Unless, of course, a similarly targeted movie opening on the same date with your movie has TV spots that are testing at 75. And then, as Mr. Goldstine, says "Your 55 is useless. It might as well be 35" [personal conversation].

This methodology (mall intercept) provides the marketer with a number and open-ended comments, but the marketer is typically engaged primarily with the number. A number that has been achieved in a contained, unreal environment. Marketers want this number, this quick report card of sorts that says you have reached or exceeded your norm. The numbers are honest. They have no agendas, no agents, no posse, no reason to please. They are numbers. But. However. Still. They are not enough and they are becoming more and more not enough.

What then? Perched on the solid foundation that a couple of digits can provide, consider launching yourself into the messy real world where your potential customers live. Surprise! You live here too. Now wallow in the primordial stew of the constant imagery assaulting each of us, the explosion of data, the instant availability of everything from global news to the last pair of Lucy and Ethel salt-and-pepper shakers auctioning now on E-bay. And Carrie Fisher's line from Mike Nichols' 1989 hit movie *Postcards from the Edge* seems prescient, "Instant gratification takes too long."

"It all becomes noise," says Mr. Shmuger. "What great marketing needs to do is create melody out of the noise." And the only way to do that is to accept the noise and know the noise. And that is why it is essential now more than ever to research the execution of our ideas—ad materials—in the real world—in an environment true to how they will ultimately interact with the advertising. "The message, the environment and the audience are inseparable, but we are always separating them" [personal conversation].

Mr. Paulos says in his thought provoking book *A Mathematician Reads the Newspaper* that "mathematicians can help determine the consequences of our assumptions and values, but we, not some mathematical divinity, are the origin of these assumptions and values" [Paulos 1995,46]. There!—permission granted to take a few steps away from the numbers and a few steps toward engaging the film-goers on their turf and see just how strong the values are and how smart the assumptions ○172 DEASY.

When we mix it up with the average movie-goer in a focus group or in a new form of quantitative testing that allows movie-goers to respond in their own environment, is there a risk that they will become professional critics, experts instead of movie lovers? Will they all become like that one loudmouth in nearly every group that the moderator dances with for an hour trying to unobtrusively take back control of the group? Possibly, but our customers are experts. The greater risk is not to engage with them. Advertising occupies an important and unique place in our customer's world. They know their advertising. They know marketing ○23 IRELAND.

In 1991, *TriStar Pictures* released, *Philadelphia*, a somewhat controversial film for the time. Audience reaction in Los Angeles and in New York was great. People loved the movie. But how would people in the middle of the country react to the main character having AIDS and suing his employer in the process? No problem. Days later a preview was set in the middle of the country—Independence, Missouri. The movie "played" great. The first comment offered by the focus group after the screening was, "This will be a marketing challenge." Marketing challenge? Do people really talk like this outside of Los Angeles and New York? Apparently they do. Now, twelve years later, imagine how much savvier, snottier, more fabulous the audience is now. And if you aren't talking to them where they live and breathe, then you are missing an important link in your journey to connect. After all, marketing is about creating a powerful connection with your audience. Though Sven Birketts is talking about a novel in his intriguing and marvelous book *The Gutenberg Elegies*, the sense of what he says is applicable to movies and to movie's clever messengers, the ads: "For what a novel [film] transmits, over and beyond its plot and character, is the bewitching assumption of connectedness" [Birketts 1994, 90].

Several marketing executives have said they don't have one specific methodology or metric that they rely on. Instead, Mr. Shmuger says he "draws from anywhere and everywhere from overhearing people talking, to hot websites, to visiting theatres and seeing his trailers play, to numbers, to regular focus groups" until a matrix of information and impressions unfolds [personal conversation]. He is creating marketing from a much richer perspective where he is participating in an ongoing dialogue with what his intuition is telling him, what the audience is teaching him and where his creativity is leading him ●145 RHEA.

Creating a research program to inform the design of movie marketing is a staggering task. It would seem important not to throw the baby out with the bathwater, but it may be that we need to change the bath water, keep the baby, but definitely get her a new bathtub. Today's audience receives and retrieves images and information differently and more expertly than any previous generation. Research must find ways to more fully and deeply integrate the process of collecting impressions from movie goers in the real world environment ●23 IRELAND. And it must do this for several reasons. One: the world is simply more complex now. We are all tied together in an incredibly sophisticated web. Six Degrees of Separation from Kevin Bacon is not just a parlor game. It is a metaphor for the unseen links and connections between and among our audience. Two: the continued reliance on numbers will push movie advertising further toward the sameness it struggles with now. Mr. Shumger suggests that when "similar creative tools such as driving music, and deft, pulse-quickening montages are used to stoke excitement" and this representation of excitement is rewarded with high testing numbers, we are perilously close to creating more noise, creating a sameness that is deadening [personal conversation]. Our audience finds it deadening even as they continue to stream into the theaters, setting both box office and attendance records in 2002. For now, their love affair with the movies is letting us off the hook. But they know that advertising is supposed to cut through the clutter, not to blend in with it. And we know it too.

"Wisdom has nothing to do with the organizing or gathering of facts. Wisdom is seeing through facts" [Birketts, 75]. Marketers are wise and they can be wiser. We don't want less from research: we want more. We want to live in this world, be part of it and not a part of it. We want to be able to strategize campaigns, create distinctive advertising and to communicate with our audience in a world that is real, fresh, complicated, loud, messy and filled with real movie-goers ●30 PLOWMAN. And in that world, research will exist along side of us, helping us, nudging us, criticizing us, focusing us, maybe even linking us to that deeper side of ourselves—the side of intuitive, nearly unconscious thinking.

Mr. Birketts reminds us of Virginia Woolf's words from *A Room of One's Own* "Thought . . . had let its line down into the stream. It swayed . . . letting the water lift it and sink it, until . . . the little tug—the sudden conglomeration of an idea at the end of one's line" [Woolf 1957, 5]. Research can be the water lifting and sinking our thoughts as we struggle toward that "sudden conglomeration of an idea" that will connect the audience to the filmmaker's vision.

Research and Design for Kids

JAN CRAIGE SINGER

Research has become a cornerstone in the strategy of designing products and brands for kids. Companies who appeal to kids as their primary target have become increasingly sophisticated. They're using every possible tool available to them and in some cases creating new ones. Most design, development, identity and marketing plans begin with research to gain insight into what appeals to kids of many ages in order to create a brand, sell a product, and gain viewers.

This level of finely tuned kid focused research hasn't always been around. Once upon a time, there was no such thing as a "tween." The age range from approximately 8 to 12 years old, now referred to as "tweens," was formerly grouped with any kid younger than 13. All kids were clumped together in a category called "KIDS 0 to 12." It didn't much matter in the minds of companies if the kids were 3 or 11; a kid was a kid. From toothpaste to shoes to toys, stuff for kids was designed and marketed with a fairly standard formula: add sugar, batteries, mix in a character or two and promote on Saturday morning cartoons. If you really wanted to do something special, write the word K-I-D-S in multi-colors and maybe even add a rainbow and throw a prize inside.

Kids have become big business—a multi-billion dollar big business. They are a target audience so powerful that they now have their own TV networks, their own websites and their own stores catering just to them. Kids influence where their families go on vacation, what car their parents drive and even where their family chooses to live. This unprecedented clout starts young and grows incrementally.

Along with this power has come the realization that kids are actually a segmented audience. The swing from being treated as a homogenous clump to finely sliced subdivisions has been swift and sweeping. Now, companies dealing with kids are hypersensitive to age and gender. They've discovered the deeper psychographics of children as well as their psychological, cognitive and social developmental stages. Layered upon these newfound nuances are the specialties of the different media: TV, radio and Web. Throw in branding, positioning, packaging, advertising and nothing is left to chance because there is just too much at stake.

It's not unusual to find a marketing group at a toy company filled with MBAs, MFAs, and PhDs. Such groups are conducting research, not only on how to market their company's wares, but also on how to design the products themselves. The marketer MBA has to figure out the business: how to sell the toys. The PhDs figure out how kids play, why they play the way they do, and how the toy company's current line of products may or may not work for that audience.

The industrial designers come to the table armed with the different information and create concepts that fit the requirements. The MFAs create the identity, design the look and feel of the packaging that will appeal to the target group. Research makes sure the name, color, texture and concept will not only appeal to kids but will also make kids want to buy it.

Research ultimately affects the design process because it helps define the challenge. The best design is always a great solution to a problem. This is not to say there is one single solution. Far from it. The lessons learned from the following case studies are examples of how different types of design research can help define problems, present new ones, ask different questions and ultimately create pathways to successful solutions.

Nickelodeon

In 1992 BIG BLUE DOT officially became a design group dedicated to kids. But long before we helped create the identity for what is now considered to be one of the world's best-known kid's brands, Nickelodeon. How the brand came to be has to do with research but not in the conventional sense of the term.

Before Nickelodeon became branded as the ubiquitous splat of orange with the knocked-out balloon type, it was a sleepy little cable television network aiming to give kids a place on TV they could call their own. In the beginning the fare was unusual and uneven, with programming as disparate as *Pink Panther* cartoons and people reading comic books aloud on air. This was back in 1979 when basic cable was still in its infancy. The only consistent competitors for kids' attention on TV were Saturday morning cartoons and PBS. Children's commercial television was roundly criticized at the time for running full-length commercials "starring" licensed characters. Peggy Charren and her group ACT (Action for Children's Television) were just beginning to make noise in Washington.

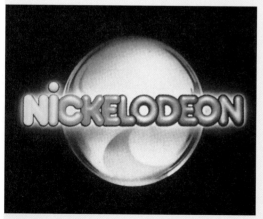

Original Nickelodeon logo

The early years of Nickelodeon were anemic. What little reputation it had managed to garner was mostly a "good-for-you" service. Why the name "Nickelodeon" was originally chosen was a bit baffling. A grown-up somewhere thought that Nickelodeon was a fun name. Perhaps in his or her own youth it was. By the late 1970s there wasn't a kid around who could tell you what a Nickelodeon was. And to make matters worse, the original design for the identity was a shiny pinball with rainbow colors spelling out the name.

Along came Geraldine Laybourne, a veteran television executive, to head up the fledgling network. She had a notion kids should be a part of something all their own. No parents. No teenagers. No grown-ups. No teachers. A kind of "Us vs. Them" attitude where the "Us", i.e. kids, always rule. At about this same time some pretty outrageous programming was happening for kids in Canada. A show called "You Can't Do That on Television" made grown-up game shows look tame by comparison. The show allowed kids to take the lead and be gooey and gross, slimy and sloppy as much as they pleased. Nickelodeon executives saw this as an opportunity to relaunch the channel with a new attitude, new shows and a whole new identity.

With the concept securely in place "The First Network For Kids" needed to be turned into a reality. The powers at Nick were savvy enough to know they were going to need some professional help. They hired the agency Fred/Allen, famous for the original MTV identity campaign in which they recruited designers and creatives from all disciplines to put their particular spin on how the MTV logo should be represented. Tom Corey and Scott Nash, the founders of BIG BLUE DOT, had impressed Fred/Allen with earlier MTV work. They were called on once again to help out with MTV's new little sister network.

As veteran brand/identity designers, Corey and Nash had had their share of creating corporate logos, print brochures and collateral. The idea of creating something new just for kids was something they both jumped at. Fred/Allen and the folks at Nickelodeon needed to create a research program to help them determine what it was that kids might want in their newly formed universe just for kids. The whole notion of grown-ups dictating the entertainment desires of girls and boys had been a less than stellar success with the original network. This time it was important to go right to the source—the kids. It was not going to be a network for little children and it wasn't going to be for teens. The target audience for Nickelodeon would be kids. Kids translated to everyone between the ages of 6 and 12.

Everything about the identity was brought into question, beginning with the name. It was argued by many on the creative team that the term "Nickelodeon" was meaningless to the current generation of kids. Another part of the brand that needed defining and testing was the color palette to determine what could be used effectively with both boys and girls. Being inclusive was important. The corporate mantra became, "If you're a kid, you're in!"

This was the early 1980s when television focus group testing was used almost exclusively with adults, primarily to help guide content and talent choices. The smart folks at Nickelodeon were out to create more than just one television program. They were out to create an honest-to-goodness brand that could stand for an entire set of ideas. They were ready to make a promise and see it through. Applying this kind of brand strategy for a kid' television network was revolutionary.

Focus groups were set up and the process was begun. Nash of BIG BLUE DOT was absolutely convinced that the name Nickelodeon would get negative reactions from kids. He was certain it would prove old-fashioned and meaningless, funny sounding and hard to pronounce. Much to the surprise and even dismay of some, the name had neither negative nor positive connotations. According to the kids' reactions the name was neutral. With that, Nickelodeon stuck. One down, a few more to go.

Next up: color. Because the name was remarkably equivocal, the palette needed to work hard to create a true brand identity. Traditionally in the creation of a brand, a designer can expect the name to carry at least a part of the emotional identity. But in this case, the creative team was beginning the visual exploration without much of an anchor from the name. Again, the kids were not the ones to give an enthusiastic endorsement to any one color or even any conclusive groups of color. The choices seemed to split along gender lines. The girls were attracted to pinks and purple. The boys liked the deeper colors and more metallic looks. This presented a real challenge to the creative team. The true position of the network was to be absolutely inclusive of all kids. There was to be no bias, no skew. The idea of Nickelodeon needed to be simple. "If you're a kid, you're in! "

Opening up the research process to the target of audience of 6-to-12-year-olds seemed like a great idea at the time. But several tests later, the palette was still in limbo. After the first few phases of research for a name and a color, the team was essentially nowhere. This is where years of listening and remembering and thinking and creating for all those corporate clients really paid off. In the aftermath of several frustrating brainstorms, Corey and Nash had a moment of inspiration.

Left: Redesigned Nickelodeon logo-default splat.
Middle and Right: Preferred color treatments for Nickelodeon.

Most of the companies they had done identity work for had been a fairly conservative lot. With these clients a few corporate-styled constants bubbled to the surface. When presenting color studies for logos, nearly every corporate client rejected anything that was orange or green. Convinced they were onto something, Corey and Nash went back to the archives to see if their hunch held up. Sure enough, not a single client had ever chosen either color. Taking this revelation to its next level, they decided that corporate clients, a.k.a. adults, a.k.a. parents, hated orange and green. A perfect foil for the "Us vs. Them" mantra.

There began the seed of a new kid-centric identity. The old Nickelodeon logo used a shiny pinball and rainbow colored lettering. A classic mistake among grown-up designers is the attempt to project one's own childhood onto a contemporary design. What is created today has to live in the here-and-now and in the future. Nostalgia for kids doesn't work. It holds no relevance. This realization became a defining moment for what would become BIG BLUE DOT. Tracking trends and being constant students of kid culture allows for informed design for kids.

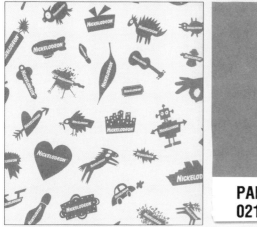

Left: Nickelodeon flexi-logo examples.
Right: Nickelodeon orange.

Originally, the big brother network MTV wanted the little sister to be called NTV. Though the name was ditched, some preliminary sketches survived. Those original sketches were jagged, rough and in-your-face. They pushed the limits of rebellion. It was critical to go overboard on the initial designs. We were onto something and we all knew it. The logo designs were helping refine the very brand itself. The anti-adult colors of orange and green won by default, not because the kids loved the color. They actually had no strong reactions either way, but in this new kid ruled universe, these colors said to grow-ups, "You're not going to like this and that's alright with us!"

The green of the palette became the viscera. It represents the slime and the goop and all those things you can't do on TV or anywhere else for that matter! Orange became the ruling color in the actual identity and it was perfect—perfect because it was ownable. In the early 1980s no one was using orange, as Corey and Nash's anecdotal research had shown.

Orange is a really tough color for television. It's difficult to get the registration correct. It's tough in print as well.

The palette became as much of a positioning statement as anything else. The logo was pushed and pushed. It really helped the conversation to set the tone for the brand. The overall look was eventually pulled back to be a little less edgy and a little less defiant. But it was necessary to go too far in the process and pull back rather than not take chances.

In the end, the new identity for Nickelodeon said to kids from a first-person point of view, "This is all mine!" The ownable orange staked its claim. The original and default Splat became a constant reference to the dumping of slime and splattering of kids which was so distinctive and appealing. The unprecedented flexibility of the orange shapes behind the name became part of the heart of the brand strategy allowing for innovation and imagination.

The always-white drop-out letters are never simply placed on the orange background; the name Nickelodeon in always-white "Balloon Bold" in all caps with the initial "N" one fifth larger on a straight baseline is integrated perfectly with the orange background shape to become a single logo unit.

The perfect integration became a critical part of the strategy because it allowed the logo to be flexible. Each shape had to follow certain basic rules such as: it has to really be a shape of something; let the logos dictate what shape should be used; the shape should look good as a solid silhouette because the orange PMS 021, added as a fifth color, needs to fill it. No outlines. No bleeds. No uncomfortable curves. No letters outside the shape.

All the rebellion and messiness seems quite tame now, but it was very radical at the time. So radical that as designers and brand strategists we were called

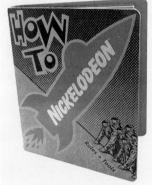

Left: Branding and Style Guide for Nickelodeon.
Right: Inside spread of "How to Nickelodeon."

upon to help create a document to guide people on "How to Nickelodeon."

It was important for the brand to be understood by everyone who touched it, from the internal creative staff to outside vendors. The original document was followed up by "How to Nickelodeon Rules and Tools" and a "Nick Manifesto."

The brand evolved over the years to have a less aggressively exclusive "Kids vs. Grown-Ups" position. The brand was allowed to alter its position from a kid's point of view because the second and third generations of 6 to 12 year olds didn't need to be the pioneers. They were growing up in a television world where Nickelodeon already existed.

The strength of Nickelodeon as a brand creation was grounded in research that was unable to answer the questions posed forthrightly. Going to the source of kids to conduct focus group research was the right start. And in the case of Nickelodeon, allowing years of design experience to help reframe the questions and guide the exploration was absolutely invaluable.

Ringling Bros. and Barnum & Bailey Circus

In another study, BIG BLUE DOT was asked to review an extensive brand equity study and positioning research project commissioned by Ringling Bros. and Barnum & Bailey Circus. The work would serve as the basis to reposition the circus to kids and their families. In addition to the branding strategy, BIG BLUE DOT was hired to refine the existing logo and redefine a unique creative approach for the circus.

How do you update one of America's best known and longest living brands? The challenge was irresistible. At 130 years old, Ringling Bros. and Barnum & Bailey Circus was the longest running show in the US. But as entertainment choices exploded, families were less and less likely to choose the circus as a live entertainment event. Ringling needed to figure out a way to fit in today's world and particularly in a kid's world.

Left: Ringling Bros. and Barnum & Bailey Circus redesigned corporate seal. Right: Ringling Bros. and Barnum & Bailey Circus's 131st edition campaign poster illustrated by Chris Van Dusen.

After months of qualitative and quantitative interviews including focus groups, in-home interviews and ethnographic studies, the research team discovered some great challenges to getting families and especially their kids to have the circus on their radar. On the positive side, Ringling's brand awareness level is very high, similar in many ways to Coke and Disney. People love the circus. The Ringling audiences are a close demographic reflection of America. The promise and tagline of "The Greatest Show On Earth" is one of the most enduring attributes. Parents who went to the circus as a child are twice as likely to take their own kids. Most people didn't know there was a new show every year, but if children were to ask to go to the circus, parents were happy to oblige.

There was an ominous message about the parents who went to the circus as kids. It was becoming harder and harder to attract families to the circus. Unless kids went to the circus at least once a year, it had little relevance to their lives. And if the kids weren't interested, parents who might have remained avid fans weren't going to take their kids. The circus was in danger of losing entire generations of potential circus-goers.

Finding a way to create relevance for families was key to the repositioning. If kids liked what they saw, they might ask to go. If they knew it was a new show every year there would a greater sense of urgency. At the same time the brand needed to have crossover appeal to those loyal circus-goers.

The traditional look of the circus was not connecting with kids today. Through a visual audit we discovered an inconsistent mix of photography and illustration. Beginning with the logo, the strongest equity was not necessarily in the Ringling name but rather in the promise of "The Greatest Show on Earth." The logo was reduced to the circular seal to serve as a seal of approval. The roundness of the logo made for greater flexibility in design and the 3-D and tilt of the earth energized and made the seal contemporary.

The true test for any circus campaign worth its salt is the poster. It synthesizes the two-hour show into a single image. The key art of the poster serves

Left: Ringling Bros. and Barnum & Bailey Circus's Animal Open House logo integrating the 131st edition's new kid friendly style. Right: Ringling Bros. and Barnum & Bailey Circus's 131st edition print advertising and collateral examples integrating Chris Van Dusen's illustrated elements.

as the building blocks for the entire edition's marketing. In order to create a kid-friendly crossover style, a children's book illustrator was chosen.

Chris Van Dusen immediately understood the challenge. His style has a cartoon touch, which worked ideally with the theme and acts of Ringling's 130th edition. He created characters both real and imagined that carried over to the entire marketing campaign, including advertising and educational work.

The strategy for Ringling Bros. and Barnum & Bailey Circus is to keep a freshness and an urgency with each edition. Each year the art will change, the style will change and the acts will change but it will still be The Greatest Show On Earth.

The massive amount of quantitative and qualitative research was invaluable in creating a new brand position for the circus. Ultimately, when it comes to smart creative solutions in designing for kids, the research can set a standard for marketing, but it's the cumulative knowledge and creative experience that determines the interpretation. There's no definitive right or wrong answer, but the essential skill is to know when to question, when to embrace, how to find the gems.

Real Brand Alignment

DAVIS MASTEN

360-Degree Brands

The most difficult aspect of branding is to align the internal culture of the company with the essence of the brand itself. A corporation wants to have an essence, a position and a point of view that is differentiated and can be leveraged in the marketplace. In order to do this efficiently and effectively it needs to express itself in consistent terms with what's commonly being referred to as "360-degree branding." In other words, at every point of interaction the company has with its constituencies, it needs to speak in a consistent voice. This voice needs to adapt to the constraints of the media in which its essence is being expressed. For instance, talking with someone face-to-face is an entirely different type of interaction than the same communication content over email, voicemail or direct mail.

Companies strive to have a clear voice because it helps align employees toward a strategic goal and provides leverage in the marketplace with the trade and consumers. The more people align internally, the more capably they can conduct their business. When they focus with clarity companies can achieve increasing efficiencies, and they can more effectively adapt their differentiable edge to the array of points they use in 360-degree branding.

Authentic Brands

In the past decade, not only has the notion of 360-degree branding taken hold in the marketing and design worlds, but also has the notion of brand authenticity. What consumers expect is the real thing, not hype. They want an experience that is what it promises to be, or if it is not, they want to understand what to expect going into the brand relationship. In this time-compressed world we live in, consumers have no patience for bait-and-switch. They may be open to being sold—in fact, they sometimes want to be sold—but they insist it be done with integrity. They want to know that the brand is who and what it says it is through the lifetime of the relationship.

Consumers have come to expect that at every point of interaction—all 360 degrees—the brand will show up clearly and in an authentic way. This approach is being preached and whole-heartedly embraced by many of the world's top designers and marketers. But as a market researcher, marketing executive, design and corporate strategist, and business person who has been involved in many of the great brands around the world, I will argue that 360-degree alignment is extremely difficult to achieve. I will also argue that, while there are many variables and obstacles to overcome, those of us in the design profession can play a unique and valuable role if we so desire. To do so, designers must learn about the business obstacles and not only how to overcome them but also how to stay with the process until the internal culture is authentically aligned. This calls for designers to play a new role in corporate strategy and execution that many will not find enticing, but those who heed the call and embrace a broader understanding of changing corporate dynamics have the potential to take their companies and their careers to new heights.

The New Dress for Success

To use a simple analogy, a great brand should be like the perfect outfit—it should fit the consumer like a glove, be attractive to the distribution channel, and provide the comfort and familiarity that allows everyone in the corporate culture to feel like they are wearing their own clothes. This is much more easily said than done. I wish it were as easy as just buying a new pair of pants, but it's not. So, what are some of the complicating factors?

First off, in a world of so-called 360-degree brands, there is no one look that fits all occasions. While consistency is desired, when taken too literally, you can be way over-dressed for the party. Branding in the 21st century demands that we be sensitive to the vehicle we are using to interface with our audiences. The Persuasive Technologies Lab at Stanford University, headed by B.J. Fogg, is based on the premise that different technologies persuade people differently; therefore it's necessary to be sensitive to the strengths and weaknesses of the particular media/technology being used to communicate.

A Challenged Wardrobe

The brand wardrobe has some other challenges as well, like intergenerational corporate cultures and interdisciplinary teams. Many corporations have employees ranging in age from 20 to 70. The needs of people under 25 are way different from those of almost anyone older. By the time they have achieved the ripe old age of 25 employees typically have made a life-choice decision. I had coffee with the son of one of my best friends the other day to do a bit of career counseling. He is 21 and feels the pressure to have made up his mind about what he wants to do by age 26. Intuitively, he understands the age dynamic—once someone has made this life choice as an adult, he becomes much more focused on what to do and is more open about what dues need to be paid to get there. On the other hand, someone 50 will not feel comfortable in the clothes of a 25-year-old no matter how mature that 25-year-old is. The same goes for their needs in terms of goals, reactions to authority, willingness or ability to embrace computing, etc. These are non-trivial issues.

Another major issue is life stage. Sometimes age has less to do with issues and decisions than the specific conditions in your life. I remember my wife's and my first kiss. At that time in my life the things that dominated my every waking minute were the wonders of her. While I was CEO of Cheskin at that point and had many professional obligations to fulfill, my personal attention was elsewhere. At the same time, we see people in their 40s recognize their own mortality and question their life's purpose as they see their parents and friends die. The point is that capturing the attention of someone who is preoccupied is a challenge every day of the week in corporations.

Everyone's lives are increasingly complex and time-compressed, so the notion that someone will not only notice but also embrace a brand message is a long shot. Messaging needs to be repeated time and again. The same message often needs to be dressed up in different ways to be accepted. Ideally people are able to interact with the brand "tailors" and experience an outcome that suits them more personally. Even so, over time the message needs to be refreshed.

Dressing for Sales

In the heyday of SGI I was doing some positioning work for a new platform of workstations. As part of this drill, we met with the top sales people and had them simulate sales calls. Three people played the client and three people represented the sales team. We told the "client" teams what kind of company they represented, what they were looking for, and the positions of those who were going to meet with these sales people. The sales people were told they were sales teams from SGI, Sun or HP. They acted out the selling situation. During the sales simulations, I would stop the teams and ask who they were, what the meeting dynamic and politics were, etc. It was so funny—the SGI guys came roaring up to the meeting in exotic sports cars, very casually dressed, and walked with a bit of a swagger. By contrast, the HP sales simulators drove up in a Ford Taurus, were professionally dressed, and reeked of technical competence. Different cultures have different attitudes, and one must speak and dress to externalize the attitude in clothes and body language.

Interdisciplinary Dress Code

I think I was in my first interdisciplinary team in a large company at AT&T in 1986. Nowadays such teams are a regular part of everyday business, but with brand they are still something of a novelty. I have come to realize that there are many groups that "own" brand. Traditionally, Marketing drives brand. But I have also talked with many people in Human Resources Departments who believe that they, not Marketing, own the internal brand culture. At the same time, I know many people in Advanced Development who believe that they, not Marketing, provide the real benefits that keep customers happy and loyal. In my experience, few designers are ever brought to the table in the early strategic interactions between these groups. In order for a company to weave a suit of clothes that will work for the consumer, the technology and the corporate culture, it needs to understand the weaknesses, strengths and legitimate contributions of each. In my experience, if Finance or Operations were to dress the corporation, it would fail to attract enough new customers. If HR were to dress the company it would be too inward-focused—while it might work well for employees, the look would not be receptive enough to the outside. If Marketing were the only people to dress the company, it might be an image that customers love but that the corporate culture itself might not be able to wear comfortably. State-of-the-art teams today incorporate all of the major disciplines early in the discussions.

Why Design a New Set of Clothes?

People who design things have a place in this conversation. You can participate as people who are told what the clothes should look like or you can help answer the strategic question of why to design a new set of clothes in the first place. Designers have a unique ability to imagine the future and make it tangible. With the tools of design research, they have the added ability to assert the future, combining the multidimensional threads and needs of many disparate constituents. Design researchers can articulate the options, not just in the form of "stratobabble," but through a process that helps the various constituents sense the opportunities.

I am currently working with the Executive Committee of a multibillion-dollar company. One brand represents the lion's share of their volume. In order to achieve increased top-line growth they have hired Cheskin to lead them in a design research process. While we are using many techniques, the most applicable is that of involving the members of the executive committee in ethnographic studies. These executive clients have been accompanying our ethnographic teams as they visit homes and explore lifestyles across America. The goal is to discover things together that will shed new light on the fundamental experience of their business. As this happens, senior management's responsibility is to restructure the company to be better aligned with the customer experience. Not only will this give them greater top-line growth; it will also result in increased internal communications, resulting in efficiencies across their company.

Each executive committee member is there because they possess a unique set of strengths and weaknesses. Our processes are designed to bring out the creativity of every one of these players. It would be grossly inappropriate to expect these people to be experts in research or design. That's our team's role. In fact, I would venture to say that the only reason they are doing this is to drive towards their business goals. If there were other techniques that had nothing to do with the customer that seemed like a better bet, they would have undoubtedly gone there instead. However, I believe that the most appropriate approach is to inspire each of these people to new heights of intuitive understanding so they can do a better job of driving the business forward.

In my role, I need to be comfortable with the language of P&L, cash flow, ROI, leverage, PE, etc. so I can redesign the outcome of our process to move the client team forward in a language they understand and are motivated by. While I am definitely considered a "California idea guy," I am not in any need of owning the creative outcomes. The important thing is that *they* embrace the process and build their business. Their business, like all businesses, is complicated—and while I can help them understand things other don't and gain competitive advantage from it, I know that I am not the guy who is going to reconceptualize how to get a better discounted cash flow in a company reorganization.

A Fresh Set of Threads

One of the outcomes of our process is to define the most important core attributes that a brand offers in the marketplace. These attributes combine into a positioning that will provide leverage against the competition. These attributes will also hook onto relevant macro-trends that are becoming increasingly influential. As the brand attributes interweave with the attributes of these macro-trends, the brand will be woven into major growth areas. And if I have learned anything in my almost three decades of business, it is to hook onto high-growth areas, if only because the money is easier and the margins are typically larger.

Let me explain this is slightly different way. Think of the core brand attributes as threads. These threads need to combine with others to make a great looking suit that will charismatically appeal to the desired marketplace. These attribute threads become interwoven into the fabric of macro-trends to become something rich and long lasting. In other words, the suit should fit appropriately and wear very well for years.

Foreign Styles

Foreign markets filled with local management create another challenge to the process of internal alignment. Early in my career, I thought it was not a big deal that I am a Californian with European roots. After all, I was an open-minded guy and had taken anthropology and psychology in college. My, how life humbles one into understanding one's own bias. People now represent Cheskin from 22 different cultures. In another example, I attended a meeting not too long ago where there were 7 senior women in the company. Now I am a pretty friendly, high-energy guy, but I was just returning from a global trip and apologized that I just did not have the energy to greet each of them in the appropriate manner. I knew the Brazilians would be offended if I did not hug them and the Chinese would be if I did. Others would fall somewhere in between. I have learned that subtle cues are incredibly important in communication. In a culturally diverse world, it is so easy to misinterpret a gesture.

Localization becomes another challenge. I just finished a project for a technology client where we involved management from more than a dozen countries. This was not some token effort from corporate headquarters to involve the divisions and then ignore them in the final decisions. The client understood that this technology is more developed in some of the markets outside the U.S. than it is in the U.S. As of this writing, Scandinavia is the world's leader in wireless experimentation. However, the U.S. has the lead in 802.11 Wi-fi technology. Korea and Singapore are the world's leaders in broadband. Japan is the world's foremost leader in consumer electronics. India and China have consumers who are excited to have CDMA phones and many can discuss them knowledgeably by name. Given that we were dealing with all of these issues, it was critical to the success of this product to listen and understand the local market development teams and give each of the local markets the right clothes to wear for local market conditions. All of these styles of clothes came from the same brand wardrobe, but each wove the brand attribute threads into the local fabric.

Don't Just Dress in Black

In order to be involved in this process in a way that captures the essence of a brand and helps drive strategy, a designer must learn how to become integrated into the process in a different way—don't just dress in black. "What?!" you say. Relax. I didn't say stop wearing black altogether, just use it selectively. And I'm speaking both literally and figuratively here. In your own brand portfolio of expressions that are true to yourself, it is important that you have a "wardrobe" that represents you appropriately in a variety of contexts. To be considered an equal—that is, to earn respect for your talent and contributions—you must be someone people want to deal with seriously on day-to-day basis. Clients need to trust that you are not only capable of dealing with their issues but also interested in them as people. If you dress like an outsider, you will be spotted on sight as "not one of us." The group you are emulating and with whom you want to participate in strategic decision-making processes respect distinct personalities. But keep in mind that they are more a part of the "general committee" running things than an élite force.

David Liddle, a successful venture capitalist and key driver in the early days of both Xerox PARC and the Santa Fe Institute, said it best. At a dinner that Clement Mok and I hosted to discuss breakdowns in the creative service industry and attended by David Kelley of IDEO, Paul Saffo of the Institute of the Future, Ray Riley of Nike and Susan Rockrise of Intel, among others, David floated his "Green Beret" hypothesis. As long as designers choose to dress and act as if they are special, just as Green Berets represent themselves as somehow superior to those around them, they will never reach the kind of power they desire. The real power in the armed forces lies in being a member of Central Command, not a member of the special forces. The real strategy is being designed without designers who live like Green Berets. These Green Berets will be relegated to lower pay, with the big money and notoriety going to the few stars of the culture. So before you decide to tell people you are a hotshot strategist who drives fundamental change within corporations, ask yourself if you are accepted by central command as a regular player on the core strategy team. And think back over the past month about how many times you have dressed like a designer rather than as a member of general management with a great sense of design.

- Lasting, authentic brands come from successful leadership.
- Good leadership means seeing clearly, knowing your talents as well as your limitations.
- Recognize that this is a long term, challenging task. Under-promise and over-deliver.
- Set your sights on what is actually doable. Be credible in your expectations. Don't claim that your brand is going to shift the culture if you do not have a good plan and sustainable resources to do it. Get senior management involved.
- Focus on the customer experience and make it come to life for cross-sections of people within the company. Embrace their creativity and help them see the possibilities. Show the culture how it can more effectively embrace the opportunities in an experience economy.
- Appreciate the differences between you and the rest of the company, the trade and your customer. It will hone your instincts, enabling you to make more insightful creative leaps.
- Listen deeply to the complexity of your client's problems. There are so many dynamic issues of culture, technology, politics and finance that it is easy to under-estimate the depth of the issues. Everybody likes to be listened to, especially if they think you can make a real contribution.
- Be gracious and non-defensive. Keep in mind that most executives understand that they are going to be wrong a lot of the time. The kind of help they are looking for are people they can trust to deliver results consistently over time.
- Build processes that have short-term wins to help show the internal culture that you can build results, not just talk. The more tangible you make your results the less risky you seem. People will want to go with a winner.
- Be honest about what you are good at. Just because you are a great designer or researcher does NOT mean that you are a strategist or a CEO.

We still need design stars. In fact, in these increasingly complex times, we need them more than ever. But these new stars should not be Green Berets; rather, they must be people who truly help drive the meaningful decisions in a company on a day-to-day basis. There is plenty of room for true brand leadership if you are up to the challenge.

Beauty, Brains and Bravery

BRENDA LAUREL

Well, that was quite a trip, wasn't it? If you've read this book from beginning to end, you can see that what we call Design Research is a cornucopia of powerful ideas and processes, many of which are incompatible with one another. Through the explanations and case studies that accompany them, I hope you begin to see how specific research approaches map to specific contexts and purposes. Seeing these relationships enables a designer to choose research methods that are appropriate to the task at hand. One need not belong to a "school" of Design Research throughout one's professional life; in fact, that would likely lead to monotony and stagnation. A vibrant practice deploys research methods appropriately and flexibly. Knowing that such variety exists creates the potential for embracing a broader palette of investigation. It allows you to match the "how" to the "why." Design Research is how you bring intent and capability into context.

To design things of beauty is a purpose that I think we all have in common. The *Random House Unabridged Dictionary* [1993] defines it this way:

> [Beauty is] the quality present in a thing or person that gives intense pleasure or deep satisfaction to the mind, whether arising from sensory manifestations (as shape, color, sound, etc.), a meaningful design or pattern, or something else (as a personality in which high spiritual qualities are manifest).

I think the key words are "intense pleasure and deep satisfaction to the mind." In the authors' conference that led to the completion of this book, we found that "delight" was a purpose for design upon which we could all agree. Every approach described in the foregoing pages looks toward this goal, whether it be the pragmatic "delight" offered by an object that serves its purpose exceedingly well (Aristotle would call this "virtue"), the pleasure offered by an object that richly engages the senses, or the mindful delight that arises in reflection of the designer's excellent actualization. Delight contains an element of surprise, a *coup* that causes us to exclaim over something that has punctured the low ceiling of the ordinary.

The old aphorism, "beauty is more than skin-deep," applies to design in that it points to the intent, process and craft of the designer as they are manifest in our work. This deep sort of beauty arises in no small part from the practice of Design Research. In this way, Design Research is the "brains" of the process. As with any human brain, the brains of designers are infused with spiritual, ethical and emotional qualities as well as abstract, pragmatic and operational ideas. The point is not so much the specific "content" of our designerly brains, but rather how we use them. The hypothesis that drives this book is that there is a direct relationship between the quality of design and the willingness of the designer to take on mindful explorations of what lies beneath a beautiful surface. Every writer in this book has taken on this challenge.

What does it mean to "make a design statement"? Sometimes it is merely an in-your-face attitude. Attitude-based design statements tend to be extremely situated; their meaning dissipates quickly in the deep, roiling currents of our dynamic culture. A more lasting design statement is one that manifests an understanding of the currents themselves, finding new flows and new ways to work with them, perhaps changing their force and direction or introducing new currents altogether. To work so deeply requires bravery—a willingness to take the plunge and an implicit assertion that one is up to the task.

So there you are. Go forth and design with beauty, brains and bravery. Why? Because it's time to reclaim our place at the table. Muscular designers can rightfully own the power of design to intend, to manifest and to lead.

REFERENCES AND ACKNOWLEDGMENTS

SECTION ONE

8–15 LUNENFELD, PETER
Preface: The Design Cluster
Adorno, Theodor W. "Functionalism Today," *Rethinking Architecture: A Reader in Cultural Theory,* Ed. Neil Leach. London: Routledge, 1997. pp. 5–19.
De Winter, Koen. *Thoughts on Originality.* www.mosne.lacab.it/art-design/dispense/ragazzo/Originality.html. 2002, cited 1 June, 2003.
Dreyfuss, Henry. *Designing for People.* New York: Simon and Schuster, 1955.
Eames, Charles and Ray. *Design Q&A.* Color film. 1972.
Frayling, Christopher. "Research in Art and Design," *Royal College of Art Research Papers* 1, No. 1, (1993–1994).
Kuhn, Thomas. *The Structure of Scientific Revolutions* 3rd ed. Chicago: University of Chicago Press, 1996 (orig. 1962).
Loewy, Raymond. *Never Leave Well Enough Alone: The Personal Record of an Industrial Designer.* New York: Simon and Schuster, 1951.
Lunenfeld, Peter. *Snap to Grid: a User's Guide to Digital Arts, Media, and Cultures.* Cambridge, MA: MIT Press, 2000.
McLuhan, Marshall. *The Gutenberg Galaxy: The Making of Typographic Man.* Toronto: University of Toronto Press, 1962.
Mitchell, William J., Alan S. Inouye, and Marjory S. Blumenthal, eds. *Beyond Productivity: Information Technology, Innovation, and Creativity.* Washington, D.C.: The National Academies Press, 2003. www7.nationalacademies.org/cstb/pub_creativity.html.
Moholy-Nagy, László. *Painting, Photography, Film.* Cambridge, MA: MIT Press, 1969.

23–29 IRELAND, CHRISTOPHER
Qualitative Methods: From Boring to Brilliant
Cooper, Alan. *The Inmates are Running the Asylum.* Indianapolis: SAMS, 1999.

30–38 PLOWMAN, TIM
Ethnography and Critical Design Practice
Althusser, L. *Lenin and Philosophy, and Other Essays.* New York: Monthly Review Press, 1972.

Blomberg, J., et al. "An Ethnographic Approach to Design." *The Human-Computer Interaction Handbook.* Eds. Julie Jacko and Andrews Sears, Mahwah, NJ: Lawrence Erlbaum Associates, Publishers, 2003.
de Certeau, M., Luce Giard, and Pierre Mayol. *The Practice of Everyday Life, Volume 2: Living and Cooking.* Minneapolis: University of Minnesota, 1998.
DaMatta, R. Conta de Mentiroso: *Sete Ensaios de Antropologia Brasileira.* Rio de Janeiro: Rocco, 1993.
Dreyfuss, H. *Designing for People.* New York: Grossman Publishers, 1974.
Dourish, P. *Where the Action is: the Foundations of Embodied Interaction.* Cambridge, MA: MIT Press, 2001.
Fogg, BJ. *Persuasive Technology: Using Computers to Change What We Think and Do.* Amsterdam, Boston: Morgan Kaufman Publishers, 2003.
Geertz, C. *The Interpretation of Culture: Selected Essays.* New York: Basic Books, 1973.
Malinowski, B. *Argonauts of the Western Pacific.* New York: E.P. Dutton, 1961 [1922].
Margolin, V. *The Politics of the Artificial: Essays on Design and Design Studies.* Chicago: University of Chicago Press, 2002.
Miller, D. *Material Culture and Mass Consumption.* Basil Blackwell: Oxford, 1987.
Rabinow, P. French *DNA: Trouble in Purgatory.* University of Chicago Press: Chicago, 1999.
Rothstein, P. "The Re-emergence of Ethnography in Industrial Design Today." *Chicago 99 Design Education Conference: Repeating the Future, Industrial Designers of America.* Chicago, 1999. pp. 163–177.
Wentworth, R. *Making Do and Getting By: A Series of Everyday Encounters 1970–1985.* Video. The Lisson Gallery, London, 1985.

39–40 MCDANIEL JOHNSON, BONNIE
The Paradox of Design Research: The Role of Informance
Leonard, Dorothy, Jeffrey Rayport. "Sparking Innovation with Empathic Design." *Harvard Business Review* 75, No.6 (1997): pp. 103–115.

41–48 DISHMAN, ERIC
Designing for the New Old: Asking, Observing and Performing Future Elders
Burns, Colin, Eric Dishman, Bill Verplank, and Bud Lassiter. "Actors, Hair-dos and Videotape—Informance Design." *CHI'94 Conference Companion* (1994): pp. 119–120.
Dishman, Eric. "Performative In(ter)ventions: Designing Future Technologies Through Synergetic Performance." *Teaching Performance Studies*. Ed. Nathan Stucky and Cynthia Wimmer, Carbondale, IL: Southern Illinois University Press, 2002. pp. 235–246.
Eagleton, Terry. *Literary Theory: An Introduction*. Minneapolis: University of Minnesota Press, 1983.
Laurel, Brenda. *Computers as Theatre*. New York: Addison-Wesley Publishing Company, 1991.
Meek, James. "The Future's Bright, the Future's Grey." *Guardian*. August 2, 2001. www.globalpolicy.org/socecon/global/0802elder.htm.

55–62 SANTOS, CARLOS
Hispanic Culture in Design Research: More than Language
2002 Yankelovich-Cheskin Hispanic Monitor. secure.yankelovich.com/solutions/monitor/his_monitor.asp.
Acknowledgements
I would like to acknowledge the following Cheskin colleagues for sharing their insights and experience: Carolina Echeverria, Ricardo Flores, Lyle Personette, and Astrid Cruz.

70–80 DON, ABBE & PETRICK, JEFF
User Requirements: By Any Means Necessary
Brechin, Elain. "Reconciling Market Segments and Personas." www.cooper.com/newsletters/2002_02/reconciling_market_segments_and_personas.htm, 2002.
Cooper, Alan. *The Inmates Are Running the Asylum*. Indianapolis, IN: SAMS, 1999.
Cooper, Alan and Robert Reimann. *About Face 2.0: The Essentials of Interaction Design*. Indianapolis, IN: Wiley Publishing, 2003.
Goodwin, Kim. "Perfecting Your Personas." www.cooper.com/newsletters/2001_07/perfecting_your_personas.htm, 2001.
Nielsen, Jakob. "How to Conduct a Heuristic Evaluation." www.useit.com/papers/heuristic/heuristic_evaluation.html.
Pruitt, John and Jonathan Grudin. "Personas: Practice and Theory." *DUX: Designing User Experiences Proceedings*. San Francisco, CA, June 5–7, 2003.

SECTION TWO

83–93 GROCOTT, LISA
Speculation, Serendipity and Studio Anybody
Dilnot, C. "The Science of Uncertainty: the Potential Contribution of Design to Knowledge." *Proceedings of Doctoral Education in Design*. Ohio State University, 1998.
Lave, J. and E. Wenger, *Situated Learning: Legitimate Peripheral Participation*. New York: Cambridge University Press, 1991.
Marshall, T. and S. Newton, "Scholarly Design as a Paradigm for Practice-Based Research." *Proceedings of Research into Practice*. University of Hertfordshire, 2000.
Rosenberg, T. "The Reservoir: Towards a Poetic Model of Research in Design." *Proceedings of Research into Practice*. University of Hertfordshire, 2000.
Schön, D.A. *The Reflective Practitioner: How Professionals Think in Action*. New York: Basic Books, 1983.
Seago, A. and A. Dunne, "New Methodology in Art and Design Research: the Object as Discourse." *Design Issues: Special Issue Design Research*. Issue 2, 1999.

94–100 GONZALES CRISP, DENISE
Toward A Definition of the Decorational (In Real Time)
Blake, P. *Form Follows Fiasco*. Boston: Little, Brown and Co., 1974.
Foster, H. Design and Crime. London: Verso, 2002.
Le Corbusier. *The Decorative Art of Today*. Trans. James I. Dunnett. Cambridge: MIT Press, 1987.
Lindinger, H. ed. Britt, D., trans. *Ulm Design: The Morality of Objects*. Cambridge: MIT Press, 1987.
Loos, A. "Ornament and Crime." Ed. I. Frank, trans. D. Britt, *The Theory of Decorative Art: An Anthology of European and American Writings*. New Haven: Yale University Press, 2000 (original 1908).

118–128 STRICKLAND, RACHEL
Spontaneous Cinema as Design Practice: How to Walk Without Watching Your Step
Cavell, Stanley. *The World Viewed: Reflections on the Ontology of Film*. Cambridge, MA: Harvard University Press, 1971.
Davis, Marc. "Media Streams: Representing Video for Retrieval and Repurposing." Ph.D. Thesis, Massachusetts Institute of Technology, 1995.
Godard, Jean-Luc. *Histoire(s) du Cinéma*. München, Germany: ECM Records, 1999.
Gombrich, E.H. *Art and Illusion: A Study in the Psychology of Pictorial Representation*. New York: Pantheon Books, 1960.
Gould, Eric and Rachel Strickland. "Method and Storage Device for Expanding and Contracting Continuous Play Media Seamlessly." U.S. Patent 6393158, 2002.

Hockings, Paul, ed. *Principles of Visual Anthropology*. The Hague: Mouton Publishers, 1975.

Klee, Paul. "Lecture Delivered on the Occasion of an Exhibition at the Jena Kustverein." *Paul Klee Notebooks: The Thinking Eye*. Ed. Jürg Spiller and trans. Ralph Manheim. London: Lund Humphries, 1961, pp. 81–82 (original 1924).

MacDougall, David. *Transcultural Cinema*. Princeton: Princeton University Press, 1998.

Manovich, Lev. *The Language of New Media*. Cambridge: MIT Press, 2001.

Nichols, Bill. *Representing Reality: Issues and Concepts in Documentary*. Bloomington: Indiana University Press, 1991.

Sobchack, Vivian. *The Address of the Eye: A Phenomenology of Film Experience*. Princeton: Princeton University Press, 1992.

Strickland, Rachel et al. "Portable Effects: A Survey of Nomadic Design Practice." www.portablefx.com, 2000.

Vaughan, Dai. *For Documentary: Twelve Essays*. Berkeley: University of California Press, 1999.

Whyte, William Holley. *City: Rediscovering the Center*. New York: Doubleday, 1988.

Winston, Brian. *Claiming the Real: The Documentary Film Revisited*. London: British Film Institute, 1995.

135–144 TOW, ROB
Strategy, Tactics, and Heuristics for Research:
A Structuralist Approach
Coram, Robert. *Boyd: The Fighter Pilot Who Changed the Art of War*. Little Brown & Company, 2002.

Culler, Jonathan. *On Deconstruction: Theory and Criticism After Structuralism*. Ithaca: Cornell University Press, 1983.

Darwin, Charles. *The Expression of the Emotions in Man and Animals*. London: John Murray, Albemarle Street, 1872. See also Charles Darwin. *The Expression of the Emotions in Man and Animals*. Introduction, Afterword and Commentaries by Paul Ekman. New York: Oxford University Press, 1998.

Edwards, Paul N. *The Closed World: Computers and the Politics of Discourse in Cold War America (Inside Technology)*. Cambridge: MIT Press, reprint edition 1997.

Hart, Basil Henry Liddell. *Strategy*. 2nd edition. New York: Meridian Books, 1991.

Laurel, Brenda, Rachel Strickland and Rob Tow. "Placeholder: Landscape and Narrative in Virtual Environments." *ACM Computer Graphics Quarterly* 28, No. 2 (May 1994): pp. 118–126. See also www.tauzero.com/Rob_Tow/Placeholder/Placeholder.html.

McGrew, W. C. *Chimpanzee Material Culture: Implications for Human Evolution*. Cambridge: Cambridge University Press, 1992.

Scheeff, Mark, John Pinto, Kris Rahardia, Scott Snibbe, Rob Tow, "Experiences with Sparky, a Social Robot." *Proceedings of the Workshop on Interactive Robotics and Entertainment (WIRE)*, 2000.

Schivelbusch, Wolfgang. *Disenchanted Night: The Industrialization of Light in the Nineteenth Century*. Berkeley: University of California Press, 1995.

Sun Tzu. *The Art of War*. Trans. Brig. General Samuel Griffith, forward by B. Liddle Hart. Oxford: Oxford University Press, 1971.

Tow, Robert F. "Affect-based Robot Communication Methods and Systems." U.S. Patent No 5,832,189, November, 1998.

Tow, Robert F. "Methods and Means for Embedding Machine Readable Digital Data in Halftone Images." U.S. Patent 5,315,098, May 1994.

SECTION THREE

153–162 SHEDROFF, NATHAN
Research Methods for Designing Effective Experiences
Andersen, Kristina and Margot Jacobs, Laura Polazzi, "Playing Games in the Emotional Space." *Funology: From Usability to Enjoyment*, Blythe, M.A., Overbeeke, K., Monk, A.F. and Wright, P.C. Eds. Dordrecht, the Netherlands: Kluwer, 2003. See also www.ifonly.org.

Ceppi, Giulio and Analia Cervini, Juan Kayser, and Mack Thomas. "Mobile Embodiments." www.interaction-ivrea.it/en/academicprogramme/projects/index.asp#mobile.

Coupland, Douglas. *Generation X: Tales for an Accelerated Culture*. New York: St. Martin's Press, 1994. See also www.nathan.com/thoughts/storm/takeaways.html.

Miller, D. "Wrapt: Sound to Fit the Wearer." people.interaction-ivrea.it/d.miller.

Ossevoort, Stijn. "Wearable Dreams." [stijn88@ife.ee.ethz.ch].

Reeves, Byron and Clifford Nass. *The Media Equation: How People Treat Computers, Television, and New Media like Real People and Places*. Stanford: CSLI Publications, 1996.

163–171 DONAHUE, SEAN
Research-Centered Design: Perspectives and Models
for Design Research in Practice
Albers, Josef. *Interaction of Color*. New Haven: Yale University Press, 1963.

Blauvelt, Andrew. "In and Around: Cultures of Design and the Design of Cultures." *Emigre* 33, (1995): pp. 2–23.

Burdick, Anne. "Introduction/Inscription." *Emigre* 36, (1995).

Crisp, Denise Gonzales. "Ways of Looking Closer." *Emigre* 35, (1995).

Gaut, Berys and Dominic McIver Lopes, eds. *The Routlege Companion to Asthetics*. London: Routledge, 2001.

Hofmann, A. and W. Weingart. "Thoughts on the Study and Making of Visual Signs." *Design Quarterly* 130 (1985): pp. 1–20.

Hollis, Richard. *Graphic Design a Concise History*. London: Thames & Hudson, 1994.

Laurel, Brenda. *Utopian Entrepreneur*. Cambridge: MIT Press, 2001.

Lighthouse International. www.lighthouse.org. May 10, 2002.

Maldonado, Tomàs. "Communication and Semiotics" *Ulm* 5 (1958): pp. 69–78.

McCoy, Katherine. "American Graphic Design Expression." *Design Quarterly* 148. (1990).

Mermoz, Gerard. "Typography and Reference." *Emigre* 36 (1995).

Pedrosa, Adriano. "Writing and Design and the Subject." *Emigre* 35 (1995).

Potter, Norman. *What Is a Designer*. London: Hyphen Press, 1969.

Rand, Paul. *Design, Form, and Chaos*. New Haven: Yale University Press, 1993.

Renner, Paul. *The Art of Typography*. New York: Princeton Architectural Press, 1998.

Stumpf, Bill. *The Ice Palace That Melted Away*. Minneapolis: University of Minnesota Press, 1998.

Tschichold, Jan. *The New Typography: A Handbook for Modern Designers*. Trans. by Ruari McLean, introduction by Robin Kinross. CA: University of California Press, 1995.

176–184 ZIMMERMAN, ERIC
Play as Research: The Iterative Design Process

SiSSYFiGHT 2000. Word.com, 2000.
    Project team: Marisa Bowe, Ranjit Bhatnagar, Tomas Clark, Michelle Golden, Lucas Gonze, Lem Jay Ignacio, Jason Mohr, Daron Murphy, Yoshi Sodeka, Wade Tinney, Eric Zimmerman

LOOP. gameLab, 2001, published by Shockwave.com
    Project Team: Ranjit Bhatnagar, Peter Lee, Frank Lantz, Eric Zimmerman and Michael Sweet / Audiobrain

LEGO Junkbot. gameLab, 2001, published by LEGO.com
    Project Team: Ranjit Bhatnagar, Nick Fortugno, Peter Lee, Frank Lantz, Eric Zimmerman and Michael Sweet / Audiobrain

Images of SiSSYFiGHT 2000 ©2000 Zapata
Images of LOOP ©2001 Shockwave.com
Images of LEGO Junkbot ©2002 LEGO

193–200 SVENSSON, PATRIK
Interdisciplinary Design Research

Börner, K., R. Hazlewood, and S.-M. Lin. "Visualizing the Spatial and Temporal Distribution of User Interaction Data Collected in Three-Dimensional Virtual Worlds." *Sixth International Conference on Information Visualization*. London, England, July 10–12. IEEE Press, 2002. pp. 25–31.

Damer, Bruce. "Meeting by Interruption." www.digitalspace.com/papers/interruptculture1.html. 2001.

Fosnot, Catherine Twomey, ed. *Constructivism: Theory, Perspectives and Practice*. New York: Teachers College Press, 1996.

Gladwell, Malcolm. *The Tipping Point: How Little Things Can Make a Big Difference*. London: Abacus, 2000.

Grau, Oliver. *Virtual Art: From Illusion to Immersion*. Cambridge: MIT Press, 2003.

Ihde, Don. *Technology and the Lifeworld: From Garden to Earth*. Bloomington: Indiana University Press, 1990.

Klein, Julie Thompson. *Crossing Boundaries: Knowledge, Disciplinarities, and Interdisciplinarities*. Charlottesville: University Press of Virginia, 1996.

Langer, Judith A. *Envisioning Literature: Literary Understanding and Literature Instruction*. New York: Teachers College Press, 1995.

McCloud, Scott. *Understanding Comics: The Invisible Art*. New York: Harper Collins, 1993.

Moore, Geoffrey A. *Crossing the Chasm: Marketing and Selling High-Tech Products to Mainstream Customers*. New York: Harper Collins, 2002.

Nissani, Moti. "Ten Cheers for Interdisciplinarity: The Case for Interdisciplinary Knowledge and Research". *Social Science Journal,* 34 (1997): 201–216.

Walton, Kendall L. *Mimesis as Make-Believe: On the Foundations of the Representational Arts*. Cambridge: Harvard University Press, 1990.

Wiederhold, B. K. and M. D. Wiederhold. "Lessons Learned from 600 Virtual Reality Sessions." *CyberPsychology & Behavior* 3, (2000): pp. 393–400.

Wray, Richard. "First with the Message". Interview with Cor Stutterheim. *The Guardian*, March 16, 2002.

212–220 LOCH, CHRISTOPH
Moving Your Idea Through Your Organization:
Beauty Is in the Eye of the Beholder

Ancona, Deborah, et al. "Three Lenses on Organizational Analysis and Action." Module 2 of *Managing for the Future: Organizational Behavior and Process* (2nd ed). Cincinnati, OH: South-Western College Publishing, 1999, pp. 1–75.

Bangle, Christopher. "The Ultimate Creativity Machine: How BMW Turns Art into Profit." *Harvard Business Review* (January–February 2001): pp. 5–11.

Gladwell, Malcolm. *The Tipping Point*. Boston: Little Brown and Company, 2000.

Loch, Christoph H., Michael Yaziji and Christian Langen. "The Fight for the Alpha Position: Channelling Status Competition in Organizations." *European Management Journal* 19 (2000): pp.16–25.

Loch, Christoph H. and Staffan Tapper. "Implementing a Strategy-Driven Performance Measurement System for an Applied Research Group." *Journal of Product Innovation Management* 19 (2002): pp. 185–198.

Loch, Christoph H. and Svenja C. Sommer. "Vol de Nuit: the Dream of the Flying Car at Lemond Automobiles SA." INSEAD Case Study 02/2003 5086, 2003.

Maney, Kevin. *The Maverick and His Machine: Thomas Watson Sr. and the Making of IBM*. New York: John Wiley and Sons, 2003.

Rich, Ben R. Skunk Works: *A Personal Memoir of My Years at Lockheed*. Boston: Little Brown and Company, 1994.

Schein, Edgar H. *Organizational Culture and Leadership*. San Francisco: Jossey Bass, 1985.

SECTION FOUR

244–252 JENKINS, HENRY ET AL
"You Can't Bring that Game to School!": Designing *Supercharged!*
Barab, S. A., M. G. Barnett, & K. Squire. "Building a Community of Teachers: Navigating the Essential Tensions in Practice." *Journal of The Learning Sciences* 11:3, 2003.

Belcher, J., J. Murray, and M. Zahn. "Force Field: Using Animation in Teaching Electromagnetism." NSF Award Abstract #9950380. Washington, DC: National Science Foundation, 1999. web.mit.edu/jbelcher/www/NSF.html.

Brown, Ann. "Design Experiments: Theoretical and Methodological Challenges in Creating Complex Interventions in Classroom Settings." *Journal of the Learning Sciences* 2, (2002): pp. 141–178.

Cobb, P.,et al. "Design Experiments in Educational Research." *Educational Researcher*, 32 (2003): pp. 9–13.

Collins, Alan. "Toward a Design Science of Education." Eds. E. Scanlon and T. O'Shea. *New Directions in Educational Technology*. New York: Springer-Verlag, 1992.

Dewey, John. "The Pattern of Inquiry." *Logic: The Theory of Inquiry*. New York: Holt, 1938, pp. 101–119. Rpt. in *Pragmatism: The Classic Writings*. H.S. Thayer, ed. Indianapolis: Hacket, 1982, pp. 316–334.

Fiske, John. *Reading the Popular*. London and New York: Routledge, 1989.

Games-to-Teach Design Team. "Designing Educational Games: Design Principles from the Games-to-Teach Project." To appear in *Educational Technology* (September–October, 2003).

Gee, James Paul. *What Video Games Have to Teach Us about Learning and Literacy*. New York: Palgrave, 2003.

Holland, W., H. Jenkins, and K. Squire. "Theory by Design." *Video Game Theory*. Eds. B. Perron and M. Wolf. Routledge, in press.

Jenkins, Henry and Kurt Squire. "The Art of Contested Spaces." Lucien King, ed. *Game On: The History and Culture of Videogames*, London: Laurence King Publishing Ltd., 2003.

Squire, Kurt. "Game Analysis: Sid Meier's Pirates!" www.joystick101.org/story/2000/10/30/7616/8742. May 30, 2003.

260–267 RAPOZA, DARION
Social Impact by Design: Tailoring Gameplay for At-Risk Players
Bartholomew, L. K., et al. "Watch, Discover, Think, and Act: Evaluation of Computer-Assisted Instruction to Improved Asthma Self-Management in Inner-City Children." *Patient Education & Counseling* 39 (2000): pp. 269–80.

Bartle, Richard A. "Hearts, Clubs, Diamonds, Spades: Players Who Suit MUDs." *The Journal of Virtual Environments 1, No. 1*, 1997. http://www.brandeis.edu/pubs/jove/HTML/v1/v1n1.html. June 25, 2003

Conrod, Patricia J., et al. "Efficacy of Brief Coping Skills Interventions That Match Different Personality Profiles of Female Substance Abusers." *Psychology of Addictive Behaviors* 14, No. 3 (2000): pp. 231–242.

Grossman, H.Y., S. Brink, and S.T. Hauser. "Self-Efficacy in Adolescent Girls and Boys with Insulin-dependent Diabetes Mellitus." *Diabetes Care* 19 (1987): pp. 324–329.

Harrington, N.G., and R. L. Donohew. "Jumpstart: a Targeted Substance Abuse Prevention Program." *Health Education & Behavior* 24, No. 5 (1997): pp. 568–586.

Homer, C., O. Susskind, H. R. Alpert, M. Owusu, L. Schneider, L. A. Rappaport, D. H. Rubin. "An Evaluation of an Innovative Multimedia Software Program for Asthma Management: Report of a Randomized, Controlled Trial." *Pediatrics* 106 No. 1, Pt. 2 (July 2000): pp. 210–215.

Johnston, J. and J. S. Ettema. "Using Television to Best Advantage: Research for Prosocial Television." *Perspectives on Media Effects*. Eds. J. Bryant and D. Zillman. Hillsdale, New Jersey: Lawrence Erlbaum, 1986.

Lieberman, Debra A. "Health Education Videogames for Children and Adolescents: Theory, Design, and Research Findings." *Paper presented at the annual meeting of the International Communication Association*, Jerusalem, 1998.

Malone, Thomas Wendell. "What Makes Things Fun to Learn? A Study of Intrinsically Motivating Computer Games." Ph.D. dissertation, Stanford University, 1980.

McDermott, S. and B. Greenberg. "Parents, Peers and Television as Determinants of Black Children's Esteem." *Communication Yearbook* 8. Ed. R. Bostrom. Beverly Hills: Sage, 1985.

Oei, T. P. S. and A. R. Baldwin. "Smoking Education and Prevention: a Developmental Model." *Journal of Drug Education* 22, No. 2 (1992): pp. 155–181.

Rubin, D., J. Leventhal, et al. "Educational Intervention by Computer in Childhood Asthma: A Randomized Clinical Trial Testing the Use of a New Teaching Intervention in Childhood Asthma." *Pediatrics.* 77 (1986): pp. 1–10.

Yawn, B.P. et al., "An in-school CD-ROM Asthma Education Program. *Journal of School Health*, 70, No. 4. (April 2000): pp. 153–159.

Yee, Nicholas. "Facets: 5 Motivation Factors for Why People Play MMORPG's." 2002. http://www.nickyee.com/facets/home.html.

Yee, Nicholas. "Codename Blue: An Ongoing Study of MMORPG Players." April 2002. http://www.nickyee.com/codeblue/home.html.

Zukerman, M. et al. "What is the Sensation Seeker? Personality Ttrait and Experience Correlates of the Sensation-Seeking Scales." *Journal of Consulting and Clinical Psychology* 39 No. 2, (1972): pp. 308–321.

268–275 DAVIS, MARGARET ET AL
Researching *America's Army*

Greenwald, T. "An Analysis of Auditory Cues for Inclusion in a Virtual Close Quarters Combat Room Clearing Operation." Master's thesis. MOVES Institute, Naval Postgraduate School. Monterey: 2002.

Perkins, K. "Implementing Realistic Helicopter Physics in 3D Game Environments." Master's thesis. MOVES Institute, Naval Postgraduate School. Monterey: 2002.

Sanders, R., and Scorgie, R. "The Effect of Sound Delivery Methods on the User's Sense of Presence in a Virtual Environment." Master's thesis. MOVES Institute, Naval Postgraduate School. Monterey: 2002.

Ulate, S. "The Impact of Emotional Arousal on Learning in Virtual Environments." Master's thesis. MOVES Institute, Naval Postgraduate School. Monterey: 2002.

Shilling, R. "Contribution of Professional Sound Design Techniques to Performance and Presence in Virtual Environments: Objective Measures." *Proceedings of 47th Department of Defense Human Factors Engineering Technical Advisory Group Meeting*, San Diego, 2002.

Shilling, R. "Entertainment Industry Sound Design Techniques to Improve Presence and Training Performance." in VE. European Simulation Interoperability Workshop, *MSIAC M&S Journal*. London: 2002.

Shilling, R., Zyda, M., Wardynski, C. "Introducing Emotion into Military Simulation and Videogame Design: America's Army: Operations and VIRTE." *Proceedings of the GameOn Conference*. London: 2002.

Zyda, M., et al. "The MOVES Institute's *America's Army*: Operations Game." *Proceedings of ACM SIGGRAPH 2003 Symposium on Interactive 3D Graphics*. Monterey: 2003.

Zyda, M., et al. "Entertainment R&D for Defense." *IEEE Computer Graphics and Applications* (January/February 2003).

276–284 DAMER, BRUCE
A Virtual Walk on the Moon: Experimental Design Research in a New Medium

Robinson, D. *From Peepshow to Palace, The Birth of American Film*. New York: Columbia University Press, 1997.

Damer, B. F. *DigiBarn Computer Museum, A History of the Graphical User Interface*, www.digibarn.com. 2001.

Damer, B. F. *Avatars! Exploring and Building Virtual Worlds on the Internet*. Berkeley: Peach Pit Press, 1997.

Laurel, B. *Computers as Theatre*. Reading, MA: Addison Wesley, 1991.

Britton, B. CERHAS Moon Project Home Page www.moon.uc.edu/. 1999.

Damer, B. F. *Digital Space Commons Virtual Walk on the Moon* www.digitalspace.com/worlds/apollo/index.html. 1999.

293–300 SHUTT, BUFFY
Research and the Movies

Birketts, Sven. *The Gutenberg Elegies*. Boston: Faber and Faber, 1994.

Paulos, John Allen. *A Mathematician Reads the Newspaper*. New York: Basic Books, 1995.

Reuters. "A Formula for Boffo Box Office?" *Los Angeles Times* [Los Angeles, CA], May 14, 2003.

Schatz, Thomas. *The Genius of the System*. New York: Pantheon Books, 1988.

Sklar, Robert. *Movie Made America*. New York: Vintage Books, 1994.

Woolf, Virginia. *A Room of One's Own*. New York: Harcourt, Brace and World, 1957.

INDEX

BIOGRAPHIES OF CONTRIBUTING AUTHORS

PHILLIP BOSSANT is the art director of *American's Army*. As a fine artist, he has exhibited extensively in the U.S. and Japan. As an artist-animator for children's software, he worked on many Brøderbund and Living Books titles, including *Carmen San Diego, Dr. Seuss, Green Eggs and Ham*, the *ABC Book*, and Nickelodeon's *RugRats*. As a lead artist at Electronic Arts, Philip worked on *Nuclear Strike*, Red Orb's *Prince of Persia 3D* and *James Bond: The World Is Not Enough*. Philip holds BFA degrees in painting/print-making from Kansas City Art Institute, Missouri and in printmaking/animation from the Osaka University of Arts, Japan.

CHRISTIAN BUHL is senior programmer for *America's Army* and a research associate and Master's student at the MOVES Institute. As a high-school student, he began working for the Naval Air Warfare Center's Training Systems Division in Orlando, Florida, developing virtual-reality based experiments for Navy psychologists. He was one of the principal programmers on the Conning Officer's Virtual Environment (COVE), now used by the U.S. Navy Surface Warfare Officer School. Christian is a graduate of the University of Central Florida with a BS in computer engineering.

ANNE BURDICK operates a triple-threat practice: she designs, writes and/or edits both client-based and self-initiated projects out of the Los Angeles-based Offices of Anne Burdick. As an outgrowth of her research interest in the intersection of writing and design, she has been involved with the electronic literature community as the site designer and design editor of the online literary journal *electronic book review* www.electronic-bookreview.com since the mid-90s. Her collaborations span media and environments, from poetry installations to net.art to "the Most Beautiful Book in the World," *The Fackel Wörterbuch: Redensarten*. Anne's writing and design has been featured nationally and internationally in *Emigre Magazine, Eye Magazine* and *I.D. Magazine,* among others. Her work has appeared in numerous exhibitions, most recently "West Coast Dreams" in Paris. Anne is currently a core faculty member of the graduate Media Design Program at Art Center College of Design. She is also the lead designer of this book.

DAVID CANAAN has nearly 30 years' experience in brand identity and image development in a wide variety of industries. For the 11 years prior to forming the independent Laurel Group, he was Senior Managing Partner at Enterprise IG, San Francisco leading the brand strategy practice. His imagery work for clients such as Universal Studios, Sundance Film Institute, Citibank, Apple and Mitsukoshi Department Stores is recognized around the world. He has served as a faculty member of Brigham Young University and the University of Utah; an academic advisor to the Academy of Art, San Francisco; and member of the Board of Trustees for the Santa Fe College of Design and the national marketing advisory board for United Way of America.

EVAN CHAMPLIN joined the *America's Army* team as an art intern after his junior year in high school, returning home in the fall to finish his diploma, and graduated midyear to come back to *AA* and resume intern duties. He is now a full artist. With an extensive knowledge of firearms, Evan is the team's weapons modeler and onsite expert.

CHRISTOPHER CHANG is *America's Army*'s character modeler. From humble beginnings, he learned his third trade through his brother Christian, who also works on *AA*. His art is mainly self-taught, first through copying then by creating his own style. He applies his study of figure drawing and human anatomy to his work on the project.

BRUCE DAMER is Principal and founder of DigitalSpace Commons and a founding director of the Contact Consortium, organizations dedicated to the development of multi-user graphical virtual worlds on the Internet. The Consortium hosts conferences and colloquia on topics of advanced virtual communities. Projects include a 3D virtual town (*Sherwood Forest*), a virtual university and architecture competition (*The U*), a virtual garden world (*Nerve Garden*), virtual learning spaces (Vlearn3D.org), the Digital Biology Project and Conference (Biota.org) and a global cyber-conference, Avatars98 through 2000. The DigitalSpace Commons works for such clients as NASA (a virtual habitat on Mars) and Adobe Systems Inc. (Adobe's *Atmosphere* community). Bruce is a graduate of the University of Southern California.

MARGARET DAVIS is the MOVES Institute's writer and webmaster. She is the former owner of Clarity Communications, a custom-writing service with clients ranging from Sun Microsystems to a European walking-tour company, and projects as varied as technical writing, historical narrative, humor and criticism. She holds a BA in English from Cal State Los Angeles and an MA in British literature from California Polytechnic, San Luis Obispo. Her daughter, Rachel, is *AA*'s intern artist.

DOROTHY DEASY is a design and marketing research professional with 23 years experience, committed to understanding what lies beneath. Her approach is to develop a deep knowledge base of an audience's needs, behaviors and motivations and to use that insight to inform evolving desires. She uses a variety of qualitative research techniques (depth interviewing, group discussions, ethnography, audits, etc.) and draws from expert involvement and cross-disciplinary learning. She has been on research teams for award winning products as well as contributing to branding, marketing and communications strategy. Formerly at Cheskin, Dorothy has now founded ddeasy inc., based in Portland, Oregon.

ERIC DISHMAN is a social scientist who has been leading qualitative research studies for the past 10 years. He directs Intel's Proactive Health Research Lab on aging-in-place technologies and chairs Intel's Health Subcommittee, which funds university grants on consumer health and disability, cancer, cardiovascular conditions, and nutrition and fitness concerns. Eric is a frequent lecturer on home healthcare, elder care, ubiquitous computing, and using ethnography and performance to help design future technologies. He received three BA degrees from the University of North Carolina at Chapel Hill in Speech Communication, English (with Honors) and Drama. He earned an MS in Speech Communication from Southern Illinois University and is a PhD candidate in Communication from the University of Utah.

ABBE DON is founder and principal of Abbe Don Interactive, specializing in user research, interface design and software product development. She is currently Director of User Experience at Classroom Connect. As Director of Interactive Design at Walt Disney Parks and Resorts Online, she developed an in-house team to redesign disneyland.com. She began her interface design career in 1988 in the Human Interface Group at Apple Computer, while also working as a media artist in interactive digital storytelling. She holds a BA from Pomona College in photography and writing, a BFA from The California Institute for the Arts, and a master's degree from the Interactive Telecommunications Program at New York University.

SEAN DONAHUE—part design practitioner, part design publisher and part design advocate—has a uniquely balanced, expanded design practice. He is founder and Principal of ResearchCenteredDesign in Los Angeles, with a portfolio of projects that begin with questioning how design is able to make a significant contribution. His persistence in moving from theory to practice has resulted in the development of projects ranging from media master plans for city development to digital tools for studying "concurrent" history. He has lectured and published internationally on media design and design research. Sean holds an MFA from the Media Design Program at Art Center College of Design.

SCOTT DOSED is lead animator for *America's Army*. He grew up in a fishing town on an island in Southeast Alaska. He balances his love of the great outdoors with interests in science, art and animation. His education includes a BFA degree from the

University of Utah and a certificate from the 3D Animation Program at Vancouver Film School. His work has been shown at SIGGRAPH and the Los Angeles Film Festival.

BJ FOGG, PhD is the founder of Stanford University's Persuasive Technology Lab, a research and design center that explores how interactive technology can motivate and influence people. Since 1993, BJ's research has involved more than 6,500 participants in lab experiments, field studies, online investigations and design explorations. An experimental psychologist, he has been appointed to Stanford's consulting faculty in both the School of Engineering and the School of Education. He is the principal of Grapevine Strategy, a consulting company that helps clients harness the power of computers to motivate and persuade users. BJ is author of *Persuasive Technology: Using Computers to Change What People Think and Do*. He holds seven patents for innovations in user experience.

DENISE GONZALES CRISP is the Chair of Graphic Design at the College of Design, North Carolina State University. From 1997 to 2001, she was the senior designer for Art Center College of Design in Pasadena, California, where was also core faculty in the graduate Media Design Program. Her studio SuperStove! has served clients including *Artext* magazine, Southern California Institute of Architecture, and small presses. Her design and writing have appeared in national and international publications including the Russian *KAK*, *Graphis*, *Émigré*, *Eye*, *Print* and *I.D.*, and were featured in the 2002 Paris design exhibition "West Coast Dreams." She earned an MFA in graphic design from California Institute of the Arts in 1996.

LISA GROCOTT has two indivisible roles—designer at Melbourne company Studio Anybody and researches coordinator in Communication Design at RMIT University. Studio Anybody's participation in the visual arts and education strongly directs Lisa works as creative director for the critically acclaimed collective whose work has been published in Australia, the States, Japan and the UK. The Studio's speculative projects disseminate practitioner-led research, which weaves back into her role as coordinator of RMIT's Master of Design by Research. Lisa holds a MFA in painting and a Masters in Design. Her PhD research examines the nexus of research, innovation and professional practice.

CHRISTOPHER IRELAND is Principal and CEO of Cheskin. She is noted for her unique ability to create simple explanations of complex human behavior. She has directed teams over the last 20 years to investigate such fundamental concepts as "play," "collaboration," "work," "trend adoption" and "design evolution." She has worked closely with teams at Microsoft and numerous other Fortune 500 companies. She earned her MBA from the Andersen School of Management at UCLA. Christopher has authored several articles examining the relationship between companies and consumers and lectures at leading universities, including Stanford, MIT and UCLA She is a member of the advisory board of the Comparative Media Studies Program at MIT.

HENRY JENKINS, PhD is the Ann Fetter Friedlaender Professor of Humanities and Director of the Comparative Media Studies Program at MIT. Henry is noted for his pioneering work in the study of fan communities and popular culture and has testified before the U.S. Congress regarding computer games. He is the author or editor of 9 books on various aspects of media and popular culture, including *Textual Poachers: Television Fans and Participatory Culture*, *From Barbie to Mortal Kombat: Gender and Computer Games*, *Hop on Pop: The Politics and Pleasures of Popular Culture* and *Rethinking New Media: The Aesthetics of Transition*. He is the principal investigator of the MIT Microsoft Games-to-Teach Project.

BONNIE JOHNSON, PhD is a veteran researcher who has had a strong influence on high-tech culture. Beginning as an educator in communication and organizational psychology, she went on to become a member of the Strategic Staff at Intel. She was co-founder of Focus Systems, Inc. and became vice president of Humanware, Inc., a company specializing in consulting and system integration. In 1992 she joined Interval Research as one of its founding members where she worked for eight years. At Interval she organized an area of 20 researchers, videographers and statisticians to conduct primary research in home technology use. Most recently she served as a Senior Expert at McKinsey & Company.

SOMI KIM works as a brand strategist at ReVerb, which she co-founded in 1990. Recipient of a 1995 Chrysler Design Award, ReVerb has evolved from a design firm into a creative think tank with a blended approach to communications planning supported by ethnographic consumer research. Somi received her MFA from CalArts and BA from Harvard University. Her writings are included in *Sunday Dinner: Food, Land and Free Time* (forthcoming); "Who Owns Cultural Imagery?" (*AIGA Journal*, 1996) and *Lift and Separate: Graphic Design and the Quote Unquote Vernacular* (Herb Lubalin Center, 1993). She has lectured at Jan van Eyck Akademie, in Maastricht, Walker Art Center, Stanford University and other cultural and academic institutions.

BRENDA LAUREL, PhD chairs the graduate Media Design Program at Art Center College of Design in Pasadena, California. She has worked since 1976 in computer games and human-computer interaction for companies including Atari, Activision, Epyx, Apple, Sony, Fujitsu and Interval Research. She co-founded Telepresence Research in 1990 and Purple Moon, a research-driven transmedia company devoted to girls, in 1996. She also works as a design research consultant, public speaker and writer. Brenda is editor of *The Art of Human-Computer Interface Design* and author of *Computers as Theatre* and *Utopian Entrepreneur*.

She serves on advisory boards of organizations including Cheskin, the MIT Comparative Media Studies program and the Berkeley Institute of Design and is a member of the Board of Governors of the Communication Research Institute of Australia. She holds a BA from DePauw University and an MFA and PhD in Theatre from the Ohio State University.

CHRISTOPH LOCH, PhD is Professor of Technology Management at INSEAD. His research revolves around the management of R&D and the product innovation process, particularly technology strategy, project selection, concurrent engineering, project management under high uncertainty, collaborative problem solving and performance measurement. He also studies status competition and its interaction with culture in organizations and consults on technology management. He is associate editor of *Management Science and Operations Research* and a senior editor of *Manufacturing & Service Operations Management*. His work has appeared in journals including *Organization Science*, the *Journal of Product Innovation Management*, *Sloan Management Review*, and the *Financial Times*. He holds a PhD from the Graduate School of Business at Stanford University.

PETER LUNENFELD, PhD is a writer/critic specializing in the history and theory of media technologies and a member of the Core Faculty of the Media Design Program at Art Center College of Design. He holds a BA from Columbia University, MA from SUNY at Buffalo, and PhD from UCLA. Peter founded *mediawork*: The Southern California New Media Working Group. He serves as Director, Institute for Technology & Aesthetics (ITA). Author: *USER* (MIT, 2004), *Snap to Grid: A User's Guide to Digital Arts, Media & Cultures* (MIT, 2000). Editor, *The Digital Dialectic: New Essays in New Media* (MIT, 1999). He is the editorial director of the highly designed Mediawork pamphlet series for the MIT Press. These "theoretical fetish objects" cover the intersections of art, design, technology, and market culture (mitpress.mit.edu/mediawork).

DAVIS MASTEN, in his role as Catalyst at Cheskin, creates customer-inspired breakthroughs for his clients. Davis joined Cheskin Associates, Inc. in 1975 and worked closely with founder and motivation research pioneer Louis Cheskin. He stepped down as the CEO of Cheskin+Masten to gain increasing flexibility to pursue his passions. Focusing on youth culture, branding, trust, market trends and product development, Davis has offered his expertise to more than 2,500 projects in innovation for retail, packaging, interactive environments, corporate positioning and industrial design. Current clients include Microsoft and Coca-Cola. In 2003, Davis was selected as a mentor at the Oxford School of Business and a member of the President's Circle of the National Academy of Sciences.

ALEX MAYBERRY is the executive producer/director of *America's Army* and the creative director of the MOVES Institute.

Alex began in games with Internet modifications of the hit products *Doom* and *Doom II* by id Software, and served as lead level designer and game designer for Xatrix Entertainment, with credits such as *Redneck Rampage, Redneck Rampage Rides Again, Redneck Hunting, Quake 2: The Reckoning,* and *Kingpin: Life of Crime.* After a stint as creative director at Electronic Arts, where he worked on *James Bond: The World is Not Enough,* Alex did conceptual work on new intellectual properties for KalistoUSA.

JESSE MCCREE became interested in game development while studying art history and anthropology. As a member of the Internet mod community, Jesse created numerous levels and art assets for various games, and ran the popular www.gamedesign.net website. His first job in the industry was with Electronic Arts, where he contributed to *James Bond: The World is Not Enough.* After a short stint at KalistoUSA, McCree joined the *America's Army* team as a level designer and artist. He now heads up the overall design effort for the project.

TRACY MOON is the Principal and Creative Director of StudioMoon, a San Francisco design firm specializing in Visual Identity. Trained first in biochemistry, Tracy completed a degree in Graphic Design at the University of Washington, Seattle. While working as a Design Director for firms such as Landor Associates, S&O/Addison Design Consultants and Frankfurt Balkind Partners/NY, Tracy designed and directed identity projects for large corporate clients such as PG&E, Touchstone Pictures, AT&T and Citicorp. She formed her own studio in 1991 to offer a more intimate and economical identity product to smaller companies. Her work has been recognized by *Communication Arts*, *Print*, *Critique*, *HOW*, *Step by Step* and others. Tracy currently teaches Visual Identity at The Academy of Art, San Francisco.

MICHAEL NAIMARK is an independent media artist and researcher with over two decades of experience investigating place representation and its consequences. He has worked extensively with field cinematography, interactive systems and immersive projection, and has been a longtime member of the Society for Visual Anthropology. Michael's art projects have been exhibited internationally. His 3D interactive installation *Be Now Here*, produced with the cooperation of the UNESCO World Heritage Centre, is currently on tour in the ZKM's "Future Cinema" exhibition. Michael is the 2002 recipient of the World Technology Award for the Arts.

JIN HYUN PARK hails from Seoul, Korea and has achieved the rare distinction of being an Art Center "lifer." He received his undergraduate degree in Environmental Design and continued with an MFA in the Media Design Program at Art Center College of Design, graduating in 2003. He is a design advisor at Onyang Museum Cultural History. He also practices as a motion graphic designer, working in both the U.S. and Korea. He has worked with several motion graphics and dance companies as motion graphic designer and art director. He recently collaborated with Milmul Modern Dance Company in Korea to create Hangul (Korean Language and alphabet) in motion, performed at the National Theater of Korea.

JEFF PETRICK is currently the Senior User Experience Designer at Classroom Connect, a leading provider of professional development and online curriculum resources. Previously, he has served as Interaction Design Manger at Walt Disney Parks and Resorts Online and a consultant at Scient Corp., where he provided overall user experience strategy for clients and led information architecture/interaction design teams. Jeff has worked with a number of major consumer brands to create online experiences integrating content and commerce, including Disney, Major League Baseball, Netscape, Estée Lauder and the LVMH Group. He holds a BA in English Literature from the University of California, Berkeley.

TIM PLOWMAN, PhD is a design anthropologist specializing in exploratory and design-based research. He designs and conducts ethnographic analyses of behavior streams and user experiences that support the conception, design, refinement and branding of products and processes. He has worked in applications research, human factors testing and multi-modal interface design. Tim has conducted long-term ethnographic research in southern Brazil on subjectivity and juridical processes. He has also conducted fieldwork in Puerto Rico and the United States. He has taught at U.C. Berkeley, Santa Clara University, and the Art Center College of Design. Tim received his undergraduate and doctoral training in anthropology from U.C. Berkeley and U.C. San Francisco.

STACEY PURPURA is currently a research director at NetFlix. As a research director at Cheskin, she specialized in quantitative design research methodology. She has diverse experience in both teaching and using quantitative methodologies. Stacey began her career in research as a Research Scientist at Harris Interactive, developing methodologies for large-scale online market research studies. Out of a desire to impact product development, Stacey then joined Razorfish (an Internet consulting company) as a Senior Usability and User Intelligence Researcher. In addition to her practical experience, Stacey has also been an instructor for SPSS where her courses included advanced statistical methods and research methodology. Stacey holds an MA and M. Phil. in sociology from Columbia University.

DARION RAPOZA, PhD received his degree in biopsychology from The University of Chicago. He is President of both Entertainment Science and Attitude Games, companies he co-founded with the missions of studying the real-life behavioral impact of videogames, and of developing videogames with empirically demonstrable positive behavioral impact. Through

Entertainment Science and Attitude Games, he is currently engaged in two projects to develop theory-based drug-abuse prevention videogames for the educational and mass markets. He also holds a position in Experimental Neurosurgery at Duke University, where he is studying hand function in primates as they play videogames for fruit juice rewards.

DARREL RHEA has pioneered the incoporation of market research into the design and development process for more than 25 years. He is a Principal and former CEO of Cheskin and is considered one of the North America's leading strategic design consultants, with extensive experience managing global programs for industrial design, product development and innovation, graphic design and brand identity creation. Darrel has developed a pragmatic approach to achieving design breakthroughs that uses research to align teams of people. He holds degrees in design and psychology, and is on the advisory board of the Design Management Institute. He frequently speaks at leading design and business schools and professional business and design organizations.

CARLOS SANTOS has been involved in Consumer Research since 1992. As a Strategic Director at Cheskin, he is responsible for both qualitative and quantitative research projects, including multi-national and multi-phase. Carlos has a strong background in the technology sector, having been involved in several early product development efforts for products such as color printers, digital cameras and home networks. As a bilingual researcher, Carlos has conducted research studies with Hispanic consumers both in the US and abroad. He holds an undergraduate degree in Business from the University of Texas and an MBA from the University of Arizona, with doctoral studies in Consumer Behavior and Cognitive Psychology at UCLA.

NATHAN SHEDROFF is one of the pioneers in Experience Design, an approach to design that encompasses multiple senses and requirements as well as the related fields of Interaction Design and Information Design. His speaking, books, and projects all support this new direction of design. Part designer and part entrepreneur, his skills lend themselves to strategic thinking and design for companies who want to exploit their strengths in order to build better experiences for their customers and themselves in a variety of media, including: print, digital, online and product design. Nathan is also an advisor to Interaction Institute Ivrea. He currently lives in San Francisco where it is easy to have a silly-sounding title like Experience Strategist and actually make a living.

RUSSELL SHILLING, PhD is the lead audio engineer/sound designer and a principal investigator for *America's Army*. His interest in audio design began when he was commissioned as Navy aerospace experimental psychologist and assigned to the Naval Air Warfare Center, where he researched networked VE sys-

tems. His MOVES Institute and systems-engineering department students investigate the contributions of immersive and spatial sound to task performance in VE, radio, radar, air-traffic control and videogames. Russ maintains collaborations with THX, Lucasfilm Skywalker Sound, Dolby Interactive, Creative Labs and various videogame developers. He holds a BA in psychology from Wake Forest University and a PhD in experimental psychology from the University of North Carolina, Greensboro.

BUFFY SHUTT is partnered with Kathy Jones in a feature and television production company. Shutt/Jones Productions is based at Universal Studios in Universal City. Their first feature, *Blue Crush*, produced with Imagine Entertainment, was released by Universal in the summer of 2002. Current projects include a feature comedy collaboration with Tom Shadyac of Shady Acres Entertainment as well as projects with Lifetime, USA and ShowTime. Buffy formerly served as President of Marketing for Universal Pictures. With her partner Kathy Jones, she spearheaded all marketing activities for Universal's feature films, including creative advertising, media/co-op advertising, research, publicity, promotion and field operations, and all phases of marketing pictures. In 1996, she received Women in Film's prestigious Crystal Award, presented to outstanding women in the entertainment industry.

JAN CRAIGE SINGER is President and Partner of BIG BLUE DOT, where she has worked with clients including Nickelodeon, Disney, Discovery Kids, Kodak, Unilever, Oral-B, Feld Entertainment/Ringling Bros. and Barnum & Bailey Circus, ShoPro Entertainment, PBS Kids, Procter & Gamble, and Buena Vista Television. Formerly as VP with Discovery Communications, she created the network identities for Discovery and The Learning Channel. She served as the original executive producer for the commercial-free pre-school block *Ready, Set, Learn!* Her work has been recognized by such organizations such as BDA, PROMAX, EMMYs, New York Film and Television Awards, and for Outstanding Achievement in Children's Programming for the NEA. Jan holds a Master's in Education from Harvard University.

KURT SQUIRE has recently joined the faculty of the University of Wisconsin, Madison as an Assistant Professor in Educational Communications and Technology. He was formerly a project manager in the Comparative Media Studies Department at MIT working on the Games-to-Teach Project. Kurt is a co-founder of Joystick101.org, a web magazine/community focusing on the in-depth study of game design, culture and industry. He is currently finishing his PhD in Instructional Systems Technology at Indiana University.

RACHEL STRICKLAND is a documentary filmmaker, architect and time-based media designer, whose work of the past 25 years has focused on cinematic dimensions of the sense of place, animate and ephemeral dimensions of architectural space, and new paradigms for narrative construction in digital media. Strickland earned a Master of Architecture degree at Massachusetts Institute of Technology, with a concentration in *cinéma vérité* filmmaking. She has taught film and video production at MIT, U.C. Santa Cruz, and Southern California Institute of Architecture. She has been employed as a research videographer by Atari, Apple, and Sun, and she directed experimental cinema projects at Interval Research Corporation.

PATRIK SVENSSON, PhD is the director of HUMlab at Umeå University in Sweden. He has a background in linguistics and cognitive science, and is now working toward creating a meeting place for the humanities, culture and information technology. He focuses on immersion and symbolism in virtual environments, creativity and learning, visualization and virtualization of language. He is involved in starting up a Scandinavian network for digital culture, and has just finished a three-year project where students of English design a graphical virtual environment instead of writing a traditional final degree essay.

PHILIP TAN is a graduate student in MIT Comparative Media Studies and has led several game design and production projects under the auspices of the MIT-Microsoft Games-to-Teach Research Project, for which he has been working as Research Manager since Summer 2003. Philip is a 2000 Burchard Scholar of the School of Humanities and Social Sciences, a 1997 Scholar of the Infocomm Development Authority of Singapore and a 2001 member of Phi Beta Kappa.

ROB TOW is an inventor/scientist/programmer with 23 years of wide experience in software and hardware systems design and development at major research labs including Northrop Aviation, Compression Labs, Schlumberger Palo Alto Research, Xerox PARC, Interval Research and AT&T Labs. He has generated patents in amorphous silicon chip design, image processing, UI design and robotics, and has worked in the design of VR systems and wearable computers. The major prior art cited in his two patents for the design of emotional communication between robots and humans is Charles Darwin. He is currently head of R&D at VIP Mobile, Inc.

EMMA WESTECOTT is Studio Director, The Zero Game Studio, Interactive Institute, Malmø, Sweden. She has worked as a creative producer, producing and programming games for 10 years as well as lecturing in game and interaction design around the world. Her most recent game credit is as Producer on *Starship Titanic* www.starshiptitanic.com, Douglas Adams' best-selling CD-ROM adventure game. She is responsible for the launch of The Digital Village's flagship web-based community h2g2.com, based on *The Hitch Hiker's Guide To The Galaxy* and now part of BBC Online. At Zero Game, Emma directs a new type of applied research lab specializing in games for the Interactive Institute zerogame.interactiveinstitute.se.

TRAVIS WIGLESWORTH is a level designer for *America's Army*. His previous work included numerous maps for *Unreal* and *Unreal Tournament*. He worked at Sony Online Entertainment as a game master for *EverQuest* and was an apprentice-level designer for the *EverQuest* Expansion: *Shadows of Luclin*.

WILL WRIGHT is the creator of both the *SimCity* and *The Sims* franchises. *SimCity* was released in 1989, and within a few months because a hit. The latest incarnation and definitive version of *SimCity*, *SimCity 3000 Unlimited*, continues the tradition. Wright's game *The Sims* puts players in charge of the lives of a neighborhood of simulated people. Released in 2000, *The Sims* has become a cultural phenomenon, and has become the best selling PC game of all time. *The Sims Online*, released in 2002, is architected to encourage and support diverse communities both in the game itself and in the independent fan sites it has spawned.

ERIC ZIMMERMAN is Co-Founder and CEO of gameLab, a New York-based online game developer www.gmlb.com. gameLab's award-winning titles include *Blix*, *Loop* and *LEGO JunkBot*. Some of Eric's pre-gameLab titles include the critically acclaimed *Sissyfight 2000* (www.sissyfight.com, created with Word.com) and the PC game *Gearheads*. Eric has taught game design and interactive narrative design in the MIT Comparative Media Studies program, New York University's Interactive Telecommunications Program and the Digital Design MFA program at Parsons School of Design. He lectures and publishes extensively about game design and digital culture. Eric is currently co-authoring two books about game design, to be published in 2003.

MICHAEL ZYDA is the Director of The MOVES Institute at the Naval Postgraduate School, Monterey, California and a Professor in the Department of Computer Science at NPS. His research interests include computer graphics, large-scale networked 3D virtual environments, agent-based simulation, modeling human and organizational behavior, interactive computer-generated story and characters, video production, entertainment/defense collaboration and modeling and simulation. He is the principal investigator of the *America's Army* PC game funded by the Assistant Secretary of the Army for Manpower and Reserve Affairs. He holds a BA in Bioengineering from U.C. San Diego, an MS in Computer Science from the University of Massachusetts, Amherst and a DSc in Computer Science from Washington University, St. Louis, Missouri.